THE LAW AND POLITICS
OF CIVIL RIGHTS
AND LIBERTIES

THE LAW AND POLITICS
OF CIVIL RIGHTS
AND LIBERTIES

Richard E. Morgan

Bowdoin College

ALFRED A. KNOPF

New York

Library of Congress Cataloging in Publication Data

Morgan, Richard E., 1937–
   The law and politics of civil rights and liberties.

   Includes index.
   1. Civil rights—United States. 2. Civil rights—
United States—Cases. I. Title.
KF4749.M65   1985b   342.73'085   84-25082
ISBN 0-394-35108-8   347.30285

Manufactured in the United States of America

To the beloved old firm
of P. P. and T.

PREFACE

This book is an act of pedagogical self-examination. That is, I have tried to set down for others how I go about introducing undergraduate students to the study of civil rights and liberties in America. Thus I have provided excerpts from the cases I use to teach legal doctrine and from the statutes I consider to be of central importance and interest. The background material provided is what I consider necessary to locate my own students in political and intellectual space and time with respect to the materials. The case studies are the discussion topics I use to encourage my classes to explore the frontier issues in various areas of law.

There is no material here of merely antiquarian interest. For instance, there is only passing reference to the reapportionment cases. This is because I regard the matter of apportionment (as opposed to matters of districting and ethnic vote dilution) as essentially settled and off the agenda of contemporary constitutional politics—material for constitutional historians and not for political scientists and lawyers. Even when (as in Part II) I insist on taking the reader back to the English Civil War, I do so because it is necessary for an understanding of some contemporary civil liberty or civil rights dispute.

The task has been immensely worthwhile. Until you try to write up your favorite and presumably familiar old course and get it ready to offer to others, you do not really appreciate how much you have been doing, year after year, that you had never really thought through. If I did not fear the competition, I would recommend the exercise to all my colleagues. Furthermore, I am confident that the annual supplements to this volume will reflect not only new court decisions, statutes, and executive orders, but also new background material and alternative ways of approaching old problems.

My thanks to Barbara Kelly, Debra Rosenthal, and Ann O'Reilly, who were my research assistants in the years this work was in progress. Suzanne Theberge performed with her usual heroism as secretary, typist, and literary traffic manager. My thanks also to the following reviewers: John Brigham, University of Massachusetts—Amherst; James D. Calder, University of Texas at San Antonio; Beth M. Henschen, Purdue University; Neil D. McFeeley, University of Idaho;

William P. McLauchlan, Purdue University; Jeffrey Morris, University of Pennsylvania; H. G. Peter Wallach, Central Connecticut State University; and John T. Wold, California State College—Stanislaws. Finally, my wife Eva, along with the enterprise referred to in the dedication, grudgingly tolerated my numerous absences over the period of composition.

North Harpswell, Maine   R.E.M.
October 1984

CONTENTS

Part I   Freedom of Speech

Part II   Freedom of Religion

Part III   Rights of the Accused

Part IV   Equality before the Law

Part V   Rights of Privacy

CHAPTER · 1

INTRODUCTION

THE theme of this book is that civil rights and civil liberties are not brought by the stork. What we often refer to as "our rights as Americans," "our inalienable rights," and even, embarrassingly, "our unalienable rights," are not written in letters of fire in the sky or clearly chiselled in the granite of our past. Rather, civil rights and civil liberties, as enforceable legal rights in our society, are the results of choices made by generations of judges, legislators, and appointed administrators (bureaucrats) who were pushed and hauled in various directions by successive generations of lawyers, political publicists, visionaries, and representatives of the myriad special interests that have together made up American society. The choices made by these past and present Americans were, in most cases, not at all self-evident. There were strongly conflicting arguments and good reasons (although perhaps not equally good) put forward in support of alternative outcomes.

Rights and liberties represent a specialized kind of American public policy. Like other kinds of public policy, they are the product of conflict and consensus building. Some of the people involved in this conflict and consensus building are of the long-dead type called "framers" of the Constitution. Equally prominent are justices of the United States Supreme Court (who also are spoken of with reverence if they have been dead long enough). Others involved in the continuing process of defining rights and liberties are familiar or "garden variety" politicians—congressmen, senators, presidents, and cabinet secretaries. In addition, there are a variety of specialized participants. These include representatives of interest groups such as the National Association for the Advancement of Colored People (NAACP) and the American Civil Liberties Union (ACLU). Also important are law professors and other prestigious commentators on public affairs. Finally, the news media—both the popular and specialized varieties—are important to the conflict over how rights and liberties should be defined.

"Framers"

We shall examine courts and judges in the next chapter, but it is useful to dwell a moment here on the question of who are the "constitutional framers" whose "intentions" are debated so heatedly in the course of defining civil rights and liberties. These shadowy figures are constantly being invoked in American constitutional politics, but attention is seldom paid to who, precisely, they were. There are, in fact, many different sets of people to whom the term refers.

"Framers" may refer to the members (or to the more active and influential members) of the Philadelphia Convention of 1787, who produced the original six articles. Or, as used by others, the term might include the members of the state ratifying conventions, who voted to adopt the new charter.

In still another context, "framers" might refer to the members (or to the more active and influential members) of the First Congress of the United States, who produced the first ten amendments—the Bill of Rights. And here again, some commentators also might look to the state legislatures that ratified the amendments in attempting to determine the "intent of the framers."

As we shall see, a great deal of the contemporary constitutional law of civil rights and liberties is based on interpretations of the language of the Fourteenth Amendment. Proposed by Congress in 1866 and ratified in 1868, the "Fourteenth" involves us with yet another set of framers several generations removed from the first sets.

And what, finally, of the revolutionary generation? Many prominent figures in the struggle for independence had no direct role in constitution or amendment making—Tom Paine and Thomas Jefferson are obvious examples. But are they, therefore, altogether excluded from the universe of framers? Such figures usually *are* included under the rubric "founding fathers," which in common parlance often is used interchangeably with "framers."

The point is that some care is in order when invoking the honored dead. When making an argument involving the "intentions of the framers," it is important to say who you are talking about, as well as how you presume to know what they thought.

Interest Groups

In pressing for the creation of new civil liberties and civil rights or the expansion of old ones, interest groups today are of central importance. Familiar groups such as the ACLU have been concerned principally with prohibitions on government and on the requirements of procedural fairness. Other groups such as the NAACP and the National Organization for Women (NOW) have been concerned principally with civil rights in combating invidious discrimination against the classes of persons they represent. Such specializations are not exclusive. The ACLU has supported numerous antidiscrimination cases, and the NAACP has made free speech and establishment clause arguments in many of its briefs.

The ACLU was founded in 1920 by Roger Baldwin, a pacifist social worker, who was an opponent of American entry into World War I and of conscription for military service in that war. The Union helped defend pacifists and political radicals against the overreaction of government authorities during the wartime emergency and the immediate postwar concern about domestic subversion and terrorism. Baldwin drew into the work of the Union such diverse individuals as Harvard Law School Professor Felix Frankfurter, American Communist leader William Z. Foster, the Rev. John A. Ryan, a Catholic priest, and the philosopher, John Dewey. Clarence Darrow undertook volunteer legal work.

Today the national ACLU and a number of state affiliates are active in court, in legislative lobbying, and in the media in the service of causes that range from abortion rights to the rights of school children. It maintains an active and influential Washington office, and while its principal support is drawn from the left of the American political spectrum, the Union and its affiliates do come to the aid of persons and groups on the right when important points of law are at stake.*

The NAACP was founded in 1910 by seven prominent white Americans and one black, W.E.B. DuBois. In its early years the principal concern of the Association was the lynching (execution by mob violence) of blacks. In the middle of the twentieth century it was the NAACP, operating through the tax free Legal Defense and Educational Fund (the "INK Fund"), which spearheaded the judicial assault on school segregation. The chief legal architect of this effort was Thurgood Marshall, special counsel of the NAACP and later to become an associate justice of the Supreme Court. In fact, a number of highly talented activist lawyers who have been associated with the NAACP and the "INK Fund" have gone on to become federal judges.† William H. Hastie, who was closely associated with the legal work of the organization during the 1930s, was appointed to the Court of Appeals for the Third Circuit in 1949. Later Constance Baker Motley and Robert L. Carter, both of whom worked for the national office, became federal district judges. Among distinguished white participants in the legal work of the NAACP have been Lewis Marshall (1895–1929), an early and energetic opponent of racial and religious discrimination, who also served as the first president of the American Jewish Committee. Another white, Jack Greenberg, was the long-time head of the "INK Fund."

Although the ACLU and NAACP probably are the best known interest groups in the field of rights and liberties, they are but the tip of the iceberg. Groups such as the American Jewish Congress and the American Jewish Committee are involved in both the legislative and judicial processes and in

---

* In January of 1984 the Washington office newsletter was given over to an article by chief lobbyist John Shattuck on "1984: The Reagan War on Civil Liberties," and the following month the office issued a special report titled *In Contempt of Congress and the Courts: The Reagan Civil Rights Record.*
† By the early 1980s the two organizations had separated completely, and the parent NAACP sued the Fund to prevent its further use of the "NAACP" identification.

both civil rights and civil liberties issues. The same is true of the National Council of Churches of Christ in America. From its headquarters on Riverside Drive in New York City (often referred to by cynics as the "Protestant Vatican"), the National Council has been involved not only in religious liberty cases and controversies throughout the country but in many important civil rights cases. In the same way, the United States Catholic Conference (formerly the National Catholic Welfare Conference) lobbies for civil rights legislation, joins civil rights suits, and opposes interpretations of the religious clauses of the First Amendment that it regards as unsound and inimical to the interests of Catholics.

In recent years many new groups have entered the arena. Some of these groups, such as the National Organization for Women, the National Senior Citizens Law Center, and the Gay and Lesbian Advocates and Defenders (GLAD), defend newly perceived interests; others, such as the Lawyers Committee for Civil Rights, supplement and extend the work of existing organizations. All told, there are now about 160 organizations affiliated with the Leadership Conference on Civil Rights in Washington. The Conference, which attempts to coordinate congressional lobbying on major issues by the affiliated groups, has as its general counsel Joseph L. Rough, Jr., an activist lawyer who is also vice-president of Americans for Democratic Action—a liberal interest group with concerns including, but not limited to, civil rights and liberties.

It should not be supposed that all the groups active in the field are on the left of the American political spectrum or favor the continuous expansion of civil rights and liberties. Citizens for Effective Law Enforcement, led by Illinois Governor and former Northwestern University Law Professor James "Big Jim" Thompson, is entering criminal procedure cases. Citizens for Decent Literature has a long track record in defending the constitutionality of obscenity laws. In addition, conservative "think tanks" such as the American Enterprise Institute and the Heritage Foundation, while not participating directly in litigation or lobbying, sponsor research and develop materials that are used by others in legal/political struggles. And while not generally thought of as a civil liberties group, there is no denying the effectiveness of the National Rifle Association in advancing its conception of the Second Amendment's right to bear arms. Finally, liberal-conservative lines are not all that clear and straightly drawn today (if, indeed, they ever were). On the issue of affirmative action, for instance, some traditionally liberal-activist groups (e.g., the American Jewish Congress) have become openly skeptical and have criticized erstwhile allies. In the chapters that follow we will encounter these and other organized groups active in the politics of civil rights and liberties.

Activist Lawyers

Overlapping somewhat with interest groups is the category of activist lawyers. These individuals sometimes work with interest groups but often work alone out of private law firms to shape new rights and liberties in the courts. William Kuntsler and Leonard Boudin (father of Weather Underground terrorist Kathy Boudin) have long been active in representing persons on the extreme left of the political spectrum and in attempting to make new law in the process. New York lawyer Ephrim London, with many clients in the publishing industry, has been involved in many important censorship cases over the years. Harrisburg Lawyer William Ball, sometimes in cooperation with the U.S. Catholic Conference and sometimes alone, has a long record of opposing what he regards an unreasonably strict separation of church and state. Ball is counterbalanced on the other side of the issue by Leo Pfeffer, who has worked with a variety of groups but deserves to be regarded as an institution in his own right in the field of church-state relations. A particularly colorful activist lawyer is Florence Kennedy. Delighting in calling herself "Old Black Flo," Kennedy has been involved in many race and sex equality cases and has been particularly interested in the treatment of prostitutes by the legal system. In one of her more famous moments, she led a meeting of working girls in a spirited rendition of "Everybody Needs a Hooker Now and Then."

Writing of the Warren Court years, Jonathan Casper perceptively distinguished "reformer" lawyers, who "view the law as a mechanism for social change," from more traditionalist lawyers who view the law as essentially a mechanism for resolving private conflicts. This pattern of activist lawyers urging judges (and legislators and bureaucrats) to action and innovation is by no means a recent development. Clement Vose has identified the activist bar as crucial to the process of constitutional change in the early decades of this century, and Benjamin Twiss and Arnold Paul have studied the process in the late nineteenth century.

The influence of well-placed "private" lawyers must not be underestimated. Joseph Califano, Secretary of Health and Human Services in the Carter administration and one of the breed himself, has said that "the Washington lawyer rarely litigates cases; rather he tries to appoint judges." Activist lawyers and their interest group allies understand this and have been very effective in the judicial nominating process—especially during the Carter administration, when a large number of newly created federal judgeships were filled.

The Professors

Another important set of actors in the politics of civil rights and liberties is the academic lawyers. Professors in the prestigious national law schools not only produce most of the students who go on to clerk for Supreme Court justices and other appellate judges, but their books and articles are a primary mode of urging innovation on judges and other decision makers.

An excellent example is the role played by Professor Yale Kimisar, of the University of Michigan Law School, in developing arguments that ultimately led the Supreme Court to its controversial decision in the case of *Miranda*

v. *Arizona*. Another is Professor Anthony Amsterdam, of the New York University Law School, who has been a prime mover in the effort to persuade the Supreme Court that the death penalty is unconstitutional. Perhaps most prominent among the academic activists is Archibald Cox, of the Harvard Law School. As Solicitor General of the United States, Watergate Special Prosecutor, volunteer advocate of expanded civil rights before the Supreme Court, and president of Common Cause, Cox has played important roles in shaping public law. And again, the pattern of activism and influence is not restricted to one part of the political spectrum. Former Solicitor General and Yale Professor Robert Bork, a conservative critic of what he regards as a hyperactivist federal judiciary, is now a federal judge, as is his Yale colleague, Ralph K. Winter, who was associated with the American Enterprise Institute before his elevation to the federal bench.

Especially important to the behavior of the contemporary courts is the writing of academic experts on the acceptable limits of judicial activism and on acceptable styles of constitutional interpretation. Of course, law professors do not write solely to influence judges and other lawyers. Like other scholars they are genuinely concerned with the truth of the matter before them. But in the realm of civil rights and liberties "the truth of the matter" often constitutes a policy position, and much of the work of the law professors is what Professor Paul Brest of the Stanford Law School calls "advocacy scholarship."

It is well to remember that these activists engage one another in all of the varied arenas of the politics of rights and liberties—courts, legislatures, bureaucracies, and in the forums for informed opinion across the country.

The Politicians

That issues of civil rights and liberties are deeply involved in the struggle for elective office in America hardly needs laboring. Jimmy Carter had been President barely a year when the ACLU taxed him with a poor civil rights record and black groups, which had strongly supported his candidacy, began complaining of lack of access to the Oval Office. Ultimately, however, rights activists gained a great deal during the Carter years—especially in appointments to the federal bench and to the permanent bureaucracy.

That changed with Ronald Reagan. Groups committed to expanding rights and liberties inveighed against him. He opposed abortion, saw the proposed ERA as a trojan horse of radical feminism, supported school prayer and aid to church-related schools, and felt the courts had gone too far in creating procedural rights for criminal defendants at the expense of society. It was no surprise when in the spring of 1981 presidential counselor Edwin Meese blasted the ACLU in a speech before the California Peace Officers Association as something approaching a lobby for criminals. The ACLU and other civil liberties groups responded with information that their memberships were up because of the "Reagan threat to the Constitution."

Reagan's judicial and bureaucratic appointments and controversial appointments to the U.S. Commission on Civil Rights reflected his administration's sense that in many areas of rights policy things had moved too far too fast in the preceding decade. This Reagan approach, especially in appointments, will have policy consequences beyond his presidency (just as his predecessor's influence persisted beyond his term of office). Issues such as the wisdom of affirmative action have been sharpened and will be hotly debated in future election campaigns, with future electoral aspirants attempting to advance their prospects by supporting or opposing the Reagan record. The dialectic of rights policy will move as part of the larger dialectic of American electoral politics, and successive administrations will seek to break, accelerate, or alter course according to the victors' perception of public need and public opinion.

This interrelationship of rights policy and electoral dynamics is apparent on Capitol Hill as well. After the Republicans gained a majority in the Senate in the 1980 elections, Senator Strom Thurmond, Republican of South Carolina, succeeded Senator Edward F. Kennedy, Democrat of Massachusetts, as Chairman of the Senate Judiciary Committee. This meant a major change in the orientation of the Committee and its staff, which has jurisdiction over much rights-related legislation and judicial nominations. Under Kennedy, the Senate Judiciary had been a liberal-activist committee. While some activist staff members were able to retain their positions (through the patronage of minority Democratic senators), the style of the Committee was greatly altered, with new emphasis on issues such as crime control and the American response to international terrorism.

The Careerists

It is useful to dwell a moment on the bureaucratic careerists and congressional staff personnel, who are put in place by the elective politicians and often continue after them. In the areas of civil rights and liberties, these are usually highly skilled specialists, often with law school or interest group backgrounds (or both). They come to Washington on the basis of established competence. And they come with established policy commitments, established relationships to interest groups, and established memberships in academic and intellectual reference groups, which parallel their loyalties to their agencies, senators, or congressmen.

When careerists have been recruited on the basis of expertise and policy commitment, and have implemented and helped make policy to which they are sympathetic, it would be unrealistic to expect them to behave as neutral civil servants and dutifully turn in new policy directions when their political "masters" change after an election. Indeed, they do not.

Thus when Assistant Attorney General William Bradford Reynolds took over as head of the Civil Rights Division of the Justice Department in the Reagan administration, he was faced with a not-so-quiet rebellion on the part of the career staff composed largely of civil rights activists. The careerists argued that certain changes in Division policy, such as withdrawing support for busing as a judicially mandated means of achieving racial balance in schools, were "contrary to law." Reynolds argued that the new administration had an electoral mandate to change the direction of the rights policy of the executive branch, and that existing law allowed for such changes in directions.

Internal Civil Rights Division documents began to leak to the press along with comments by staff lawyers that their new bosses were ignoring them and ignoring the law. When Reynolds called a staff meeting to insist that the leaking stop, he was sharply challenged on his policies. When Reynolds affirmed his intention to make changes, some staffers announced they might be forced to resign in protest. A ruffled Reynolds replied that he would then get a new staff. And so the internal bureaucratic struggle went on.

It is not difficult to imagine that in some future administration committed to civil rights activism, a new assistant attorney general will confront greying, "new right" lawyers, who came in under Reagan, who will drag their feet noisily in implementing new policy.

The reality of Washington is that staffers, both executive branch and congressional, can serve as "stay behind" forces for an administration swept from power, harrassing and disrupting the new administration from within.

The Media

As with other aspects of our politics, the struggle over the ways in which civil rights and liberties are to be defined is affected by the way that struggle is portrayed in the communications media.

Thus it was surely a source of institutional support to the Warren Court of the late 1950s and early 1960s, when powerful forces were arrayed against it in Congress and the state legislatures, that it usually was portrayed favorably in the national "prestige media" (*New York Times, Washington Post,* the TV networks, and the major news magazines).

Furthermore, popular books can create a climate of opinion favorable to innovation in new areas of rights policy. An excellent example is *Gideon's Trumpet,* by *New York Times* journalist Anthony Lewis. Published in 1964, this was the story behind the decision of the Supreme Court in the case of *Gideon* v. *Wainwright,* 372 U.S. 335 (1963), which extended to state trials the Sixth Amendment's requirement (previously applicable only to federal trials) that indigent defendants be provided lawyers at government expense in all serious criminal cases.

Lewis artfully described the way in which Clarence Earl Gideon, a life-long drifter and jailbird, had been tried and convicted of breaking into the Bay Harbor Poolroom in Panama City, Florida, and stealing some cigarettes and the change from the Coke machine. Gideon asked the trial judge for a court-appointed lawyer but was informed that Florida law provided for appointment of counsel only in capital cases (i.e., where the punishment might be death). After his conviction, Gideon filed an *in forma pauperis* petition to have the U.S. Supreme Court hear his case. Under the Court's rules such a petition may be hand written and filing fees are waived. The Court receives several thousand of these each year.

Gideon argued that Florida's denial of court-appointed counsel violated his federal constitutional rights as enunciated in the case of *Betts* v. *Brady,* 316 U.S. 455 (1942). But *Betts* had held that, in state trials, free counsel was only required by the federal Constitution when some special circumstance obtained—a young or mentally impaired defendant, a particularly complex charge, a language barrier, or something of that sort. Since Gideon had defended himself in a reasonably intelligent fashion against a simple charge, he clearly did not qualify under *Betts.* If counsel were to be provided to defendants such as Gideon, the Court would have to break new ground in extending to the states rules that hitherto had operated only in federal courts.

In response to Gideon's petition the Supreme Court appointed Abe Fortas, a highly successful Washington lawyer and future associate justice, to argue Gideon's case. Clarence Earl Gideon went from having no lawyer to having one of the most expensive in the world. Fortas prepared carefully and won the day (as at least some of the justices had expected when they voted to consider Gideon's petition over hundreds of others, and appointed Fortas to represent him).

Fortas and the Court were the real heroes of the book, with Gideon an obscure but likeable old rogue who had the gumption to stand up for his rights and change the law of the land. The book was an instant success, especially as supplementary reading in courses on American government. A documentary film for schools was made from it with Gideon playing himself, and later a TV movie was made starring Henry Fonda. Thus *Gideon* v. *Wainwright* enjoyed two lives, one as an important Supreme Court decision and a second as a media event.

This occurred early in a period in which the Court was accomplishing a small revolution in American public policy by extending federal rules of criminal procedure to the states and reducing the discretion of state judges and legislatures. *Gideon's Trumpet* both portrayed and helped to legitimate this process of nationalization for a much wider public than ever could have been reached by the purely legal debate. It humanized and domesticated the business of constitutional change for many thousands of readers and viewers in living rooms and classrooms, and in this not inconsiderable way, contributed to that change.

Finally, in the day-to-day politics of rights and liberties, the media exercise considerable influence by deciding what leaks to play in what ways. This can, in today's atmosphere of journalistic free-for-all, be a considerable power as the Reagan civil rights appointees discovered. There have even been media attempts to develop "back channels" into the Supreme Court itself. Nina Totenberg, of National Public Radio, and Tim O'Brien, of ABC News, have both experimented with stories of what went on in the secret conferences of the Court and have announced the votes in cases before they "came down." Others, such as CBS's Fred Graham, the unofficial dean of Supreme Court reporters, and Linda Greenhouse, of the *New York Times,* have disdained such practices. But whether the bolder techniques of investigative reporting will or will not be applied routinely to the Court still remains to be seen.

Clarifying Terms

In undertaking the study of civil rights and liberties it is important to recognize that these rights occur in a variety of legal forms. Most familiar to us is the form of constitutional rights—the provisions of the original Constitution and its Amendments as authoritatively interpreted by the Supreme Court. Constitutional rights are obviously very important, but while granting them center stage, they must not be allowed to steal the show. Also important are statutory rights and liberties created by the Congress of the United States at the national level, by state legislatures, and even by municipal authorities. Finally, a note in the considerable body of civil rights and civil liberties law is created by administrative interpretation of court decisions and statutes. These rights take the form of bureaucratic regulations, guidelines, and enforcement decisions— what William Bradford Reynolds and his staff were feuding over.

Before pressing further, it also is well to pause a moment on the words "rights" and "liberties." *Civil liberty* is usually employed to describe prohibitions on government behavior with respect to individuals. Thus government may not interfere with free speech except under very special circumstances and may not enter homes to search for evidence or contraband (e.g., stolen goods) except pursuant to well-delineated procedures. Government may not interfere with certain spheres of individual activity, and when it does proceed against an individual's liberty or property must do so in accordance with certain canons of fairness. *Civil right* generally refers to requirements that persons be treated equally by government. That is, certain kinds of distinctions and discriminations among people are forbidden to government. Persons must not be singled out for special treatment on the basis of these forbidden characteristics; they must be allowed to participate equally in the enjoyment of public services (such as schooling) and political participation (such as voting and running for office).

Since the U.S. Constitution and the judiciary are so important in the working out of these definitions and distinctions, it is to a brief survey of this institutional landscape that we now turn.

SELECTED READINGS

Califano, Joseph A., Jr. *Governing America* (New York: Simon and Schuster, 1981). A good chapter on civil rights enforcement policy.

Casper, Jonathan D. *Lawyers Before the Warren Court: Civil Liberties and Civil Rights, 1957–66* (Urbana: University of Illinois, 1972). An excellent treatment of the roles of interest groups and individual activist lawyers in several different legal issue areas.

Krislov, Samuel. "The Amicus Curial Brief: From Friendship to Advocacy." 62 *Yale Law Journal* 694 (1963).

Lewis, Anthony. *Gideon's Trumpet* (New York: Random House, 1964). A very popular account of a landmark Supreme Court case in the area of criminal defendants' rights.

Manwaring, David R. *Render Unto Caesar: The Flag-Salute Controversy* (Chicago: University of Chicago Press, 1962). An account of the role of the Jehovah's Witnesses in forcing the Supreme Court to confront and then reconsider a painful constitutional question.

Morgan, Richard E. *The Politics of Religious Conflict: Church and State in America,* 2d ed. (Washington, D.C.: University Press of America, 1980). Focuses on the groups and individual actors with special reference to the battle over the "Blaine Amendment" in New York.

Paul, Arnold M. *Conservative Crisis and the Role of Law: Attitudes of Bar and Bench, 1887–1895* (Ithaca, N.Y.: Cornell University Press, 1960). Defenders of laissez-faire economic doctrine effectively protecting what they regarded as civil liberties.

Sigler, Jay A. *American Rights Politics* (Homewood, Ill.: The Dorsey Press, 1975). A survey of the field with some attention to interest group involvement.

Sorauf, Frank J. *The Wall of Separation: The Constitutional Politics of Church and State* (Princeton, N.J.: Princeton University Press, 1976). A close examination of the participation of interest groups in establishment clause cases.

Truman, David B. *The Governmental Process: Political Interests and Public Opinion,* 2d ed. (New York: Knopf, 1971). Contains a ground-breaking chapter on interest groups in the judicial process.

Twiss, Benjamin R. *Lawyers and the Constitution: How Laissez Faire Came to the Supreme Court* (Princeton, N.J.: Princeton University Press, 1942). Excellent study of activist lawyers in the service of the doctrine of unregulated free enterprise.

Vose, Clement E. *Caucasians Only: The Supreme Court, the NAACP, and the Restrictive Covenant Cases* (Berkeley: University of California Press, 1959). One of the best case studies of interest group involvement in the judicial process.

————. *Constitutional Change: Amendment, Politics, and Supreme Court Litigation Since 1900* (Lexington, Mass.: D.C. Heath, 1972). A fascinating picture of groups and activist lawyers at work to make and unmake constitutional law.

CHAPTER · 2

THE INSTITUTIONAL SETTING

THE pattern of American constitutional arrangements is important in many different ways in the struggle over rights and liberties. As was just noted in Chapter 1, many rights and liberties are of constitutional origin; that is, they are purported to be based on particular constitutional provisions such as the speech guarantee of the First Amendment or the due process clause of the Fourteenth. But our constitutional structure is relevant to the politics of civil rights and liberties in other ways as well.

Article III contains the basic grant of power to the federal judiciary in general and to the Supreme Court in particular. Article I not only lays the foundation for the powers of Congress, but it embodies in broad outline the division of powers between the central government and the states—the federal arrangement—which the framers saw as one aspect of their "new science of politics." These grants of responsibility and powers to the branches of the national government, and this division of powers between the nation and the states, are of great importance to the development of rights and liberties, both constitutional and statutory.

Judicial Review

Much of our body of constitutional rights and liberties developed in cases where the Supreme Court interpreted a constitutional provision in a case where the constitutionality of the act of a state legislature or of the national Congress was challenged. Thus the question of the legitimacy and scope of judicial review by the Supreme Court over acts of the states and acts of the coordinate branches of the national government is crucial. Article III provides that the judicial power of the United States shall be vested in a Supreme Court and such inferior courts as Congress shall create. The original jurisdiction of the Supreme Court (where it may serve as the actual trial court to which cases may be brought directly) is spelled out in considerable detail. In all other instances, says Article III, the jurisdiction of the Supreme Court shall be appellate. There is no specific mention of judicial review—of a power to disregard or nullify an act of Congress or of the President or of one of the states on the grounds that it contravenes some prohibition of the Constitution.

It is true that Article VI states that the Constitution and federal laws and treaties passed under the authority of the United States shall be the supreme law of the land. And if the judicial power of the United States is vested in the Supreme Court, one can argue that this court must necessarily possess power to enforce the supremacy clause. But this is a far cry from a specific provision for judicial review, and in any case it goes only to the question of Supreme Court review of acts of the states. What power did the framers of the Constitution intend the Supreme Court to exercise?

While the question cannot be answered categorically, the truth seems to be that a significant number of the more active and influential members of the Constitutional Convention did envision some form of judicial review, both over acts of the states and of coordinate branches of the national government. Interesting in this regard is the story of the historian Charles Beard and his classic study of *The Supreme Court and Judicial Review.* Beard was a man of strong progressive political views, and he was infuriated by the way in which the Supreme Court in the early twentieth century struck down acts of the states and of the national Congress that were intended to regulate the economy and protect workers and consumers against big business. So Beard set out to demonstrate that this power of judicial review, at least insofar as it extended to acts of the national Congress, was illegitimate—that it had not been intended by the framers.

But honest and diligent historian that he was, Beard was forced to the opposite conclusion, and this was eventually embodied in his short, lucid book. A strong bit of evidence that the framers intended the Court to exercise something like the power of judicial review is contained in Alexander Hamilton's *Federalist No. 78.* Here Hamilton discusses the proposed federal judiciary and argues that it will police the Constitution with respect to the other branches as a matter of checks and balances.

It is also interesting to note that James Wilson of Pennsylvania, one of the most influential members of the Constitutional Convention and Chairman of the Committee on Detail (responsible for the drafting of the constitutional language), floated at the Convention the unsuccessful proposal that the Supreme Court be allowed to automatically review acts of Congress for constitutionality in advance of their implementation. Wilson also had fixed his sights on becoming Chief Justice of the United States and only his personal ill-fortune (he was deeply in debt and his life was disrupted by the necessity of evading his creditors) resulted in his having to settle for an associate justiceship from the new President Washington. That Wilson aspired so ardently to the Court would be indication enough of his understanding of its power, but in a series of lectures in 1790–91 at the College of Philadelphia (soon to become the University of Pennsylvania) Wilson explained that the Court had the power to find acts of Congress and of the states unconstitutional, and set forth an argument for that power similar in many respects to that which would be advanced in 1803 by the third Chief Justice of the United States, John Marshall, in the landmark case of *Marbury* v. *Madison,* 1 Cranch 137 (1803).

Certain myths have grown up around *Marbury* v. *Madison* that need dispelling. In the 1940s and 1950s some were schooled to think that *Marbury* was an audacious *coup de main* by John Marshall in which, like Prometheus, he stole from the gods of American democracy the fire of judicial review to which the Court was not entitled. More seriously, *Marbury* is often presented as the origin of the American theory of judicial review. Both ideas are quite false. It does not detract from the brilliance of John Marshall's performance to remember that notions of judicial review were bruted at the Convention, discussed in some detail in the *Federalist Papers,* and adumbrated by James Wilson in his law lectures. In addition, there were several cases before John Marshall's accession to the Chief Justiceship in which the Supreme Court, while not exercising the power of judicial review over acts of the national Congress, had made positive reference to such a power as belonging to the Court.

This is not to say that there is no tension between the elitist character of judicial review and the underlying majoritarian premises of our governmental arrangements. The Justices are not elected by anyone. They have in common some modicum of legal training and the fact that for one reason or another they appealed sufficiently to a sitting President to secure nomination and confirmation by the Senate. They serve for life (absent some high crime or misdemeanor), they cannot be forced to retire, and there are few ways in which the electorate can register disapproval of what they do.

At various points in our history, when the Court has seemed to frustrate political initiatives that have widespread support in the country, commentators have been quick to call attention to the counter-majoritarian character of judicial review. And throughout our history important political leaders have doubted the wisdom of judicial review. Jefferson, Jackson, Lincoln, and Franklin Roosevelt at various times were all frustrated and hostile to the practice. In our own time, perhaps the most significant and influential attack on judicial review was delivered in the spring of 1955 when Judge Learned Hand of the Second Circuit Court of Appeals, one of the most respected of American jurists, delivered the Oliver Wendell Holmes, Jr., lecture at the Harvard Law School. The lecture was published later as a slender volume entitled *The Bill of Rights.* Hand argued that while judicial review was here to stay, its counter-majoritarian character and ambiguous historical origins made it in-cumbent on the Supreme Court to exercise the power only in the clearest instances and only when no other way of disposing of the case before it was available. Over the past thirty years a great deal of legal scholarship has been addressed to rebutting, quarrelling with, or attempting to dismiss Hand's thesis.

Today, there can be no doubt of the essential legitimacy of the power of judicial review by the Court over acts of the national government and over acts of the states. But very important debate continues over the question of when the Court is justified in resorting to the power to declare acts of popularly elected officials—Congress, state legislatures, presidents, and governors—unconstitutional. While there are few today who would have the justices exercise the iron self-restraint advocated by Hand, many are concerned that the contemporary Court has been far too willing to resort to the ultimate weapon of judicial review to impose its own views of sound public policy on other agencies of American government.

Federalism

On the issue of Supreme Court review of acts of the states for constitutionality, we have seen that there was a stronger textual case for judicial review than existed at the national level. The matter was not conclusively settled, however, until the Supreme Court's decision in 1812 in the case of *Martin* v. *Hunter's Lessee.* The case was a complicated property action which involved the peace treaty with Great Britain that ended the Revolution (the Treaty of Paris in 1782) and the disputed ownership of a valuable tract of land in northern Virginia. John Marshall had a personal interest in the case and did not participate; he "recused himself" in the language of the Court. Justice Joseph Story, who also served as professor at the Harvard Law School and wrote a learned set of *Commentaries on the Constitution,* wrote the opinion of the Court, but it was very much in the Marshall tradition and style. Story held that the Court of Appeals of Virginia (the state's highest) had incorrectly decided a federal constitutional question in disposing of the case. Story ordered the Virginia decision reversed. In 1821, in the case of *Cohens* v. *Virginia,* a similar decision was announced by John Marshall in a criminal case. Thus the power of judicial review over decisions of the courts of the states was firmly established.

But this was far from ending the involvement of the Supreme Court of the United States with questions of nation-state relationships; that is, with questions of *federalism.* It fell to the Court to define the scope of the powers of the national government and to identify those areas of peculiar state responsibility into which the federal government might not intrude. The first half of the nineteenth century saw clashes before the Court over the power of Congress to establish a national central bank and maintain it against the taxing powers of the states (*McCulloch* v. *Maryland,* in 1822), the relative powers of the states and the nation to regulate commerce between the states (*Gibbons* v. *Ogden,* in 1824), and, most terribly, the powers of the states and nation wth respect to the issue of human slavery (*Dred Scott* v. *Sanford,* in 1858).

The ratification of the Fourteenth Amendment in 1868 opened a whole new vista of federalism questions for the Court. Prohibitions of the Fourteenth Amendment applied to the states, and the Court, by its interpretation of the majestic phrases "due process of law" and "equal protection of the laws," was to fashion a whole new constellation of federal constitutional restraints on the states.

In the last quarter of the nineteenth century the Court, using the Fourteenth Amendment's prohibition against deprivation of "life, liberty or property without due process of law," read into the word liberty a notion of liberty of contract or liberty of economic entrepreneurship. On this, an elaborate jurisprudence of restraint was erected in which the states were forestalled from undertaking certain kinds of regulation of business activity on the grounds that to do so would deprive individuals who wished to enter into economic arrangements of liberty of contract. This notion also was applied to acts of the federal government through the due process clause of the Fifth Amendment, and a variety of state and federal statutes dealing with working conditions, maximum hours, minimum wages, and permitted price variations were struck down as violating the Constitution. This reading into the due process clause of particular conceptions of liberty, not specifically delineated by the Fourteenth Amendment, came to be called *substantive due process*.

Since the late 1930s the Court has not used the weapon of liberty of contract to strike down either state or national economic regulations, and, for a period in the 1940s and 1950s, the notion of unspecified substantive liberties inhering in the due process clause fell into disrepute. However, as we shall see in Chapter 22, the mode of substantive due process analysis has not been abandoned by the justices. In place of the now neglected liberty of contract the contemporary Supreme Court has found in the due process clause a substantive liberty of sexual and familial freedom that is used to limit the regulatory powers of the states in such areas as abortions.

Nationalizing the Bill of Rights

Even more important than the nineteenth century discovery of certain substantive liberties in the due process clause (and the revival of this notion lately) was the use made of it by the Court in the middle decades of the twentieth century to nationalize the specific provisions of the federal Bill of Rights and make most of them applicable to the states. By its original terms, the Bill of Rights (the first ten Amendments to the Constitution) applied to the national government. That these strictures were not intended to bind the states was affirmed by John Marshall in 1833 in the case of *Barron* v. *Baltimore,* 7 Peters 243, and this view was maintained at least until the adoption of the Fourteenth Amendment in 1868. While it was clear that the due process clause of the Fourteenth Amendment protected individuals against fundamentally unfair treatment by state government in the same way that they were protected against unfair federal treatment by the due process clause of the Fifth Amendment, it also came to be suggested that the due process language of the Fourteenth Amendment should be understood to include or to "incorporate" some, or perhaps even all, of the specific guarantees of Amendments I through X. Students of the framing of the Fourteenth Amendment have been deeply divided over the intentions of its framers. Justice Hugo Black, in a famous dissenting opinion in the case of *Adamson* v. *California,* 332 U.S. 46 (1947), took the position that the framers of the Fourteenth Amendment had specifically intended the incorporation into the due process clause of the protections afforded to individuals against the federal government by Amendments I through VIII. This position had been asserted by the first Justice Harlan, who sat on the Court from 1877–1911, and had been developed in a book, *The Adoption of the Fourteenth Amendment,* published by Professor Horace Flack in 1908. And it was espoused as recently as 1955 in a similarly titled volume by Professor James L. James.

The weight of modern scholarship, however, is against the proposition that the framers of the Fourteenth Amendment (or more than a few of them) intended to "incorporate" the Bill of Rights and make its strictures applicable to the states. Two articles in the April 1949 issue of the *Stanford Law Review,* one by Professor Charles Fairman of the Harvard Law School and one by Professor Charles Morrison of Stanford, persuasively argued that the evidence for "framer incorporation" was thin and confusing. They further argued that the one dominant and broadly shared purpose of those involved was to ensure equal legal rights for the newly freed black people of the South. Even more important, it is clear that contemporaries of the framers of the Fourteenth Amendment, and the generation of interpreters which immediately followed them, did not think that the Fourteenth Amendment incorporated the Bill of Rights. Professor James' effort to rebut Fairman and Morrison was deeply flawed and this was demonstrated by the work of Raoul Berger in his history of the Fourteenth Amendment, which appeared in 1978 (see Part IV). But if the case for an "original incorporation" of the Bill of Rights in the Fourteenth Amendment is weak, the reality of contemporary constitutional politics is that the Supreme Court, in a series of decisions beginning in 1925 and culminating in 1969, extended most of the important provisions of Amendments IV through VIII to the states by holding that they were protected against infringement by the due process clause of the Fourteenth Amendment. The end result of this process of "selective incorporation" was to get the Court to just about where it would have been had it been persuaded by Mr. Justice Black's spirited historical argument in 1947. This nationalization of the Bill of Rights is one of the most important constitutional developments of our time. It profoundly altered the nature of American federalism and has resulted in the Supreme Court's deep involvement in monitoring the criminal justice processes of the states.

Finally, the equal protection clause of the Fourteenth Amendment resulted in another alteration of the pattern of American federalism; namely, it involves the federal judiciary in monitoring matters that, throughout most of our history, were regarded as local. We shall explore this development in Part IV.

What this all means is that, in many important civil rights and liberties matters that come before it, the Supreme Court—and, indeed, Congress and executive branch officials—must be concerned not only with the "intention of the framers," with tradition and precedent, and with the rights and wrongs of the immediate situation at hand, but also must grapple with the structural question of what level of American government should have primary responsibility. American federalism is a unique governmental arrangement, one that is uniquely complicated. It is not surprising that there is a significant "federalism" dimension to debates over rights policy.

Getting to the Supreme Court

Article III spells out the original or trial jurisdiction of the Court. Today, the original jurisdiction is infrequently invoked and then usually in situations where one state sues another. The Supreme Court reviews (except for the one or two original cases each term) decisions of law suits and criminal convictions made somewhere "below." Over four thousand cases are docketed each year for some sort of consideration by the Supreme Court. Where do they come from?

The Federal Courts

Article III provided for a Supreme Court and such inferior courts as Congress "shall from time to time ordain and establish." Under the Judiciary Act of 1789, Congress established national courts in each state so that federal laws could be enforced in friendly forums, not in sometimes hostile state courts. Over the years, Congress has modified and expanded this system through successive amendments to the Judiciary Act. Since 1891 we have had a three-tiered system of federal courts: district courts, courts of appeals (sometimes called circuit courts), and one Supreme Court.

The lowest level of the federal system, the courts of first instance, are the United States district courts. These courts are where trials in criminal cases and civil suits actually take place. There is at least one district for each state, and the large states, such as New York and California, are split into multiple federal district court jurisdictions. There are over five hundred district judges working in over ninety districts. These district judges characteristically sit alone. But in special cases, in which the constitutionality of a federal or state statute is at issue, district judges may sit in three-judge panels. In populous districts, such as the Central District of California, there may be between thirty and forty district judges.

At the intermediate level of the federal judicial system are the courts of appeals. There are United States courts of appeals in twelve circuits, including one for the District of Columbia. Each circuit court, depending on the workload of the area it services, has between four and twenty-three judges. Courts of appeals characteristically sit as three-judge panels. But on occasion, in highly charged cases, they may sit *en banc,* meaning all together as a full bench.

The jurisdiction of federal courts is based on the language of Article III of the Constitution. Cases involving federal statutes, claims under the Constitution, or treaties of the United States are appropriately brought in federal district courts. In addition, suits between persons residing in different states, where the amount at issue exceeds a minimum amount (presently $10,000), may be brought in federal courts.

The State Courts

By far the largest part of the legal work of America, however, is done in state judicial systems. Most crimes and "causes of action" for civil suits are created by *state* laws and are the responsibility of state courts. As a generalization, it is fair to say that most state court systems are organized in a three-tier structure similar to that of the federal courts—trial courts, intermediate appellate courts, and a state supreme court. To illustrate the workings of these parallel but distinct federal and state court systems and the way they relate to the national Supreme Court, spend a moment examining Fig. 2.2. Cases in the state courts *must* proceed through the state system of appeal and review before the Supreme Court of the United States will consider them.

The Court at Work

Our usual mental picture of the Supreme Court is of the nine justices seated behind the bench in the marble Supreme Court Building across the park from the Capitol Building. They are listening to lawyers' arguments and announcing opinions. But this is only the public face of the Court. The real work takes place in the offices, the library, and the conference room—down corridors blocked by velvet ropes and uniformed guards where the public cannot go.

Not only do the justices do their most important work out of public view, but they also perform most of their work independently from one another. The Court sits *en banc,* together behind the bench, to hear oral arguments several times each week during the term of the Court, which runs from October through the following June. The justices also meet in conference, usually once a week, to argue among themselves, vote, and make decisions about cases.

During conference deliberations no one but the justices is allowed in the conference room. If a book or a message must be sent in, the junior associate justice, now Sandra Day O'Connor, gets up, answers the knock, and takes the material. The secrecy of these conferences is almost never breached. No matter how skeptical individual justices may be about secrecy in the other branches of government (Justice Douglas, for instance, was a persistent critic of secrecy as undemocratic), they support it as necessary for their own operations.

Circuit	States Included	Federal Judges Appellate	District
1st	Maine, New Hampshire, Massachusetts, Rhode Island, Puerto Rico	4	23
2nd	New York, Connecticut, Vermont	11	50
3rd	Pennsylvania, New Jersey, Delaware, Virgin Islands	10	50
4th	Virginia, West Virginia, Maryland, North Carolina, South Carolina	10	44
5th	Texas, Louisiana, Mississippi	14	57
6th	Michigan, Ohio, Kentucky, Tennessee	11	51
7th	Illinois, Indiana, Wisconsin	9	36
8th	Missouri, Iowa, Minnesota, North Dakota, South Dakota, Nebraska, Arkansas	9	35
9th	California, Alaska, Hawaii, Washington, Oregon, Idaho, Montana, Arizona, Nevada, Guam	23	75
10th	Colorado, Kansas, Oklahoma, New Mexico, Utah, Wyoming	8	27
11th	Alabama, Georgia, Florida	12	52
D.C.	District of Columbia	11	15

FIGURE 2.1 The Circuit Courts of Appeal in the United States.

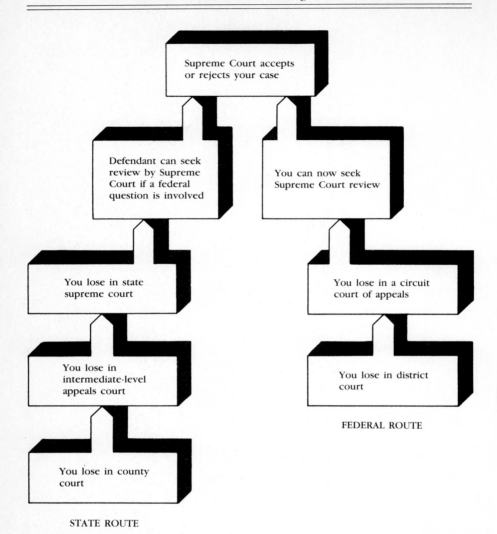

FIGURE 2.2   The Two Most Common Routes to the Supreme Court for Someone Who Has Lost a Lawsuit or Been Convicted of a Crime.

Once a case has been briefed and argued before the Court, full discussion takes place in conference and a vote is taken proceeding from the chief justice to the most junior associate justice. After a particular case has been voted on, the task of writing an opinion is assigned by the Chief Justice if he is with the majority on the case, or if not, by the senior associate justice within the majority. Justices desiring to write dissenting or concurring opinions may begin immediately after the conference vote, or they may wait until the draft of the majority opinion has been circulated to them.

Not all the decisions reached in the conference require written opinions,

TABLE 2.1   THE WORKLOAD OF THE COURT

	Disposed of	Remaining on Docket
ORIGINAL DOCKET	3	14
APPELLATE DOCKET	2174	536
On Merits	282	
Appeals and petitions for review denied, dismissed, or withdrawn (*Review Granted:* 292 (13.5%))	1892	
MISCELLANEOUS DOCKET	2011	341
On merits	16	
Appeals and petitions for review denied, dismissed, or withdrawn (*Review Granted:* 12 (0.6%))	1995	
TOTAL	4188	891

METHOD OF DISPOSITION			
By written opinion (*Number of Written Opinions:* 162)	182	By denial, dismissal or withdrawal of appeals or petitions for review	3887
By Per Curiam or Memorandum Decision	119		
Total			4188

Source: *Harvard Law Review,* Vol. 97, No. 1, November 1983. Copyright © 1983 by the Harvard Law Review Association.

of course. As we have noted, around four thousand cases a year are docketed, meaning received for preliminary consideration. Most of these cases subsequently are rejected by the Court as not presenting questions sufficiently new or interesting to warrant taking up, a decision that must be made by vote of the justices in conference. It requires four votes to qualify a docketed case for oral argument and, presumably, decision. Only about 5 percent of docketed cases are voted for such full consideration.

The justices are assisted in deciding which cases should be given full consideration by their law clerks, who are selected from the best and the brightest recent graduates of the foremost law schools. The Chief Justice enjoys the services of four clerks, while the associate justices have two or three apiece.

A request for consideration by the Supreme Court is initially reviewed by a clerk for each justice. The clerks then make recommendations to their justices as to whether review should be granted. If four or more clerks think so, and four or more justices agree the case is worthy, the case will be voted up when its number is called in conference. Then briefs are called for and a date is set for oral argument. If fewer than four justices are persuaded that the case is worthy, that ends the matter.

Since 1975 the Supreme Court has enjoyed almost total discretion over which of the docketed cases to accept for argument and decision. Most requests for consideration come to the Supreme Court in the form of a petition for a writ of *certiorari* (an order to a lower court to send a case up). A smaller number of cases come to the Court on appeal. The Court is altogether at liberty to accept or reject cases coming on petitions for *certiorari* but is technically obligated to take all cases that present valid appeals.* To the distress of legal purists, however, there seems to be little operational difference between the way the justices handle *certiorari* and the way they handle appeals. It takes four votes to grant petition for *certiorari* and four votes to confirm that an appeal is valid. Thus if you persuade four justices you get review, and if after argument you persuade five (assuming the Court to be at full strength), you win your case.

On Reading Citations

Throughout this book you will encounter citations to legal materials. These look like awful misprints at first glance, but they really are quite easy to understand and use. After all, they have been developed to enable busy people to find their way to what they need quickly. The most frequently encountered "cite" will be to the *United States Reports,* the official rendition of the opinions and acts of the U.S. Supreme Court. Taking the example of the case of *Brown* v. *Board of Education,* 347 U.S. 483 (1954), the first number (347) is the volume number, U.S. is the abbreviation for *United States Reports,* 483 is the page on which *Brown* begins, and 1954 is the year in which the case was decided. This is the pattern for *all appellate court citations;* only the abbreviation in the middle changes to indicate what set of reports is referred to.

Decisions of the U.S. Supreme Court, for instance, also are reported in two commercially prepared and annotated series, *The Supreme Court Reporter* and the *Lawyer's Edition*—abbreviated S.Ct. and L.Ed., respectively. Since these are excellent sources (in many ways better than the *United States Reports*) and are available in many college and university libraries, we have included these citations for all cases excerpted here.

While there are only a few references in this text to lower federal court decisions and to decisions of the state high courts, it will be helpful to you to recognize the citations. The *Federal Supplement* (F. Supp) covers decisions

---

* The special circumstances under which an appeal may be taken are set out in 28 U.S.C. 1257. A party seeking to appeal is required to submit a "statement of probable jurisdiction." The justices treat these in much the same way they treat petitions for writs of *certiorari.* There is an infrequently used third form in which Supreme Court review is invoked—certification. By this procedure a federal circuit court or the Court of Claims places a complex point of law before the Supreme Court. Issues of civil rights and liberties are rarely decided this way.

of the U.S. district courts, and the *Federal Reporter* (F.) covers those of the U.S. courts of appeals. The *Federal Reporter* is in a "second series" (the numbering having been started over again); thus F.2d. Many college and university libraries will have these sets.

As for state supreme courts, there usually is an official set of reports published by each state, and regionally organized sets of reports are prepared commercially. Thus the 1972 decision of the Court of Appeals of New York in *Newport Associates* v. *Solon* is 30 N.Y.2d 263 (*New York Reports,* second series) and 283 N.E.2d 600 (*North East Reporter,* second series). State court decisions usually can be found only in law libraries.

A word also is in order about statutes—at least federal statutes. They appear in three forms: the Public Laws of the United States (the individual acts as signed into law), the *U.S. Statutes At Large* (an annual compilation), and the *United States Code* (all the federal law presently in effect organized topically and cross referenced). Taking the Foreign Intelligence Surveillance Act of 1978, for example, it was Public Law 95-511, 95th Congress. It appears at 92 Stat. 1783 (yes, volume and page!), and its provisions have been fitted into the *U.S. Code* at 50 U.S.C. 1801. In the case of the Code citation, however, the first number refers to a topical *Title* of the Code, and the second number to a *section* of that Title. Subsections are further identified by a lower case letter, and paragraphs within subsections by an arabic number. Thus the description of unlawful employment practices by private employers covered by the Civil Rights Act of 1964 is at 42 U.S.C. 2000(e) (1).

In referring to law review articles in this text, we have generally followed the convention of legal writing by "citing" the volume number, the name of the review, the first page number, and the year. A very useful research tool in the area of rights policy (or any public law area) is the *Index to Legal Periodicals,* which indexes about 300 journals including all of the important law reviews.

A final useful tool for research in the area of rights and liberties is *U.S. Law Week.* This covers each term of the Supreme Court (as well as other important legal developments) on a weekly basis. It is the easiest, quickest source of the texts of recently decided cases. Many college and university libraries maintain *U.S. Law Week* in their reference sections.

SELECTED READINGS

Beard, Charles A. *The Supreme Court and the Constitution* (New York: Macmillan, 1912). Said Beard of this book, "the ghost of usurpation was fairly laid." Reissued in 1962 by Prentice-Hall as Spectrum paperback.

Beverage, Albert J. *The Life of John Marshall,* 4 vols. (Boston: Houghton Mifflin, 1916). Classic biography of the most influential figure in the early development of the federal judiciary by a latter-day "Federalist."

Bickel, Alexander M. *The Supreme Court and the Idea of Progress* (New York: Harper and Row, 1970). This is an expanded version of Bickel's 1969 Holmes lectures at Harvard, which constitute the most influential attack on judicial activism since Learned Hand's 1955 performance.

Choper, Jesse H. *Judicial Review and the National Political Process* (Chicago: University of Chicago Press, 1980). An argument for removing basic federalism questions from the ambit of judicial review.

Ely, John Hart. *Democracy and Distrust: A Theory of Judicial Review* (Cambridge: Harvard University Press, 1980). A suggested "middle-way" between activism and restraint by the Dean of the Stanford Law School.

Fairman, Charles. "Does the Fourteenth Amendment Incorporate the Bill of Rights?" 2 *Stanford Law Review* (1949).

Flack, Horace. *The Adoption of the Fourteenth Amendment* (Baltimore: Johns Hopkins University Press, 1908). Still cited as authority for the intention by the framers of the Fourteenth Amendment to "incorporate" the Bill of Rights.

Haines, Charles Grove. *The Role of the Supreme Court in American Government*, 2 vols. (Berkeley: University of California Press, 1957). Detailed treatment of the development of the Court by a political scientist.

Halperin, Stephen C., and Lamb, Charles M., eds. *Supreme Court Activism and Restraint* (Lexington, Mass.: Lexington Books, 1982). An excellent collection of recent essays on the subject.

Hand, Learned. *The Bill of Rights* (Cambridge: Harvard University Press, 1958). Forty-five years after Beard, Hand again raised the spectre of usurpation by the Court of the power of judicial review.

James, James B. *The Framing of the Fourteenth Amendment* (Urbana: University of Illinois Press, 1956). Attempted to repair the damage to Flack's thesis by Fairman and Morrison.

Kurland, Philip B.; Casper, Gerhard; and Hutchinson, Dennis J. *The Supreme Court Review.* This has been published annually by the University of Chicago Press since 1960. An excellent source of secondary material.

McCloskey, Robert G. *The American Supreme Court* (Chicago: University of Chicago Press, 1960). An excellent short history of the early development of the Court. Available in paperback.

Morrison, Stanley. "Does the Fourteenth Amendment Incorporate the Bill of Rights?" 2 *Stanford Law Review* (1949).

Murphy, Bruce Allen. *The Brandeis/Frankfurter Connection: The Secret Political Activities of Two Supreme Court Justices* (New York: Oxford University Press, 1982). A lively portrayal of the interrelationship of Justices, law professors, and political opinion makers, with reference to the relationship indicated by the title.

Murphy, Walter F. *The Vicar of Christ* (New York: Macmillan, 1979). A novel by a distinguished academic student of the Court in which a Marine Corps hero becomes, successively, Chief Justice of the United States and Pope. The passages on the internal life of the Court are entertaining.

Warren, Charles. *The Supreme Court in United States History,* 2 vols. (Boston: Little, Brown, 1922). Treatment of the Court up to 1918 by a distinguished historian.

Wechsler, Herbert. *Principles, Politics, and Fundamental Law* (Cambridge: Harvard University Press, 1961). This volume contains Wechsler's 1958–59 Holmes lecture, "Toward Neutral Principles of Constitutional Law," in which he affirmed the legitimacy and utility of judicial review (*pace* Hand) as long as it was exercised in a disciplined and principled fashion.

Woodward, Bob, and Armstrong, Scott. *The Brethren* (New York: Simon and Schuster, 1979). Backstairs gossip of the Court, largely pieced together from the conversation of incautious clerks. Altogether unreliable, but fascinating.

PART I

FREEDOM OF SPEECH

Congress shall make no law ... abridging the freedom of speech, or of the press; ....

THIS was the language of Amendment I proposed by the first Congress of the United States and ratified by two-thirds of the state legislatures in 1791. In 1925, in the case of *Gitlow* v. *New York,* the Supreme Court held that the freedoms of speech and of the press, protected by the First Amendment from abridgement by Congress, were among the "fundamental personal rights and liberties protected by the due process clause of the Fourteenth Amendment from abridgement by the states." Thus the majestic language of the First Amendment binds all levels of American government from the national to the local. But just what is it that all governments are prohibited from abridging, and what constitutes an abridgement? Freedom of speech and freedom of the press are at one and the same time among the most important and the most opaque concepts in American constitutional law.

Does "speech" mean any squeaking or croaking of the vocal cords? Does "press" mean any crooked little markings on paper? What about pictures— visual portrayal of ideas? And what about certain kinds of behavior associated with the expression of ideas—walking the picket line or blocking access to the construction site of a nuclear power plant? Does the concept of the press include the mimeographed scribblings of basement pornographers or racists? Or does it require some level of organized, professional communications activity for one to be denominated a member of the press? And does freedom of the speech and of the press mean the capacity to say and write anything? If not, where may government draw the line consistent with the commands of the First and Fourteenth Amendments?

As students of constitutional interpretation, our first recourse must be to the history of the speech and press clauses. But here, surprisingly and unhappily, there is little to guide us. Some students of the history of free speech in

America, notably Professor Zachariah Chafee, Jr., of the Harvard Law School, in his famous *Free Speech in the United States,* suggested that the intentions of the framers were to wipe out the common law of seditious libel (writing intended to stimulate hatred and contempt for public officials) and make prosecutions for criticism of the government, without any incitement to law breaking, impossible. There are a number of key words in this conclusion. "Sedition" is the incitement to violate the laws of the land, and this, Chafee concluded, was not an offense protected by the First Amendment. Seditious libel, however, was the common law offense of traducing or vilifying officials of the government. This, according to Chafee, the framers intended to exclude.

In the common law of England, which was, on the whole, exported to the colonies and appropriated by the new states upon independence, the truth of a statement made about an individual or government official was none the less libel for it being true. In fact, in the common law tradition, the truth of the statement exacerbated its libelous character. The theory was that any statement that brought an individual or member of the government into contempt or brought down political ridicule upon that person was actionable. An action at law, either civil or criminal, was in the common law tradition a substitute for individual acts of vengeance. In the ancient logic of common law, vengeance was even more likely if the defamatory statement were true. The core of Chafee's argument was that, at least for attacks on government officials, the First Amendment reversed the presumption of the common law. Inflammatory statements about a public official could not be made the subject of a criminal prosecution; if they were, truth would be a defense against conviction.

If Chafee had been correct, this would indeed have been a substantial building block of intention on which an edifice of First Amendment interpretation could be based. The difficulty is that the evidence for such intention by the framers is dubious. In 1960 the eminent constitutional historian Leonard W. Levy published a short book, *Freedom of Speech and Press in Early American History: Legacy of Suppression.* After a careful review of the evidence from the colonial period and from the period of the framing of the First Amendment, Levy concludes that far from intending to repeal the common law of seditious libel "it would be closer to the truth to say that freedom of speech and press were so little known that even libertarian theory regarded the right to express seditious sentiments as an intolerable indulgence in licenticiousness." Indeed, Levy remarks, the notion of truth as an absolute defense against libel was "in the air" in the colonial period, but it was far from being generally accepted, and the appropriate historical conclusion is that the framers as a group had only a very vague and general conception of what they intended by the speech and press clauses of Amendment I.

But even if Levy is correct, does this mean that there is nothing in the intentions of the framers of the First Amendment to guide and constrain today's interpretation of the speech clause? Not necessarily. It may be argued that Chafee, Levy, and others who preoccupied themselves with the question of whether the framers specifically intended to alter the common law of seditious libel were asking the wrong question. They were seeking a specific intent that could not be found, and this has persuaded some commentators that there is little helpful to today's interpreters in the First Amendment's history. The fault was looking for a specific intention when a general purpose is relatively easy to establish from their historical materials and is not at all unhelpful or without meaning for today's struggles over interpreting the speech clause.

Levy certainly recognized there was a general idea of free speech in the air, both in late eighteenth century England and in America. In December 1792, Thomas Paine, the radical political theorist and pamphleteer of the American Revolution, was tried in England for sedition. Paine had travelled to England in 1787, and published a two-volume work defending the French Revolution titled, *The Rights of Man.* It was the second volume of this work that resulted in a charge for inciting the public to resist the laws of England and overturn its government. Paine was defended by Lord Erskine, a leading lawyer and politician of the day. Erskine admitted to the court that Paine's writings could not be defended on their merits, but went on to argue that "according to the laws of England, a writer is at liberty to address the reason of the nation upon the constitution and government, and is criminal only if he seeks to incite them to disobey the law or calumniates living magistrates." Since Paine had done neither of the latter, Erskine argued that his ideas, no matter how offensive or radical in the abstract, could not be deemed criminal. Erskine drew on the writings of John Locke, John Milton, and Edmund Burke in his appeal to the jury.

Paine was found guilty—on the conclusion of the jury that he had in fact incited disobedience of the laws—and promptly fled to Paris. But Erskine's argument on his behalf beautifully captures the conception of free speech entertained by libertarians in the eighteenth century; namely, the expression of political views could never be criminalized unless they incited law breaking or libeled living officials. Both the common law offenses of sedition and seditious libel were thus recognized as valid, but the core idea of free political discourse up to these thresholds was a striking and important one.

One finds in eighteenth century America, in the writings of those who reflected upon free speech, echoes of Erskine's argument. Free political speech is linked again and again with republican government. Republican government, it is reasoned, is impossible without open political discourse, and within the broad limits of sedition and seditious libel, political views could not be punished. Such an argument was in direct contradiction to the prevailing views in seventeenth and early eighteenth century America and England, where opinion could be punished merely because it was dangerous or offensive or "of a pernicious tendency."

The idea of largely free political speech was a development of major importance. This was the core idea of the speech clause of the First Amendment and is the proper and useful starting point for an examination of the evolving doctrine of free speech in America.

SELECTED READINGS

Berns, Walter. *The First Amendment and the Future of American Democracy* (New York: Basic Books, 1976). An elegant critique of some recent trends in First Amendment interpretation.

Chafee, Zachariah, Jr. *Free Speech in the United States* (Cambridge: Harvard University Press, 1941). The first really scholarly study of free speech. If it now appears flawed, it is well to remember that Chafee was an intellectual pioneer who defended free speech in a period of anti-radical repression and at the risk of his own career.

Emerson, Thomas I. *The System of Freedom of Expression* (New York: Random House, 1970). A survey of contemporary free speech issues by a scholar committed to a very broad interpretation of the speech-press clause.

Haiman, Franklyn S. *Speech and Law in a Free Society* (Chicago: University of Chicago Press, 1981). The author, a professor of communications, takes the position that unless an utterance will cause immediate "material" harm to other persons, it should be protected.

Levy, Leonard W. *Freedom of Speech and Press in Early American History: Legacy of Suppression* (Cambridge: Harvard University Press, 1960). Now a minor classic, Levy's work advanced our understanding of the origins of the First Amendment's speech-press provision.

May, Thomas Erskine. *The Constitutional History of England Since the Accession of George the Third* 2 vols. (New York: Armstrong, 1899). Volume II, covering the period 1780–1800, has much interesting English background on free speech, including a discussion of Paine's trial.

Meiklejohn, Alexander. *Political Freedom* (New York: Harper and Row, 1960). A philosopher's eloquent defense of absolute protection for political speech.

Tussman, Joseph. *Government and the Mind* (New York: Oxford University Press, 1977). Lays the theoretical foundation for a conservative theory of free speech. Interesting contrast to Emerson and Berns.

CHAPTER · 3

"SUBVERSIVE SPEECH"—THE SEARCH FOR SEDITION

WHATEVER may be unclear about the tradition of free speech in America from the framing of the First Amendment through the nineteenth century, it is clear that sedition—incitement to resist the laws and to revolt against the authority of the legally established government—was not protected. When the domestic tensions generated by American entry into World War I in 1917 finally produced a clash before the Supreme Court that required the tribunal to authoritatively interpret the meaning of the speech clause of the First Amendment for the first time, the cases before the Court involved something with a superficial resemblance to sedition but not sedition itself.

In 1917 Congress enacted an Espionage Act. This statute defined the crime of espionage as furnishing information to an enemy of the United States with intent to damage the interests of this country. This portion of the statute remains in force today. Another portion of the statute, which has long since lapsed, made it a crime to cause or attempt to cause insubordination in the military or naval forces of the United States or to obstruct recruitment and enlistment into military service while the United States was at war with the German empire. The following year, 1918, the statute was amended to create the further crime of urging curtailment of war production with the intent to hinder the prosecution of the war against Germany.

In the wake of World War I and the adoption of the Espionage Act, a number of states adopted statutes that criminalized advocating, or conspiring to advocate, the violent overthrow of government. And in 1940, with war clouds once again darkening the American horizon, the national government in the Smith Act of that year made it a federal crime to advocate or conspire to advocate the violent overthrow of government within the United States.

None of these statutes required specific incitement to violate specific laws, nor the incitement of others to overthrow the government in any immediate sense. The speech that was criminalized was a step removed from actual incitement to action. In the abridged and summarized cases that follow, you will see how the Supreme Court grappled with the problem presented by these "subversive speech" laws.

In *Schenck* v. *United States,* the Court grappled with the provision of the Espionage Act criminalizing attempts to cause insubordination of military and naval forces. In the *Abrams* case, the 1918 Amendments concerning war production were at issue. In *Gitlow* v. *New York,* prosecution was for violating the New York Criminal Anarchy Act, which prohibited advocacy of violent overthrow. In *Whitney* v. *California,* that state's Criminal Syndicalism Act was at issue. *Dennis* v. *United States,* and the trilogy of *Yates, Scales,* and *Noto,* involved the Smith Act of 1940 and the federal "advocacy offense."

Justice Oliver Wendell Holmes, Jr., first for the Court in *Schenck,* and then in dissent in *Abrams* and *Gitlow,* attempted to develop some principle to limit the extent to which speech that was not actual incitement to action could be criminalized consistent with the First Amendment. In *Dennis,* the Court struggled further with this problem. The *Yates, Scales* and *Noto* trilogy sees Justice John Marshall Harlan persevere in the effort to contain speech crimes to those utterances that are closely linked to incitement to specific action.

Schenck v. *United States*
249 U.S. 47, 39 S.Ct. 247, 63 L.Ed. 470 (1919)

In June of 1917, in the wake of the American entry into World War I, Congress passed, and President Woodrow Wilson signed into law, the Espionage Act. Some parts of this statute (those dealing with actual spying) remain in force today. Certain other provisions have long since lapsed. Among these were the following three offenses:

> (1) Whoever, when the United States is at war, shall willfully make or convey false reports or false statements with intent to interfere with the operation or success of the military or naval forces of the United States or to promote the success of its enemies and (2) whoever, when the United States is at war, shall willfully cause or attempt to cause insubordination, disloyalty, mutiny, or refusal of duty, in the military or naval forces of the United States, or (3) shall willfully obstruct the recruiting or enlistment Service of the United States, to the injury of the service or of the United States, shall be punished by a fine of not more than $10,000 or imprisonment for not more than twenty years, or both.

There were several convictions under these provisions, including that of Eugene V. Debs, five-time presidential candidate of the American Socialist Party, for a speech to a crowd in a railway yard in Canton, Ohio, in which he urged active opposition to the war effort. His conviction was upheld by the Supreme Court, along with those of others, in a group of decisions in which Justice Oliver Wendell Holmes, Jr. wrote for the Court. Holmes' opinion in *Schenck* displays the reasoning he applied to all of this "first round" of Espionage Act cases.

Mr. Justice Holmes delivered the opinion of the court.

This is an indictment in three counts. The first charges a conspiracy to violate the Espionage Act . . . by causing and attempting to cause insubordination, &c., in the military and naval forces of the United States, and to obstruct the recruiting and enlistment service of the United States, when the United States was at war with the German Empire, to-wit, that the defendants wilfully conspired to have printed and circulated to men who had been called and accepted for military service under the Act of May 18, 1917, a document set forth and alleged to be calculated to cause such insubordination and obstruction. . . . The defendants set up the First Amendment to the Constitution forbidding Congress to make any law abridging the freedom of speech, or of the press, and bringing the case here on that ground have argued some other points also of which we must dispose.

The document in question upon its first printed side recited the first section of the Thirteenth Amendment, said that the idea embodied in it was violated by the Conscription Act and that a conscript is little better than a convict. In impassioned language it intimated that conscription was despotism in its worst form and a monstrous wrong against humanity in the interest of Wall Street's chosen few. It said "Do not submit to intimidation," but in form at least confined itself to peaceful measures such as a petition for the repeal of the act. The other and later printed side of the sheet was headed "Assert Your Rights." It stated reasons for alleging that any one violated the Constitution when he refused to recognize "your right to assert your opposition to the draft," and went on "If you do not assert and support your rights, you are helping to deny or disparage rights which it is the solemn duty of all citizens and residents of the United States to retain." It described the arguments on the other side as coming from cunning politicians and a mercenary capitalist press, and even silent consent to the conscription law as helping to support an infamous conspiracy. It denied the power to send our citizens away to foreign shores to shoot up the people of other lands, and added that words could not express the condemnation such cold-blooded ruthlessness deserves, &c., &c., winding up "You must do your share to maintain, support and uphold the rights of the people of this country." Of course the document would not have been sent unless it had been intended to have some effect, and we do not see what effect it could be expected to have upon persons subject to the draft except to influence them to obstruct the carrying of it out. The defendants do not deny that the jury might find against them on this point.

But it is said, suppose that that was the tendency of this circular, it is protected by the First Amendment to the Constitution. . . . We admit that in many places and in ordinary times the defendants in saying all that was said in the circular would have been within their constitutional rights. But the character of every act depends upon the circumstances in which it is done. . . . The most stringent protection of free speech would not protect a man in falsely shouting fire in a theatre and causing a panic. It does not even protect a man from an injunction against uttering words that may have all the effect of force. . . . The question in every case is whether the words used are used in such circumstances and are of such a nature as to create a clear and present danger that they will bring about the substantive evils that Congress has a right to prevent. It is a question of proximity and degree. When a nation is at war many things that might be said in time of peace are such a hindrance to its effort that their utterance will not be endured so long as men fight and that no Court could regard them as protected by any constitutional right. It seems to be admitted that if an actual obstruction of the recruiting service were proved, liability for words that produced that effect might be enforced. The statute of 1917 . . . punishes conspiracies to obstruct as well as actual obstruction. If the act, (speaking, or circulating a paper,) its tendency and the intent with which it is done are the same, we perceive no ground for saying that success alone warrants making the act a crime. . . .

Judgments affirmed.

Abrams v. United States
250 U.S. 616, 40 S.Ct. 17, 63 L.Ed. 1173 (1919)

This case involved the 1918 amendment to the Espionage Act. Offenses created here included uttering, printing, writing, or publishing any disloyal, profane, scurrilous, or abusive language or language intended to cause contempt, scorn, contumely, or disrepute as regards the form of government of the United States; any language intended to incite resistance to the United States or promote the cause of its enemies; or any language urging curtailment of production of any things necessary to the prosecution of war with the intent to hinder such prosecution. Abrams was convicted of conspiring to violate these provisions of the 1918 amendment for distributing in New York City some five thousand circulars, which allegedly were intended to bring the form of government of the United States into contempt, encourage resistance to the United States in World War I, and incite curtailment of war production. In the circulars the workers of the world were urged to awake and put down the common enemy—capitalism. A general strike was advocated as the necessary reply to the "barbaric intervention" in Russia. Further, the toilers of America were encouraged to pledge themselves "to create so great a disturbance that the autocrats of America should be compelled to keep their armies at home, and not be able to spare any for Russia." Justice John Clarke's opinion for the Court argued that the question of the constitutionality of the Espionage Act had been disposed of by *Schenck.* The only question that remained was whether the materials distributed by Abrams would have the tendency of diminishing war production. Clarke had no difficulty holding that they would. For Justice Holmes, the author of *Schenck,* the matter was not that simple.

Mr. Justice Holmes, dissenting.

This indictment is founded wholly upon the publication of two leaflets which I shall describe in a moment. The first count charges a conspiracy pending the war with Germany to publish abusive language about the form of government of the United States, laying the preparation and publishing of the first leaflet as overt acts. The second count charges a conspiracy pending the war to publish language intended to bring the form of government into contempt, laying the preparation and publishing of the two leaflets as overt acts. The third count alleges a conspiracy to encourage resistance to the United States in the same war and to attempt to effectuate the purpose by publishing the same leaflets. The fourth count lays a conspiracy to incite curtailment of production of things necessary to the prosecution of the war and to attempt to accomplish it by publishing the second leaflet to which I have referred.

The first of these leaflets says that the President's cowardly silence about the intervention in Russia reveals the hypocrisy of the plutocratic gang in Washington. It intimates that "German militarism combined with allied capitalism to crush the Russian revolution"—goes on that the tyrants of the world fight each other until they see a common enemy—working class enlightenment, when they combine to crush it; and that now militarism and capitalism combined, though not openly, to crush the Russian revolution. It says that there is only one enemy of the workers of the world and that is capitalism; that it is a crime for workers of America, &c., to fight the workers' republic of Russia, and ends "Awake! Awake, you Workers of the World! Revolutionists." A note adds "It is absurd to call us pro-German. We hate and despise German militarism more than do you hypocritical tyrants. We have more reasons for denouncing German militarism than has the coward of the White House."

The other leaflet, headed "Workers—Wake Up," with abusive language says that America together with the Allies will march for Russia to help the Czecko-Slovaks in their struggle against the Bolsheviki, and that this time the hypocrites shall not fool the Russian emigrants and friends of Russia in America. It tells the Russian emigrants that they now must spit in the face of the false military propaganda by which their sympathy and help to the prosecution of the war have been called forth and says that with the money they have lent or are going to lend "they will make bullets not only for the Germans but also for the Workers Soviets of Russia," and further, "Workers in the ammunition factories, you are producing bullets, bayonets, cannon, to murder not only the Germans, but also your dearest, best, who are in Russia and are fighting for freedom." It then appeals to the same Russian emigrants at some length not to consent to the "inquisitionary expedition to Russia," and says that the destruction of the Russian revolution is "the politics of the march to Russia." The leaflet winds up by saying "Workers, our reply to this barbaric intervention has to be a general strike!," and after a few words on the spirit of revolution, exhortations not to be afraid, and some usual tall talk ends "Woe unto those who will be in the way of progress. Let solidarity live! The Rebels."

No argument seems to me necessary to show that these pronunciamentos in no way attack the form of government of the United States, or that they do not support either of the first two counts. What little I have to say about the third count may be postponed until I have considered the fourth. With regard to that it seems too plain to be denied that the suggestion to workers in the ammunition factories that they are producing bullets to murder their dearest, and the further advocacy of a general strike, both in the second leaflet, do urge curtailment of production of things necessary to the prosecution of the war within the meaning of the Act. . . . But to make the conduct criminal that statute requires that it should be "with intent by such curtailment to cripple or hinder the United States in the prosecution of the war." It seems to me that no such intent is proved.

I am aware of course that the word intent as vaguely used in ordinary legal discussion means no more than knowledge at the time of the act that the consequences said to be intended will ensue. Even less than that will satisfy the general principle of civil and criminal liability. A man may have to pay damages, may be sent to prison, at common law might be hanged, if at the time of his act he knew facts from which common experience showed that the consequences would follow, whether he individually could foresee them or not. But, when words are used exactly, a deed is not done with intent to produce a consequence unless that consequence is the aim of the deed. It may be obvious, and obvious to the actor, that the consequence will follow, and he may be liable for it even if he regrets it, but he does not do the act with intent to produce it unless the aim to produce it is the proximate motive of the specific act, although there may be some deeper motive behind.

It seems to me that this statute must be taken to use its words in a strict and accurate sense. They would be absurd in any other. A patriot might think that we were wasting money on aeroplanes, or making more cannon of a certain kind than we needed, and might advocate curtailment with success, yet even if it turned out that the curtailment hindered and was thought by other minds to have been obviously likely to hinder the United States in the prosecution of the war, no one would hold such conduct a crime. I admit that my illustration does not answer all that might be said but it is enough to show what I think and to let me pass to a more important aspect of the case. I refer to the First Amendment to the Constitution that Congress shall make no law abridging the freedom of speech.

I never have seen any reason to doubt that the questions of law that alone were before this Court in the cases of *Schenck, Frohwerk* and *Debs,* 249 U.S. 47, 204, 211, were rightly decided. I do not doubt for a moment that by the same reasoning that would justify punishing persuasion to murder, the United States constitutionally may punish speech that produces or is intended to produce a clear and imminent danger that it will bring about forthwith certain substantive evils that the United States constitutionally may seek to prevent. The power undoubtedly is greater in time of war than in time of peace because war opens dangers that do not exist at other times.

But as against dangers peculiar to war, as against others, the principle of the right to free speech is always the same. It is only the present danger of immediate evil or an intent to bring it about that warrants Congress in setting a limit to the expression of opinion where private rights are not concerned. Congress certainly cannot forbid all effort to change the mind of the country. Now nobody can suppose that the surreptitious publishing of a silly leaflet by an unknown man, without more, would present any immediate danger that its opinions would hinder the success of the government arms or have any appreciable tendency to do so. . . .

. . . .

Persecution for the expression of opinions seems to me perfectly logical. If you have no doubt of your premises or your power and want a certain result with all your heart you naturally express your wishes in law and sweep away all opposition. To allow opposition by speech seems to indicate that you think the speech impotent, as when a man says that he has squared the circle, or that you do not care whole-heartedly for the result, or that you doubt either your power or your premises. But when men have realized that time has upset many fighting faiths, they may come to believe even more than they believe the very foundations of their own conduct that the ultimate good desired is better reached by free trade in ideas—that the best test of truth is the power of the thought to get itself accepted in the competition of the market, and that truth is the only ground upon which their wishes safely can be carried out. That at any rate is the theory of our Constitution. It is an experiment, as all life is an experiment. Every year if not every day we have to wager our salvation upon some prophecy based upon imperfect knowledge. While that experiment is part of our system I think that we should be eternally vigilant against attempts to check the expression of opinions that we loathe and believe to be fraught with death, unless they so imminently threaten immediate interference with the lawful and pressing purposes of the law that an immediate check is required to save the country. . . .

Mr. Justice Brandeis concurs with the foregoing opinion.

Gitlow v. *New York*
268 U.S. 652, 45 S.Ct. 625, 69 L.Ed. 1138 (1925)

In this case the conflict over what seditious or subversive speech may be restricted by government moves into a *state* context. At issue is the New York Criminal Anarchy Law of 1902, which had been enacted after President William McKinley was assassinated by an anarchist gunman. Justice Edward T. Sanford's opinion for the Court is notable for the almost casual fashion in which he concludes that any speech that has a tendency to produce violent acts may be proscribed, and for his equally casual acceptance of the theory that the speech and press clauses of our First Amendment also apply to acts of the states through the due process clause of the Fourteenth Amendment. In his dissent, Justice Holmes further refines his "clear and present danger" approach. Benjamin Gitlow went on to become a long-time functionary of the Communist Party of the United States.

Mr. Justice Sanford delivered the opinion of the Court.

Benjamin Gitlow was indicted in the Supreme Court of New York, with three others, for the statutory crime of criminal anarchy. . . .

. . . The indictment was in two counts. The first charged that the defendant had advocated, advised and taught the duty, necessity and propriety of overthrowing and overturning organized government by force, violence and unlawful means, by certain writings therein set forth entitled "The Left Wing Manifesto"; the second that he had printed, published and knowingly circulated and distributed a certain paper called "The Revolutionary Age," containing the writings set forth in the first count advocating, advising and teaching the doctrine that organized government should be overthrown by force, violence and unlawful means. . . .

. . . .

. . . . There was no evidence of any effect resulting from the publication and circulation of the Manifesto. . . .

The sole contention here is, essentially, that as there was no evidence of any concrete result flowing from the publication of the Manifesto or of circumstances showing the likelihood of such result, the statute as construed and applied by the trial court penalizes the mere utterance, as such, of "doctrine" having no quality of incitement, without regard either to the circumstances of its utterance or to the likelihood of unlawful sequences; and that, as the exercise of the right of free expression with relation to government is only punishable "in circumstances involving likelihood of substantive evil," the statute contravenes the due process clause of the Fourteenth Amendment. . . .

The statute does not penalize the utterance or publication of abstract "doctrine" or academic discussion having no quality of incitement to any concrete action. It is not aimed against mere historical or philosophical essays. It does not restrain the advocacy of changes in the form of government by constitutional and lawful means. What it prohibits is language advocating, advising or teaching the overthrow of organized government by unlawful means. These words imply urging to action. . . .

The Manifesto, plainly, is neither the statement of abstract doctrine nor, as suggested by counsel, mere prediction that industrial disturbances and revolutionary mass strikes will result spontaneously in an inevitable process of evolution in the economic system. It advocates and urges in fervent language mass action which shall progressively foment industrial disturbances and through political mass strikes and revolutionary mass action overthrow and destroy organized parliamentary government. It concludes with a call to action in these words:

"The proletariat revolution and the Communist reconstruction of society—
the struggle for these—is now indispensable. . . . The Communist Internaional
calls the proletariat of the world to the final struggle!"

This is not the expression of philosophical abstraction, the mere prediction of future events; it is the language of direct incitement.

The means advocated for bringing about the destruction of organized parliamentary government, namely, mass industrial revolts usurping the functions of municipal government, political mass strikes directed against the parliamentary state, and revolutionary mass action for its final destruction, necessarily imply the use of force and violence, and in their essential nature are inherently unlawful in a constitutional government of law and order. That the jury were warranted in finding that the Manifesto advocated not merely the abstract doctrine of overthrowing organized government by force, violence and unlawful means, but action to that end, is clear.

For present purposes we may and do assume that freedom of speech and of the press—which are protected by the First Amendment from abridgment by Congress—are among the fundamental personal rights and "liberties" protected by the due process clause of the Fourteenth Amendment from impairment by the States. . . .

By enacting the present statute the State has determined, through its legislative body, that utterances advocating the overthrow of organized government by force, violence and unlawful means, are so inimical to the general welfare and involve such danger of substantive evil that they may be penalized in the exercise of its police power. That determination must be given great weight. . . . That utterances inciting to the overthrow of organized government by unlawful means, present a sufficient danger of substantive evil to bring their punishment within the range of legislative discretion, is clear. Such utterances, by their very nature, involve danger to the public peace and to the security of the State. They threaten breaches of the peace and ultimate revolution. And the immediate danger is none the less real and substantial because the effect of a given utterance cannot be accurately foreseen. . . .

We cannot hold that the present statute is an arbitrary or unreasonable exercise of the police power of the State unwarrantably infringing the freedom of speech or press; and we must and do sustain its constitutionality.

Affirmed.

Mr. Justice Holmes, dissenting.

Mr. Justice Brandeis and I are of opinion that this judgment should be reversed. The general principle of free speech, it seems to me, must be taken to be included in the Fourteenth Amendment, in view of the scope that has been given to the word "liberty" as there used, although perhaps it may be accepted with a somewhat larger latitude of interpretation than is allowed to Congress by the sweeping language that governs or ought to govern the laws of the United States. If I am right then I think that the criterion sanctioned by the full Court in *Schenck v. United States* applies. . . . It is true that in my opinion this criterion was departed from in *Abrams v. United States*. . . . but the convictions that I expressed in that case are too deep for it to be possible for me as yet to believe that it [has] . . . settled the law. If what I think the correct test is applied, it is manifest that there was no present danger of an attempt to overthrow the government by force on the part of the admittedly small minority who shared the defendant's views. It is said that this manifesto was more than a theory, that it was an incitement. Every idea is an incitement. It offers itself for belief and if believed it is acted on unless some other belief outweighs it or some failure of energy stifles the movement at its birth. The only difference between the expression of an opinion and an incitement in the narrower sense is the speaker's enthusiasm for the result. Eloquence may set fire to reason. But whatever may be thought of the redundant discourse before us it had no chance of starting a present conflagration. If in the long run the beliefs expressed in proletarian dictatorship are destined to be accepted by the dominant forces of the community, the only meaning of free speech is that they should be given their chance and have their way.

If the publication of this document had been laid as an attempt to induce an uprising against government at once and not at some indefinite time in the future it would have presented a different question. The object would have been one with which the law might deal, subject to the doubt whether there was any danger that the publication could produce any result, or in other words whether it was not futile and too remote from possible consequences. But the indictment alleges the publication and nothing more.

Whitney v. California
274 U.S. 357, 47 S.Ct. 641, 71 L.Ed. 1095 (1927)

Miss Whitney, an organizer of the Communist Labor Party, was convicted under the California Criminal Syndicalism Act of 1919. "Criminal syndicalism" was defined very much as New York defined criminal anarchy; that is, as "advocating . . . unlawful acts of force and violence or unlawful methods of terrorism as a means of accomplishing a change in industrial ownership or control, or effecting any political change." Whitney's defense simply challenged the constitutionality of the act on its face. It did not raise (as *Schenck, Abrams,* and *Gitlow* had) the further question of whether this particular defendant had done things to which the law could be applied constitutionally. The Supreme Court, in other words, was faced with the "bare bones" question of whether California's law could ever be applied constitutionally to anyone. This was easy for Justice Sanford, the author of *Gitlow,* to answer positively. Justice Louis D. Brandeis wrote a reluctant concurrance; Justice Holmes joined. Brandeis explored some of the difficulties and unanswered questions of the clear and present danger approach. He would strengthen it, it seems, to allow punishment of speech and related activity only when there is a "probability" of serious and imminent injury to the state, not just a likelihood of such occurring.

Mr. Justice Brandeis, concurring.

Miss Whitney was convicted of the felony of assisting in organizing, in the year 1919, the Communist Labor Party of California, of being a member of it, and of assembling with it.

The right of free speech, the right to teach and the right of assembly are, of course, fundamental rights. . . . These may not be denied or abridged. But, although the rights of free speech and assembly are fundamental, they are not in their nature absolute. Their exercise is subject to restriction, if the particular restriction proposed is required in order to protect the State from destruction or from serious injury, political, economic or moral. That the necessity which is essential to a valid restriction does not exist unless speech would produce, or is intended to produce, a clear and imminent danger of some substantive evil which the State constitutionally may seek to prevent has been settled. See *Schenck v. United States.* . . .

It is said to be the function of the legislature to determine whether at a particular time and under the particular circumstances the formation of, or assembly with, a society organized to advocate criminal syndicalism constitutes a clear and present danger of substantive evil; and that by enacting the law here in question the legislature of California determined that question in the affirmative. Compare *Gitlow v. New York.* . . . The legislature must obviously decide, in the first instance, whether a danger exists which calls for a particular protective measure. But where a statute is valid only in case certain conditions exist, the enactment of the statute cannot alone establish the facts which are essential to its validity.

Prohibitory legislation has repeatedly been held invalid, because unnecessary, where the denial of liberty involved was that of engaging in a particular business. The power of the courts to strike down an offending law is no less when the interests involved are not property rights, but the fundamental personal rights of free speech and assembly.

This Court has not yet fixed the standard by which to determine when a danger shall be deemed clear; how remote the danger may be and yet be deemed present; and what degree of evil shall be deemed sufficiently substantial to justify resort to abridgement of free speech and assembly as the means of protection. To reach sound conclusions on these matters, we must bear in mind why a State is, ordinarily, denied the power to prohibit dissemination of social, economic and political doctrine which a vast majority of its citizens believes to be false and fraught with evil consequence.

Those who won our independence believed that the final end of the State was to make men free to develop their faculties; and that in its government the deliberative forces should prevail over the arbitrary. They valued liberty both as an end and as a means. They believed liberty to be the secret of happiness and courage to be the secret of liberty. They believed that freedom to think as you will and to speak as you think are means indispensable to the discovery and spread of political truth; that without free speech and assembly discussion would be futile; that with them, discussion affords ordinarily adequate protection against the dissemination of noxious doctrine; that the greatest menace to freedom is an inert people; that public discussion is a political duty; and that this should be a fundamental principle of the American government. They recognized the risks to which all human institutions are subject. But they knew that order cannot be secured merely through fear of punishment for its infraction; that it is hazardous to discourage thought, hope and imagination; that fear breeds repression; that repression breeds hate; that hate menaces stable government; that the path of safety lies in the opportunity to discuss freely supposed grievances and proposed remedies; and that the fitting remedy for evil counsels is good ones. Believing in the power of reason as applied through public discussion, they eschewed silence coerced by law—the argument of force in its worst form. Recognizing the occasional tyrannies of governing majorities, they amended the Constitution so that free speech and assembly should be guaranteed.

Fear of serious injury cannot alone justify suppression of free speech and assembly. Men feared witches and burnt women. It is the function of speech to free men from the bondage of irrational fears. To justify suppression of free speech there must be reasonable ground to fear that serious evil will result if free speech is practiced. There must be reasonable ground to believe that the danger apprehended is imminent. There must be reasonable ground to believe that the evil to be prevented is a serious one. Every denunciation of existing law tends in some measure to increase the probability that there will be violation of it. Condonation of a breach enhances the probability. Expressions of approval add to the probability. Propagation of the criminal state of mind by teaching syndicalism increases it. Advocacy of law-breaking heightens it still further. But even advocacy of violation, however reprehensible morally, is not a justification for denying free speech where the advocacy falls short of incitement and there is nothing to indicate that the advocacy would be immediately acted on. The wide difference between advocacy and incitement, between preparation and attempt, between assembling and conspiracy, must be borne in mind. In order to support a finding of clear and present danger it must be shown either that immediate serious violence was to be expected or was advocated, or that the past conduct furnished reason to believe that such advocacy was then contemplated. ...

....

... The fact that speech is likely to result in some violence or in destruction of property is not enough to justify its suppression. There must be the probability of serious injury to the State.

Mr. Justice Holmes joins in this opinion.

Dennis v. *United States*
341 U.S. 494, 71 S.Ct. 857, 95 L.Ed. 1137 (1951)

In the late 1930s, with Europe slipping once again toward war, and with expansion of Japanese power in the Pacific, concern grew in Washington over the possible danger of domestic subversion and sabotage should the United States be forced into hostilities. The provisions of the Espionage Act that gave rise to the *Schenck* and *Abrams* cases had long since lapsed, but in 1940 Congress passed, and President Roosevelt signed, the Alien Registration Act. Popularly known as the Smith Act for one of its principal sponsors, this statute, among other things, made it a crime:

(1) to knowingly or willfully advocate, abet, advise, or teach the duty, necessity, desirability, or propriety of overthrowing or destroying any government in the United States by force or violence, or by the assassination of any officer of any such government ...

(2) to organize or help to organize any society, group, or assembly of persons who teach, advocate, or encourage the overthrow or destruction of any government in the United States by force or violence; or to be or become a member of, or affiliate with, any such society, group, or assembly of persons, knowing the purposes thereof. ...

The statute also made it a crime to *conspire* to do any of the above. In law, a conspiracy involves two or more people who agree to cooperate to achieve an illegal end. The top leaders of the Communist Party of the United States, including Dennis, were charged with violating the conspiracy provision of the Smith Act and were convicted in federal district court in New York City. The defendants argued that the Smith Act, by making *advocacy* of something a crime, violated the speech clause. On appeal in the U.S. Court of Appeals for the Second Circuit, Judge Learned Hand wrote an opinion for that Court sustaining the convictions. Hand purported to apply the "clear and present danger test" to determine the question of constitutionality, but he gave the famous phrase a twist that surely would have surprised Holmes or Brandeis. Hand interpreted the "test" as follows: "In each case (the judge) must ask whether the gravity of the 'evil,' discounted by its improbability, justifies such invasion of free speech as is necessary to avoid the danger." In *Dennis,* presumably, the "danger" was the destruction of the government by violence. This was sufficiently grave, apparently, to outweigh some degree of "improbability." At the Supreme Court, the Justices also affirmed the conviction but could not agree on a majority opinion. Justices Stanley Reed, Harold Burton, and Sherman Minton joined Chief Justice Fred Vinson in what is called a "plurality" opinion—one which receives the most support among the justices voting for the winning outcome of the case. Vinson's opinion followed Hand's reasoning. Justice Felix Frankfurter wrote a long concurring opinion in which he emphasized the need to balance claims of First Amendment liberty against the legitimate needs of domestic security. The legislative branch was primarily responsible for striking this balance, Frankfurter argued, and the judicial branch was required by our constitutional scheme to defer to the legislative unless the balance struck was clearly unreasonable. Justice Roberts also filed a concurrence which sustained the convictions on different reasoning.

Mr. Justice Jackson, concurring.

> This prosecution is the latest of never-ending, because never successful, quests for some legal formula that will secure an existing order against revolutionary radicalism. It requires us to reappraise, in the light of our own times and conditions, constitutional doctrines devised under other circumstances to strike a balance between authority and liberty.
>
> Activity here charged to be criminal is conspiracy—that defendants conspired to teach and advocate, and to organize the Communist Party to teach and advocate, overthrow and destruction of the Government by force and violence. There is no charge of actual violence or attempt at overthrow.
>
> The principal reliance of the defense in this Court is that the conviction cannot stand under the Constitution because the conspiracy of these defendants presents no "clear and present danger" of imminent or foreseeable overthrow. . . .
>
>   . . . .
>
> Communism . . . appears today as a closed system of thought representing Stalin's version of Lenin's version of Marxism. As an ideology, it is not one of spontaneous protest arising from American working-class experience. It is a complicated system of assumptions, based on European history and conditions, shrouded in an obscure and ambiguous vocabulary, which allures our ultrasophisticated intelligentsia more than our hard-headed working people. From time to time it champions all manner of causes and grievances and makes alliances that may add to its foothold in government or embarrass the authorities.
>
> The Communist Party, nevertheless, does not seek its strength primarily in numbers. Its aim is a relatively small party whose strength is in selected, dedicated, indoctrinated, and rigidly disciplined members. From established policy it tolerates no deviation and no debate. It seeks members that are, or may be, secreted in strategic posts in transportation, communications, industry, government, and especially in labor unions where it can compel employers to accept and retain its members. It also seeks to infiltrate and control organizations of professional and other groups. Through these placements in positions of power it seeks a leverage

over society that will make up in power of coercion what it lacks in power of persuasion.

The Communists have no scruples against sabotage, terrorism, assassination, or mob disorder; but violence is not with them, as with the anarchists, an end in itself. The Communist Party advocates force only when prudent and profitable. Their strategy of stealth precludes premature or uncoordinated outbursts of violence, except, of course, when the blame will be placed on shoulders other than their own. They resort to violence as to truth, not as a principle but as an expedient. Force or violence, as they would resort to it, may never be necessary, because infiltration and deception may be enough.

Force would be utilized by the Communist Party not to destroy government but for its capture. The Communist recognizes that an established government in control of modern technology cannot be overthrown by force until it is about ready to fall of its own weight. Concerted uprising, therefore, is to await that contingency and revolution is seen, not as a sudden episode, but as the consummation of a long process.

The United States, fortunately, has experienced Communism only in its preparatory stages and for its pattern of final action must look abroad. Russia, of course, was the pilot Communist revolution, which to the Marxist confirms the Party's assumptions and points its destiny. But Communist technique in the overturn of a free government was disclosed by the *coup d'etat* in which they seized power in Czechoslovakia. There the Communist Party during its preparatory stage claimed and received protection for its freedoms of speech, press, and assembly. Pretending to be but another political party, it eventually was conceded participation in government, where it entrenched reliable members chiefly in control of police and information services. When the government faced a foreign and domestic crisis, the Communist Party had established a leverage strong enough to threaten civil war. In a period of confusion the Communist plan unfolded and the underground organization came to the surface throughout the country in the form chiefly of labor "action committees." Communist officers of the unions took over transportation and allowed only persons with party permits to travel. Communist printers took over the newspapers and radio and put out only party-approved versions of events. Possession was taken of telegraph and telephone systems and communications were cut off wherever directed by party heads. Communist unions took over the factories, and in the cities a partisan distribution of food was managed by the Communist organization. A virtually bloodless abdication by the elected government admitted the Communists to power, whereupon they instituted a reign of oppression and terror, and ruthlessly denied to all others the freedoms which had sheltered their conspiracy. . . .

. . . .

The "clear and present danger" test was an innovation by Mr. Justice Holmes in the *Schenck* case, reiterated and refined by him and Mr. Justice Brandeis in later cases, all arising before the era of World War II revealed the subtlety and efficacy of modernized revolutionary techniques used by totalitarian parties. In those cases, they were faced with convictions under so-called criminal syndicalism statutes aimed at anarchists but which, loosely construed, had been applied to punish socialism, pacifism, and left-wing ideologies, the charges often resting on farfetched inferences which, if true, would establish only technical or trivial violations. They proposed "clear and present danger" as a test for the sufficiency of evidence in particular cases.

I would save it, unmodified, for application as a "rule of reason" in the kind of case for which it was devised. When the issue is criminality of a hot-headed speech on a street corner, or circulation of a few incendiary pamphlets, or parading by some zealots behind a red flag, or refusal of a handful of school children to salute our flag, it is not beyond the capacity of the judicial process to gather, comprehend, and weigh the necessary materials for decision whether it is a clear and present danger of substantive evil or a harmless letting off of steam. It is not a prophecy, for the danger in such cases has matured by the time of trial or it was never present. The test applies and has meaning where a conviction is sought to be based on a speech or writing which does not directly or explicitly advocate a crime but to which such tendency is sought to be attributed by construction or by implication from external circumstances. The formula in such cases favors freedoms that are vital to our society, and, even if sometimes applied too generously, the consequences cannot be grave. But its recent expansion has extended, in particular to Communists, unprecendented immunities. Unless we are to hold our Government captive in a judgemade verbal trap, we must approach the problem of a well-organized, nation-wide conspiracy, such as I have described, as realistically as our predecessors faced the trivialities that were being prosecuted until they were checked with a rule of reason.

I think reason is lacking for applying that test to this case. . . .

. . . .

The authors of the clear and present danger test never applied it to a case like this, nor would I. If applied as it is proposed here, it means that the Communist plotting is protected during its period of incubation; its preliminary stages of organization and preparation are immune from the law; the Government can move only after imminent action is manifest, when it would, of course, be too late. . . .

Among the dissenters, Justice Hugo Black's opinion advanced the theory of free speech that was to become firmly associated with his name; namely, that the First Amendment's protection of speech was absolute. There was no room for Frankfurterian balancing or even for a clear and present danger test so long as the activity in question was speech. Only when *action* or *conduct* of some sort was involved could government intervene. However, when Black saw an action dimension—when something other than pure speech was involved—he was quicker than most of his brethren to allow regulation. Of greater interest is Justice Douglas' dissent. He met head on, in his first sentence, the question of what sort of speech was punishable. But he disagreed fundamentally with Jackson as to the nature and track record of the C.P.U.S.A. Where Jackson had seen an organizational weapon, Douglas saw something closer to a literary society. That historians of the period are still deeply divided over which view was closer to the truth is revealing of the kinds of deeply controversial matters the justices are routinely called upon to decide.

Mr. Justice Douglas, dissenting.

If this were a case where those who claimed protection under the First Amendment were teaching the techniques of sabotage, the assassination of the President, the filching of documents from public files, the planting of bombs, the art of street warfare, and the like, I would have no doubts. The freedom to speak is not absolute; the teaching of methods of terror and other seditious conduct should be beyond the pale along with obscenity and immorality. This case was argued as if those were the facts. The argument imported much seditious conduct into the record. That is easy and it has popular appeal, for the activities of Communists in plotting and scheming against the free world are common knowledge. But the fact is that no such evidence was introduced at the trial. There is a statute which makes a seditious conspiracy unlawful. Petitioners, however, were not charged with a "conspiracy to overthrow" the Government. They were charged with a conspiracy to form a party and groups and assemblies of people who teach and advocate the overthrow of our Government by force or violence and with a conspiracy to advocate and teach its overthrow by force and violence. It may well be that indoctrination in the techniques of terror to destroy the Government would be indictable under either statute. But the teaching which is condemned here is of a different character.

So far as the present record is concerned, what petitioners did was to organize people to teach and themselves teach the Marxist-Leninist doctrine contained chiefly in four books: Stalin, Foundations of Leninism (1924); Marx and Engels, Manifesto of the Communist Party (1848); Lenin, The State and Revolution (1917); History of the Communist Party of the Soviet Union (B.) (1939). . . .

. . . .

The opinion of the Court does not outlaw these texts nor condemn them to the fire, as the Communists do literature offensive to their creed. But if the books themselves are not outlawed, if they can lawfully remain on library shelves, by what reasoning does their use in a classroom become a crime? It would not be a crime under the Act to introduce these books to a class, though that would be teaching what the creed of violent overthrow of the Government is. The Act, as construed, requires the element of intent—that those who teach the creed believe in it. The crime then depends not on what is taught but on who the teacher is. That is to make freedom of speech turn not on *what is said*, but on the *intent* with which it is said. Once we start down that road we enter territory dangerous to the liberties of every citizen. . . .

. . . .

The vice of treating speech as the equivalent of overt acts of a treasonable or seditious character is emphasized by a concurring opinion, which by invoking the law of conspiracy makes speech do service for deeds which are dangerous to society. The doctrine of conspiracy has served divers and oppressive purposes and in its broad reach can be made to do great evil. But never until today has anyone seriously thought that the ancient law of conspiracy could constitutionally be used to turn speech into seditious conduct. Yet that is precisely what is suggested. I repeat that we deal here with speech alone, not with speech *plus* acts of sabotage or unlawful conduct. Not a single seditious act is charged in the indictment. To make a lawful speech unlawful because two men conceive it is to raise the law of conspiracy to appalling proportions. That course is to make a radical break with the past and to violate one of the cardinal principles of our constitutional scheme. . . .

. . . .

There comes a time when even speech loses its constitutional immunity. Speech innocuous one year may at another time fan such destructive flames that it must be halted in the interests of the safety of the Republic. That is the meaning of the clear and present danger test. When conditions are so critical that there will be no time to avoid the evil that the speech threatens, it is time to call a halt. Otherwise, free speech which is the strength of the Nation will be the cause of its destruction.

Yet free speech is the rule, not the exception. The restraint to be constitutional must be based on more than fear, on more than passionate opposition against the speech, on more than a revolted dislike for its contents. There must be some immediate injury to society that is likely if speech is allowed. . . .

The *Yates, Scales,* and *Noto* Trilogy

Yates v. *United States*
354 U.S. 298, 77 S.Ct. 1064, 1 L.Ed.2d. 1356 (1957)

Scales v. *United States*
367 U.S. 203, 81 S.Ct. 1469, 6 L.Ed.2d. 782 (1961)

Noto v. *United States*
367 U.S. 290, 81 S.Ct. 1517, 6 L.Ed.2d. 836 (1961)

Dennis was the kind of case—and we will encounter them frequently in this volume—that raises more questions than it answers. It deeply divided the American political and intellectual elites, it was played out in the glare of intense publicity, and the Court rendered no clear decision. The various concurrences and dissents impressed contending factions within the constitutionally attentive public more than the plurality opinion. Could "advocacy" be criminalized? The apparent answer of *Dennis* was yes, but it took the careful craftmanship of Justice John Marshall Harlan ("the second Justice Harlan"; his grandfather, of the same name, served on the Court with great distinction from 1877 to 1911) to clarify *when* the Smith Act could be applied constitutionally. *Yates* was a prosecution of lower echelon American Communists, as opposed to the top leadership. The Supreme Court reversed the convictions, Justices Burton and Black (joined by Douglas) wrote separately, and Justice Clark dissented. Harlan, in the opinion of the Court, drew a sharp distinction between advocacy of abstract doctrine and advocacy of action. He made it clear the Smith Act convictions would not be easy to sustain, and that the government must bear the heavy burden of showing advocacy as the organizing of action.

Mr. Justice Harlan delivered the opinion of the Court.

We brought these cases here to consider certain questions arising under the Smith Act which have not heretofore been passed upon by this Court, and otherwise to review the convictions of these petitioners for conspiracy to violate that Act. Among other things, the convictions are claimed to rest upon an application of the Smith Act which is hostile to the principles upon which its constitutionality was upheld in *Dennis* v. *United States,* 341 U.S. 494.

These 14 petitioners stand convicted, after a jury trial in the United States District Court for the Southern District of California, upon a single count indictment charging them with conspiring (1) to advocate and teach the duty and necessity of overthrowing the Government of the United States by force and violence, and (2) to organize, as the Communist Party of the United States, a society of persons who so advocate and teach, all with the intent of causing the overthrow of the Government by force and violence as speedily as circumstances would permit. . . .

Petitioners contend that the instructions to the jury were fatally defective in that the trial court refused to charge that, in order to convict, the jury must find that the advocacy which the defendants conspired to promote was of a kind calculated to "incite" persons to action for the forcible overthrow of the Government. It is argued that advocacy of forcible overthrow as mere *abstract doctrine* is within the free speech protection of the First Amendment; that the Smith Act, consistently with that constitutional provision, must be taken as proscribing only the sort of advocacy which incites to illegal *action;* and that the trial court's charge, by permitting conviction for mere advocacy, unrelated to its tendency to produce forcible action, resulted in an unconstitutional application of the Smith Act. The Government, which at the trial also requested the court to charge in terms of "incitement," now takes the position, however, that the true constitutional dividing line is not between inciting and abstract advocacy of forcible overthrow, but rather between advocacy as such, irrespective of its inciting qualities, and the mere discussion or exposition of violent overthrow as an abstract theory. . . .

There can be no doubt from the record that in so instructing the jury the court regarded as immaterial, and intended to withdraw from the jury's consideration, any issue as to the character of the advocacy in terms of its capacity to stir listeners to forcible action. . . .

We are thus faced with the question whether the Smith Act prohibits advocacy and teaching of forcible overthrow as an abstract principle, divorced from any effort to instigate action to that end, so long as such advocacy or teaching is engaged in with evil intent. We hold that it does not. . . .

. . . .

In failing to distinguish between advocacy of forcible overthrow as an abstract doctrine and advocacy of action to that end, the District Court appears to have been led astray by the holding in *Dennis* that advocacy of violent action to be taken at some future time was enough. It seems to have considered that, since "inciting" speech is usually thought of as something calculated to induce immediate action, and since *Dennis* held advocacy of action for future overthrow sufficient, this meant that advocacy, irrespective of its tendency to generate action, is punishable, provided only that it is uttered with a specific intent to accomplish overthrow. In other words, the District Court apparently thought that *Dennis* obliterated the traditional dividing line between advocacy of abstract doctrine and advocacy of action.

This misconceives the situation confronting the Court in *Dennis* and what was held there. . . . The essence of the *Dennis* holding was that indoctrination of a group in preparation for future violent action, as well as exhortation to immediate action, by advocacy found to be directed to "action for the accomplishment" of forcible overthrow, to violence as "a rule or principle of action," and employing "language of incitement," is not constitutionally protected when the group is of sufficient size and cohesiveness, is sufficiently oriented towards action, and other circumstances are such as reasonably to justify apprehension that action will occur. This is quite a different thing from the view of the District Court here that mere doctrinal justification of forcible overthrow, if engaged in with the intent to accomplish overthrow, is punishable *per se* under the Smith Act. That sort of advocacy, even though uttered with the hope that it may ultimately lead to violent revolution, is too remote from concrete action to be regarded as the kind of indoctrination preparatory to action which was condemned in *Dennis.* As one of the concurring opinions in *Dennis* put it: "Throughout our decisions there has recurred a distinction between the statement of an idea which may prompt its hearers to take unlawful action, and advocacy that such action be taken." There is nothing in Dennis which makes that historic distinction obsolete. . . .

The essential distinction is that those to whom the advocacy is addressed must be urged to *do* something, now or in the future, rather than merely to *believe* in something. . . .

In *Scales* the defendant was Chairman of the North and South Carolina Districts of the Communist Party. He was convicted of violating the membership clause of the Smith Act, which made it a crime to become a member of an organization advocating the overthrow of the government by force or violence, knowing the purposes of such organization. The trial judge had instructed the jury that to convict it must find (1) that the Communist Party advocated the violent overthrow of the government, in the sense of present "advocacy of action" to accomplish that end as soon as circumstances were propitious; and (2) that Scales was an "active" member of the Party—not merely "a nominal, passive, inactive, or purely technical" member with knowledge of the Party's illegal advocacy—with specific intent to bring about overthrow "as speedily as circumstances would permit." The Supreme Court affirmed Scales' conviction. There were dissenting opinions from Justices Black and Douglas, from Justice William Brennan, and from Chief Justice Earl Warren. Once again, Justice Harlan spoke for the majority, holding that the trial judge, by insisting on the distinction between active and nominal membership, and by insisting on a specific evidenciary showing as to Scales' activity, had construed and applied the membership clause in a constitutional fashion. In the companion case of *Noto,* Justice Harlan reversed a conviction under the membership clause because "the evidence of illegal Party advocacy was insufficient." Harlan pointed out that specific evidence of "advocacy of action" was "sparse indeed." He concluded that it "lacked the compelling quality which in *Scales* was supplied by the petitioner's utterances and systematic conduct as a high party official."

CASE STUDY: *BRANDENBURG* AND "ADVOCACY-PLUS"

What emerges from the gloss of interpretation placed on *Dennis* by Harlan in the *Yates–Scales–Noto* trilogy? Certainly Harlan made it clear that for "advocacy" of violence to be criminalized it must be specific and must involve a pattern of purposeful activity by the accused clearly directed at preparing organizationally for illegal action in the future. Abstract advocacy, nominal membership, or unwitting association with a revolutionary movement were protected by the First Amendment. The Court emphasized the strictness of the "advocacy-plus" standard in the rather strange case of *Brandenburg* v. *Ohio*, 395 U.S. 444 (1969).

Brandenburg was leader of a local Ku Klux Klan "klavan." He was convicted under the Ohio Criminal Syndicalism statute for "advocat(ing) . . . the duty, necessity, or propriety of crime, sabotage, violence, or unlawful methods of terrorism as a means of accomplishing industrial or political reform" and for "voluntarily assemb(ling) with any society, group, or assemblage of persons formed to teach or advocate the doctrines of criminal syndicalism." He was fined $1,000 and sentenced to one to ten years' imprisonment. Brandenburg challenged the constitutionality of the criminal syndicalism statute under the First and Fourteenth Amendments to the United States Constitution but lost in the appellate courts of Ohio.

The trial record shows that a man, identified at trial as Brandenburg, telephoned an announcer-reporter on the staff of a Cincinnati television station and invited him to come to a Ku Klux Klan rally to be held at a farm in Hamilton County. With the cooperation of the organizers, the reporter and a cameraman attended the meeting and filmed the events. Portions of the film were later broadcast on the local station and on a national network.

The prosecution's case rested on the films and on testimony identifying Brandenburg as the person who called the reporter and spoke at the rally. The prosecution also introduced into evidence several articles appearing in the film, including a pistol, a rifle, a shotgun, ammunition, a Bible, and a red hood worn by the speaker in the films.

One film showed twelve hooded figures, some of whom carried firearms. They were gathered around a large wooden cross, which they burned. No one was present other than the participants and the newsmen who made the film. Most of the words uttered during the scene were incomprehensible when the film was projected, but scattered phrases could be understood that were derogatory of Negroes and, in one instance, of Jews. The significant portions that could be understood were:

> How far is the nigger going to—yeah.
> This is what we are going to do to the niggers.
> A dirty nigger.
> Send the Jews back to Israel.
> Let's give them back to the dark garden.
> Save America.
> Let's go back to constitutional betterment.
> Bury the niggers.
> We intend to do our part.
> Give us our state rights.
> Freedom for whites.
> Nigger will have to fight for every inch he gets from now on.

Another scene on the same film showed the appellant, in Klan regalia, making a speech:

> This is an organizer's meeting. We have had quite a few members here today which are—we have hundreds, hundreds of members throughout the state of Ohio. I can quote from a newspaper clipping from the Columbus, Ohio *Dispatch,* five weeks ago Sunday morning. The klan has more members in the state of Ohio than does any other organization. We're not a revengent organization, but if our President, our Congress, our Supreme Court, continues to suppress the white, Caucasian race, it's possible that there might have to be some reveangance taken.
>
> We are marching on Congress July the Fourth, four hundred thousand strong. From there we are dividing into two groups, one group to march on St. Augustine, Florida, the other group to march into Mississippi. Thank you.

The second film showed six hooded figures one of whom, later identified as the appellant, repeated a speech very similar to that recorded on the first film. The reference to the possibility of "reveangance" was omitted, and one sentence was added: "Personally, I believe the nigger should be returned to Africa, the Jew returned to Israel." Though some of the figures in the film carried weapons, the speaker did not.

The Court reversed Brandenburg's conviction in an unsigned, *per curium* opinion. Usually this technique of disposition is reserved for unremarkable cases in which only a few references to established doctrine are needed to explain the result. This anonymous opinion concluded that, on its face, the Ohio Criminal Syndicalism Act was intended to punish "mere advocacy" and abstract teaching. The majority declined to read the more sophisticated federal concept of advocacy-plus, which Harlan had teased out of the Smith Act, into the Ohio statute. Therefore it was unnecessary, apparently, to consider whether the actual, gun-toting behavior of Brandenburg and his friends went beyond "mere advocacy."

One result of *Brandenburg* is that all state "advocacy" statutes appear constitutionally doomed. And some commentators have argued that the decision casts doubt over the Smith Act itself, despite the fact that the *per curium* purports to be based on *Dennis!*

What is clear is that, over the years since 1951, successive majorities have replaced the notion of subversive speech or advocacy, embodied in many state laws and in the Smith Act, with a narrowed, judicially crafted substitute that resembles the ancient crime of sedition—incitement to rebellion and resistance to the laws. As things stand now, the clear and present danger test really has been abandoned as the principal approach to reconciling First Amendment imperatives and the perceived need of government to respond to revolutionary rhetoric and organizing. The clear and present danger test remains, as Justice Jackson, in his *Dennis* concurrence, suggested it might, a better guide to dealing with the street corner orator and the riotous crowd than the long-term radical organizer. It is to the problem of speech in the streets we now turn.

CHAPTER · 4

SPEECH IN THE STREETS— THE PROBLEM OF THE "PUBLIC FORUM"

THE constitutional law of free speech has a number of different facets. We have just examined the problem of when utterance, per se, may be criminalized because it constitutes an incitement to revolutionary action. In this chapter, we are concerned, not with the content of speech, but with the circumstances in which it is uttered. Governments within the United States, municipal, state, and federal, have an interest in the safety and good order of their public places—the spaces such as streets and parks owned by government but available to all of us for reasonable uses.

For instance, the Court has recognized that municipalities have a legitimate interest in protecting the use of their public spaces by licensing and permit schemes that determine in advance when and where speech and related activities, such as soliciting funds or parading, may take place. The unifying principle of the Court's decisions in permit and licensing cases is that the discretion of the public official or authority empowered to issue the permit must be strictly circumscribed. Licensing authorities may have no discretion as to whether or not to grant permits; neither may they discriminate in any way between the individuals and groups seeking to use public space as public forums. The licensing authorities must confine themselves solely to reasonable considerations of time and place and manner.

A second problem that arises in connection with speech in public places involves the ancient common law offense of disturbing the peace. Certainly government, usually at the level of municipalities, has an interest in preventing outbreaks of violence and disorder in its streets and parks. But spirited and forceful utterance often will arouse hostile feelings in listeners. Under what circumstances may speakers in public spaces be arrested for disturbing the peace?

A third public-forum problem involves the use of space around special purpose government facilities such as prisons, hospitals, and military installations.

Of the cases that follow, *Lovell* v. *Griffin* is concerned with the problem of permits for use of the streets. *Feiner* v. *New York* and *Edwards* v. *South Carolina* are concerned with the circumstances under which persons speaking and demonstrating in the streets may be subjected to prosecution for the common law crimes of disturbing the peace and disorderly conduct. *Cox* v. *Louisiana* and *Adderley* v. *Florida* involve the issue of special purpose public facilities.

Lovell v. Griffin
303 U.S. 444, 58 S.Ct. 666, 82 L.Ed. 949 (1938)

A city ordinance prohibited the distribution of "circulars, handbooks, advertising or literature of any kind ... without first obtaining written permission from the City Manager." The defendant, a Jehovah's Witness, distributed religious tracts without applying for or receiving a permit. She admitted violation of the ordinance, while challenging its constitutionality, and was convicted. The Court reversed. Chief Justice Charles Evans Hughes, speaking for the Court, stressed the broad discretion vested in the city manager to grant or deny a permit, and the absence of standards in the ordinance to guide that official in making decisions. The principle that emerges from Hughes' opinion is that municipalities have legitimate interests in regulating the time, manner, and places of speech in the streets. But the First Amendment protection of speech requires that these interests be protected by very narrowly drawn laws, which provide specific guidance to the permit-granting authority. The granting authority may consider only such time, place, and manner criteria as are specified in the law. There must be no discretion in the granting authority to withhold the permit based on the content of the proposed speech or the character of the speaker.

Mr. Chief Justice Hughes delivered the opinion of the Court.

Appellant, Alma Lovell, was convicted in the Recorder's Court of the City of Griffin, Georgia, of the violation of a city ordinance and was sentenced to imprisonment for fifty days in default of the payment of a fine of fifty dollars.

The ordinance in question is as follows:

"Section 1. That the practice of distributing, either by hand or otherwise, circulars, handbooks, advertising, or literature of any kind, whether said articles are being delivered free, or whether same are being sold, within the limits of the City of Griffin, without first obtaining written permission from the City Manager of the City of Griffin, such practice shall be deemed a nuisance, and punishable as an offense against the City of Griffin.

"Section 2. The Chief of Police of the City of Griffin and the police force of the City of Griffin are hereby required and directed to suppress the same and to abate any nuisance as is described in the first section of this ordinance."

The violation, which is not denied, consisted of the distribution without the required permission of a pamphlet and magazine in the nature of religious tracts, setting forth the gospel of the "Kingdom of Jehovah." Appellant did not apply for a permit, as she regarded herself as sent "by Jehovah to do His work" and that such an application would have been "an act of disobedience to His commandment."

Upon the trial, with permission of the court, appellant demurred to the charge and moved to dismiss it upon a number of grounds, among which was the contention that the ordinance violated the Fourteenth Amendment of the Constitution of the United States in abridging "the freedom of the press" and prohibiting "the free exercise of petitioner's religion." This contention was thus expressed:

"Because said ordinance is contrary to and in violation of the first amendment to the Constitution of the United States. . . ."

. . . .

Freedom of speech and freedom of the press, which are protected by the First Amendment from infringement by Congress, are among the fundamental personal rights and liberties which are protected by the Fourteenth Amendment from invasion by state action. . . .

The ordinance in its broad sweep prohibits the distribution of "circulars, handbooks, advertising, or literature of any kind." It manifestly applies to pamphlets, magazines and periodicals. The evidence against appellant was that she distributed a certain pamphlet and a magazine called the "Golden Age." Whether in actual administration the ordinance is applied, as apparently it could be, to newspapers does not appear. The City Manager testified that "every one applies to me for a license to distribute literature in this City. None of these people (including defendant) secured a permit from me to distribute literature in the City of Griffin." The ordinance is not limited to "literature" that is obscene or offensive to public morals or that advocates unlawful conduct. There is no suggestion that the pamphlet and magazine distributed in the instant case were of that character. The ordinance embraces "literature" in the widest sense.

The ordinance is comprehensive with respect to the method of distribution. It covers every sort of circulation "either by hand or otherwise." There is thus no restriction in its application with respect to time or place. It is not limited to ways which might be regarded as inconsistent with the maintenance of public order or as involving disorderly conduct, the molestation of the inhabitants, or the misuse or littering of the streets. The ordinance prohibits the distribution of literature of any kind at any time, at any place, and in any manner without a permit from the City Manager.

We think that the ordinance is invalid on its face. Whatever the motive which induced its adoption, its character is such that it strikes at the very foundation of the freedom of the press by subjecting it to license and censorship. The struggle for the freedom of the press was primarily directed against the power of the licensor. It was against that power that John Milton directed his assault by his "Appeal for the Liberty of Unlicensed Printing." And the liberty of the press became initially a right to publish "*without* a license what formerly could be published only *with* one." While this freedom from previous restraint upon publication cannot be regarded as exhausting the guaranty of liberty, the prevention of that restraint was a leading purpose in the adoption of the constitutional provision.

The liberty of the press is not confined to newspapers and periodicals. It necessarily embraces pamphlets and leaflets. These indeed have been historic weapons in the defense of liberty, as the pamphlets of Thomas Paine and others in our own history abundantly attest. The press in its historic connotation comprehends every sort of publication which affords a vehicle of information and opinion. What we have had recent occasion to say with respect to the vital importance of protecting this essential liberty from every sort of infringement need not be repeated. . . .

As the ordinance is void on its face, it was not necessary for appellant to seek a permit under it. She was entitled to contest its validity in answer to the charge against her. . . .

The judgment is reversed and the cause is remanded for further proceedings not inconsistent with this opinion.

Reversed.

Feiner v. New York
340 U.S. 315, 71 S.Ct. 303, 95 L.Ed. 295 (1951)

On a March evening in 1949, Feiner was addressing an open-air meeting on a street corner in Syracuse, New York, when two police officers arrived to investigate. They found about seventy-five or eighty people, both black and white, filling the sidewalk and spreading out into the street. Feiner, standing on a box on the sidewalk, was addressing the crowd through an amplifier in a "loud high-pitched voice." Although the purpose of his speech was to urge listeners to attend a meeting later that night, he was making derogatory remarks concerning President Truman (calling him "a bum"), the Mayor of Syracuse (also labelling him "a bum"), and the American Legion (calling it "a Nazi Gestapo"). According to testimony, he also said: "The Negroes don't have equal rights; they should rise up in arms and fight for their rights." There was some pushing and shoving in the crowd but no disorder. After Feiner had been speaking about twenty minutes, a man said to the police officers, "If you don't get the son of a bitch off, I will go over and get him off there myself." In order to break up the crowd, the police then requested Feiner to stop speaking and, when he repeatedly refused to do so, arrested him. He was prosecuted and convicted of a misdemeanor under the New York disorderly conduct law. The justices were divided deeply in their perceptions of the danger on that Syracuse street on that evening in 1949. The majority saw Feiner refusing a request by police in a tight spot and unable to avoid violence in any other way. The minority justices asked why the police did not protect the speaker from the crowd. The *Feiner* decision has come to stand for the principle that police may only request that a speaker stop (and make a valid arrest for breach of the peace if the request is refused) as a matter of last resort—where violence and disorder can reasonably be avoided in no other way.

Mr. Chief Justice Vinson delivered the opinion of the Court.

We are not faced here with blind condonation by state court of arbitrary police action. Petitioner was accorded a full, fair trial. The trial judge heard testimony supporting and contradicting the judgment of the police officers that a clear danger of disorder was threatened. After weighing this contradictory evidence, the trial judge reached the conclusion that the police officers were justified in taking action to prevent a breach of the peace. The exercise of the police officers' proper discretionary power to prevent a breach of the peace was thus approved by the trial court and later by two courts on review. The courts below recognized petitioner's right to hold a street meeting at this locality, to make use of loud-speaking equipment in giving his speech, and to make derogatory remarks concerning public officials and the American Legion. They found that the officers in making the arrest were motivated solely by a proper concern for the preservation of order and protection of the general welfare, and that there was no evidence which could lend color to a claim that the acts of the police were a cover for suppression of petitioner's views and opinions. Petitioner was thus neither arrested nor convicted for the making or the content of his speech. Rather, it was the reaction which it actually engendered. . . .

. . . It is one thing to say that the police cannot be used as an instrument for the suppression of unpopular views, and another to say that, when as here the speaker passes the bounds of argument or persuasion and undertakes incitement to riot, they are powerless to prevent a breach of the peace. Nor in this case can we condemn the considered judgment of three New York courts approving the means which the police, faced with a crisis, used in the exercise of their power and duty to preserve peace and order. The findings of the state courts as to the existing situation and the imminence of greater disorder coupled with petitioner's deliberate defiance of the police officers convince us that we should not reverse this conviction in the name of free speech.

Affirmed.

Justices Frankfurter and Jackson concurred in separate opinions.

Mr. Justice Black, dissenting.

The record before us convinces me that petitioner, a young college student, has been sentenced to the penitentiary for the unpopular views he expressed. . . . The police of course have power to prevent breaches of the peace. But if, in the name of preserving order, they ever can interfere with a lawful public speaker, they first must make all reasonable efforts to protect him. Here the policemen did not even pretend to try to protect petitioner. According to the officers' testimony, the crowd was restless but there is no showing of any attempt to quiet it; pedestrians were forced to walk into the street, but there was no effort to clear a path on the sidewalk; one person threatened to assault petitioner but the officers did nothing to discourage this when even a word might have sufficed. Their duty was to protect petitioner's right to talk, even to the extent of arresting the man who threatened to interfere. Instead, they shirked that duty and acted only to suppress the right to speak. . . .

Mr. Justice Douglas, with whom Mr. Justice Minton concurs, dissenting.

A speaker may not, of course, incite a riot any more than he may incite a breach of the peace by the use of "fighting words". . . . But this record shows no such extremes. It shows an unsympathetic audience and the threat of one man to haul the speaker from the stage. It is against that kind of threat that speakers need police protection. If they do not receive it and instead the police throw their weight on the side of those who would break up the meetings, the police become the new censors of speech. . . .

Edwards v. South Carolina
372 U.S. 229, 83 S.Ct. 680, 9 L.Ed.2d. 697 (1963)

The situation in *Edwards,* we learn, was "a far cry" from Feiner, where the majority of the Court perceived a threat of imminent riot. Jack Greenberg, of the "Ink" Fund, argued the case for the defendants, along with Constance Baker Motley.

Mr. Justice Stewart delivered the opinion of the Court.

The petitioners, 187 in number, were convicted in a magistrate's court in Columbia, South Carolina, of the common-law crime of breach of the peace. Their convictions were ultimately affirmed by the South Carolina Supreme Court. . . . We granted certiorari . . . to consider the claim that these convictions cannot be squared with the Fourteenth Amendment of the United States Constitution.

There was no substantial conflict in the trial evidence. Late in the morning of March 2, 1961, the petitioners, high school and college students of the Negro race, met at the Zion Baptist Church in Columbia. From there, at about noon, they walked in separate groups of about 15 to the South Carolina State House grounds, an area of two city blocks open to the general public. Their purpose was "to submit a protest to the citizens of South Carolina, along with the Legislative Bodies of South Carolina, our feelings and our dissatisfaction with the present condition of discriminatory actions against Negroes, in general, and to let them know that we were dissatisfied and that we would like for the laws which prohibited Negro privileges in this State to be removed."

Already on the State House grounds when the petitioners arrived were 30 or more law enforcement officers, who had advance knowledge that the petitioners were coming. Each group of petitioners entered the grounds through a driveway and parking area known in the record as the "horseshoe." As they entered, they were told by the law enforcement officials that "they had a right, as a citizen, to go through the State House grounds, as any other citizen has, as long as they were peaceful." During the next half hour or 45 minutes, the petitioners, in the same small groups, walked single file or two abreast in an orderly way through the grounds, each group carrying placards bearing such messages as "I am proud to be a Negro" and "Down with segregation."

During this time a crowd of some 200 to 300 onlookers had collected in the horseshoe area and on the adjacent sidewalks. There was no evidence to suggest that these onlookers were anything but curious, and no evidence at all of any threatening remarks, hostile gestures, or offensive language on the part of any member of the crowd. The City Manager testified that he recognized some of the onlookers, whom he did not identify, as "possible trouble makers," but his subsequent testimony made clear that nobody among the crowd actually caused or threatened any trouble. There was no obstruction of pedestrian or vehicular traffic within the State House grounds. No vehicle was prevented from entering or leaving the horseshoe area. Although vehicular traffic at a nearby street intersection was slowed down somewhat, an officer was dispatched to keep traffic moving. There were a number of bystanders on the public sidewalks adjacent to the State House grounds, but they all moved on when asked to do so, and there was no impediment of pedestrian traffic. Police protection at the scene was at all times sufficient to meet any foreseeable possibility of disorder.

In the situation and under the circumstances thus described, the police authorities advised the petitioners that they would be arrested if they did not disperse within 15 minutes. Instead of dispersing, the petitioners engaged in what the City Manager described as "boisterous," "loud," and "flamboyant" conduct, which, as his later testimony made clear, consisted of listening to a "religious harangue" by one of their leaders, and loudly singing "The Star Spangled Banner" and other patriotic and religious songs, while stamping their feet and clapping their hands. After 15 minutes had passed, the police arrested the petitioners and marched them off to jail. . . .

This, therefore, was a far cry from the situation in *Feiner* v. *New York,* 340 U.S. 315, where two policemen were faced with a crowd which was "pushing, shoving and milling around," *id.,* at 317, where at least one member of the crowd "threatened violence if the police did not act," *id.,* at 317, where "the crowd was pressing closer around petitioner and the officer," *id.,* at 318, and where "the speaker passes the bounds of argument or persuasion and undertakes incitement to riot." . . .

The Fourteenth Amendment does not permit a State to make criminal the peaceful expression of unpopular views. "[A] function of free speech under our system of government is to invite dispute. It may indeed best serve its high purpose when it induces a condition of unrest, creates dissatisfaction with conditions as they are, or even stirs people to anger. Speech is often provocative and challenging. It may strike at prejudices and preconceptions and have profound unsettling effects as it presses for acceptance of an idea. That is why freedom of speech . . . is . . . protected against censorship or punishment, unless shown likely to produce a clear and present danger of a serious substantive evil that rises far above public inconvenience, annoyance, or unrest. . . . There is no room under our Constitution for a more restrictive view.

For these reasons we conclude that these criminal convictions cannot stand.

Reversed.

There was, however, one member of the Court who saw the facts differently.

Mr. Justice Clark, dissenting.

The convictions of the petitioners, Negro high school and college students, for breach of the peace under South Carolina law . . . are held violative of "petitioners' constitutionally protected rights of free speech, free assembly, and freedom to petition for redress of their grievances." Petitioners, of course, had a right to peaceable assembly, to espouse their cause and to petition, but in my view the manner in which they exercised those rights was by no means the passive demonstration which this Court relates; rather, as the City Manager of Columbia testified, "a dangerous situation was really building up" which South Carolina's courts expressly found had created "an actual interference with traffic and an imminently threatened disturbance of the peace of the community." Since the Court does not attack the state courts' findings . . . it is difficult for me to understand its understatement of the facts and reversal of the convictions.

The priceless character of First Amendment freedoms cannot be gainsaid, but it does not follow that they are absolutes immune from necessary state action reasonably designed for the protection of society. . . . South Carolina's courts have found: "There is no indication whatever in this case that the acts of the police officers were taken as a subterfuge or excuse for the suppression of the appellants' views and opinions." It is undisputed that the city officials specifically granted petitioners permission to assemble, imposing only the requirement that they be "peaceful." Petitioners then gathered on the State House grounds, during a General Assembly session, in a large number of almost 200, marching and carrying placards with slogans such as "Down with segregation" and "You may jail our bodies but not our souls." Some of them were singing.

The activity continued for approximately 45 minutes, during the busy noon-hour period, while a crowd of some 300 persons congregated in front of the State House and around the area directly in front of its entrance, known as the "horseshoe," which was used for vehicular as well as pedestrian ingress and egress. During this time there were no efforts made by the city officials to hinder the petitioners in their rights of free speech and assembly; rather, the police directed their efforts to the traffic problems resulting from petitioners' activities. It was only after the large crowd had gathered, among which the City Manager and Chief of Police recognized potential troublemakers, and which together with the students had become massed on and around the "horseshoe" so closely that vehicular and pedestrian traffic was materially impeded, that any action against the petitioners was taken. Then the City Manager, in what both the state intermediate and Supreme Court found to be the utmost good faith, decided that danger to peace and safety was imminent. Even at this juncture no orders were issued by the City Manager for the police to break up the crowd, now about 500 persons, and no arrests were made. Instead, he approached the recognized leader of the petitioners and requested him to tell the various groups of petitioners to disperse within 15 minutes, failing which they would be arrested. Even though the City Manager might have been honestly mistaken as to the imminence of danger, this was certainly a reasonable request by the city's top executive officer in an effort to avoid a public brawl. But the response of petitioners and their leader was defiance rather than cooperation. The leader immediately moved from group to group among the students, delivering a "harangue" which, according to testimony in the record, "aroused [them] to a fever pitch causing this boisterousness, this singing and stomping."

For the next 15 minutes the petitioners sang "I Shall Not Be Moved" and various religious songs, stamped their feet, clapped their hands, and conducted what the South Carolina Supreme Court found to be a "noisy demonstration in defiance of [the dispersal] orders." ... Ultimately, the petitioners were arrested, as they apparently planned from the beginning, and convicted on evidence the sufficiency of which the Court does not challenge. The question thus seems to me whether a State is constitutionally prohibited from enforcing laws to prevent breach of the peace in a situation where city officials in good faith believe, and the record shows, that disorder and violence are imminent, merely because the activities constituting that breach contain claimed elements of constitutionally protected speech and assembly. To me the answer under our cases is clearly in the negative. ... [In] *Feiner* v. *New York* ... we upheld a conviction for breach of the peace in a situation no more dangerous than that found here. There the demonstration was conducted by only one person and the crowd was limited to approximately 80, as compared with the present lineup of some 200 demonstrators and 300 onlookers. There the petitioner was "endeavoring to arouse the Negro people against the whites, urging that they rise up in arms and fight for equal rights." ... Only one person—in a city having an entirely different historical background—was exhorting adults. Here 200 youthful Negro demonstrators were being aroused to a "fever pitch" before a crowd of some 300 people who undoubtedly were hostile. Perhaps their speech was not so animated but in this setting their actions, their placards reading "You may jail our bodies but not our souls" and their chanting of "I Shall Not Be Moved," accompanied by stamping feet and clapping hands, created a much greater danger of riot and disorder. It is my belief that anyone conversant with the almost spontaneous combustion in some Southern communities in such a situation will agree that the City Manager's action may well have averted a major catastrophe.

The gravity of the danger here surely needs no further explication. The imminence of that danger has been emphasized at every stage of this proceeding, from the complaints charging that the demonstrations "tended directly to immediate violence" to the State Supreme Court's affirmance on the authority of *Feiner, supra.* This record, then, shows no steps backward from a standard of "clear and present danger." But to say that the police may not intervene until the riot has occurred is like keeping out the doctor until the patient dies. I cannot subscribe to such a doctrine. ... I would affirm the convictions.

Cox v. *Louisiana* (I)
379 U.S. 536, 85 S.Ct. 453, 13 L.Ed.2d. 471 (1965)

Cox v. *Louisiana* (II)
379 U.S. 559, 85 S.Ct. 476, 13 L.Ed.2d. 487 (1965)

Bearing in mind the *Feiner-Edwards* dichotomy as to when government may intervene against speech in streets and parks, how is the constitutional situation changed when the public space sought by speakers as a forum is devoted to a specialized governmental purpose? Suppose, for example, the space is immediately around a courthouse, or a hospital, or a jail, or the gate of a military base, or the halls of the Department of Justice Building in Washington. Attempted use of special purpose space as a public forum lessens First Amendment protection, but how much, and under what circumstances, are questions which vex the justices. *Cox* presented just such questions.

On December 14, 1961, twenty-three black students were arrested in downtown Baton Rouge for picketing stores that maintained segregated lunch counters. The next morning about two thousand students assembled at the old State Capitol Building; led by B. Elton Cox, a field secretary of The Congress of Racial Equality (CORE), they marched to the courthouse where the twenty-three students were jailed. After discussion with Cox, police officers agreed, according to some witnesses, to permit a peaceful demonstration provided the demonstrators stayed across the street from the courthouse. The students lined up across the street, thus blocking the sidewalk but not the street, sang songs and listened to a short speech by Cox in which he stated that the demonstration was a protest against the "illegal arrest" of the students. Since it was nearly lunchtime, Cox urged his listeners to go eat and called attention to the stores that had segregated lunch counters. There was "muttering" and "grumbling" by the white onlookers. Deeming the appeal to the students to sit at the lunchcounters to be "inflammatory," the Sheriff ordered the gathering to disperse and used tear gas to enforce his order. Cox was arrested the next day and charged with three statutory offenses: disturbing the peace, obstructing public passages, and courthouse picketing. The Supreme Court reversed convictions on all three charges. Only the courthouse picketing conviction is considered here. The first conviction was disposed of rather easily by reference to *Edwards*. On the second, the majority concluded that while the obstruction of way ordinance was constitutional on its face, it had been enforced in the past by Baton Rouge in a selective and discriminatory fashion, and it could not be applied constitutionally to Cox and his followers. Justices White and Harlan dissented from this conclusion. It is the third conviction, for courthouse picketing, which concerns us here. This split the Court deeply. Justice Arthur Goldberg wrote for the majority. Justices Black, Clark, White and Harlan dissented, with Black and Clark writing opinions.

Mr. Justice Goldberg delivered the opinion of the Court.

> Appellant was convicted of violating a Louisiana statute which provides:

> "Whoever, with the intent of interfering with, obstructing, or impeding the administration of justice, or with the intent of influencing any judge, juror, witness, or court officer, in the discharge of his duty pickets or parades in or near a building housing a court of the State of Louisiana . . . shall be fined not more than five thousand dollars or imprisoned not more than one year, or both." . . .

This charge was based upon the same set of facts as the "disturbing the peace" and "obstructing a public passage" charges. . . .

. . . .

There can be no question that a State has a legitimate interest in protecting its judicial system from the pressures which picketing near a courthouse might create. Since we are committed to a government of laws and not of men, it is of the utmost importance that the administration of justice be absolutely fair and orderly. This Court has recognized that the unhindered and untrammeled functioning of our courts is part of the very foundation of our constitutional democracy. . . .

A State may adopt safeguards necessary and appropriate to assure that the administration of justice at all stages is free from outside control and influence. A narrowly drawn statute such as the one under review is obviously a safeguard both necessary and appropriate to vindicate the State's interest in assuring justice under law.

Nor does such a statute infringe upon the constitutionally protected rights of free speech and free assembly. The conduct which is the subject of this statute— picketing and parading—is subject to regulation even though intertwined with expression and association. The examples are many of the application by this Court of the principle that certain forms of conduct mixed with speech may be regulated or prohibited. The most classic of these was pointed out long ago by Mr. Justice Holmes: "The most stringent protection of free speech would not protect a man in falsely shouting fire in a theatre and causing a panic." *Schenck* v. *United States.* . . .

We hold that this statute on its face is a valid law dealing with conduct subject to regulation so as to vindicate important interests of society and that the fact that free speech is intermingled with such conduct does not bring with it constitutional protection.

We now deal with the Louisiana statute as applied to the conduct in this case. The group of 2,000, led by appellant, paraded and demonstrated before the courthouse. Judges and court officers were in attendance to discharge their respective functions. It is undisputed that a major purpose of the demonstration was to protest what the demonstrators considered an "illegal" arrest of 23 students the previous day. While the students had not been arraigned or their trial set for any day certain, they were charged with violation of the law, and the judges responsible for trying them and passing upon the legality of their arrest were then in the building.

It is, of course, true that most judges will be influenced only by what they see and hear in court. However, judges are human; and the legislature has the right to recognize the danger that some judges, jurors, and other court officials, will be consciously or unconsciously influenced by demonstrations in or near their courtrooms both prior to and at the time of the trial. . . .

. . . .

We therefore reject the clear and present danger argument of appellant. . . .

. . . .

There are, however, more substantial constitutional objections arising from appellant's conviction on the particular facts of this case. Appellant was convicted for demonstrating not "in," but "near" the courthouse. It is undisputed that the demonstration took place on the west sidewalk, the far side of the street, exactly 101 feet from the courthouse steps and, judging from the pictures in the record, approximately 125 feet from the courthouse itself. The question is raised as to whether the failure of the statute to define the word "near" renders it unconstitutionally vague. It is clear that there is some lack of specificity in a word such as "near." While this lack of specificity may not render the statute unconstitutionally vague, at least as applied to a demonstration within the sight and hearing of those in the courthouse, it is clear that the statute, with respect to the determination of how near the courthouse a particular demonstration can be, foresees a degree of on-the-spot administrative interpretation by officials charged with responsibility for administering and enforcing it. It is apparent that demonstrators, such as those involved here, would justifiably tend to rely on this administrative interpretation of how "near" the courthouse a particular demonstration might take place. Louisiana's statutory policy of preserving order around the courthouse would counsel encouragement of just such reliance. This administrative discretion to construe the term "near" concerns a limited control of the streets and other areas in the immediate vicinity of the courthouse and is the type of narrow discretion which this Court has recognized as the proper role of responsible officials in making determinations concerning the time, place, duration, and manner of demonstrations. . . .

. . . The record here clearly shows that the officials present gave permission for the demonstration to take place across the street from the courthouse. . . .

The record shows that at no time did the police recommend, or even suggest, that the demonstration be held further from the courthouse than it actually was. The police admittedly had prior notice that the demonstration was planned to be held in the vicinity of the courthouse. They were prepared for it at that point and so stationed themselves and their equipment as to keep the demonstrators on the far side of the street. As Cox approached the vicinity of the courthouse, he was met by the Chief of Police and other officials. At this point not only was it not suggested that they hold their assembly elsewhere, or disband, but they were affirmatively told that they could hold the demonstration on the sidewalk of the far side of the street, 101 feet from the courthouse steps. This area was effectively blocked off by the police and traffic rerouted.

Thus, the highest police officials of the city, in the presence of the Sheriff and Mayor, in effect told the demonstrators that they could meet where they did, 101 feet from the courthouse steps, but could not meet closer to the courthouse. In effect, appellant was advised that a demonstration at the place it was held would not be one "near" the courthouse within the terms of the statute.

This is not to say that had the appellant, entirely on his own, held the demonstration across the street from the courthouse within the sight and hearing of those inside, or *a fortiori*, had he defied an order of the police requiring him to hold this demonstration at some point further away out of the sight and hearing of those inside the courthouse, we would reverse the conviction as in this case. In such cases a state interpretation of the statute to apply to the demonstration as being "near" the courthouse would be subject to quite different considerations. . . .

. . . .

The application of these principles requires us to reverse the judgment of the Supreme Court of Louisiana.

Reversed.

Justice Black concurred in dismissing the breach of peace and obstruction of way convictions. However, he would have sustained the conviction for courthouse picketing. Justice Clark agreed with him but wrote separately. Justices White and Harlan agreed with Black on courthouse picketing and also would have sustained the obstruction of way conviction. Justice White's opinion is omitted.

Mr. Justice Black, concurring in part and dissenting in part.

I concur in the Court's judgment reversing appellant Cox's convictions for violation of the Louisiana statutes prohibiting breach of the peace and obstructing public passages. . . .

I would sustain the conviction of appellant for violation of Louisiana's [law] which makes it an offense for anyone, under any conditions, to picket or parade near a courthouse, residence or other building used by a judge, juror, witness, or court officer, "with the intent of influencing" any of them. Certainly the record shows beyond all doubt that the purpose of the 2,000 or more people who stood right across the street from the courthouse and jail was to protest the arrest of members of their group who were then in jail. As the Court's opinion states, appellant Cox so testified. Certainly the most obvious reason for their protest at the courthouse was to influence the judge and other court officials who used the courthouse and performed their official duties there. The Court attempts to support its holding by its inference that the Chief of Police gave his consent to picketing the courthouse. But quite apart from the fact that a police chief cannot authorize violations of his State's criminal laws, there was strong, emphatic testimony that if any consent was given it was limited to telling Cox and his group to come no closer to the courthouse than they had already come without the consent of any official, city, state, or federal. And there was also testimony that when told to leave appellant Cox defied the order by telling the crowd not to move. I fail to understand how the Court can justify the reversal of this conviction because of a permission which testimony in the record denies was given, which could not have been authoritatively given anyway, and which even if given was soon afterwards revoked. . . .

Experience demonstrates that it is not a far step from what to many seems the earnest, honest, patriotic, kind-spirited multitude of today, to the fanatical, threatening, lawless mob of tomorrow. And the crowds that press in the streets for noble goals today can be supplanted tomorrow by street mobs pressuring the courts for precisely opposite ends. . . .

Justice Clark would also have sustained the third conviction.

Mr. Justice Clark, dissenting.

According to the record, the opinions of all of Louisiana's courts and even the majority opinion of this Court, the appellant, in an effort to influence and intimidate the courts and legal officials of Baton Rouge and procure the release of 23 prisoners being held for trial, agitated and led a mob of over 2,000 students in the staging of a modern Donnybrook Fair across from the courthouse and jail. He preferred to resolve the controversy in the streets rather than submit the question to the normal judicial procedures by contacting the judge and attempting to secure bail and an early trial for the prisoners. . . .

But the Court excuses Cox's brazen defiance of the statute—the validity of which the Court upholds—on a much more subtle ground. It seizes upon the acquiescence of the Chief of Police arising from the laudable motive to avoid violence and possible bloodshed to find that he made an on-the-spot administrative determination that a demonstration confined to the west side of St. Louis Street— 101 feet from the courthouse steps—would not be "near" enough to the court building to violate the statute. It then holds that the arrest and conviction of appellant for demonstrating there constitutes an "indefensible sort of entrapment." . . .

With due deference, the record will not support this novel theory. . . . This mob of young Negroes led by Cox—2,000 strong—was not only within sight but in hearing distance of the courthouse. The record is replete with evidence that the demonstrators with their singing, cheering, clapping and waving of banners drew the attention of the whole courthouse square as well as the occupants and officials of the court building itself. Indeed, one judge was obliged to leave the building. . . .

. . . .

Reading the facts in a way most favorable to the appellant would, in my opinion, establish only that the Chief of Police consented to the demonstration at that location. However, if the Chief's action be consent, I never knew until today that a law enforcement official—city, state or national—could forgive a breach of the criminal laws. I missed that in my law school, in my practice and for the two years while I was head of the Criminal Division of the Department of Justice. . . .

I have always been taught that this Nation was dedicated to freedom *under law* not under mobs, whether they be integrationists or white supremacists. Our concept of equal justice under law encompasses no such protection as the Court gives Cox today. The contemporary drive for personal liberty can only be successful when conducted within the framework of due process of law. Goals, no matter how laudable, pursued by mobocracy in the end must always lead to further restraints of free expression. To permit, and even condone, the use of such anarchistic devices to influence the administration of justice can but lead us to disaster. For the Court to place its imprimatur upon it is a misfortune that those who love the law will always regret.

Adderley v. *Florida*
385 U.S. 39, 87 S.Ct. 242, 17 L.Ed.2d. 149 (1966)

In *Adderley* the Court tipped the other way on a demonstration near a specialized public facility, and Justice Black's stricter views on control of demonstrations prevailed. Whereas Black accorded "pure speech" absolute protection, picketing and demonstration involved speech plus action. As we just saw in *Cox,* Black anchored the wing of the Court more disposed to accept governmental restriction of such expression.

Mr. Justice Black delivered the opinion of the Court.

Petitioners [32 students at Florida A. & M. University in Tallahassee] were convicted [of] "trespass with a malicious and mischievous intent" upon the premises of the county jail contrary to [Florida law]. [They] had gone from the school to the jail about a mile away, along with many other students, to "demonstrate" at the jail their protests of arrests of other protesting students the day before, and perhaps to protest more generally against state and local policies and practices of racial segregation, including segregation of the jail. The county sheriff, legal custodian of the jail and jail grounds, tried to persuade [them to leave]. When this did not work he notified them that they must leave, that if they did not leave he would arrest them for trespassing, and that if they resisted he would charge them with that as well. Some of the students left but others, including petitioners, remained and they were arrested. . . .

Petitioners [argue this case is] controlled [by *Edwards*]. . . . We cannot agree. [In] *Edwards*, the demonstrators went to the South Carolina State Capitol grounds to protest. In this case they went to the jail. Traditionally, state capitol grounds are open to the public. Jails, built for security purposes, are not. . . . [The *Edwards* demonstrators were charged with] . . . breach of the peace. . . . [But the Florida trespass law here] . . . is aimed at conduct of one limited kind, that is, [trespassing] upon the property of another with a malicious and mischievous intent. There is no lack of notice in this law, nothing to entrap or fool the unwary. . . .

[The . . . question is whether the conviction violates petitioners' First Amendment rights.] We hold it does not. The sheriff, as jail custodian, had power [to] direct that this large crowd of people get off the grounds. There is not a shred of evidence in this record that this power was exercised [because] the sheriff objected to what was being sung or said by the demonstrators or because he disagreed with the objectives of their protest. The record reveals that he objected only to their presence on that part of the jail grounds reserved for jail uses. There is no evidence at all that on any other occasion had similarly large groups of the public been permitted to gather on this portion of the jail grounds for any purpose. Nothing in the [Constitution] prevents Florida from even-handed enforcement of its general trespass statute against those refusing to obey the sheriff's order to remove themselves from what amounted to the curtilage of the jailhouse. The State, no less than a private owner of property, has power to preserve the property under its control for the use to which it is lawfully dedicated. For this reason there is no merit to the petitioners' argument that they had a constitutional right to stay on the property, over the jail custodian's objections, because this "area chosen for the peaceful civil rights demonstration was not only 'reasonable' but also particularly appropriate." Such an argument has as its major unarticulated premise the assumption that people who want to propagandize protests or views have a constitutional right to do so whenever and however and wherever they please. That concept of constitutional law was vigorously and forthrightfully rejected [before]. .... We reject it again. The [Constitution] does not forbid a State to control the use of its own property for its own lawful nondiscriminatory purpose.

Affirmed.

There was prestigious dissent, and the issue survives to be fought over on many a day and many a factual context to come.

Mr. Justice Douglas, with whom The *Chief Justice* [Warren], Mr. Justice Brennan, and Mr. Justice Fortas concur, dissenting.

[T]he Court errs in treating the case as if it were an ordinary trespass case or an ordinary picketing case. The jailhouse, like an executive mansion, a legislative chamber, a courthouse, or the statehouse itself [*Edwards*], is one of the seats of government, whether it be the Tower of London, the Bastille, or a small county jail. And when it houses political prisoners or those whom many think are unjustly held, it is an obvious center for protest. The right to petition for the redress of grievances has an ancient history and is not limited to writing a letter or sending a telegram to a congressman; it is not confined to appearing before the local city council, or writing letters to the President or Governor or Mayor. Conventional methods of petitioning may be, and often have been, shut off to large groups of our citizens. Legislators may turn deaf ears; formal complaints may be routed endlessly through a bureaucratic maze; courts may let the wheels of justice grind very slowly. Those who do not control television and radio, those who cannot afford to advertise in newspapers or circulate elaborate pamphlets may have only a more limited type of access to public officials. Their methods should not be condemned as tactics of obstruction and harassment as long as the assembly and petition are peaceable, as these were.

There is no question that petitioners had as their purpose a protest against the arrest of Florida A. & M. students for trying to integrate public theatres. [The] group was protesting the arrests, and state and local policies of segregation, including segregation of the jail. [The] fact that no one gave a formal speech, that no elaborate handbills were distributed, and that the group was not laden with signs would seem to be immaterial. Such methods are not the sine qua non of petitioning for the redress of grievances. The group did sing "freedom" songs. And history shows that a song can be a powerful tool of protest. [There] was no violence; no threat of violence; no attempted jail break; no storming of a prison; no plan or plot to do anything but protest. The evidence is uncontradicted that the petitioners' conduct did not upset the jailhouse routine. [There] was no shoving, no pushing, no disorder or threat of riot. It is said that some of the group blocked part of the driveway leading to the jail entrance. [If] there was congestion, the solution was a further request to move to lawns or parking areas, not complete ejection and arrest. [Finally], the fact that some of the protestants may have felt their cause so just that they were willing to be arrested for making their protest outside the jail seems wholly irrelevant. A petition is nonetheless a petition, though its futility may make martyrdom attractive.

We do violence to the First Amendment when we permit this "petition for redress of grievances" to be turned into a trespass action. It does not help to analogize this problem to the problem of picketing. Picketing is a form of protest usually directed against private interests. I do not see how rules governing picketing in general are relevant to this express constitutional right to assemble and to petition for redress of grievances. In the first place the jailhouse grounds were not marked with "NO TRESPASSING!" signs, nor does respondent claim that the public was generally excluded from the grounds. Only the sheriff's fiat transformed lawful conduct into an unlawful trespass. To say that a private owner could have done the same if the rally had taken place on private property is to speak of a different case, as an assembly and a petition for redress of grievances run to government, not to private proprietors. . . .

CASE STUDY: SKOKIE AND THE NAZIS

Skokie, Illinois (population 70,000), is a rather drab industrial suburb of Chicago that, until 1940, had rejoiced in the name of Niles Center. It was an unlikely stage for the playing out of a national drama over the limits of free speech. But Skokie has one distinguishing feature—its population is heavily Jewish, and among these Jews are a number of survivors of the Nazi holocaust, which cost the lives of over six million of their coreligionists during World War II.

The National Socialist Party of America (the American Nazis), a virulently anti-Semitic formation, was founded by George Lincoln Rockwell in 1958. The party has never been a serious force in Illinois—or, indeed, anywhere else. One member assassinated Rockwell in 1967. Nonetheless, the American Nazis have remained a hardy little weed in the garden of American politics. In the late 1970s the party was making a special recruiting effort in Illinois and had apparently enjoyed some success in the Chicago area. It was then the Nazis began planning a parade through the streets of Skokie.

The municipal authorities of Skokie were horrified. The old, savage symbols of swastika and brown shirt would be displayed in ways sure to give offense to many residents. Written material would be distributed calumniating Jews and other American minorities. And beyond the pain that such an intrusion into the community would cause, could Skokie's police keep the peace? Might not violent crowd reaction simply overwhelm what law enforcement resources could be mustered? On the other hand, what the Nazis sought was nothing more than the peaceful use of the streets, which the Court in *Lovell, Edwards,* and *Cox* recognized as protected to a high degree by the First Amendment against governmental encroachment. As we have seen, some regulation of time, place, and manner was allowed; regulation based on the content of the proposed speech was not.

Undaunted, Skokie officials went into the state courts of Illinois seeking an injunction to stop the demonstration. The initial trial court issued an injunction forbidding the Nazis from engaging in specific activities in Skokie— parading in uniform, displaying the swastika, and distributing pamphlets of an anti-Semitic nature. Nazis immediately announced that they would appeal on the grounds that the injunction violated their First Amendment rights and asked the Illinois appellate court to stay the injunction (postpone its legally binding effect) until substantive arguments were heard on the appeal. The appellate court refused the stay. Then the Illinois Supreme Court denied a petition that it hear the substantive appeal immediately, and it also refused a stay. With the proposed date for the parade drawing near, the Nazis then sought a stay from the Supreme Court of the United States. The Court treated this request as a petition for *certiorari,* considered the case, and granted the stay on June 14, 1977.

The decision in *National Socialist Party of America* v. *Village of Skokie,* 432 U.S. 43 (1977), was 5-4, and the majority spoke through a *per curiam* opinion that stressed the need for "strict procedural safeguards" in cases involving restrictions on speech. By denying either immediate appellate review, or a stay pending such review, the Illinois Supreme Court had failed to meet that standard. The thrust of the *per curiam* opinion was that without "strict safeguards" it would be possible for trial courts to throw off the timetables of proposed demonstrators and perhaps achieve the ultimate cancellation of demonstrations by issuing constitutionally defeative injunctions. Eventually such injunctions would be voided, but by the time the regular, slow appeals process had run its course (over many months or even years), the reason a group sought to express itself at a particular time and place may have evaporated. The issue or occasion prompting the protest may have become history. Without swift review for constitutionality, the injunction could serve as a device by which local authorities and sympathetic local trial courts postponed unwanted appearances in their "public forums" into the indefinite future.

Justice Byron White simply noted that he favored the stay, but Justice William Rehnquist, with whom Chief Justice Warren Burger and Justice Potter Stewart joined, filed a dissent. Rehnquist recognized that the terms of the original injunction were "extremely broad" and probably constitutionally defective. Nevertheless, it was not for the U.S. Supreme Court to intervene until the Illinois courts had authoritatively and finally passed on the constitutional questions involved. Then, if Illinois' answer was wrong, it could be corrected by the Court. Whether or not stays were granted pending such final Illinois adjudication of the substantive constitutional issues was a matter of policy for the Illinois court system with which the U.S. Supreme Court had no jurisdiction to interfere. "Erroneous" injunctions by state trial courts were regrettable, but it did not encourage "long run respect for the Constitution or for the law" for the Justices to disregard the jurisdictional limitations placed on them by Congress and short circuit the orderly operation of the parallel federal and state court systems in order to correct particular mistakes immediately.

Meanwhile, other initiatives were taken in Skokie to block the Nazis. In May of 1977, the village adopted three ordinances. The first set up a permit system for parades and other demonstrations under which applicants for permits were required to obtain $300,000 in liability insurance and $50,000 in property damage insurance. (This requirement not only mandated the cost of the insurance coverage, but left it to the applicant to find a willing underwriter.) The second ordinance prohibited the "dissemination of any materials . . . which (intentionally) promote and incite hatred against persons by reason of their race, national origin, or religion." The third ordinance prohibited political demonstrations by persons wearing "military-style" uniforms.

Nazi leader Frank Collin, represented by an attorney provided by the American Civil Liberties Union, challenged these ordinances in federal district court on First Amendment grounds. That court found the ordinances unconstitutional, concluding that "it is better to allow those who preach racial hate to expend their venom in rhetoric rather than to be panicked into embarking on the dangerous course of permitting the government to decide what its citizens may say and hear." *Collin* v. *Smith,* 447 F.Supp. 676 (1978). The Court of Appeals for the Seventh Circuit affirmed this decision and on June 12, 1978, with the Nazi march scheduled for June 25, the Supreme Court denied Skokie's petition for a stay of the Court of Appeals decision. *Smith* v. *Collins,* 436 U.S. 953 (1978). Justice Harry Blackmun, joined by Justice William Rehnquist, dissented from the denial. Blackmun relied on the twenty-five year old precedent of *Beauharnais* v. *Illinois,* 343 U.S. 250 (1952). There, in a 5-4 decision, the Court had upheld a so-called "group libel" law prohibiting the "public display or distribution of any publication which portrays depravity, criminality, unchastity, or lack of virtue of a class of citizens, of any race, color, creed, or religion," or which "exposes the citizens of any race, color, creed or religion to contempt, derision, or obloquy. . . ." Blackmun reasoned that the Court of Appeals decision was "in some tension with this Court's decision . . . in *Beauharnais,*" and noted that "*Beauharnais* has never been overruled or formally limited in any way." (That particular Illinois group libel law had long since lapsed and had not been reenacted. That is why it was not available to help the Skokie authorities.)

All legal obstacles to the Nazi demonstration were now removed, but on June 22 Collin cancelled the Skokie plan, announcing that it had been "pure agitation to restore our right to free speech." The elders of Skokie breathed easier, but not the leaders of the A.C.L.U. Civil libertarians had been deeply split on the issue of whether the efforts of Skokie to prevent a full-fledged Nazi parade constituted a true free speech crisis in which the Union (as a matter of fidelity to principle) ought to involve itself. The majority decision of the leadership had been to intervene, but there were deep resentments generated by the group's "siding with Nazis." There were resignations and a decline in contributions to the organization.

The final act of the Skokie drama was played out on October 16, 1978, when the Supreme Court refused to review the merits of the Court of Appeals decision invalidating the Skokie ordinances (the refusal of June 12, 1978 had been only of petition for a stay of the effect of Seventh Circuit's decision pending review of the merits). *Smith* v. *Collin,* 439 U.S. 916 (1978).

Again Justice Blackmun dissented from the denial of *certiorari,* this time joined by Justice Byron White. Blackmun wanted the apparent conflict between the Seventh Circuit's decision and the *Beauharnais* case cleared up, but he also felt "that the present case affords the Court an opportunity to consider whether . . . there is no limit whatsoever to the exercise of free speech. There indeed may be no such limit, but when citizens assert, not casually but with deep conviction, that the proposed demonstration is scheduled at a place and in a manner that is taunting and overwhelmingly offensive to the citizens of that place, that assertion, uncomfortable though it may be for judges, deserves to be examined. It might just fall into the same category as one's 'right' (falsely) to cry 'fire' in a crowded theater, for 'the character of every act depends upon the circumstances in which it is done.' *Schenck.*"

CHAPTER · 5

SYMBOLIC SPEECH—THE PROBLEM OF LADY GODIVA

THAT we are expressing an idea by taking some dramatic physical action does not, by itself, confer First Amendment protection on that action. What, after all, is more expressive than a well delivered punch to the nose? Lady Godiva was the wife of Leofric, an eleventh century Earl of Mercia, in England. She is supposed to have ridden naked through the town of Coventry to put pressure on her husband to lower the heavy taxes he levied on the townspeople. (Legend has it that the only man who looked became known as Peeping Tom.) The good lady's example has been followed by dissidents through the ages who believed strongly in some cause and concluded that verbal expression was inadequate to convey their feelings or would not attract the attention they desired.

In the cases that follow, *U.S.* v. *O'Brien* involves the action of a young man who burned his draft card at a political demonstration on the steps of the South Boston Courthouse to demonstrate his opposition to American military involvement in Vietnam. The second case, *Tinker* v. *Des Moines,* also involved the Vietnam conflict. The Tinker children wore black arm bands to high school to protest the continued American involvement in Southeast Asia. The third case, *Spence* v. *Washington,* involved the use of an American flag contrary to a Washington state statute.

In these cases, where the speech component is inextricably intertwined with action, the question of whether the display is protected by the First Amendment seems to turn on such factors as (1) the extent to which a coherent message is actually being communicated, (2) the extent of the disruption of legitimate activities caused by the behavior, and, (3) the availability of alternate channels for communicating the desired message.

This problem of action to achieve expression is complicated today by the importance of organized communications media—especially the electronic media (radio and TV)—in the political process and the formation of political opinion. Bizarre behavior, the more offensive to majority sensibilities the better, is also the sort of behavior likely to win the "speaker" a few precious minutes on the evening news. To what extent, if at all, should this political imperative be a factor in determining whether the speech content of a particular expressive action is sufficiently substantial to warrant First Amendment protection?

United States v. *O'Brien*
391 U.S. 367, 88 S.Ct. 1673, 20 L.Ed.2d. 672 (1968)

The Universal Military Training and Service Act of 1948 (the old "draft law") required registrants to keep their registration certificates in their "personal possession at all times." Presumably, this was to allow authorities to quickly determine the draft status of persons in enforcing the law; that is, an easy way to catch a "draft dodger" would be to ask to see the person's draft card. In 1965, with Vietnam related resistance to the draft escalating, Congress added some amendments to the draft law. One of these, Section 462 (b) (3), made it an offense for anyone to knowingly destroy or knowingly mutilate a draft card. It was under this provision that O'Brien was charged after burning his card on the courthouse steps in the course of a carefully staged media event. O'Brien was convicted at trial, but the Court of Appeals for the First Circuit reversed with a majority opinion by Judge Frank Coffin. *O'Brien* v. *U.S.,* 376 F. 2d 538 (C.A. 1st Cir. 1976). Coffin reasoned that the legitimate interests of Congress in protecting the administrative integrity of the selective service system was adequately served by the possession requirement, and that the additional crime of knowing destruction could only be understood as a criminal sanction directed at the *message* being communicated by the act of destruction. Before the Supreme Court, O'Brien's case was argued by Marvin Karpatkin, one of the leading radical attorneys of the 1960s; other ACLU stalwarts, such as Mel Wolf, were "on the brief." Despite this O'Brien lost and the First Circuit was reversed.

Mr. Chief Justice Warren delivered the opinion of the Court.

O'Brien first argues that the [statute] is unconstitutional as applied to him because his act of burning his registration certificate was protected "symbolic speech" within the First Amendment. His argument is that the freedom of expression which the First Amendment guarantees includes all modes of "communication of ideas by conduct," and that his conduct is within this definition because he did it in "demonstration against the war and against the draft."

We cannot accept the view that an apparently limitless variety of conduct can be labelled "speech" whenever the person engaging in the conduct intends thereby to express an idea. However, even on the assumption that the alleged communicative element in O'Brien's conduct is sufficient to bring into play the First Amendment, it does not necessarily follow that the destruction of a registration certificate is constitutionally protected activity. This court has held that when "speech" and "nonspeech" elements are combined in the same course of conduct, a sufficiently important governmental interest in regulating the nonspeech element can justify incidental limitations on First Amendment freedoms. To characterize the quality of the governmental interest which must appear, the Court has employed a variety of descriptive terms: compelling; substantial; subordinating; paramount; cogent; strong. Whatever imprecision inheres in these terms, we think it clear that a government regulation is sufficiently justified if it is within the constitutional power of the Government; if it furthers an important or substantial governmental interest; if the governmental interest is unrelated to the suppression of free expression; and if the incidental restriction on alleged First Amendment freedom is no greater than is essential to the furtherance of that interest. We find that the [statute] meets all of these requirements, and consequently that O'Brien can be constitutionally convicted for violating it.

. . . .

The many functions performed by Selective Service certificates establish beyond doubt that Congress has a legitimate and substantial interest in preventing their wanton and unrestrained destruction and assuring their continuing availability by punishing people who knowingly and wilfully destroy or mutilate them. . . .

. . . The governmental interest and the scope of the [statute] are limited to preventing a harm to the smooth and efficient functioning of the Selective Service System. When O'Brien deliberately rendered unavailable his registration certificate, he wilfully frustrated this governmental interest. For this noncommunicative impact of his conduct, and nothing else, he was convicted. . . .

. . . .

O'Brien finally argues that the 1965 Amendment is unconstitutional as enacted because what he calls the "purpose" of Congress was "to suppress freedom of speech." We reject this argument because under settled principles the purpose of Congress, as O'Brien uses that term, is not a basis for declaring this legislation unconstitutional.

It is a familiar principle of constitutional law that this Court will not strike down an otherwise constitutional statute on the basis of an alleged illicit legislative motive. . . .

Inquiries into congressional motives or purposes are a hazardous matter. When the issue is simply the interpretation of legislation, the Court will look to statements by legislators for guidance as to the purpose of the legislature, because the benefit to sound decision-making in this circumstance is thought sufficient to risk the possibility of misreading Congress' purpose. It is entirely a different matter when we are asked to void a statute that is, under well-settled criteria, constitutional on its face, on the basis of what fewer than a handful of Congressmen said about it. What motivates one legislator to make a speech about a statute is not necessarily what motives scores of others to enact it, and the stakes are sufficiently high for us to eschew guess-work. We decline to void essentially on the ground that it is unwise legislation which Congress had the undoubted power to enact and which could be reenacted in its exact form if the same or another legislator made a "wiser" speech about it.

. . . .

We think it not amiss, in passing, to comment upon O'Brien's legislative-purpose argument. There was little floor debate on this legislation in either House. Only Senator Thurmond commented on its substantive features in the Senate. . . .

In the House debate only two Congressmen addressed themselves to the Amendment—Congressmen Rivers and Bray. ... It is principally on the basis of the statements by these three Congressmen that O'Brien makes his congressional-"purpose" argument. We note that if we were to examine legislative purpose in the instant case, we would be obliged to consider not only these statements but also the more authoritative reports of the Senate and House Armed Services Commitees. The portions of those reports explaining the purpose of the Amendments are reproduced in the Appendix in their entirety. While both reports make clear a concern with the "defiant" destruction of so-called "draft cards" and with "open" encouragement to others to destroy their cards, both reports also indicate that this concern stemmed from an apprehension that unrestrained destruction of cards would disrupt the smooth functioning of the Selective Service System. ...

Justice Harlan concurred briefly. Justice Douglas, who was alone in thinking a peace-time draft unconstitutional, dissented.

Tinker v. *Des Moines School District*
393 U.S. 503, 89 S.Ct. 733, 21 L.Ed.2d. 731 (1969)

In December, 1965, the Tinker children, high school and junior high school students in Des Moines, Iowa, wore black armbands to school to publicize their objections to United States operations in Vietnam. Anticipating such action, the school authorities had adopted a policy that any student wearing an armband to school would be requested to remove it, and if the student refused, he or she would be suspended until returning without the armband. The Tinkers refused to remove their armbands and were suspended. In federal district court they sought an injunction restraining the school officials from disciplining them. The lower federal courts upheld the action of the school authorities on the ground that it was reasonable to prevent disturbance of school discipline.

Mr. Justice Fortas delivered the opinion of the Court.

The District Court recognized that the wearing of an armband for the purpose of expressing certain views is the type of symbolic act that is within the Free Speech Clause of the First Amendment. ... As we shall discuss, the wearing of armbands in the circumstances of this case was entirely divorced from actually or potentially disruptive conduct by those participating in it. It was closely akin to "pure speech" which, we have repeatedly held, is entitled to comprehensive protection under the First Amendment. Cf. *Cox* v. *Louisiana*, 379 U.S. 536, 555 (1965); *Adderley* v. *Florida*, 385 U.S. 39 (1966) [which were "speech-plus cases"].

First Amendment rights, applied in light of the special characteristics of the school environment, are available to teachers and students. It can hardly be argued that either students or teachers shed their constitutional rights to freedom of speech or expression at the schoolhouse gate. ...

On the other hand, the Court has repeatedly emphasized the need for affirming the comprehensive authority of the States and of school authorities, consistent with fundamental constitutional safeguards, to prescribe and control conduct in the schools. ... Our problem lies in the area where students in the exercise of First Amendment rights collide with the rules of the school authorities.

The problem presented by the present case does not relate to regulation of the length of skirts or the type of clothing, to hair style or deportment. ... It does not concern aggressive, disruptive action or even group demonstrations. Our problem involves direct, primary First Amendment rights akin to "pure speech."

The school officials banned and sought to punish petitioners for a silent, passive, expression of opinion, unaccompanied by any disorder or disturbance on the part of petitioners. There is here no evidence whatever of petitioners' interference, actual or nascent, with the school's work or of collision with the rights of other students to be secure and to be let alone. ...

The District Court concluded that the action of the school authorities was reasonable because it was based upon their fear of a disturbance from the wearing of the armbands. But, in our system, undifferentiated fear or apprehension of disturbance is not enough to overcome the right to freedom of expression. Any departure from absolute regimentation may cause trouble. ...

In order for the State in the person of school officials to justify prohibition of a particular expression of opinion, it must be able to show that its action was caused by something more than a mere desire to avoid the discomfort and unpleasantness that always accompany an unpopular viewpoint. Certainly where there is no finding and no showing that the exercise of the forbidden right would "materially and substantially interfere with the requirements of appropriate discipline in the operation of the school," the prohibition cannot be sustained. ...

In the present case, the District Court made no such finding, and our independent examination of the record fails to yield evidence that the school authorities had reason to anticipate that the wearing of the armbands would substantially interfere with the work of the school or impinge upon the rights of other students. Even an official memorandum prepared after the suspension that listed the reasons for the ban on wearing the armbands made no reference to the anticipation of such disruption.

On the contrary, the action of the school authorities appears to have been based upon an urgent wish to avoid the controversy which might result from the expression even by the silent symbol of armbands, of opposition to this Nation's part in the conflagration in Vietnam. ...

As we have discussed, the record does not demonstrate any facts which might reasonably have led school authorities to forecast substantial disruption of or material interference with school activities, and no disturbances or disorders on the school premises in fact occured. These petitioners merely went about their ordained rounds in school. Their deviation consisted only in wearing on their sleeve a band of black cloth, not more than two inches wide. They wore it to exhibit their disapproval of the Vietnam hostilities and their advocacy of a truce, to make their views known, and by their example, to influence others to adopt them. They neither interrupted school activities nor sought to intrude in the school affairs or the lives of others. They caused discussion outside of the classroom, but no interference with work and no disorder. In the circumstances, our Constitution does not permit officials of the State to deny their form of expression. . . .

Reversed and remanded.

Mr. Justice Stewart, concurring.

Although I agree with much of what is said in the Court's opinion, and with its judgment in this case, I cannot share the Court's uncritical assumption that, school discipline aside, the First Amendment rights of children are co-extensive with those of adults. . . .

Mr. Justice White, concurring.

While I join the Court's opinion, I deem it appropriate to note, first, that the Court continues to recognize a distinction between communicating by words and communicating by acts or conduct which sufficiently impinge on some valid state interest. . . .

Mr. Justice Black, dissenting.

While the record does not show that any of these armband students shouted, used profane language or were violent in any manner, detailed testimony by some of them shows their armbands caused comments, warnings by other students, the poking of fun at them, and a warning by an older football player that other, nonprotesting students had better let them alone. There is also evidence that the professor of mathematics had his lesson period practically "wrecked" chiefly by disputes with Mary Beth Tinker, who wore her armband for her "demonstration." Even a casual reading of the record shows that this armband did divert students' minds from their regular lessons, and that talks, comments, etc., made John Tinker "self-conscious" in attending school with his armband. While the absence of obscene or boisterous and loud disorder perhaps justifies the Court's statement that the few armband students did not actually "disrupt" the classwork, I think the record overwhelmingly shows that the armbands did exactly what the elected school officials and principals foresaw it would, that is, took the students' minds off their classwork and diverted them to thoughts about the highly emotional subject of the Vietnam war. . . .

[It has not] been the "unmistakable holding of this Court for almost 50 years" that "students" and "teachers" take with them into the "schoolhouse gate" constitutional rights to "freedom of speech or expression." . . . The truth is that a teacher of kindergarten, grammar school, or high school pupils no more carries into a school with him a complete right to freedom of speech and expression than an anti-Catholic or anti-Semitic carries with him a complete freedom of speech and religion into a Catholic church or Jewish synagogue. Nor does a person carry with him into the United States Senate or House, or to the Supreme Court, or any other court, a complete constitutional right to go into those places contrary to their rules and speak his mind on any subject he pleases. It is a myth to say that any person has a constitutional right to say what he pleases, where he pleases, and when he pleases. Our Court has decided precisely the opposite. . . .

Mr. Justice Harlan, dissenting.

    ... [I] am reluctant to believe that there is any disagreement between the majority and myself on the proposition that school officials should be accorded the widest authority in maintaining discipline and good order in their institutions. To translate that proposition into a workable constitutional rule, I would, in cases like this, cast upon those complaining the burden of showing that a particular school measure was motivated by other than legitimate school concerns—for example, a desire to prohibit the expression of an unpopular point of view, while permitting expression of the dominant opinion.

    Finding nothing in this record which impugns the good faith of respondents in promulgating the armband regulation, I would affirm the judgment below.

Spence v. *Washington*
418 U.S. 405, 94 S.Ct. 2727, 41 L.Ed.2d. 842 (1974)

    On May 10, 1970, Spence, a college student, hung an American flag from the window of his Seattle apartment. The flag was upside down and attached to the front and back, in black plastic tape, was a "peace symbol"—a circle enclosing a trident. The symbol occupied roughly half the surface of the flag. Spence was convicted under a Washington statute prohibiting the exhibition of a U.S. flag to which superimposed figures or other extraneous material is attached. Again, we encounter the device of the *per curiam* opinion (supposedly reserved for easy, noncontroversial cases) in a situation where the Court was, in fact, deeply divided.

    [Spence] was not charged under Washington's flag desecration statute. Rather, the State relied on the so-called "improper use" statute. [He] testified that he put a peace symbol on the flag and displayed it to public view as a protest to the invasion of Cambodia and the killings at Kent State University, events which occurred a few days prior to his arrest. He said that his purpose was to associate the American flag with peace instead of war and violence: "I felt there had been so much killing and that this was not what America stood for. I felt that the flag stood for America and I wanted people to know that I thought America stood for peace." [Spence] further testified that he chose to fashion the peace symbol from tape so that it could be removed without damaging the flag.

    A number of factors are important in the instant case. First, this was a privately owned flag. In a technical property sense it was not the property of any government. [Second, Spence] displayed his flag on private property. He engaged in no trespass or disorderly conduct. Nor is this a case that might be analyzed in terms of reasonable time, place, or manner restraints on access to a public area. Third, the record is devoid of proof of any risk of breach of the peace. [Fourth], the state concedes [that Spence] engaged in a form of communication. [That] concession is inevitable on this record. [To] be sure, [Spence] did not choose to articulate his views through printed or spoken words. It is therefore necessary to determine whether his activity was sufficiently imbued with elements of communication to fall within the scope of the First [Amendment]. [The] nature of [Spence's] activity, combined with the factual context and environment in which it was undertaken, lead to the conclusion that he engaged in a form of protected expression.

Moreover, the context in which a symbol is used for purposes of expression is important, for the context may give meaning to the symbol. In his case, [Spence's] activity was roughly simultaneous with and concededly triggered by the Cambodian incursion and the Kent State tragedy, [matters] of great public moment. A flag bearing a peace symbol and displayed upside down by a student today might be interpreted as nothing more than bizarre behavior, but it would have been difficult for the great majority of citizens to miss the ... point at the time that he made it. It may be noted, further, that this was not an act of mindless nihilism. Rather, it was a pointed expression of anguish [about] the then current domestic and foreign affairs of his government. An intent to convey a particularized message was present, and in the surrounding circumstances the likelihood was great that the message would be understood by those who viewed it.

We are confronted then with a case of prosecution for the expression of an idea through activity. Moreover, the activity occurred on private property. [Accordingly], we must examine with particular care [the] range of various state interests that might be thought to support the challenged conviction, drawing upon the arguments before us, the opinions below, and the Court's opinion in Street v. New York. The first interest at issue is prevention of breach of the peace. [It] is totally without support in the record.

We are also unable to affirm the judgment below on the ground that the State may have desired to protect the sensibilities of passersby. "It is firmly settled that under our Constitution the public expression of ideas may not be prohibited merely because the ideas are themselves offensive to some of their hearers." ... Moreover, appellant did not impose his ideas upon a captive audience. Anyone who might have been offended could easily have avoided the display. See [Cohen]. Nor may appellant be punished for failing to show proper respect for our national emblem.

We are brought, then, to the state court's thesis that Washington has an interest in preserving the national flag as an unalloyed symbol of our country. The court did not define this interest; it simply asserted it. The dissenting opinion today adopts essentially the same approach. Presumably, this interest might be seen as an effort to prevent the appropriation of a revered national symbol by an individual, interest group, or enterprise where there was a risk that association of the symbol with a particular product or viewpoint might be taken erroneously as evidence of governmental endorsement. Alternatively, it might be argued that the interest asserted by the state court is based on the uniquely universal character of the national flag as a symbol. For the great majority of us, the flag is a symbol of patriotism, of pride in the history of our country, and of the service, sacrifice, and valor of the millions of Americans who in peace and war have joined together to build and to defend a Nation in which self-government and personal liberty endure. It evidences both the unity and diversity which are America. For others the flag carries in varying degrees a different message. "A person gets from a symbol the meaning he puts into it, and what is one man's comfort and inspiration is another's jest and scorn." It might be said that we all draw something from our national symbol, for it is capable of conveying simultaneously a spectrum of meanings. If it may be destroyed or permanently disfigured, it could be argued that it will lose its capability of mirroring the sentiments of all who view it.

But we need not decide in this case whether the interest advanced by the court below is valid. We assume, arguendo, that it is. The statute is nontheless unconstitutional as applied to appellant's activity. There was no risk that appellant's acts would mislead viewers into assuming that the Government endorsed his viewpoint. To the contrary, he was plainly and peacefully protesting the fact that it did not. Appellant was not charged under the desecration statute, nor did he permanently disfigure the flag or destroy it. He displayed it as a flag of his country in a way closely analogous to the manner in which flags have always been used to convey ideas. Moreover, his message was direct, likely to be understood, and within the contours of the First Amendment. Given the protected character of his expression and in light of the fact that no interest the State may have in preserving the physical integrity of a privately-owned flag was significantly impaired on these facts, the conviction must be invalidated.

Reversed.

Mr. Justice Rehnquist, with whom The Chief Justice [Burger] and Mr. Justice White join, dissenting.

Since a state concededly may impose some limitations on speech directly, it would seem to follow a fortiori that a State may legislate to protect important state interests even though an incidental limitation on free speech results. Virtually any law enacted by the State, when viewed with sufficient ingenuity, could be thought to interfere with some citizen's preferred means of expression. But no one would argue, I presume, that a State could not prevent the painting of public buildings simply because a particular class of protesters believed their message would best be conveyed through that medium. [Yet] the Court today holds that [the State] cannot limit use of the American flag, at least insofar as its statute prevents appellant from using a privately owned flag to convey his personal message. [The majority] demonstrates a total misunderstanding of the State's interest in the integrity of the American flag, and [places itself] in the position either of ultimately favoring appellant's message ... [or], alternatively, of making the flag available for limitless succession of political and commercial messages. I shall treat these issues in reverse order.

The statute under which appellant was convicted is no stranger to this Court, a virtually identical statute having been before the Court in Halter [where] the Court held that Nebraska could enforce its statute to prevent use of flag representation on beer bottles. ... "Such an use tends to degrade and cheapen the flag in the estimation of the people, as well as to defeat the object of maintaining it as an emblem of National power and National honor." The Court today finds Halter irrelevant. ... [I]f the Court is suggesting that Halter would now be decided differently, and that the State's interest in the flag falls before any speech which is "direct, likely to be understood, and within the contours of the First Amendment," that view would mean the flag could be auctioned as a background to anyone willing and able to buy or copy one. I find it hard to believe the Court intends to presage that result.

Turning to the question of the State's interest in the flag, it seems to me that the Court's treatment lacks all substance. The suggestion that the State's interest somehow diminishes when the flag is decorated with [removable] tape trivializes something which is not trivial. The [State] is hardly seeking to protect the flag's resale value. . . . The [State] has chosen to set the flag apart for a special purpose, and has directed that it not be turned into a common background for an endless variety of superimposed messages. The physical condition of the flag itself is irrelevant to that purpose.

The true nature of the State's interest in this case is not only one of preserving "the physical integrity of the flag," but also one of preserving the flag as "an important symbol of nationhood and unity." Although the Court treats this important interest with a studied inattention, it is hardly one of recent invention and has previously been accorded considerable respect by this Court. There was no question in Halter of physical impairment of a flag since no actual flag was even involved. And it certainly would have made no difference to the Court's discussion of the State's interest if [Halter] had chosen to advertise his product by decorating the flag with beer bottles fashioned from some removable substance. It is the character, not the cloth, of the flag which the State seeks to protect. The value of this interest has been emphasized in recent as well as distant times. . . . What appellant here seeks is simply license to use the flag however he pleases, so long as the activity can be tied to a concept of speech, regardless of any state interest in having the flag used only for more limited purposes. I find no reasoning in the Court's opinion which convinces me that the Constitution require such license to be given.

The fact that the State has a valid interest in preserving the character of the flag does not mean, of course, that it can employ all conceivable means to enforce it. It certainly could not require all citizens to own the flag or compel citizens to salute one. . . . It presumably cannot punish criticism of the flag, or the principles for which it stands, any more than it could punish criticism of this country's policies or ideas. But the statute in this case demands no such allegiance. Its operation does not depend upon whether the flag is used for communicative or noncommunicative purposes; upon whether a particular message is deemed commercial or political; upon whether the use of the flag is respectful or contemptuous; or upon whether any particular segment of the State's citizenry might applaud or oppose the intended message. It simply withdraws a unique national symbol from the roster of materials that may be used as a background for communications. Since I do not believe the Constitution prohibits Washington from making that decision, I dissent.

CASE STUDY: IS RUGBY "SPEECH"?

The constitutional presumption is that government may regulate physical behavior—conduct—unless it has a speech component or is protected by one of very few other constitutional provisions (for instance, the guarantees of "free exercise" of religion). Just how far can the notion of action protected as expression be stretched?

This question was presented in an interesting way by the visit to the United States in the fall of 1981 of the South African national rugby team—

the Springboks. The views of individual Springbok players on apartheid were unknown, although the squad included both blacks and whites. Yet protests by American opponents of apartheid erupted at matches played by the South African team as it toured under the auspices of the Eastern Rugby Union. When the tour reached Albany, New York, the authorities of that state stepped in. Governor Hugh Carey, fearing that a riot might break out in the state's capitol, "determined that the rugby game should not be held in Albany," and that city's Mayor, Erastus Corning, 3d, withdrew previously granted permission to use the municipal stadium.

But the governor had not reckoned with the New York Civil Liberties Union (an affiliate of the national ACLU). NYCLU attorney Steven R. S. Shapiro asked the federal district court in Albany to void the governor's order. Shapiro argued that "There is no obvious reason why nude dancing viewed through a coin operated booth in an adult establishment should be entitled to greater (First Amendment) protection" than an athletic contest. Judge Howard G. Munson agreed and voided Carey's order. The match went on, but so did comments by expert constitutional politicians.

Professor Laurence H. Tribe, of the Harvard Law School, protested that "Neither rugby nor soccer (or, presumably, cricket) are speech protected by the First Amendment. " Professor Tribe concluded, "When the state reasonably determines that there is a serious threat of violence, it surely has the authority to withhold access to a municipal facility for the athletic event that poses the threat."

Professor A. E. Dick Howard, of the University of Virginia Law School, disagreed. "It's not the event that's political so much as the reaction to it," Howard argued. He added, "The protestors are in effect infusing it (the rugby tour) with a public interest, and the First Amendment gets involved, if only through the back door."

On the danger of violence, Professor Gerald Gunther, of the Stanford Law School, observed that "only the prospect of mass violence is an adequate justification for the government to step in." But Professor Vincent Blasi, of the Columbia University Law School, was worried about the expense of police protection if courts extended First Amendment protection too far: " . . . if necessary you can bring out tanks and troops to protect them (unpopular performers), but that's something a legal system can't push too far, particularly when there aren't intrinsic First Amendment activities at issue."

With the courts having gone as far as they now have, this is a controversy waiting to break out on other days in other contexts. Many communist bloc countries boycotted the 1984 Olympics, but their teams will be touring in America soon and groups will be organizing to pressure local governments to keep them out. Does the restriction of an ostensibly non-speech activity for a political reason confer some speech protection on that activity?

CHAPTER · 6

SEXUALLY EXPLICIT SPEECH—THE PROBLEM OF KNOWING IT WHEN YOU SEE IT

IN traditional understandings of free speech, both in England and America, sexually explicit speech was considered "obscene" and not protected from legal regulation. The major difficulty with this was always one of determining what, precisely, was obscene. Until 1957, the generally accepted rule had been that announced in Britain in 1868 in the case of *Regina* v. *Hicklin*. The approach was exceedingly restrictive of descriptions of human sexual behavior. Material was obscene if any part of it would have the effect of sexually arousing the most susceptible (oversexed? undersexed?) of its possible readers.

The application of the so-called Hicklin Rule produced some absurd results. Material that was sexually explicit but of clear and considerable artistic and cultural value was banned from the literary market place. Perhaps the most dramatic example involved James Joyce's masterpiece *Ulysses*. The novel, written in a then innovative "stream of consciousness style," explored the thoughts and interlocking personalities of its characters through the course of a single day. In places the language was explicit both as to sexual and excretory functions. Under a provision of the U.S. customs laws prohibiting the importation of obscene material, *Ulysses* was effectively banned from this country until 1933. Even after the federal court decision holding that the novel was not obscene within the meaning of the U.S. law, the *Ulysses* case served as a powerful demonstration of the mischievous narrowness of the prevailing *Hicklin* approach—focusing on isolated passages without considering the character of the work itself.

In the first of the cases below, *Roth* v. *U.S.* (decided in 1957 along with the case of *Alberts* v. *California*), the Supreme Court abandoned the *Hicklin* test for deciding what was obscene for First Amendment purposes. In its place Justice William Brennan sketched a three-pronged approach that has been the focus of ferocious controversy ever since. Material was obscene, and therefore unprotected by the First Amendment speech clause, only if (1) the dominant theme of the material, taken as a whole, appealed to the "prurient interest" of the average reader; (2) the explicit character of the words or descriptions exceeded "contemporary community standards of candor"; and (3) the material was without redeeming social or artistic value.

In the *Ginzburg, Memoirs, Mishkin* trilogy, the difficulty of applying this "test" in a coherent and consistent manner became painfully obvious. By 1968, with *Redrup* v. *New York,* it seemed that the Court was retreating from the *Roth* test and would confine itself to upholding only specialized regulations that served the narrow purposes of protecting minors or prohibiting the obtrusive advertising of sexually explicit entertainment. In the 1973 case of *Miller* v. *California,* however, the Court (now under Chief Justice Warren Burger) reaffirmed the validity of the *Roth* test and tightened it in several important respects. Many state and local governments were emboldened, in the wake of *Miller,* to undertake aggressive censorship from which they had felt themselves barred in the years since *Roth.* But the Court, in *Jenkins* v. *Georgia* in 1974, checked this enthusiasm and made it clear that local majorities were not wholly free to determine for themselves what was obscene. *Roth,* as revised by *Miller,* affords greater discretion to localities than did the unvarnished *Roth* approach of 1957 to 1973, but only modestly so.

Roth v. United States
Alberts v. California
354 U.S. 476, 77 S.Ct. 1304, 1 L.Ed.2d. 1498 (1957)

Roth, a New York publisher, was convicted of violating the federal statute that prohibits the mailing of obscene books or other writings. Alberts, a Los Angeles operator of a mail order business, was convicted of violating the California obscenity statute by keeping obscene books for sale and publishing an obscene advertisement of them. Both convictions were affirmed by the Supreme Court.

Mr. Justice Brennan delivered the opinion of the Court.

The dispositive question is whether obscenity is utterance within the area of protected speech and press. Although this is the first time the question has been squarely presented to this Court, either under the First Amendment or under the Fourteenth Amendment, expressions found in numerous opinions indicate that this Court has always assumed that obscenity is not protected by the freedoms of speech and press. . . .

The guarantees of freedom of expression in effect in 10 of the 14 States which by 1792 had ratified the Constitution, gave no absolute protection for every utterance. Thirteen of the 14 States provided for the prosecution of libel and all of those States made either blasphemy or profanity, or both, statutory crimes. As early as 1712, Massachusetts made it criminal to publish "any filthy, obscene, or profane song, pamphlet, libel or mock sermon" in imitation or mimicking of religious services. . . .

In light of this history, it is apparent that the unconditional phrasing of the First Amendment was not intended to protect every utterance. This phrasing did not prevent this Court from concluding that libelous utterances are not within the area of constitutionally protected speech. . . . At the time of the adoption of the First Amendment, obscenity law was not as fully developed as libel law, but there is sufficiently contemporaneous evidence to show that obscenity, too, was outside the protection intended for speech and press. . . .

All ideas having even the slightest redeeming social importance—unorthodox ideas, controversial ideas, even ideas hateful to the prevailing climate of opinion—have the full protection of the guarantees, unless excludable because they encroach upon the limited area of more important interests. But implicit in the history of the First Amendment is the rejection of obscenity as utterly without redeeming social importance. This rejection for that reason is mirrored in the international agreement of over 50 nations, in the obscenity laws of all the 48 states, and in the 20 obscenity laws enacted by the Congress from 1842 to 1956. . . .

We hold that obscenity is not within the area of constitutionally protected speech or press. . . .

. . . .

However, sex and obscenity are not synonymous. Obscene material is material which deals with sex in a manner appealing to prurient interest. The portrayal of sex, *e.g.,* in art, literature and scientific works, is not itself sufficient reason to deny material the constitutional protection of freedom of speech and press. Sex, a great and mysterious motive force in human life, has indisputably been a subject of absorbing interest to mankind through the ages; it is one of the vital problems of human interest and public concern.

The fundamental freedoms of speech and press have contributed greatly to the development and well-being of our free society and are indispensable to its continued growth. Ceaseless vigilance is the watchword to prevent their erosion by Congress or by the States. The door barring federal and state intrusion into this area cannot be left ajar; it must be kept tightly closed and opened only the slightest crack necessary to prevent encroachment upon more important interests. It is therefore vital that the standards for judging obscenity safeguard the protection of freedom of speech and press for material which does not treat sex in a manner appealing to prurient interest.

The early leading standard of obscenity allowed material to be judged merely by the effect of an isolated excerpt upon particularly susceptible persons. *Regina* v. *Hicklin* [1868]. . . . Some American courts adopted this standard but later decisions have rejected it and substituted this test: whether to the average person, applying contemporary community standards the dominant theme of the material taken as a whole appeals to prurient interest. The Hicklin test, judging obscenity by the effect of isolated passages upon the most susceptible persons, might well encompass material legitimately treating with sex, and so it must be rejected as unconstitutionally restrictive of the freedoms of speech and press. On the other hand, the substituted standard provides safeguards adequate to withstand the charge of constitutional infirmity.

Both trial courts below sufficiently followed the proper standard. . . . The test in each case is the effect of the book, picture or publication considered as a whole, not upon any particular class, but upon all those whom it is likely to reach. In other words, you determine its impact upon the average person in the community. The books, pictures and circulars must be judged as a whole, in their entire context, and you are not to consider detached or separate portions in reaching a conclusion. You judge the circulars, pictures and publications which have been put in evidence by present-day standards of the community. You may ask yourselves does it offend the common conscience of the community by present-day standards. . . .

In summary then, we hold that these statutes, applied according to the proper standard for judging obscenity, do not offend constitutional safeguards against convictions based upon protected material, or fail to give men in acting adequate notice of what is prohibited. . . .

The judgments are affirmed.

Affirmed

Chief Justice Warren concurred in the result, stressing the commercially exploitive behavior of the sellers as a factor in determining what was punishable and what was not. This line of reasoning was to lead the Court into troubled waters in the *Ginzburg* case nine years later.

Justices Black and Douglas dissented. They rejected the very idea of obscenity as an unprotected category of utterance and found Brennan's approach particularly troubling because it turned on the quality of thoughts triggered in the mind of the reader.

Justice Harlan concurred in the result of *Alberts* (the state case), but dissented in *Roth* (the federal case). In Harlan's view the First Amendment, operating directly on the national government, was more restrictive of the power to censor than when the speech and press clause operated on the state through the due process clause of the Fourteenth Amendment.

Not only is the federal interest in protecting the Nation against pornography attenuated, but the dangers of federal censorship in this field are far greater than anything the states may do. (I)t seems to me that no overwhelming danger to our freedom to experiment and to gratify our tastes in literature is likely to result from the suppression of a borderline book in one of the states, so long as there is no uniform nation-wide suppression of the book, and so long as other states are free to experiment with same or bolder books.

The Mishkin, Ginzburg, Memoirs Trilogy

Ginzburg v. *United States*
383 U.S. 463, 86 S.Ct. 942,16 L.Ed.2d. 31 (1966)

Memoirs v. *Massachusetts*
383 U.S. 413, 86 S.Ct. 975, 16 L.Ed.2d. 1(1966)

Mishkin v. *New York*
383 U.S. 502, 86 S.Ct. 958, 16 L.Ed.2d. 56 (1966)

In the spring of 1966 the Court decided three cases that one commentator described as reducing the law of obscenity to "a constitutional disaster area."*

The first involved the zany media entrepreneur Ralph Ginzburg, who launched a hardcover sex magazine called *Eros* (physically modeled on *American Heritage*), and threw in with each subscription a biweekly newsletter called "Liaison," plus a short book titled *The Housewife's Handbook on Selective Promiscuity.* To further hype his product, Ginzburg obtained mailing privileges from the postmasters of Intercourse and Blue Ball, Pennsylvania. Ginzburg was charged with the Federal offense of introducing obscene materials into the mails and convicted. He went to the federal penitentiary at Danbury, Connecticut, to pick tomatoes for a time.

Justice Brennan wrote for the Supreme Court, sustaining the conviction despite *amici curiae* briefs from the Author's League of America, the American Book Publishers Council, and the ACLU—alone, on the other side, was Citizens for Decent Literature. Brennan argued that while Ginzburg's material was not intrinsically obscene by the *Roth* standard (*Eros* was really pretty tame stuff), the salacious way in which Ginzburg had advertised and marketed his product made it obscene. The entire operation was permeated by the "leer of the sensualist." Black and Douglas both dissented on the argument that there is no such thing as obscenity. Justice Harlan dissented because the material itself passed the *Roth* test, and he did not see how Ginzburg's highjinks could make something obscene that wasn't. Justice Stewart dissented on his distinctive argument (first offered in 1964 in *Jacobellis* v. *Ohio,* 378 U.S. 184) that only "hard core pornography" could be proscribed. Stewart did not attempt to define "hard core pornography" but was confident he knew it when he saw it.

The second case involved that favorite of preparatory school dormitories, John Cleland's eighteenth century pornographic send up *Memoirs of a Woman of Pleasure,* more familiarly known as *Fanny Hill.* A Massachusetts statute provided for civil actions to have books declared obscene and thus subject to seizure and destruction by the state. Citizens for Decent Literature supported Massachusetts; but only the publisher, G. P. Putnam's Sons, stood up for *Fanny.* At the trial, professors of English from Williams, Harvard, Boston University, M.I.T., and Brandeis testified to the book's value as an early, if minor, example of the picaresque novel. Justice Brennan spoke for the Court, reversing the Massachusetts decision. He concluded that *Fanny* had literary and historical value and was therefore not obscene under *Roth.* Black and Stewart concurred

---

*   C. Peter McGrath, "The Obscenity Cases: Grapes of Roth," 1966 *Supreme Court Review* 7.

on familiar grounds, and Justice Douglas appended to his concurring opinion a sermon by a Universalist minister which observed that Fanny, while admittedly lacking self-control, "came to appreciate the value of self-expression." The minister also pointed out that "her clients were not looked upon as means to an end," and Fanny "was concerned about them as persons." In lonely dissent Justice Clark declared that he had " 'stomached' past cases for almost ten years without much outcry," but that "this book is too much even for me." Fanny, Clark concluded, "was nothing but a harlot." Justice Harlan and Justice White also dissented on the ground that *Fanny* flunked the *Roth* test. They were unpersuaded by Brennan's argument for redeeming social value. Nevertheless *Memoirs* continued to prosper in Massachusetts.

The last case, *Mishkin,* involved the prosecution of a producer-seller specializing in fetishist and sado-masochistic literature under a New York law criminalizing the publication of obscene books. Titles such as "Dance with the Dominant Whip" and "the Violated Wrestler" convey the flavor of the offering. Mishkin's counsel, Emanuel Redfield, made the intriguing argument that his client's materials were not obscene under *Roth* because they did not appeal to the prurient interest of the average person—they appealed to deviant readers, fetishists, and sadists. Unconvinced, Justice Brennan held for the Court that when material is "disseminated to a clearly defined deviant sexual group . . . the prurient-appeal requirement of the *Roth* test is satisfied if the dominant appeal of the material taken as a whole appeals to the prurient interest in sex of the members of that group." Justice Harlan concurred but wondered how "Peggy's Distress on Planet Venus" could be distinguished from *Fanny Hill.* Justices Black, Douglas, and Stewart dissented on their familiar grounds, and Mishkin's conviction was upheld.

What was one to make of these opinions—especially Justice Brennan's *Ginzburg* effort? Was the Court evolving coherent principles to distinguish protected from unprotected depiction of sex?

Stanley v. *Georgia*
394 U.S. 557, 89 S.Ct. 1243, 22 L.Ed.2d. 542 (1969)

In the wake of the *Ginzburg-Memoirs-Mishkin* embarrassment, the Court appeared to back off from attempts to distinguish between protected and unprotected material. Instead, signals were given in several cases that henceforth only narrow government restrictions aimed at protecting unconsenting adults and children against intrusive advertising of pornography would be upheld. In *Redrup* v. *New York,* 386 U.S. 767 (1967), the Court reversed three findings of obscenity. The *per curiam* opinion commented on the difficulty the justices were experiencing in agreeing on a definition of obscenity.

Two members of the Court (Black and Douglas) consistently argued that the State is utterly without power to suppress, control, or punish the distribution of any writings or pictures upon the ground of their "obscenity". A third

(Stewart) held to the opinion that a state's power in this area is narrowly limited to a distinct and clearly identifiable class of material. Other justices have subscribed to a similar standard, holding that a state may not constitutionally inhibit the distribution of literary material as obscene unless "(a) the dominant theme of the material taken as a whole appeals to a prurient interest in sex; (b) the material is patently offensive because it affronts contemporary community standards relating to the description or representation of sexual matters; and (c) the material is utterly without redeeming social value," emphasizing that the "three elements must coalesce," and that no such material can "be proscribed unless it is found to be utterly without redeeming social value." *Memoirs* v. *Massachusetts,* 383 U.S. 413, 481–419. (Brennan opinion.) Another justice (White) has not viewed the "social value" element as an independent factor in the judgment of obscenity. *Stanley* v. *Georgia,* decided two years after *Redrup,* was read at the time (the twilight of the "Warren Court") as indicating that a majority of the justices were moving away from the doctrine of obscenity as altogether unprotected utterance.

Mr. Justice Marshall delivered the opinion of the Court.

An investigation of appellant's alleged bookmaking activities led to the issuance of a search warrant for appellant's home. Under authority of this warrant, federal and state agents secured entrance. They found very little evidence of bookmaking activity, but while looking through a desk drawer in an upstairs bedroom, one of the federal agents, accompanied by a state officer, found three reels of eight-millimeter film. Using a projector and screen found in an upstairs living room, they viewed the films. The state officer concluded that they were obscene and seized them. [Appellant] was later indicted for "knowingly hav[ing] possession of obscene matter" in violation of Georgia law. Appellant was tried before a jury and convicted. . . .

Appellant argues here, and argued below, that the Georgia obscenity statute, insofar as it punishes mere private possession of obscene matter, violates the First Amendment, as made applicable to the states by the Fourteenth Amendment. For the reason set forth below, we agree that the mere private possession of obscene matter cannot constitutionally be made a crime. . . .

Georgia concedes that the present case appears to be one of "first impression . . . on this exact point," but contends that since "obscenity is not within the area of constitutionally protected speech or press," *Roth* v. *United States* . . . the States are free, subject to the limits of other provisions of the Constitution . . ., to deal with it any way deemed necessary, just as they may deal with possession of other things thought to be detrimental to the welfare of their citizens. If the State can protect the body of a citizen, may it not, argues Georgia, protect his mind?

It is true that *Roth* does declare, seemingly without qualification, that obscenity is not protected by the First Amendment. . . . However, neither Roth nor any subsequent decision of this Court dealt with the precise problem involved in the present case. . . . Those cases dealt with the power of the State and Federal Governments to prohibit or regulate certain public actions taken or intended to be taken with respect to obscene matter. . . .

In this context, we do not believe that this case can be decided simply by citing *Roth*. *Roth* and its progeny certainly do mean that the First and Fourteenth Amendments recognize a valid governmental interest in dealing with the problem of obscenity. But the assertion of that interest cannot, in every context, be insulated from all constitutional protections. *Roth* cannot foreclose an examination of the constitutional implications of a statute forbidding mere private possession of such material.

[The] right to receive information and ideas, regardless of their social worth . . . is fundamental to our free society. Moreover, in the context of this case—a prosecution for mere possession of printed or filmed matter in the privacy of a person's own home—that right takes on an added dimension. For also fundamental is the right to be free, except in very limited circumstances, from unwanted governmental intrusions into one's privacy. . . .

These are the rights that appellant is asserting in the case before us. He is asserting the right to read or observe what he pleases—the right to satisfy his intellectual and emotional needs in the privacy of his own home. He is asserting the right to be free from state inquiry into the contents of his library. Georgia contends that appellant does not have these rights, that there are certain types of materials that the individual may not read or even possess. Georgia justifies this assertion by arguing that the films in the present case are obscene. But we think that mere categorization of these films as "obscene" is insufficient justification for such a drastic invasion of personal liberties guaranteed by the First and Fourteenth Amendments. Whatever may be the justifications for other statutes regulating obscenity, we do not think they reach into the privacy of one's own home. If the First Amendment means anything, it means that a State has no business telling a man sitting alone in his own house, what books he may read or what films he may watch. Our whole constitutional heritage rebels at the thought of giving government the power to control men's minds.

And yet, in the face of these traditional notions of individual liberty, Georgia asserts the right to protect the individual's mind from the effects of obscenity. We are not certain that this argument amounts to anything more than the assertion that the State has the right to control the moral content of a person's thoughts. To some, this may be a noble purpose, but it is wholly inconsistent with the philosophy of the First Amendment.

Finally, we are faced with the argument that prohibition of possession of obscenity is a necessary incident to statutory schemes prohibiting distribution. That argument is based on alleged difficulties of proving an intent to distribute or in producing evidence of actual distribution. We are not convinced that such difficulties exist, but even if they did we do not think that they would justify infringement of the individual's right to read or observe what he pleases. Because that right is so fundamental to our scheme of individual liberty, its restriction may not be justified by the need to ease the administration of otherwise valid criminal laws.

We hold that the First and Fourteenth Amendments prohibit making mere private possession of obscene material a crime. Roth and the cases following that decision are not impaired by today's holding. As we have said, the States retain broad power to regulate obscenity; that power simply does not extend to mere possession by the individual in the privacy of his own home. Accordingly, the judgment of the court below is reversed and the case is remanded for proceedings not inconsistent with this opinion.

It is so ordered.

Justice Black wrote a brief concurring opinion, and Justice Stewart, joined by Brennan and White, concurred on Fourth and Fourteenth Amendment grounds—that the police should not have looked at Stanley's film since their warrant authorized a search for bookmaking materials.

Miller v. *California*
413 U.S. 15, 93 S.Ct. 2607, 37 L.Ed.2d. 419 (1973)

In *Miller,* and its companion case of *Paris Adult Theatre I* v. *Slaton,* 413 U.S. 49 (1973), the court returned to the *Roth* test in a tightened form. But Justice Brennan, the author of *Roth,* dissented and announced he was abandoning his former handiwork. In his opinion for the court in *Miller,* Chief Justice Burger established that material need not be *utterly* without social or literary value to be found obscene (material could not be saved by isolated passages), and that "community standards" did not mean the national "community" but allowed for some local variation.

Mr. Chief Justice Burger delivered the opinion of the court.

This is one of a group of "obscenity-pornography" cases being reviewed by the Court in a re-examination of standards enunciated in earlier cases involving what Mr. Justice Harlan called "the intractable obscenity problem." [This] case involves the application of a State's criminal obscenity statute to a situation in which sexually explicit materials have been thrust by aggressive sales action upon unwilling recipients who had in no way indicated any desire to receive such materials. This Court has recognized that the States have a legitimate interest in prohibiting dissemination or exhibition of obscene material when the mode of dissemination carries with it a significant danger of offending the sensibilities of unwilling recipients or of exposure to juveniles. It is in this context that we are called on to define the standards which must be used to identify obscene material that a State may regulate.

Mr. Justice Brennan [in his dissent] reviews the background of the obscenity problem, but since the Court now undertakes to formulate standards more concrete than those in the past, it is useful for us to focus on two of the landmark cases in the somewhat tortured history of the Court's obscenity decisions. [While] *Roth* presumed "obscenity" to be "utterly without redeeming social value," [*Memoirs* v. *Massachusetts*] ... required that to prove obscenity it must be affirmatively established that the material is "*utterly*" without redeeming social value." Thus, even as they repeated the words of *Roth*, the *Memoirs* plurality produced a drastically altered test that called on the prosecution to prove a negative, i.e., that the material was "*utterly* without redeeming social value"— a burden virtually impossible to discharge. [Apart] from the initial formulation in the *Roth* case, no majority of the Court has at any given time been able to agree on a standard to determine what constitutes obscene, pornographic material subject to regulation under the States' police power. . . .

This much has been categorically settled by the Court, that obscene material is unprotected by the First Amendment. [We] acknowledge, however, the inherent dangers of undertaking to regulate any form of expression. State statutes designed to regulate obscene materials must be carefully limited. As a result, we now confine the permissible scope of such regulation to works which depict or describe sexual conduct. That conduct must be specifically defined by the applicable state law, as written or authoritatively construed. A state offense must also be limited to works which, taken as a whole, appeal to the prurient interest in sex, which portray sexual conduct in a patently offensive way, and which, taken as a whole, do not have serious literary, artistic, political, or scientific value.

The basic guidelines for the trier of fact must be: (a) whether "the average person, applying contemporary community standards" would find that the work, taken as a whole, appeals to the prurient interest [*Roth*], (b) whether the work depicts or describes, in a patently offensive way, sexual conduct specifically defined by the applicable state law, and (c) whether the work, taken as a whole, lacks serious literary, artistic, political, or scientific value. We do not adopt as a constitutional standard the "[utterly] without redeeming social value" test of [Memoirs]; that concept has never commanded the adherence of more then three Justices at one time. . . .

We emphasize that it is not our function to propose regulatory schemes for the States. [It] is possible, however, to give a few plain examples of what a state statute could define for regulation under the second part (b) of the standard announced in this opinion: (a) Patently offensive representations or descriptions of ultimate sexual acts, normal or perverted, actual or simulated. (b) Patently offensive representations or descriptions of masturbation, excretory function, and lewd exhibition of the genitals.

Sex and nudity may not be exploited without limit by films or pictures exhibited or sold in places of public accommodation any more than live sex and nudity can be exhibited or sold without limit in such public places. At a minimum, prurient, patently offensive depiction or description of sexual conduct must have serious literary, artistic, political, or scientific value to merit First Amendment protection. For example, medical books for the education of physicians and related personnel necessarily use graphic illustrations and descriptions of human anatomy. In resolving the inevitably sensitive questions of fact and law, we must continue to rely on the jury system, accompanied by the safeguards that judges, rules of evidence, presumption of innocence and other protective features provide, as we do with rape, murder and a host of other offenses against society and its individual members.

Mr. Justice Brennan, author of the opinions of the Court, or the plurality opinions, in [*Roth, Jacobellis, Ginzburg, Mishkin,* and *Memoirs*], has abandoned his former position and now maintains that no formulation of this Court, the Congress, or the States can adequately distinguish obscene material unprotected by the First Amendment from protected expression. . . . Paradoxically, [Justice Brennan] indicates that suppression of unprotected obscene material is permissible to avoid exposure to unconsenting adults, as in this case, and to juveniles, although he gives no indication of how the division between protected and nonprotected materials may be drawn with greater precision for these purposes than for regulation of commercial exposure to consenting adults only. Nor does he indicate where in the Constitution he finds the authority to distinguish between a willing "adult" one month past the state law age of majority and a willing "juvenile" one month younger.

Under the holdings announced today, no one will be subject to prosecution for the sale or exposure of obscene materials unless these materials depict or describe patently offensive "hard core" sexual conduct specifically defined by the regulating state law, as written or construed. We are satisfied that these specific prerequisites will provide fair notice to a dealer in such materials that his public and commercial activities may bring prosecution. If the inability to define regulated materials with ultimate, god-like precision altogether removes the power of the States or the Congress to regulate, then "hard core" pornography may be exposed without limit to the juvenile, the passerby, and the consenting adult alike, as, indeed, Mr. Justice Douglas contends. . . .

[Now], for the first time since [Roth], a majority of this Court has agreed on concrete guidelines to isolate "hard core" pornography from expression protected by the First Amendment. Now we may abandon the casual practice of [Redrup] and attempt to provide positive guidance to the federal and state courts alike. . . .

Under a national Constitution, fundamental First Amendment limitations on the powers of the States do not vary from community to community, but this does not mean that there are, or should or can be, fixed, uniform national standards of precisely what appeals to the "prurient interest" or is "patently offensive." These are essentially questions of fact, and our nation is simply too big and too diverse for this Court to reasonably expect that such standards could be articulated for all 50 States in single formulation, even assuming the prerequisite consensus exists. [Requiring] a State to structure obscenity proceedings around evidence of a *national* "community standard" would be an exercise in futility. . . .

It is neither realistic nor constitutionally sound to read the First Amendment as requiring that the people of Maine or Mississippi accept public depiction of conduct found tolerable in Las Vegas, or New York City. [People] in different States vary in their tastes and attitudes, and this diversity is not to be strangled by the absolutism of imposed uniformity. . . .

The dissenting Justices sound the alarm of repression. But, in our view, to equate the free and robust exchange of ideas and political debate with commercial exploitation of obscene material demeans the grand conception of the First Amendment and its high purposes in the historic struggle for freedom. . . .

There is no evidence, empirical or historical, that the stern 19th century American censorship of public distribution and display of material relating to sex in any way limited or affected expression of serious literary, artistic, political, or scientific ideas. [We] do not see the harsh hand of censorship of ideas—good or bad, sound or unsound—and "repression" of political liberty lurking in every state regulation of commercial exploitation of human interest in sex. [Justice Brennan] finds "it is hard to see how state-ordered regimentation of our minds can ever be forestalled." These doleful anticipations assume that courts cannot distinguish commerce in ideas, protected by the First Amendment, from commercial exploitation of obscene material. . . .

In sum we (a) reaffirm the *Roth* holding that obscene material is not protected by the First Amendment; (b) hold that such material can be regulated by the States, subject to the specific safeguards enunciated above, without a showing that the material is "utterly without redeeming social value"; and (c) hold that obscenity is to be determined by applying "contemporary community standards," not "national standards." . . .

Vacated and remanded.

Justice Brennan dissented in both *Miller* and *Paris Adult Theatre,* along with Justice Stewart ("I know it when I see it") and Justice Marshall. Brennan was "convinced that the approach initiated 16 years ago in (*Roth*) . . . cannot bring stability to this area of law without jeopardizing fundamental First Amendment values. . . ." He would have built on the implicit principles of *Redrup* and *Stanley* to sustain only those restrictions that protected children and unconsenting adults.

Justice Douglas dissented on his familiar argument that all sexually explicit utterance was protected unless it could be shown to constitute a clear and present danger of causing antisocial acts.

Jenkins v. *Georgia*
418 U.S. 153, 94 S.Ct. 2750, 41 L.Ed.2d. 642 (1974)

Some jurisdictions overreacted to the new signal of *Miller* with respect to variable community standards. The Court was then quick to intervene and emphasize that *Miller* did not mean communities could restrict *anything* that local officials considered obscene.

Mr. Justice Rehnquist delivered the opinion of the Court.

Appellant was convicted in Georgia of the crime of distributing obscene material. His conviction, in March 1972, was for showing the film "Carnal Knowledge" in a movie theatre in Albany, Georgia. The jury that found appellant guilty was instructed on obscenity pursuant to the Georgia statute, which defines material in language similar to that of the definition of obscenity set forth in this Court's plurality opinion in *Memoirs* v. *Massachusetts*, 383 U.S. 413, 418 (1966):

"Material is obscene if considered as a whole applying community standards, its predominant appeal is to prurient interest, that is, a shameful or morbid interest in nudity, sex or excretion, and utterly without redeeming social value and, if, in addition, it goes substantially beyond customary limits of candor in describing or representing such matters." Ga.Code Ann. § 26–2101 (b) (1972).

...We conclude here that the film "Carnal Knowledge" is not obscene under the constitutional standards announced in *Miller* v. *California*, 413 U.S. 15 (1973), and the First and Fourteenth Amendments therefore require that the judgment of the Supreme Court of Georgia affirming appellant's conviction be reversed. ...

....

We agree with the Supreme Court of Georgia's implicit ruling that the Constitution does not require that juries be instructed in state obscenity cases to apply the standards of a hypothetical statewide community. Miller approved the use of such instructions; it did not mandate their use. ...

We now turn to the question of whether appellant's exhibition of the film was protected by the First and Fourteenth Amendments, ...

There is little to be found in the record about the film "Carnal Knowledge" other than the film itself. However, appellant has supplied a variety of information and critical commentary, the authenticity of which appellee does not dispute. The film appeared on many "Ten Best" lists for 1971, the year in which it was released. Many but not all of the reviews were favorable. We believe that the following passage from a review which appeared in the *Saturday Review* is a reasonably accurate description of the film:

"[It is the story] of two young college men, roommates and lifelong friends preoccupied with their sex lives. Both are first met âs virgins. Nicholson is the more knowledgeable and attractive of the two; speaking colloquially, he is a burgeoning bastard. Art Garfunkel is his friend, the nice but troubled guy straight out of those early Feiffer cartoons, but *real*. He falls in love with the lovely Susan (Candice Bergen) and unknowingly shares her with his college buddy. As the 'safer' one of the two, he is selected by Susan for marriage.

"The time changes. Both men are in their thirties, pursuing successful careers in New York. Nicholson has been running through an average of a dozen women a year but has never managed to meet the right one, the one with the full bosom, the good legs, the properly rounded bottom. More than that, each and every one is a threat to his malehood and peace of mind, until at last, in a bar, he finds Ann-Margret, an aging bachelor girl with striking cleavage and, quite obviously, something of a past. 'Why don't we shack up?' she suggests. They do and a horrendous relationship ensues, complicated mainly by her paranoidal desire to marry. Meanwhile, what of Garfunkel? The sparks have gone out of his marriage, the sex has lost its savor, and Garfunkel tries once more. And later, even more foolishly, again.' "

Appellee contends essentially that under *Miller* the obscenity *vel non* of the film "Carnal Knowledge" was a question for the jury, and that the jury having resolved the question against appellant, and there being some evidence to support its findings, the judgment of conviction should be affirmed. We turn to the language of *Miller* to evaluate appellee's contention. ...

We also took pains in *Miller* to "give a few plain examples of what a state statute could define for regulation under part (b) of the standard announced," that is, the requirement of patent offensiveness. These examples included "representations or descriptions of ultimate sexual acts, normal or perverted, actual or simulated," and "representations or descriptions of masturbation, excretory functions, and lewd exhibition of the genitals." While this did not purport to be an exhaustive catalog of what juries might find patently offensive, it was certainly intended to fix substantive constitutional limitations, deriving from the First Amendment, on the type of material subject to such a determination. It would be wholly at odds with this aspect of *Miller* to uphold an obscenity conviction based upon a defendant's depiction of a woman with a bare midriff, even though a properly charged jury unanimously agreed on a verdict of guilty.

Our own view of the film satisfies us that "Carnal Knowledge" could not be found under the *Miller* standards to depict sexual conduct in a patently offensive way. Nothing in the movie falls within either of the two examples given in *Miller* of material which may constitutionally be found to meet the "patently offensive" element of those standards, nor is there anything sufficiently similar to such material to justify similar treatment. While the subject matter of the picture is, in a broader sense, sex, and there are scenes in which sexual conduct including "ultimate sexual acts" is to be understood to be taking place, the camera does not focus on the bodies of the actors at such times. There is no exhibition whatever of the actors' genitals, lewd or otherwise, during these scenes. There are occasional scenes of nudity, but nudity alone is not enough to make material legally obscene under the *Miller* standards. . . .

Reversed.

Mr. Justice Brennan, with whom Mr. Justice Stewart and Mr. Justice Marshall join, concurring in the result.

. . . Today's decision confirms my observation in *Paris Adult Theatre I* v. *Slaton*, 413 U.S. 49 (1973), that the Court's new formulation does not extricate us from the mire of case-by-case determinations of obscenity. . . .

Justice Douglas also concurred.

CASE STUDY: KIDDIE PORN

And still the battle rages. In the mid-1970s authorities in the state of New York became concerned about the problem of child pornography. The popularity of such materials (usually in the form of motion pictures) was increasing, and this meant more and more children were being procured to perform in the stuff. Since the procuring and filming were literally one-shot operations, prohibitions on the actual behavior were almost impossible to enforce. Only by curtailing traffic in the product and lessening demand, it was reasoned, could the abuse of children be reduced. Thus in 1977, New York enacted a law prohibiting any dealing in portrayals of sexual conduct by children under sixteen, regardless of whether the portrayals were obscene or not. Sexual conduct was defined as:

> ... actual or simulated sexual intercourse, deviate sexual intercourse, sexual beastiality, masturbation, sado-masochistic abuse, or lewd exhibition of the genitals.

Paul Ira Ferber, owner of a Manhattan porn store, was arrested after selling two films devoted almost exclusively to two young boys masturbating. At trial he was convicted. New York's highest court, the Court of Appeals, reversed Ferber's conviction on the grounds that it violated the First Amendment. 52 N.Y.2d 674 (1981). By creating criminal liability without requiring a showing of obscenity, the Court of Appeals reasoned, "the statute would ... prohibit the promotion of materials which are traditionally entitled to constitutional protection from government interference under the First Amendment."

Manhattan District Attorney Robert M. Morgenthau sought U.S. Supreme Court review. The case was accepted and on July 2, 1982, the Supreme Court overruled the Court of Appeals of New York. Justice Byron White wrote the opinion of the Court in *New York* v. *Ferber*, 458 U.S. 747 (1982). White conceded that under previous Supreme Court decisions, most recently *Miller*, it was not unreasonable for the New York Court to have concluded that only obscene sexual depictions could be regulated consistent with the First Amendment. However, White went on, "this case ... constitutes our first examination of a statute directed at and limited to depictions of sexual activity involving children." A state, White concluded, should have "somewhat more freedom (than is available under the obscenity standard) in proscribing works which portray sexual acts or lewd exhibition of genitalia by children." The distribution of films depicting "sexual activity by juveniles was closely related to the sexual abuse of children." The most expeditious if not only practical method of law enforcement may be to dry up the market for this material. ...." This was a determination states were entitled to make.

The effect of the Court's decision was to render child pornography a category of material outside of the protection of the First Amendment even though it might not be obscene under *Miller*.

Justice Blackmun concurred in the result and Justice John Paul Stevens concurred, stressing his view that the First Amendment should be understood to afford "some forms of speech more protection from governmental regulation than other forms of speech."

Justice Sandra Day O'Connor also filed a short concurring opinion. She emphasized that the Court's opinion *did not* hold that New York must exempt all kiddie porn "with serious literary, scientific or educational value." States, O'Connor argued, should be able to ban distribution of depictions of minors engaged in sexual conduct, regardless of the social value of the depictions.

"A twelve-year-old child photographed while masturbating will surely suffer the same psychological harm whether the community labels the photograph 'edifying' or 'tasteless.' Pictures in medical books or pictures of children engaged in rites widely approved by their cultures, such as might appear in issues of *National Geographic*, might not trigger the compelling interests identified by the Court (in this case)." For Justice O'Connor, the key to the problem was not the nature of the finished product, but whether children were abused to get it.

CHAPTER · 7

THE PRESS—THE PROBLEM OF A "SPECIAL PROTECTION"

THE First Amendment prohibits the government from abridging the freedom of speech *or the freedom of the press.* Was this simply because the framers of the Amendment wanted to protect both spoken and written communication? Or was a separate and distinct protection created for the institutional press? While the Supreme Court has steadfastly refused to recognize such an independent press right, arguments for it continue. And in one area of constitutional law, the Court has modified the common law to allow for more spirited and freewheeling discussion of public affairs.

Also relevant to the Court's treatment of the organized press is the doctrine of "prior restraint." That the executive may not suppress publication of material (as opposed to punishing publishers after the fact if their material is found to be libelous) was part and parcel of the body of eighteenth century English ideas about free speech and was clearly important in the thinking of the framers of the First Amendment. This is clear from Sir William Blackstone's *Commentaries,* published in the late 1760s, and familiar to the entire American founding generation. In 1931 the Supreme Court significantly expanded the traditional doctrine of prior restraint by holding that a judicial order to cease publishing certain kinds of materials constituted a prior restraint (*Near* v. *Minnesota,* 293 U.S. 697).

In the cases that follow, *New York Times* v. *Sullivan* is concerned with the special constitutional restrictions that operate on the law of libel. The excruciating difficulties involved in applying the doctrine of prior restraint are explored through the vehicle of *New York Times Co.* v. *United States* (the Pentagon Papers case). The third case, *Branzburg* v. *Hayes,* raises the question of the special protection of the press in the context of a "reporter's privilege" to refuse to testify before a grand jury about criminal matters if this would require disclosing sources of information. *Nebraska Press Association* v. *Stuart* also involves a conflict between freedom of the press and the integrity of the judicial processes. At issue is the use of "gag orders" by a court to forbid publication of certain information which, should it come to the attention of prospective jurors, would make the empaneling of an impartial jury (required by the Fifth Amendment) difficult.

The final case, *Red Lion Broadcasting Co.* v. *F.C.C.,* explores the very special First Amendment problem presented by the broadcast media.

New York Times Co. v. Sullivan
376 U.S. 254, 84 S.Ct. 710, 11 L.Ed.2d. 686 (1964)

L.B. Sullivan was one of three elected Commissioners of the City of Montgomery, Alabama with the duty of supervising the police department.

In the early spring of 1960 there was a civil rights demonstration in Montgomery by students from the then all-black Alabama State College. This was part of a campaign of civil rights activity mounted as part of a movement under the general leadership of the Rev. Martin Luther King.

On March 29, 1960, the *New York Times* carried an advertisement placed by a coalition of civil rights interest groups. Entitled "Heed Their Rising Voices," the advertisement alleged that peaceful student demonstrations for constitutional rights were "being met by an unprecedented wave of terror by those who would deny and negate that document which the whole world looks upon as setting the pattern for modern freedom." The remainder of the advertisement purported to illustrate the "wave of terror" by describing certain alleged events. It concluded with an appeal for funds.

Sullivan sued for libel in an Alabama court, claiming that, as the official responsible for the conduct of the police, untrue statements in the ad about police misconduct defamed him. A jury awarded him $500,000, the full amount claimed, and the Supreme Court of Alabama affirmed.

Mr. Justice Brennan delivered the opinion of the Court.

We are required for the first time in this case to determine the extent to which the constitutional protections for speech and press limit a State's power to award damages in a libel action brought by a public official against critics of his official conduct. . . .

Although . . . by name, he contended that the word "police" in the third paragraph referred to him as the Montgomery Commissioner who supervised the Police Department, so that he was being accused of "ringing" the campus with police. He further claimed that the paragraph would be read as imputing to the police, and hence to him, the padlocking of the dining hall in order to starve the students into submission. As to the sixth paragraph, he contended that since arrests are ordinarily made by the police, the statement "They have arrested [Dr. King] seven times" would be read as referring to him; he further contended that the "They" who did the arresting would be equated with the "They" who committed the other described acts and with the "Southern violators.". . .

The campus dining hall was not padlocked on any occasion, and the only students who may have been barred from eating there were the few who had neither signed a preregistration application nor requested temporary meal tickets. Although the police were deployed near the campus in large numbers on three occasions, they did not at any time "ring" the campus, and they were not called to the campus in connection with the demonstration on the State Capitol steps, as the third paragraph implied. Dr. King had not been arrested seven times, but only four; and although he claimed to have been assaulted some years earlier in connection with his arrest for loitering outside a courtroom, one of the officers who made the arrest denied that there was such an assault.

On the premise that the charges in the sixth paragraph could be read as referring to him, respondent was allowed to prove that he had not participated in the events described. Although Dr. King's home had in fact been bombed twice when his wife and child were there, both of these occasions antedated respondent's tenure as Commissioner, and the police were not only not implicated in the bombings, but had made every effort to apprehend those who were. Three of Dr. King's four arrests took place before respondent became Commissioner. Although Dr. King had in fact been indicted (he was subsequently acquitted) on two counts of perjury, each of which carried a possible five-year sentence, respondent had nothing to do with procuring the indictment.

Respondent made no effort to prove that he suffered actual pecuniary loss as a result of the alleged libel. One of his witnesses, a former employer, testified that if he had believed the statements, he doubted whether he "would want to be associated with anybody who would be a party to such things as are stated in that ad," and that he would not re-employ respondent if he believed "that he allowed the Police Department to do things that the paper say he did." But neither this witness nor any of the others testified that he had actually believed the statements in their supposed reference to respondent. . . .

The trial judge submitted the case to the jury under instructions that the statements in the advertisement were "libelous per se" and were not privileged, so that petitioners might be held liable if the jury found that they had published the advertisement and that the statements were made "of and concerning" respondent. . . . We reverse the judgment. We hold that the rule of law applied by the Alabama courts is constitutionally deficient for failure to provide the safeguards for freedom of speech and of the press that are required by the First and Fourteenth Amendments in a libel action brought by a public official against critics of his official conduct. We further hold that under the proper safeguards the evidence presented in this case is constitutionally insufficient to support the judgment for respondent. . . .

Under Alabama law as applied in this case, a publication is "libelous per se" if the words "tend to injure a person . . . in his reputation" or to "bring [him] into public contempt"; the trial court stated that the standard was met if the words are such as to "injure him in his public office, or impute misconduct to him in his office, or want of official integrity, or want of fidelity to a public trust. . . ." The jury must find that the words were published "of and concerning" the plaintiff, but where the plaintiff is a public official his place in the governmental hierarchy is sufficient evidence to support a finding that his reputation has been affected by statements that reflect upon the agency of which he is in charge. Once "libel per se" has been established, the defendant has no defense as to stated facts unless he can persuade the jury that they were true in all their particulars. . . . Unless he can discharge the burden of proving truth, general damages are presumed, and may be awarded without proof of pecuniary injury. . . .

The question before us is whether this rule of liability, as applied to an action brought by a public official against critics of his official conduct, abridges the freedom of speech and of the press that is guaranteed by the First and Fourteenth Amendments. . . .

The state rule of law is not saved by its allowance of the defense of truth. . . . Allowance of the defense of truth, with the burden of proving it on the defendant, does not mean that only false speech will be deterred. . . . Under such a rule, would-be critics of official conduct may be deterred from voicing their criticism, even though it is believed to be true and even though it is in fact true, because of doubt whether it can be proved in court or fear of the expense of having to do so. They tend to make only statements which "steer far wider of the unlawful zone. . . . The rule thus dampens the vigor and limits the variety of public debate. It is inconsistent with the First and Fourteenth Amendments.

The constitutional guarantees require, we think, a federal rule that prohibits a public official from recovering damages for a defamatory falsehood relating to his official conduct unless he proves that the statement was made with "actual malice"—that is, with knowledge that it was false or with reckless disregard of whether it was false or not. . . .

As to the Times, we similarly conclude that the facts do not support a finding of actual malice. . . . We think the evidence against the Times supports at most a finding of negligence in failing to discover the misstatements, and is constitutionally insufficient to show the recklessness that is required for a finding of actual malice. . . .

Justice Black, with Justice Douglas joining, concurred on the basis of his "belief that the First and Fourteenth Amendments not merely 'delimit' a state's power to award damages to a 'public official against critics of his official conduct' but completely prohibit a State from exercising such power." In other words, public officials should not be able to sue for libel no matter what was said about their official conduct.

Justice Goldberg also concurred, and Justice Douglas joined him as well. Goldberg agreed with Black that there should be no liability even for actual malicious statements made about the official conduct of public officials. But Goldberg emphasized that the private conduct of a public official or a private citizen was still protected against defamatory statements.

Several interesting questions were raised by *New York Times* v. *Sullivan*, and the courts continue to grapple with them. What libel standard should operate in the case of false statements made about someone who is not a "public official" but rather a "public figure," say, a political activist or publicist? *Associated Press* v. *Walker*, 388 U.S. 130 (1967). Who is a "public figure" anyway? *Rosenbloom* v. *Metromedia*, 403 U.S. 29 (1971) and *Gertz* v. *Robert Welch*, 418 U.S. 323 (1974). And do the special constitutional standards apply to all types of defendants or only to the defendants who are part of the institutionalized communications media—"the press"? Note, "Mediaocracy and Mistrust: Extending *New York Times* Defamation Protection to Nonmedia Defendants," 95 Harvard Law Review 1876 (1982).

New York Times Co. v. United States
403 U.S. 713, 91 S.Ct. 2140, 29 L.Ed.2d. 822 (1971)

American involvement in the Vietnam War divided the nation as deeply as any crisis since the Civil War. It was inevitable, given our penchant for constitutionalizing policy conflicts, that the controversy over Vietnam would resonate in various ways in the courts. The "Pentagon Papers" case forced the Supreme Court to consider the relationship between the national security interest in secrecy and the First Amendment imperative that publication not be restrained. In 1967 Robert S. McNamara, then Secretary of Defense commissioned a TOP SECRET study by analysts in his department of how America had become involved in an unpopular and protracted war in Southeast Asia. McNamara, of course, was a principal architect of that involvement. Yet as a thoughtful man, he sought in retrospect to understand where we had gone wrong—what reports and estimates had been believed that should have been discounted, and what discounted information should have been taken more seriously.

As for the TOP SECRET classification, it reflected, as classification decisions usually do, a variety of considerations. First, since much CIA material was to be used, there was the concern over inadvertently revealing sources and methods of intelligence operations in a war in which American soldiers were still being shot at. But second, there was the felt need to keep the study from the American public. The war was bitterly controversial. If McNamara was to hope for candid analysis and a forthcoming attitude by all the government agencies involved, it was imperative that no one fear he was performing for the public. Otherwise, candor would be lost; role playing and self-justification would be the rule of the day.

After the study was completed, Daniel Ellsberg, a former "hawk" and defense expert who had undergone a change of heart and mind about the Vietnam War and America's role in world affairs, had access to a copy of the report as a consultant to the RAND corporation. Ellsberg took the report and photocopied it. He then offered his copies to various news media. The *New York Times* and the *Washington Post* took him up. On June 13, 1971, the *New York Times* began publishing portions of the *Papers,* and on June 18 the *Washington Post* began its serialization. The United States moved in federal district courts in New York City and the District of Columbia to enjoin publication. Between June 15 and June 23, two district courts and two courts of appeals considered the case, with temporary restraining orders in effect. They disagreed on the merits. The case was rushed before the Supreme Court, where Professor Alexander M. Bickel, of Yale Law School, argued for the

Times. The Court heard oral arguments on June 26, and rendered a decision on June 30, 1971, accompanied by a bewildering set of opinions.

Per Curiam.

We granted certiorari in these cases in which the United States seeks to enjoin the New York Times and the Washington Post from publishing the contents of a classified study entitled "History of U.S. Decision-Making Process on Viet Nam Policy." [commonly referred to as the "Pentagon Papers".]

"Any system of prior restraint of expression comes to this Court bearing a heavy presumption against its constitutional validity." . . . Near v. Minnesota , 283 U.S. 697 (1931). The Government "thus carries a heavy burden of showing justification for the enforcement of such a restraint." . . . The District Court for the Southern District of New York in the *New York Times* case and the District Court for the District of Columbia and the Court of Appeals for the District of Columbia Circuit in the *Washington Post* case held that their Government had not met that burden. We agree.

The judgment of the Court of Appeals for the District of Columbia Circuit is therefore affirmed. The order of the Court of Appeals for the Second Circuit is reversed and the case is remanded with directions to enter a judgment affirming the judgment of the District Court for the Southern District of New York. . . .

Mr. Justice Black, with whom Mr. Justice Douglas joins, concurring.

I adhere to the view that the Government's case against the Washington Post should have been dismissed and that the injunction against the New York Times should have been vacated without oral argument when the cases were first presented to this Court. I believe that every moment's continuance of the injunctions against these newspapers amounts to a flagrant, indefensible, and continuing violation of the First Amendment. Furthermore, after oral arguments, I agree completely that we must affirm the judgment of the Court of Appeals for the District of Columbia and reverse the judgment of the Court of Appeals for the Second Circuit for the reasons stated by my Brothers Douglas and Brennan. In my view it is unfortunate that some of my Brethren are apparently willing to hold that the publication of news may sometimes be enjoined. Such a holding would make a shambles of the First Amendment. . . .

Mr. Justice Douglas, with whom Mr. Justice Black joins, concurring.

It should be noted at the outset that the First Amendment provides that "Congress shall make no law . . . abridging the freedom of speech or of the press." That leaves, in my view, no room for governmental restraint on the press. . . .

These disclosures may have a serious impact. But that is no basis for sanctioning a previous restraint on the press. . . .

The stays in these cases that have been in effect for more than a week constitute a flouting of the principles of the First Amendment as interpreted in *Near* v. *Minnesota.*

Mr. Justice Brennan, concurring.

I write separately in these cases only to emphasize what should be apparent: that our judgment in the present cases may not be taken to indicate the propriety, in the future, of issuing temporary stays and restraining orders to block the publication of material sought to be suppressed by the Government. . . .

The error which has pervaded these cases from the outset was the granting of any injunctive relief whatsoever, interim or otherwise. The entire thrust of the Government's claim throughout these cases has been that publication of the material sought to be enjoined "could," or "might," or "may" prejudice the national interest in various ways. But the First Amendment tolerates absolutely no prior judicial restraints of the press predicated upon surmise or conjecture that untoward consequences may result. Our cases, it is true, have indicated that there is a single, extremely narrow class of cases in which the First Amendment's ban on prior judicial restraint may be overridden. Our cases have thus far indicated that such cases arise only when the Nation "is at war," . . . during which times "no one would question but that a Government might prevent actual obstruction to its recruiting service or the publication of the sailing dates of transports or the number and location of troops." . . .

Mr. Justice Stewart, with whom Mr. Justice White joins, concurring.

In the governmental structure created by our Constitution, the Executive is endowed with enormous power in the two related areas of national defense and international relations. This power, largely unchecked by the Legislative and Judicial branches, has been pressed to the very hilt since the advent of the nuclear missile age. For better or for worse, the simple fact is that a President of the United States possesses vastly greater constitutional independence in these two vital areas of power than does, say, a prime minister of a country with a parliamentary form of government.

In the absence of the governmental checks and balances present in other areas of our national life, the only effective restraint upon executive policy and power in the areas of national defense and international affairs may lie in an enlightened citizenry—in an informed and critical public opinion which alone can here protect the values of democratic government. For this reason, it is perhaps here that a press that is alert, aware, and free most vitally serves the basic purpose of the First Amendment. For without an informed and free press there cannot be an enlightened people.

Yet it is elementary that the successful conduct of international diplomacy and the maintenance of an effective national defense require both confidentiality and secrecy. Other nations can hardly deal with this Nation in an atmosphere of mutual trust unless they can be assured that their confidences will be kept. And within our own executive departments, the development of considered and intelligent international policies would be impossible if those charged with their formulation could not communicate with each other freely, frankly, and in confidence. In the area of basic national defense the frequent need for absolute secrecy is, of course, self-evident.

I think there can be but one answer to this dilemma, if dilemma it be. The responsibility must be where the power is. If the Constitution gives the Executive a large degree of unshared power in the conduct of foreign affairs and the maintenance of our national defense, then under the Constitution the Executive must have largely unshared duty to determine and preserve the degree of internal security necessary to exercise that power successfully. . . .

This is not to say that Congress and the courts have no role to play. Undoubtedly Congress has the power to enact specific and appropriate criminal laws to protect government property and preserve government secrets. Congress has passed such laws, and several of them are of very colorable relevance to the apparent circumstances of these cases. And if a criminal prosecution is instituted, it will be the responsibility of the courts to decide the applicability of the criminal law under which the charge is brought. Moreover, if Congress should pass a specific law authorizing civil proceedings in this field, the courts would likewise have the duty to decide the constitutionality of such a law as well as its applicability to the facts proved.

But in the cases before us we are asked neither to construe specific regulations nor to apply specific laws. We are asked, instead, to perform a function that the Constitution gave to the Executive, not the Judiciary. We are asked, quite simply, to prevent the publication by two newspapers of material that the Executive Branch insists should not, in the national interest, be published. I am convinced that the Executive is correct with respect to some of the documents involved. But I cannot say that disclosure of any of them will surely result in direct, immediate, and irreparable damage to our Nation or its people. That being so, there can under the First Amendment be put one judicial resolution of the issues before us. I join the judgments of the Court.

Mr. Justice White, with whom Mr. Justice Stewart joins, concurring.

I concur in today's judgments, but only because of the concededly extraordinary protection against prior restraints enjoyed by the press under our constitutional system. I do not say that in no circumstances would the First Amendment permit an injunction against publishing information about government plans or operations. Nor, after examining the materials the Government characterizes as the most sensitive and destructive, can I deny that revelation of these documents will do substantial damage to public interests. Indeed, I am confident that their disclosure will have that result. But I nevertheless agree that the United States has not satisfied the very heavy burden which it must meet to warrant an injunction against publication in these cases, at least in the absence of express and appropriately limited congressional authorization for prior restraints in circumstances such as these.

. . . .

It is not easy to reject the proposition urged by the United States and to deny relief on its good-faith claims in these cases that publication will work serious damage to the country. But that discomfiture is considerably dispelled by the infrequency of prior restraint cases. Normally, publication will occur and the damage be done before the Government has either opportunity or grounds for suppression. So here, publication has already begun and a substantial part of the threatened damage has already occurred. The fact of a massive breakdown in security is known, access to the documents by many unauthorized people is undeniable and the efficacy of equitable relief against these or other newspapers to avert anticipated damage is doubtful at best. . . .

Mr. Chief Justice Burger, dissenting.

In this case, the imperative of a free and unfettered press comes into collision with another imperative, the effective functioning of a complex modern government and specifically the effective exercise of certain constitutional powers of the Executive. Only those who view the First Amendment as an absolute in all circumstances—a view I respect, but reject—can find such a case as this to be simple or easy.

This case is not simple for another and more immediate reason. We do not know the facts of the case. . . .

I suggest we are in this posture because these cases have been conducted in unseemly haste. . . .

Here, moreover, the frenetic haste is due in large part to the manner in which the Times proceeded from the date it obtained the purloined documents. It seems reasonably clear now that the haste precluded reasonable and deliberate judicial treatment of these cases and was not warranted. . . .

The newspapers make a derivative claim under the First Amendment; they denominate this right as the public right-to-know; by implication, the Times asserts a sole trusteeship of that right by virtue of its journalist "scoop." The right is asserted as an absolute. Of course, the First Amendment right itself is not an absolute, as Justice Holmes so long ago pointed out in his aphorism concerning the right to shout of fire in a crowded theater. There are other exceptions, some of which Chief Justice Hughes mentioned by way of example in *Near* v. *Minnesota*. . . .

It is not disputed that the Times has had unauthorized possession of the documents for three to four months, during which it has had its expert analysts studying them, presumably digesting them and preparing the material for publication. . . .

. . . To me it is hardly believable that a newspaper long regarded as a great institution in American life would fail to perform one of the basic and simple duties of every citizen with respect to the discovery or possession of stolen property or secret government documents. That duty, I had thought—perhaps naively—was to report forthwith, to responsible public officers. This duty rests on taxi drivers, Justices and the New York Times. The course followed by the Times, whether so calculated or not, removed any possibility of orderly litigation of the issues. If the action of the judges up to now has been correct that result is sheer happenstance.* . . .

The consequence of all this melancholy series of events is that we literally do not know what we are acting on. As I see it we have been forced to deal

---

* Interestingly, the *Times* explained its refusal to allow the government to examine its own purloined documents by saying in substance this might compromise *its* sources and informants! The *Times* thus asserts a right to guard the secrecy of its source while denying that the Government of the United States has that power.

with litigation concerning rights of great magnitude without an adequate record, and surely without time for adequate treatment either in the prior proceedings or in this Court: ... I am not prepared to reach the merits.

Mr. Justice Harlan, with whom The Chief Justice and Mr. Justice Blackmun join, dissenting.

With all respect, I consider that the Court has been almost irresponsibly feverish in dealing with these cases.

Both the Court of Appeals for the Second Circuit and the Court of Appeals for the District of Columbia Circuit rendered judgment on June 23. The New York Times' petition for certiorari, its motion for accelerated consideration thereof, and its application for interim relief were filed in this Court on June 24 at about 11 a.m. The application of the United States for interim relief in the *Post* case was also filed here on June 24, at about 7:15 p.m. This Court's order setting a hearing before us on June 26 at 11 a.m., a course which I joined only to avoid the possibility of even more peremptory action by the Court, was issued less than 24 hours before. The record in the *Post* case was filed with the Clerk shortly before 1 p.m. on June 25; the record in the *Times* case did not arrive until 7 or 8 o'clock that same night. The briefs of the parties were received less than two hours before argument on June 26.

This frenzied train of events took place in the name of the presumption against prior restraints created by the First Amendment. Due regard for the extraordinarily important and difficult questions involved in these litigations should have led the Court to shun such a precipitate timetable. In order to decide the merits of these cases properly, some or all of the following questions should have been faced:

1. Whether the Attorney General is authorized to bring these suits in the name of the United States. ...

2. Whether the First Amendment permits the federal courts to enjoin publication of stories which would present a serious threat to national security. See *Near* v. *Minnesota.* ...

3. Whether the threat to publish highly secret documents is of itself a sufficient implication of national security to justify an injunction on the theory that regardless of the contents of the documents harm enough results simply from the demonstration of such a breach of secrecy.

4. Whether the unauthorized disclosure of any of these particular documents would seriously impair the national security.

5. What weight should be given to the opinion of high officers in the Executive Branch of the Government with respect to questions 3 and 4.

6. Whether the newspapers are entitled to retain and use the documents notwithstanding the seemingly uncontested facts that the documents, or the originals of which they are duplicates, were purloined from the Government's possession and that the newspapers received them with knowledge that they had been feloniously acquired. ...

7. Whether the threatened harm to the national security or the Government's possessory interest in the documents justifies the issuance of an injunction against publication in light of—

a. The strong First Amendment policy against prior restraints on publication;
b. The doctrine against enjoining conduct in violation of criminal statutes; and
c. The extent to which the materials at issue have apparently already been otherwise disseminated.

These are difficult questions of fact, of law, and of judgment; the potential consequences of erroneous decision are enormous. The time which has been available to us, to the lower courts, and to the parties has been wholly inadequate for giving these cases the kind of consideration they deserve. It is a reflection on the stability of the judicial process that these great issues—as important as any that have arisen during my time on the Court—should have been decided under the pressures engendered by the torrent of publicity that has attended these litigations from their inception.

Forced as I am to reach the merits of these cases, I dissent from the opinion and judgments of the Court. . . .

It is a sufficient basis for affirming the Court of Appeals for the Second Circuit in the *Times* litigation to observe that its order must rest on the conclusion that because of the time elements the Government had not been given an adequate opportunity to present its case to the District Court. At least this conclusion was not an abuse of discretion. . . .

. . . .

Pending further hearings in each case conducted under the appropriate ground rules, I would continue the restraints on publication. I cannot believe that the doctrine prohibiting prior restraint reaches to the point of preventing courts from maintaining the *status quo* long enough to act responsibly in matters of such national importance as those involved here.

Mr. Justice Blackmun, [dissenting].

I join Mr. Justice Harlan in his dissent. I also am in substantial accord with much that Mr. Justice White says, by way of admonition, in the latter part of his opinion. . . .

. . . .

The First Amendment, after all, is only one part of an entire Constitution. Article II of the great document vests in the Executive Branch primary power over the conduct of foreign affairs and places in that branch the responsibility for the Nation's safety. Each provision of the Constitution is important, and I cannot subscribe to a doctrine of unlimited absolutism for the First Amendment at the cost of downgrading other provisions. First Amendment absolutism has never commanded a majority of this Court. . . . What is needed here is a weighing, upon properly developed standards, of the broad right of the press to print and of the very narrow right of the Government to prevent. Such standards are not yet developed. The parties here are in disagreement as to what those standards should be. But even the newspapers concede that there are situations where restraint is in order and is constitutional. ...

Branzburg v. Hayes
408 U.S. 665, 92 S.Ct. 2646, 33 L.Ed.2d. 626 (1972)

An ancient assumption of the Anglo-American legal tradition is that, in seeking to determine if a crime has been committed, the law "has a right to every man's evidence." When properly ordered ("subpeonaed"), we are all obliged to testify unless (1) we reasonably fear that such testimony may personally incriminate us in violation of the Fifth Amendment guarantee against self-incrimination; or (2) our testimony involves a relationship which, as a matter of public policy, has been set aside by the state involved or (in a federal forum) by the national Congress, as "privileged." Husband-wife, lawyer-client, and priest-penitent are a few examples of the kinds of relationships some legislatures have determined to be privileged. These vary from state to state. But what of the situation where a journalist, who has written an exposé of the drug traffic in Xville, is called before a grand jury and asked about the sources of his information so that it may be determined whether indictments are in order? Branzburg was a Louisville *Courier-Journal* reporter who reported observing two persons synthesizing hashish from marijuana, a violation of Kentucky law. When asked to name names, he argued that the speech-press protection of the First Amendment should be read to create a constitutional "newsperson's privilege" to decline to divulge confidential sources. The Supreme Court responded in the negative, although in the years since *Branzburg* some states have moved to create limited reporter's privileges in their own courts—so-called "shield laws" for the press.

Opinion of the Court by Mr. Justice White.

The issue in these cases is whether requiring newsmen to appear and testify before state or federal grand juries abridges the freedom of speech and press guaranteed by the First Amendment. We hold that it does not.

[The journalists] press First Amendment claims that may be simply put: that to gather news it is often necessary to agree either not to identify the source of information published or to publish only part of the facts revealed, or both; that if the reporter is nevertheless forced to reveal these confidences to a grand jury, the source so identified and other confidential sources of other reporters will be measurably deterred from furnishing publishable information, all to the detriment of the free flow of information protected by the First Amendment. Although [the journalists] do not claim an absolute privilege against official interrogation in all circumstances, they assert that the reporter should not be forced either to appear or to testify before a grand jury or at trial until and unless sufficient grounds are shown for believing that the reporter possesses information relevant to a crime the grand jury is investigating, that the information the reporter has is unavailable from other sources, and that the need for the information is sufficiently compelling to override the claimed invasion of First Amendment interests occasioned by the disclosure. . . .

. . . [N]ews gathering [is not without] . . . First Amendment protection; without some protection for seeking out the news, freedom of the press could be eviscerated. But this case involves no intrusions upon speech or assembly, [and] no penalty, civil or criminal, related to the content of published material, is at issue here. The use of confidential sources by the press is not forbidden or restricted. No attempt is made to require the press to publish its sources of information or indiscriminately to disclose them on request. The sole issue is the obligation of reporters to respond to grand jury subpoenas as other citizens do and to answer questions relevant to an investigation into the commission of crime. [The Constitution does not protect] the average citizen from disclosing to a grand jury information that he has received in confidence. The claim is, however, that reporters are exempt. . . .

. . . [T]he First Amendment does not invalidate every incidental burdening of the press that may result from the enforcement of civil or criminal statutes of general applicability. It has generally been held that the First Amendment does not guarantee the press a constitutional right of special access to information not available to the public generally. [Despite] the fact that news gathering may be hampered, the press is regularly excluded from grand jury proceedings, our own conferences, the meetings of other official bodies gathered in executive session, and the meetings of private organizations. Newsmen have no constitutional right of access to the scenes of crime or disaster to assure a defendant a fair trial before an impartial tribunal. It is thus not surprising that the great weight of authority is that newsmen are not exempt from the normal duty of appearing before a grand jury and answering questions relevant to a criminal investigation. . . .

The prevailing constitutional view of the newsman's privilege is very much rooted in the ancient role of the grand jury. [I]ts investigative powers are necessarily broad. The longstanding principle that "the public has a right to every man's evidence," except for those persons protected by a constitutional, common law, or statutory privilege, is particularly applicable to grand jury proceedings. . . . We are asked to [interpret] the First Amendment to grant newsmen a testimonial privilege that other citizens do not enjoy. This we decline to do. On the records now before us, we perceive no basis for holding that the public interest in law enforcement and in ensuring effective grand jury proceedings is insufficient to override the consequential, but uncertain, burden on news gathering which is said to result from insisting that reporters, like other citizens, respond to relevant questions put to them in the course of a valid grand jury investigation or criminal trial.

This conclusion [does not] threaten the vast bulk of confidential relationships between reporters and their sources. [Only] where news sources themselves are implicated in crime or possess information relevant to the grand jury's task need they or the reporter be concerned about grand jury subpoenas. Nothing before us indicates that a large number or percentage of *all* confidential news sources fall into either category and would in any way be deterred by our holding. . . .

. . . [G]rand jury investigations if instituted or conducted other than in good faith, would pose wholly different issues for resolution under the First Amendment. Official harassment of the press undertaken not for purposes of law enforcement but to disrupt a reporter's relationship with his news sources would have no justification. Grand juries are subject to judicial control and subpoenas to motions to quash. We do not expect courts will forget that grand juries must operate within the limits of the First Amendment as well as the Fifth.

So ordered.

Justice Powell concurred with the caution that only the subpoenas of "good faith" grand jury investigations were covered by the majority opinion, and that "harassment of newsmen will not be tolerated." Justice Stewart, with whom Justices Brennan and Marshall joined, dissented. Stewart accused the majority of taking a "crabbed view of the First Amendment" and showing "insensitivity to the critical role of an independent press in our society." While Stewart was not prepared to admit an absolute First Amendment right for a reporter to refuse to identify his sources, he concluded that before such disclosure could be required, the government should have to demonstrate "a compelling and overriding interest in the information."

Nebraska Press Ass'n v. *Stuart*
427 U.S. 539, 96 S.Ct. 2791, 49 L.Ed.2d. 683 (1976)

One of the most vexing contemporary constitutional conflicts involves the tension between the freedom of the press to publish information about criminal justice proceedings; and the right of accused persons to fair trials before impartial juries. An important characteristic of an impartial jury member is the ability to take into consideration only what is entered into evidence at trial. The more information about a case that a prospective jury member is exposed to before trial, or out of the courtroom while the trial is in progress, the more difficult is the task of of deciding on the formally admitted evidence alone. But for a judge to order the news media not to publish information, even temporarily, is a prior restraint which, as we know from *Near* and the Pentagon Papers Case, can only be justified by the most pressing governmental need. In *Nebraska Press Association* Chief Justice Burger ruled against the "gag order" at issue but did not altogether close the First Amendment door on the device in extreme circumstances. *Amicis* briefs opposing the gag order were filed by the ACLU, the National Broadcasting Company, the American Newspaper Publishers Association, the National Press Club, and by Joseph Califano for the Washington Post Company.

Mr. Chief Justice Burger delivered the opinion of the Court.

The respondent State District Judge entered an order restraining the petitioners from publishing or broadcasting accounts of confessions or admissions made by the accused or facts "strongly implicative" of the accused in a widely reported murder of six persons. We granted certiorari to decide whether the entry of such an order on the showing made before the state court violated the constitutional guarantee of freedom of the press. . . .

On the evening of October 18, 1975, local police found the six members of the Henry Kellie family murdered in their home in Sutherland, Neb., a town of about 850 people. Police released the description of a suspect, Erwin Charles Simants, to the reporters who had hastened to the scene of the crime. Simants was arrested and arraigned in Lincoln County Court the following morning, ending a tense night for this small rural community.

The crime immediately attracted widespread news coverage, by local, regional, and national newspapers, radio and television stations. Three days after the crime, the County Attorney and Simants' attorney joined in asking the County Court to enter a restrictive order relating to "matters that may or may not be publicly reported or disclosed to the public," because of the "mass coverage by news media" and the "reasonable likelihood of prejudicial news which would make difficult, if not impossible, the impaneling of an impartial jury and tend to prevent a fair trial." The County Court heard oral arguments but took no evidence; no attorney for members of the press appeared at this stage. The County Court granted the prosecutor's motion for a restrictive order and entered it the next day, October 22. The order prohibited everyone in attendance from "releas[ing] or authoriz[ing] the release for public dissemination in any form or manner whatsoever any testimony given or evidence adduced;" . . .

. . . .

Simants' preliminary hearing was held the same day, open to the public but subject to the order. The County Court bound over the defendant for trial to the State District Court. The charges, as amended to reflect the autopsy findings, were that Simants had committed the murders in the course of a sexual assault.

Petitioners—several press and broadcast associations, publishers, and individual reporters—moved on October 23 for leave to intervene in the District Court, asking that the restrictive order imposed by the County Court be vacated. The District Court conducted a hearing, at which the County Judge testified and newspaper articles about the *Simants* case were admitted in evidence. The District Judge granted petitioners' motion to intervene and, on October 27, entered his own restrictive order. The judge found "because of the nature of the crimes charged in the complaint that there is a clear and present danger that pre-trial publicity could impinge upon the defendant's right to a fair trial." The order applied only until the jury was impaneled, and specifically prohibited petitioners from reporting five subjects: (1) the existence or contents of a confession Simants had made to law enforcement officers, which had been introduced in open court at arraignment; (2) the fact or nature of statements Simants had made to other persons; (3) the contents of a note he had written the night of the crime; (4) certain aspects of the medical testimony at the preliminary hearing; and (5) the identity of the victims of the alleged sexual assault and the nature of the assault. It also prohibited reporting the exact nature of the restrictive order itself. Like the County Court's order, this order incorporated the Nebraska Bar-Press Guidelines. Finally, the order set out a plan for attendance, seating, and courthouse traffic control during the trial. . . .

. . . .

The state trial judge in the case before us acted responsibly, out of a legitimate concern, in an effort to protect the defendant's right to a fair trial. What we must decide is not simply whether the Nebraska courts erred in seeing the possibility of real danger to the defendant's right, but whether in the circumstances of this case the means employed were foreclosed by another provision of the Constitution. . . .

In assessing the probable extent of publicity, the trial judge had before him newspapers demonstrating that the crime had already drawn intensive news coverage, and the testimony of the County Judge, who had entered the initial restraining order based on the local and national attention the case had attracted. The District Judge was required to assess the probable publicity that would be given these shocking crimes prior to the time a jury was selected and sequestered. He then had to examine the probable nature of the publicity and determine how it would affect prospective jurors.

Our review of the pretrial record persuades us that the trial judge was justified in concluding that there would be intense and pervasive pretrial publicity concerning this case. He could also reasonably conclude, based on common human experience, that publicity might impair the defendant's right to fair trial. He did not purport to say more, for he found only "a clear and present danger that pre-trial publicity *could* impinge upon the defendant's right to a fair trial." (Emphasis added.) His conclusion as to the impact of such publicity on prospective jurors was of necessity speculative, dealing as he was with factors unknown and unknowable. . . .

We find little in the record that goes to another aspect of our task, determining whether measures short of an order restraining all publication would have insured the defendant a fair trial. Although the entry of the order might be read as a judicial determination that other measures would not suffice, the trial court made no express findings to that effect. . . . Most of the alternatives to prior restraint of publication in these circumstances were discussed with obvious approval in *Sheppard* v. *Maxwell*: . . . (a) change of trial venue to a place less exposed to the intense publicity that seemed imminent in Lincoln County; (b) postponement of the trial to allow public attention to subside; (c) searching questioning of prospective jurors . . . to screen out those with fixed opinions as to guilt or innocence; (d) the use of emphatic and clear instructions on the sworn duty of each juror to decide the issues only on evidence presented in open court. Sequestration of jurors is, of course, always available. Although that measure insulates jurors only after they are sworn, it also enhances the likelihood of dissipating the impact of pretrial publicity and emphasizes the elements of the jurors' oaths. . . .

The record demonstrates, as the Nebraska courts held, that there was indeed risk that pretrial news accounts, true or false, would have some adverse impact on the attitudes of those who might be called as jurors. But on the record now before us it is not clear that further publicity, unchecked, would so distort the views of potential jurors that 12 could not be found who would, under proper instructions, fulfill their sworn duty to render a just verdict exclusively on the evidence presented in open court. We cannot say on this record that alternatives to a prior restraint on petitioners would not have sufficiently mitigated the adverse effects of pretrial publicity so as to make prior restraint unnecessary. Nor can we conclude that the restraining order actually entered would serve its intended purpose. Reasonable minds can have few doubts about the gravity of the evil pretrial publicity can work, but the probability that it would do so here was not demonstrated with the degree of certainty our cases on prior restraint require.

Of necessity our holding is confined to the record before us. . . . However difficult it may be, we need not rule out the possibility of showing the kind of threat to fair trial rights that would possess the requisite degree of certainty to justify restraint. This Court has frequently denied that First Amendment rights are absolute and has consistently rejected the proposition that a prior restraint can never be employed. . . .

Our analysis ends as it began, with a confrontation between prior restraint imposed to protect one vital constitutional guarantee and the explicit command of another that the freedom to speak and publish shall not be abridged. We reaffirm that the guarantees of freedom of expression are not an absolute prohibition under all circumstances, but the barriers to prior restraint remain high and the presumption against its use continues intact. We hold that, with respect to the order entered in this case prohibiting reporting or commentary on judicial proceedings held in public, the barriers have not been overcome. . . .

Reversed.

In a lengthy opinion, joined by Justices Stewart and Marshall, Justice Brennan concurred in the judgment. He would have preferred an absolute ban on all prior restraints, concluding that "resort to prior restraints on the freedom of the press is a constitutionally impermissible method for insuring fair trials." Justices White and Powell each joined the majority opinion but filed brief concurrences. Justice White doubted whether "orders with respect to the press such as were entered in this case would ever be justifiable." Justice Powell stressed that prior restraint was to be considered as a last resort only in cases of clear and serious threat of prejudicial publicity, where no alternative means of meeting the threat were available, and where there was a clear possibility that the gag order would work. The press was not to be restricted in situations where the prejudicial information would likely reach prospective jurors in other ways (e.g., word of mouth).

Red Lion and the Special Problem of Broadcasting
Red Lion Broadcasting Co. v. *FCC*
395 U.S. 367, 89 S.Ct. 1794, 23 L.Ed.2d. 371 (1969)

The electronic media (radio and TV) pose an interesting variation on the question of whether the First Amendment creates any special protection for the press, over and above the speech protection available to everyone. Because of the limited number of broadcast channels available, their use is regulated by the Federal Communications Commission (F.C.C.) under a 1934 act of Congress. In the interest of balanced coverage of controversial issues over limited airwaves, the F.C.C. has promulgated a "fairness doctrine" that requires licensees to assure some balance in their programming between contending positions on questions of public concern. But doesn't this requirement "abridge" the freedom of the broadcasters by forcing them to undertake coverage and make room for views that they otherwise would ignore? While this objection would have great force with respect to the print media, the Supreme Court has held that the broadcast media are different. In *Red Lion* and its companion case, *U.S.* v. *Radio Television News Directors Association,* the legal talent arrayed in opposition to the "fairness doctrine" included Archibald Cox, arguing for the R.T.N.D.A., Melvin Wolf and Eleanor Holmes Norton (future director of the Equal Employment Opportunity Commission under President Carter) on an *amicus curiae* brief for the A.C.L.U., William Ball on another for the Office of Communications of the United Church of Christ, and Herbert Wechsler on a brief for CBS.

Mr. Justice White delivered the opinion of the Court.

The Federal Communications Commission has for many years imposed on radio and television broadcasters the requirement that discussion of public issues be presented on broadcast stations, and that each side of those issues must be given fair coverage. This is known as the fairness doctrine, which originated very early in the history of broadcasting and has maintained its present outlines for some time. It is an obligation whose content has been defined in a long series of FCC rulings in particular cases, and which is distinct from the statutory requirement of § 315 of the Communications Act [of 1934] that equal time be allotted all qualified candidates for public office. Two aspects of the fairness doctrine, relating to personal attacks in the context of controversial public issues and to political editorializing, were codified more precisely in the form of FCC regulations in 1967. The two cases before us now, which were decided separately below, challenge the constitutional and statutory bases of the doctrine and component rules. *Red Lion* involves the application of the fairness doctrine to a particular broadcast, and RTNDA arises as an action to review the FCC's 1967 promulgation of the personal attack and political editorializing regulations, which were laid down after the *Red Lion* litigation had begun.

The broadcasters challenge the fairness doctrine and its specific manifestations in the personal attack and political editorial rules on conventional First Amendment grounds, alleging that the rules abridge their freedom of speech and press. Their contention is that the First Amendment protects their desire to use their allotted frequencies continuously to broadcast whatever they choose, and to exclude whomever they choose from ever using that frequency. No man may be prevented from saying or publishing what he thinks, or from refusing in his speech or other utterances to give equal weight to the views of his opponents. This right, they say, applies equally to broadcasters. . . .

Although broadcasting is clearly a medium affected by a First Amendment interest, . . . differences in the characteristics of new[s] media justify differences in the First Amendment standards applied to them. . . .

. . . .

When two people converse face to face, both should not speak at once if either is to be clearly understood. But the range of the human voice is so limited that there could be meaningful communications if half the people in the United States were talking and the other half listening. Just as clearly, half the people might publish and the other half read. But the reach of radio signals is incomparably greater than the range of the human voice and the problem of interference is a massive reality. The lack of know-how and equipment may keep many from the air, but only a tiny fraction of those with resources and intelligence can hope to communicate by radio at the same time if intelligible communication is to be had, even if the entire radio spectrum is utilized in the present state of commercially acceptable technology. . . .

. . . .

It was this reality which at the very least necessitated first the division of the radio spectrum into portions reserved respectively for public broadcasting and for other important radio uses such as amateur operation, aircraft, police, defense, and navigation; and then subdivision of each portion, and assignment of specific frequencies to individual users or groups of users. Beyond this, however, because the frequencies reserved for public broadcasting were limited in number, it was essential for the Government to tell some applicants that they could not broadcast at all because there was room for only a few. . . .

. . . It would be strange if the First Amendment, aimed at protecting and furthering communications, prevented the Government from making radio communication possible by requiring licenses to broadcast and by limiting the number of licenses so as not to overcrowd the spectrum. . . .

. . . .

. . . There is nothing in the First Amendment which prevents the Government from requiring a licensee to share his frequency with others and to conduct himself as a proxy or fiduciary with obligations to present those views and voices which are representative of his community and which would otherwise, by necessity, be barred from the airwaves. . . .

This is not to say that the First Amendment is irrelevant to public broadcasting. . . . Because of the scarcity of radio frequencies, the Government is permitted to put restraints on licensees in favor of others whose views should be expressed on this unique medium. But the people as a whole retain their interest in free speech by radio and their collective right to have the medium function consistently with the ends and purposes of the First Amendment. It is the right of the viewers and listeners, not the right of the broadcasters, which is paramount. . . .

Rather than confer frequency monopolies on a relatively small number of licensees, in a Nation of 200,000,000, the Government could surely have decreed that each frequency should be shared among all or some of those who wish to use it, each being assigned a portion of the broadcast day or the broadcast week. The ruling and regulations at issue here do not go quite so far. They assert that under specified circumstances, a licensee must offer to make available a reasonable amount of broadcast time to those who have a view different from that which has already been expressed on his station. The expression of a political endorsement, or of a personal attack while dealing with a controversial public issue, simply triggers this time sharing. As we have said, the First Amendment confers no right on licensees to prevent others from broadcasting on "their" frequencies and no right to an unconditional monopoly of a scarce resource which the Government has denied others the right to use. . . .

. . . .

In view of the scarcity of broadcast frequencies, the Government's role in allocating those frequencies, and the legitimate claims of those unable without governmental assistance to gain access to those frequencies for expression of their views, we hold the regulations and ruling at issue here are both authorized by statute and constitutional. The judgment of the Court of Appeals in *Red Lion* is affirmed and that in *RTNDA* reversed and the cases remanded for proceedings consistent with this opinion.

It is so ordered.

Not having heard oral argument in these cases, Mr. Justice Douglas took no part in the Court's decision.

CASE STUDY: "IDENTITIES" LEGISLATION

In early 1975 former CIA employee Philip Agee published, in England, a gossipy book titled *CIA Diary: Inside the Company*. Agee further announced his intention of exposing U.S. intelligence officers working abroad undercover as a way of frustrating the Agency's work and gave a number of interviews in Europe in which he named names—some true, some false.

On Christmas Eve, 1975, Richard Welch, CIA Station Chief in Athens, was shot down by unidentified gunmen as he was getting into his car. Welch had been identified in the Greek press shortly before as the head of the American CIA in Greece. Welch was buried in Arlington National Cemetery with military honors. President Ford attended, and there were rumblings in Congress to the effect that something ought to be done to better insure the security of Welch's colleagues. Although there was no evidence that Agee was responsible for Welch's public identification, the incident created a broad Washington consensus that what Agee and others were doing was reprehensible.

By late 1979, the "identities" issue had been rolled into the larger issue of comprehensive charter legislation for American intelligence activities. That enterprise was at a dead stall in the congressional process. But interest in separate "identities" legislation was reawakened by CIA antagonist Louis Wolf, who, along with William H. Schapp and Ellen Ray, edited the Washington-based *Covert Action Information Bulletin*. On July 2, 1980, Wolf held a news conference in Kingston, Jamaica, and identified fifteen Americans resident there as "CIA agents" engaged in a campaign of "destabilization" directed at the leftist regime of Premier Michael Manley. Two days later the home of the CIA station chief was peppered with bullets, and several days after that gunshots were fired at guards outside the home of another person named by Wolf.

Wolf and his coeditors maintained that they used no illicit methods to discover the identities of intelligence officers but deduced them from open government publications such as lists of foreign service officers (a cover frequently used). What they were doing, Wolf maintained, was fully protected by the First Amendment.

Now a congressional hornets' nest was buzzing. Senator John H. Chafee, Republican of Rhode Island and principal sponsor of "identities" legislation, said of Wolf: "I want to put him away." And Senate Intelligence Committee Chairman Birch Bayh, Democrat of Indiana, announced "I want to nail him." Bills were introduced in both the House and Senate, and debate began in earnest.

Argument quickly focused on the question of what could be done within the bounds of the Constitution. Senator Joseph R. Biden, Jr., Democrat of Delaware, cautioned "We're all outraged by what has happened in Jamaica. We are all outraged by Agee. But (will) our effort to get them, which we should, violate the Constitution?" The 96th Congress adjourned for the November election with skirmishing continuing. Bills were reported out of committee (S. 2216 and H.R. 5615) but failed to reach the floor.

In the 97th Congress the battle lines formed around two new proposals—S. 391 sponsored by Senator Chafee, and H.R.4, sponsored by Edward P. Boland, Democrat of Massachusetts, Chairman of the House Intelligence Committee. Both bills made it a crime for private persons to disclose the identities of U.S. intelligence officers working undercover, or of their agents—even if public sources were used to work out the identification.

Reactions were sharp. Professor Philip Kurland, of the University of Chicago Law School, called H.R.4 "the clearest violation of the First Amendment attempted by Congress in this era." But Kenneth C. Bass, III, counsel for the Intelligence Policy Group in the Justice Department, commented that "the First Amendment is not absolute," and argued that intentionally "blowing a cover" is speaking "the same kind of speech as a person who shouts fire in a crowded theater: speech that endangers ... individual lives."

The constitutional argument tilted somewhat in the direction of those favoring restrictive legislation when, on June 29, 1981, the Supreme Court decided *Haig* v. *Agee*, 101 S.Ct. 2766 (1981). The State Department (hence Haig) had revoked Agee's passport under a regulation providing for such action where "the Secretary determines that the national's activities abroad are causing or are likely to cause serious damage to the national security or the foreign policy of the United States." Agee argued that the revocation was because of what he was *saying*, and hence it was an abridgment of his freedom of speech. He lost (although Justice Brennan, joined by Justice Marshall, dissented). Chief Justice Burger, writing for the majority, commented that "Agee's First Amendment claim has no foundation. The revocation of Agee's passport rests in part on the content of his speech: specifically, his repeated disclosures of intelligence operations and names of intelligence personnel. Agee's disclosures, among other things, have the declared purpose of obstructing intelligence operations and the recruiting of intelligence personnel. They are not protected by the Constitution. The mere fact that Agee is also engaged in criticism of the government does not render his conduct beyond the reach of the law."

Despite a determined filibuster attempt by Senator Bill Bradley, Democrat of New Jersey, the Senate passed S.391 on March 17, 1982. Jerry Berman, legislative counsel for the ACLU, conceded, "We took a bath."

Meanwhile H.R.4 had passed the House, and since the two measures differed in an important respect, they had to be reconciled. On the crucial matter of when it would be criminal for someone to expose a name, S.391 made it "in the course of a pattern of activities intended to identify and expose covert agents and with reason to believe that such activities would impair or impede" U.S. intelligence operations. H.R.4, by contrast, made disclosure a crime only if undertaken with "the intent to impair or impede" intelligence operations. While the Senate standard was potentially easier for federal prosecutors to meet, the House standard specifically echoed the Chief Justice's remarks about First Amendment protection of Agee, and it ultimately proved easier to marshal agreement around it.

On June 10 the Senate cleared the House version, and a few days later President Reagan signed it into law. The ACLU, the Society of Professional Journalists, and the rest of the constellation of groups that resist any restrictions on the press, are waiting to challenge the law in court.

CHAPTER · 8

ACCESS TO GOVERNMENT INFORMATION—THE PROBLEM OF A "RIGHT TO KNOW"

EVENTS of the 1970s, especially Vietnam and Watergate, forced Americans to confront a basic question of democratic theory: To what extent may government properly refuse to disclose its internal documents, and what measures may it take to enforce its decisions? Or to phrase the matter in another way, what information is government justified in keeping secret, and how may secrecy be maintained? Today, legislation is being debated that would create new "information crimes." Judges, journalists, professors, members of Congress, and officials of the Reagan administration are scrabbling to formulate new rules for secrecy and disclosure of government information—most dramatically the names of officers of the Central Intelligence Agency serving abroad undercover. As a legal matter the "right to know" is still very much in the process of becoming. Furthermore, it is of a mixed nature—with constitutional, statutory, and administrative dimensions.

Several of the Supreme Court decisions treated in Chapter 7 suggested that, in addition to its protection of individuals against government interference with their speech, the First Amendment also created some sort of general right to know—to have access to information. *New York Times* v. *Sullivan,* which created the special libel standard for public officials and public figures, really rested on a right to know basis. And in the *Red Lion* case, Justice White spoke approvingly of "the right of the public to receive suitable access to social, political esthetic, moral, and other ideas. ..."

With the Freedom of Information Act (passed in 1966 and substantially amended in 1974) and the Privacy Act (enacted in 1974), there are now federal statutes protecting the rights of citizen access to information at the federal level, and many states have enacted access laws of their own. In addition, the security classification system established within the executive branch of the federal government constitutes another set of rules governing access to sensitive information concerned with national security.

In what follows are two Supreme Court cases, *Gannett* v. *DePasquale* and *Richmond Newspapers* v. *Virginia*, which treat the issue of a constitutional (that is, First Amendment) right of access to information. We shall explore the development of the security classification system and the problems that beset it. And we shall examine the provisions and controversy surrounding the Privacy Act and the Freedom of Information Act.

Gannett Co. v. *DePasquale*
443 U.S. 368, 99 S.Ct. 2898, 61 L.ED.2d. 608 (1979)

Richmond Newspapers v. *Virginia*
448 U.S. 555, 100 S.Ct. 2814, 65 L.Ed.2d. 973 (1980)

In *Gannett* the Court rejected a newspaper publisher's attack on an order barring the public, including the press, from a pretrial hearing concerning suppression of evidence in a murder case. Justice Stewart's opinion for the Court held that the press and public had no independent constitutional right to insist upon access to such pretrial procedures when the accused, the prosecutor, and the trial judge all had agreed to close the hearing in order to assure a fair trial. Although the Justice focused primarily on the Sixth Amendment provision that, in "all criminal prosecutions, the accused shall enjoy the right to a speedy and public trial," First Amendment concerns also were voiced in most of the opinions. The Justices agreed that the problem here was distinguishable from that in *Nebraska Press Association*, since the present issue was "not one of prior restraint on the press but, one of *access to a judicial proceeding*."

Mr. Justice Stewart delivered the opinion of the Court.

The question presented in this case is whether members of the public have an independent constitutional right to insist upon access to a pretrial judicial proceeding, even though the accused, the prosecutor, and the trial judge all have agreed to the closure of that proceeding in order to assure a fair trial. . . .

The Sixth Amendment, applicable to the States through the Fourteenth, surrounds a criminal trial with guarantees such as the rights to notice, confrontation, and compulsory process that have as their overriding purpose the protection of the accused from prosecutorial and judicial abuses. Among the guarantees that the Amendment provides to a person charged with the commission of a criminal offense, and to him alone, is the "right to speedy and public trial, by an impartial jury." The Constitution nowhere mentions any right of access to a criminal trial on the part of the public; its guarantee, like the others enumerated, is personal to the accused. . . .

Our cases have uniformly recognized the public-trial guarantee as one created for the benefit of the defendant. . . .

The petitioner [Gannett] also argues that members of the press and the public have a right of access to the pretrial hearing by reason of the First and Fourteenth Amendments. In *Pell* v. *Procunier*, 417 U.S. 817, *Saxbe* v. *Washington Post Co.*, 417 U.S. 843, and *Houchins* v. *KQED, Inc*, 438 U.S. 1, this Court upheld prison regulations that denied to members of the press access to prisons superior to that afforded to the public generally. Some Members of the Court, however, took the position in those cases that the First and Fourteenth Amendments do guarantee to the public in general, or the press in particular, a right of access that precludes their complete exclusion in the absence of a significant governmental interest. . . .

Several factors lead to the conclusion that the actions of the trial judge here were consistent with any right of access the petitioner may have had under the First and Fourteenth Amendments. First, none of the spectators present in the courtroom, including the reporter employed by the petitioner, objected when the defendants made the closure motion. Despite this failure to make a contemporaneous objection, counsel for the petitioner was given an opportunity to be heard at a proceeding where he was allowed to voice the petitioner's objections to closure of the pretrial hearing. At this proceeding, which took place after the filing of briefs, the trial court balanced the "constitutional rights of the press and the public" against the "defendants' rights to a fair trial." The trial judge concluded after making this appraisal that the press and the public could be excluded from the suppression hearing and could be denied immediate access to a transcript, because an open proceeding would pose a "reasonable probability of prejudice to these defendants." Thus, the trial court found that the representatives of the press did have a right of access of constitutional dimension, but held, under the circumstances of this case, that this right was outweighed by the defendants' right to a fair trial. In short, the closure decision was based "on an assessment of the competing societal interest involved . . . rather that on any determination that First Amendment freedoms were not implicated." . . .

Furthermore, any denial of access in this case was not absolute but only temporary. Once the danger of prejudice had dissipated, a transcript of the suppression hearing was made available. The press and the public then had a full opportunity to scrutinize the suppression hearing. Unlike the case of an absolute ban on access, therefore, the press here had the opportunity to inform the public of the details of the pretrial hearing accurately and completely. Under these circumstances, any First and Fourteenth Amendment right of the petitioner to attend a criminal trial was not violated.

We certainly do not disparage the general desirability of open judicial proceedings. But we are not asked here to declare whether open proceedings represent beneficial social policy, or whether there would be a constitutional barrier to a state law that imposed a stricter standard of closure than the one here employed by the New York courts. Rather, we are asked to hold that the Constitution itself gave the proceeding, even though all the participants in the litigation agreed that it should be closed to protect the fair-trial rights of the defendants.

For all of the reasons discussed in this opinion, we hold that the Constitution provides no such right. Accordingly, the judgment of the New York Court of Appeals is affirmed.

It is so ordered.

Mr. Chief Justice Burger, concurring.

I join the opinion of the Court, but I write separately to emphasize my view of the nature of the proceeding involved in today's decision. By definition, a hearing on a motion before trial to suppress evidence is not a *trial*; it is a *pre*trial hearing. . . .

Mr. Justice Powell, concurring.

Although I join the opinion of the Court, I would address the question that it reserves. Because of the importance of the public's having accurate information concerning the operation of its criminal justice system, I would hold explicitly that petitioner's reporter had an interest protected by the First and Fourteenth Amendments in being present at the pretrial suppression hearing. . . .

The right of access to courtroom proceedings, of course, is not absolute. It is limited both by the constitutional right of defendants to a fair trial . . . and by the needs of government to obtain just convictions and to preserve the confidentiality of sensitive information and the identity of informants. . . .

In cases such as this, where competing constitutional rights must be weighed in the context of a criminal trial, the often difficult question is whether unrestrained exercise of First Amendment rights poses a serious danger to the fairness of a defendant's trial. . . .

In my view, the procedure followed by the trial court fully comported with that required by the Constitution. Moreover, the substantive standard applied was essentially correct, and, giving due deference to the proximity of the trial judge to the surrounding circumstances, I cannot conclude that it was error in this case to exclude petitioner's reporter. I therefore agree that the judgment of the New York Court of Appeals must be affirmed.

Mr. Justice Rehnquist, concurring.

While I concur in the opinion of the Court, I write separately to emphasize what should be apparent from the Court's Sixth Amendment holding and to address the First Amendment issue that the Court appears to reserve.

The Court today holds, without qualification, that "members of the public have no constitutional right under the Sixth and Fourteenth Amendments to attend criminal trials." . . . In this case, the trial judge closed the suppression hearing because he concluded that an open hearing might have posed a danger to the defendants' ability to receive a fair trial. . . . But the Court's recitation of this fact and its discussion of the need to preserve the defendant's right to a fair trial . . . should not be interpreted to mean that under the Sixth Amendment a trial court can close a pretrial hearing or trial only when there is a danger that prejudicial publicity will harm the defendant. To the contrary, since the Court holds that the public does not have *any* Sixth Amendment right of access to such proceedings, it necessarily follows that if the parties agree on a closed proceeding, the trial court is not required by the Sixth Amendment to advance any reason whatsoever for declining to open a pretrial hearing or trial to the public. . . .

The Court states that it may assume *"arguendo"* that the First and Fourteenth Amendments guarantee the public a right of access to pretrial hearings in some situations, because it concludes that in this case this "putative right was given all appropriate deference." ... Despite the Court's seeming reservation of the question whether the First Amendment guarantees the public a right of access to pretrial proceedings, it is clear that this Court repeatedly has held that there is no First Amendment right of access in the public or the press to judicial or other governmental proceedings. ... Because this Court has refused to find a First Amendment right to access in the past, lower courts should not assume that after today's decision they must adhere to the procedure employed by the trial court in this case or to those advanced by Mr. Justice Powell in his separate opinion. ...

Mr. Justice Blackmun, with whom Mr. Justice Brennan, Mr. Justice White, and Mr. Justice Marshall join, concurring in part and dissenting in part.

I emphasize that the trial court should begin with the assumption that the Sixth Amendment requires that a pretrial suppression hearing be conducted in open court unless a defendant carries his burden to demonstrate a strict and inescapable necessity for closure. There should be no need for a representative of the public to demonstrate that the public interest is legitimate or genuine, or that the public seeks access out of something more than mere curiosity. Trials and suppression hearings by their nature are events of legitimate public interest, and the public need demonstrate no threshold of respectability in order to attend. This is not to say, of course, that a court should not take into account heightened public interest in cases of unusual importance to the community or to the public at large. The prosecution of an important office holder could intensify public interest in observing the proceedings, and the court should take that interest into account where it is warranted. It is also true, however, that as the public interest intensifies, so does the potential for prejudice.

As a rule, the right of the accused to a fair trial is compatible with the interest of the public in maintaining the publicity of pretrial proceedings. "In the over-whelming majority of criminal trials, pretrial publicity presents few unmanageable threats to this important right." *Nebraska Press Assn.* v. *Stuart* . . . .

If, after considering the essential factors, the trial court determines that the accused has carried his burden of establishing that closure is necessary, the Sixth Amendment is no barrier to reasonable restrictions on public access designed to meet that need. Any restrictions imposed, however, should extend no further than the circumstances reasonably require. ...

. . . .

Petitioner acknowledges that it seeks no greater rights than those due the general public. But it argues that, the Sixth Amendment aside, the First Amendment protects the free flow of information about judicial proceedings, and that this flow may not be cut off without meeting the standards required to justify the imposition of a prior restraint under the First Amendment. Specifically, petitioner argues that the First Amendment prohibits closure of a pretrial proceeding except in accord with the standards established in *Nebraska Press* and only after notice and hearing and a stay pending appeal.

I do not agree. As I have noted, this case involves no restraint upon publication or upon comment about information already in the possession of the public or the press. It involves an issue of access to a judicial proceeding. To the extent the Constitution protects a right of public access to the proceeding, the standards enunciated under the Sixth Amendment suffice to protect that right. I therefore need not reach the issue of First Amendment access.

The media reaction to *Gannett* was savage, and a number of influential commentators argued that the majority was wrong—some said access was guaranteed on Sixth Amendment grounds, some said on First Amendment grounds. Particularly galling was Justice Rehnquist's cocksure concurrence, which had assumed that the decision in *Gannett* applied to trials as well as pretrial hearings, and asserted that state trial judges had unlimited discretion in closing their courtrooms.

A year after *Gannett,* The 7–1 decision in *Richmond Newspapers* held that, "[a]bsent an overriding interest articulated in findings, the trial of a criminal case must be open to the public."

Chief Justice Burger's plurality opinion (joined by Justice White and Stevens) stated that the "narrow question" was "whether the right of the public and press to attend criminal trials is guaranteed under the United States Constitution." The Chief Justice built squarely on the distinction he had emphasized in *Gannett* between pretrial hearings and trials. Professor Laurence H. Tribe, of the Harvard Law School, argued before the Supreme Court for Richmond Newspapers, Inc., supported by the now familiar phalanx of *amici* and plus Edward Bennett Williams representing the *Washington Post.*

Mr. Chief Justice Burger announced the judgment of the Court and delivered an opinion, in which Mr. Justice White and Mr. Justice Stevens joined.

> The narrow question presented in this case is whether the right of the public and press to attend criminal trials is guaranteed under the United States Constitution. . . .
>
> From [an] unbroken, uncontradicted history, supported by reasons as valid today as in centuries past, we are bound to conclude that a presumption of openness inheres in the very nature of a criminal trial under our system of justice. This conclusion is hardly novel; without a direct holding on the issue, the Court has voiced its recognition of it in a variety of contexts over the years. . . . And recently in *Gannett Co.* v. *DePasquale,* . . . both the majority and dissenting opinion . . . agreed that open trials were part of the common-law tradition [*Pace* Rehnquist] . . .
>
> The First Amendment, in conjunction with the Fourteenth, prohibits governments from "abridging the freedom of speech, or of the press; or the right of the people peaceably to assemble, and to petition the Government for a redress of grievances." These expressly guaranteed freedoms share a common core purpose of assuring freedom of communication on matters relating to the functioning of government. Plainly it would be difficult to single out any aspect of government of higher concern and importance to the people than the manner in which criminal trials are conducted; as we have shown, recognition of this pervades the centuries-old history of open trials and the opinions of this Court. . . .
>
> . . . .
>
> The right of access to places traditionally open to the public, as criminal

trials have long been, may be seen as assured by the amalgam of the First Amendment guarantees of speech and press. . . .

The State argues that the Constitution nowhere spells out a guarantee for the right of the public to attend trials, and that accordingly no such right is protected. The possibility that such a contention could be made did not escape the notice of the Constitution's draftsmen; they were concerned that some important rights might be thought disparaged because not specifically guaranteed. It was even argued that because of this danger no Bill of Rights should be adopted. See, *e.g.,* The Federalist No. 84 (A. Hamilton). In a letter to Thomas Jefferson in October 1788, James Madison explained why he, although "in favor of a bill of rights," had "not viewed it in an important light" up to that time: "I conceive that in a certain degree . . . the rights in question are reserved by the manner in which the federal powers are granted." He went on to state that "there is great reason to fear that a positive declaration of some of the most essential rights could not be obtained in the requisite latitude." 5 Writings of James Madison 271 (G. Hunt ed. 1904).

But arguments such as the State makes have not precluded recognition of important rights not enumerated. Notwithstanding the appropriate caution against reading into the Constitution rights not explicitly defined, the Court has acknowledged that certain unarticulated rights are implicit in enumerated guarantees. For example, the rights of association and of privacy, the right to be presumed innocent, and the right to be judged by a standard of proof beyond a reasonable doubt in a criminal trial, as well as the right to travel, appear nowhere in the Constitution or Bill of Rights. Yet these important but unarticulated rights have nonetheless been found to share constitutional protection in common with explicit guarantees. The concerns expressed by Madison and others have thus been resolved; fundamental rights, even though not expressly guaranteed, have been recognized by the Court as indispensable to the enjoyment of rights explicitly defined.

We hold that the right to attend criminal trials is implicit in the guarantees of the First Amendment; without the freedom to attend such trials, which people have exercised for centuries, important aspects of freedom of speech and "of the press could be eviscerated." . . .

. . . .

. . . Absent an overriding interest articulated in findings, the trial of a criminal case must be open to the public. Accordingly, the judgment under review is

Reversed.

Mr. Justice Powell took no part in the consideration or decision of this case.

Mr. Justice White, concurring.

This case would have been unnecessary had *Gannett Co.* v. *DePasquale* . . . construed the Sixth Amendment to forbid excluding the public from criminal proceedings except in narrowly defined circumstances. But the Court there rejected the submission of four of us to this effect, thus requiring that the First Amendment issue involved here be addressed. On this issue, I concur in the opinion of The Chief Justice.

Mr. Justice Stevens, concurring.

This is a watershed case. Until today the Court has accorded virtually absolute protection to the dissemination of information or ideas, but never before has it squarely held that the acquistion of newsworthy matter is entitled to any constitutional protection whatsoever. . . .

Mr. Justice Brennan, with whom Mr. Justice Marshall joins, concurring in the judgment.

Gannett Co. v. *DePasquale* . . . held that the Sixth Amendment right to a public trial was personal to the accused, conferring no right of access to pretrial proceedings that is separately enforceable by the public or the press. The instant case raises the question whether the First Amendment, of its own force and as applied to the States through the Fourteenth Amendment, secures the public an independent right of access to trial proceedings. Because I believe that the First Amendment—of itself and as applied to the States through the Fourteenth Amendment—secures such a public right of access, I agree with those of my Brethren who hold that, without more, agreement of the trial judge and the parties cannot constitutionally close a trial to the public. . . .

Mr. Justice Stewart, concurring in the judgment.

In *Gannett Co.* v. *DePasquale* . . . the Court held that the Sixth Amendment, which guarantees "the accused" the right to a public trial, does not confer upon representatives of the press or members of the general public any right of access to a trial. But the Court explicitly left open the question whether such a right of access may be guaranteed by other provisions of the Constitution. . . . Mr. Justice Powell expressed the view that the First and Fourteenth Amendments do extend at least a limited right of access even to pretrial suppression hearings in criminal cases . . . (concurring opinion). Mr. Justice Rehnquist expressed a contrary view . . . (concurring opinion). The remaining members of the Court were silent on the question.

Whatever the ultimate answer to that question may be with respect to pretrial suppression hearings in criminal cases, the First and Fourteenth Amendments clearly give the press and the public a right of access to trials themselves, civil as well as criminal. . . . With us, a trial is by very definition a proceeding open to the press and to the public. . . .

Mr. Justice Blackmun concurring in the judgment.

My opinion and vote in partial dissent last Term in *Gannett Co.* v. *DePasquale* . . . compels my vote to reverse the judgment of the Supreme Court of Virginia. . . .

The Court's return to history is a welcome change in direction.

It is gratifying, second, to see the Court wash away at least some of the graffiti that marred the prevailing opinion in *Gannett.* . . .

The Court's ultimate ruling in *Gannett,* with such clarification as is provided by the opinions in this case today, apparently is now to the effect that there is no *Sixth* Amendment right on the part of the public—or the press—to an open hearing on a motion to suppress. I, of course, continue to believe that *Gannett* was in error, both in its interpretation of the Sixth Amendment generally, and in its application to the suppression hearing, for I remain convinced that the right to a public trial is to be found where the Constitution explicitly placed it—in the Sixth Amendment. ...

Mr. Justice Rehnquist, dissenting.

In the Gilbert & Sullivan operetta "Iolanthe," the Lord Chancellor recites:

"The Law is the true embodiment
of everything that's excellent,
It has no kind of fault or flaw,
And I, my Lords, embody the Law."

It is difficult not to derive more than a little of this flavor from the various opinions supporting the judgment in this case. The opinion of The Chief Justice states:

"[H]ere for the first time the Court is asked to decide whether a criminal trial itself may be closed to the public upon the unopposed request of a defendant, without any demonstration that closure is required to protect the defendant's superior right to a fair trial, or that some other overriding consideration requires closure." ...

The opinion of Mr. Justice Brennan states:

"Read with care and in context, our decisions must therefore be understood as holding only that any privilege of access to governmental information is subject to a degree of restraint dictated by the nature of the information and countervailing interests in security or confidentiality." ...

For the reasons stated in my separate concurrence in *Gannett Co.* v. *DePasquale,* ... I do not believe that either the First or Sixth Amendment, as made applicable to the States by the Fourteenth, requires that a State's reasons for denying public access to a trial, where both the prosecuting attorney and the defendant have consented to an order of closure approved by the judge, are subject to any additional constitutional review at our hands. ... We have at present 50 state judicial systems and one federal judicial system in the United States, and our authority to reverse a decision by the highest court of the State is limited to only those occasions when the state decision violates some provision of the United States Constitution. And that authority should be exercised with a full sense that the judges whose decisions we review are making the same effort as we to uphold the Constitution. As said by Mr. Justice Jackson, ... "we are not final because we are infallible, but we are infallible only because we are final."

The proper administration of justice in any nation is bound to be a matter of the highest concern to all thinking citizens. But to gradually rein in, as this Court has done over the past generation, all of the ultimate decisionmaking power over how justice shall be administered, not merely in the federal system but in each of the 50 States, is a task that no Court consisting of nine persons, however gifted, is equal to. Nor is it desirable that such authority be exercised by such a tiny numerical fragment of the 220 million people who compose the population of this country. In the same concurrence just quoted, Mr. Justice Jackson accurately observed that "[t]he generalities of the Fourteenth Amendment are so indeterminate as to what state actions are forbidden that this Court has found it a ready instrument, in one field or another, to magnify federal, and incidentally its own, authority over the states." ...

However high-minded the impulses which originally spawned this trend may have been, and which impulses have been accentuated since the time Mr. Justice Jackson wrote it is basically unhealthy to have so much authority concentrated in a small group of lawyers who have been appointed to the Supreme Court and enjoy virtual life tenure. Nothing in the reasoning of Mr. Chief Justice Marshall in *Marbury* v. *Madison,* 1 Cranch 137 (1803), requires that this Court through ever-broadening use of the Supremacy Clause smother a healthy pluralism which would ordinarily exist in a national government embracing 50 States.

The issue here is not whether the "right" to freedom of the press conferred by the First Amendment to the Constitution overrides the defendant's "right" to a fair trial conferred by other Amendments to the Constitution; it is instead whether any provision in the Constitution may fairly be read to prohibit what the trial judge in the Virginia state-court system did in this case. Being unable to find any such prohibition in the First, Sixth, Ninth, or any other Amendment to the United States Constitution, or in the Constitution itself, I dissent.

So Rehnquist was laid low, and it was Justice John Paul Steven's chance to crow that *Richmond Newspapers* was a "watershed case" that "unequivocally holds that an arbitrary interference with access to important information is an abridgement of the freedoms of speech and of the press protected by the First Amendment." But in the absence of an opinion of the court, and given the wide variety of situations in which "newsworthy matter" is sought, one may wonder whether Justice Steven's triumph will be longer lived than Rehnquist's in *Gannett.*

The Classification System

There is widespread, if not universal, agreement that government must keep some sorts of information secret because publication would impair "national security." But national security is an ambiguous term. Potential external dangers to the United States run across a broad spectrum—from the classic case of disclosure of the positions of troop ships on the high seas, to the disruption of our relations with another government because of the disclosure of confidential talks.

A further difficulty arises from the well-documented use of the "national security" concept to cover governmental blunders. But while it is simple enough to say "no covering up by classification," it is also simple-minded. The fact is that disclosures of certain blunders may prejudice America's external security. In the real world of government, hard information and mistakes, embarrassment to individuals, and damage to the international position of the United States are often inextricably intertwined. In making a secrecy decision one is often left asking "which documents," and "how much risk," and "for how long," and "in whose judgment"?

It is perhaps surprising that until the second decade of this century, American state secrets were kept by gentlemen's agreement, supported by a general provision (since repealed) of the so-called "Housekeeping Act" of 1789, which provided for setting up government files.

In 1911, Congress passed, and President Taft signed into law, a measure criminalizing certain unauthorized gathering of information related to national defense. This was followed, and preempted, by the Espionage Act of 1917, which created multiple offenses of obtaining and divulging defense information. The Act also provided for severe penalties but it is important to note that the Congress refused to include penal sanctions for disclosure of material designated by the President as sensitive. For there to be criminal liability the material in question had to relate to national defense (ambiguous, but narrower than national security), and there had to be, under most of the provisions of the Act, an intent (variously described in various subsections) to harm the interest of the United States.

During World War I, the Headquarters of the American Expeditionary Force in France developed an internal classification system employing the categories SECRET, CONFIDENTIAL, and FOR CIRCULATION ONLY. This system was carried into the inter-war years, becoming common throughout the Army and Navy. In 1940, President Roosevelt first formalized the classification system in Executive Order No. 8381 of March 22, 1940. This order made reference to the espionage laws and particularly the amendments of January 12, 1938, which had empowered the President to designate certain defense installations and equipment unlawful to photograph, map, or observe. Authority to classify documents as SECRET, CONFIDENTIAL, and RESTRICTED was conferred on the Secretaries of War and Navy.

Once again, during World War II, practice bounded ahead of the formal rules, and the classification TOP SECRET came into use within the uniformed services. This was the situation in February 1950, when President Truman issued Executive Order No. 10,104. TOP SECRET was authorized as a designation, but authority to classify continued to be restricted to the Secretary of Defense and the service secretaries. However, on September 24, 1951, a year into the Korean conflict, President Truman superceded Executive Order No. 10,104 with Executive Order No. 10,290. This extended the authority to classify to nonmilitary agencies and broadened the TOP SECRET category from defense information to information requiring protection in the interest of "national security." It was at this point that the classification system took on its contemporary form. Executive Order No. 10,104 also created a gap between what is classifiable and what is protected against malicious disclosure by the espionage laws.

In 1953, President Eisenhower issued Executive Order No, 10,501. This was a response to criticisms that under Truman's program too much material was being classified, that authority to classify was too widely diffused, and that the guidelines for classification were unclear. The Eisenhower order withdrew classification authority from twenty-eight agencies and restricted that of seventeen others. Executive Order No. 10,501 also included provisions for periodic review and declassification. As a guideline for classification, the order referred to "national defense," but this was interpreted to include "foreign relations." The classification system was never specifically approved by Congress, although it received tacit approval when its existence was recognized in the Atomic Energy Act of 1946, the National Security Act of 1947, the Internal Security Act of 1950, and most importantly, the Freedom of Information Act in 1966.

In 1972, in the wake of the furor over the Pentagon Papers disclosure, President Nixon, on the advice of a Justice Department Committee headed by future Supreme Court Justice William Rehnquist, issued a new Executive Order, No. 11,652. This adopted the national security criterion for classification but it severely limited classification authority. Indeed, by the spring of 1975, it was reported that the number of personnel in all agencies authorized to classify material had dropped from 59,316 in June 1972, to 15,466 by December 31, 1974. Executive Order 11,652 also provided an accelerated declassification schedule, although in its basic architecture the classification system went unchanged. The disjunction between the classification system and the espionage laws remained. Critics of the system on the political left were still unhappy that so much material was being classified, while those on the right continued to worry that the system was enforced only with administrative and not penal sanctions.

The Carter administration quickly moved to replace the Nixon classification order with one embodying sharper definitions of the categories of classification. If it was precisely stated what TOP SECRET, SECRET, and CONFIDENTIAL meant, it was argued, then it would be much easier to crack down on improper classification. Sharp definitions might even allow for judicial monitoring of classification practices which, in the post-Watergate atmosphere of 1979 appealed to many Carterites as a good idea. Executive Order No. 12,148 was issued on July 20, 1979; it remains in force today. The key definitions in this order are as follows:

> "Top Secret" shall be applied only to information, the unauthorized disclosure of which reasonably could be expected to cause exceptionally grave damage to the national security.
>
> "Secret" shall be applied only to information, the unauthorized disclosure of which reasonably could be expected to cause serious damage to the national security.
>
> "Confidential" shall be applied to information, the unauthorized disclosure of which reasonably could be expected to cause identifiable damage to the national security.

The Carter order also provided that the potential damage to national security contemplated in these three categories had to be "identifiable," and that officials must consider the public's right to know before imposing a security classification on material.

The Reagan administration thought this overrestrictive. In Executive Order No. 12,356 of April 2, 1982, Reagan eliminated the requirement that the public's right to know be considered in classification decisions. He also dropped the requirement that a potential danger be "identifiable," on the argument that strictly speaking, nothing that is political is precisely identifiable. However, the Reagan order retained the Carter gradations with respect to degrees of potential danger.

In their thoroughgoing 1973 article on the espionage laws, Harold Edgar and Benno C. Schmidt, Jr., refer to the "state of benign indeterminacy about the rule of law governing defense secrets."* They go on to observe that such a state of things could tolerably prevail as long as there was high consensus on foreign policy, strong gentleman's understandings on the operational rules of the classification system. But, they observe, such an arrangement of law will "not survive many trips to the courthouse." One is entitled to wonder whether the 1979 classification definitions improve things very much.

FOIA and the Privacy Act

Let us now turn to the statutory dimension of the right to know. The Freedom of Information Act (FOIA) was signed into law by Lyndon Johnson in 1966, and amended over Gerald Ford's veto late in 1974. How close does the FOIA come to being an adequate mechanism of access? How does it relate to the classification system? How well does it protect really sensitive materials? Where are its strengths and its weaknesses, and how does it relate to the Privacy Act, 5 U.S.C. 552a, adopted in 1974?

At the heart of the Freedom of Information Act, was a commitment to a policy of executive branch disclosure—unless the requested materials fell within one of nine exempted categories of information. But the breadth and ambiguity of these exemptions, along with the cumbersome access procedures established by the Act, came to be the despair of media advocates and civil libertarians.

Of the exemptions the first was the most problematical. Subsection (b)(1) allowed the Executive to withhold information that, if disclosed, would adversely affect national defense or foreign policy. In *Environmental Protection Administration* v. *Mink,* 410 U.S. 73 (1973), the Supreme Court held this

---

* Harold Edgar and Benno C. Schmidt, Jr., "The Espionage Statutes and Publication of Defense Information," 73 *Columbia Law Review* 930 (1973).

protected agencies against requests from courts handling FOIA cases that they, the judges, be given classified materials for *in camera* inspection, to determine if classification was proper or whether nonclassified portions might be sorted out.

In 1974, subsection (b)(1) was changed to exempt from disclosure only materials "specifically authorized under criteria established by an Executive Order to be kept secret in the interest of national defense or foreign policy." Those materials must be "properly classified pursuant to such Executive Order."

It seems clear that FOIA reformers thought they were narrowing the secrecy exemption by tieing it to the existing classification system. The qualification that the materials must be properly classified seems, equally clearly, to have been intended as an invitation for the courts to review materials and determine which of them met the standard of the existing classification guidelines. But this all assumes that the guidelines for classification are less ambiguous than the old subsection (b)(1) language, which refers to the Executive protecting national defense and foreign policy interests. If not, how will federal courts be able to do more than substitute their judgments about national security for the president's? We have seen that the present Executive Order is more carefully drawn than its predecessors; whether its key passages are sufficiently precise to allow for principled judicial construction remains to be seen. The danger is having judges, who are far removed from practical, situational knowledge of the possible consequences of disclosure, producing an *ad hoc* and unhelpful jurisprudence.

The seventh exemption of the FOIA is also controversial. It protects "investigatory files compiled for law enforcement purposes." However, this provision has been interpreted by the courts as not protecting all documents related to investigations; only those which, if disclosed, would result in some impairment of the law enforcement function. Section (b)(7) was amended in 1974 to specify the sorts of dangers that would justify withholding a law enforcement investigation record. These include (1) interference with enforcement proceedings, (2) possible deprivation of the right to fair trial, (3) unwarranted invasion of personal privacy, (4) disclosure of confidential sources, (5) disclosure of investigative techniques, and (6) the endangering of law enforcement personnel.

A final question with respect to the Freedom of Information Act involves its protection of personal privacy. Subsection (b)(6) exempts from disclosure "personnel, medical and similar files," but only if disclosure would constitute a "clearly unwarranted invasion of personal privacy." To protect against disclosure (in the interest of a private citizen), the agency must bear the burden of demonstrating that the file is personnel, medical, or similar, *and* that the injury to privacy outweighs (is unwarranted by) the gain in public information acquired by disclosure.

Perhaps this deficiency is less worrisome than it might be in light of the passage, in December 1974, of the Privacy Act. This statute, it is suggested, remedies the faulty sixth exemption of the FOIA. Subsection (e)(10) of the Privacy Act provides that agencies shall "establish appropriate administrative, technical and physical safeguards to insure the security and confidentiality of records and to protect against any anticipated threats or hazards to their security or integrity which could result in substantial harm, embarrassment, inconvenience, or unfairness to any individual on whom information is obtained."

But what, precisely, is "the law"? Between "inconvenience" and "embarrassment" to individuals (Privacy Act) and "unwarranted invasion" (FOIA) a gulf yawns. Furthermore, information about persons of the sort contemplated by the Privacy Act is certainly contained in files other than "personnel, medical or similar." Yet unless such personal information fell under one of the other exemptions it could have no protection from disclosure under the FOIA. May subsection (e)(10) be read as modifying the sixth exemption of the FOIA? May it be relied upon as an independent ground in refusing to disclose? Different officials within the Justice Department respond differently on the question of which act prevails. This is a textbook example of rights formation through trial and error.

Core Provisions of the Freedom of Information Act

§552. Public information; agency rules, opinions, orders, records, and proceedings

(a) Each agency shall make available to the public information as follows:

(1) Each agency shall separately state and currently publish in the Federal Register for the guidance of the public—

(A) descriptions of its central and field organization and the established places at which, the employees (and in the case of a uniformed service, the members) from whom, and the methods whereby, the public may obtain information, make submittals or requests, or obtain decisions;

(B) statements of the general course and method by which its functions are channeled and determined, including the nature and requirements of all formal and informal procedures available;

(C) rules of procedure, descriptions of forms available or the places at which forms may be obtained, and instructions as to the scope and contents of all papers, reports, or examinations;

(D) substantive rules of general applicability adopted as authorized by law, and statements of general policy or interpretations of general applicability formulated and adopted by the agency; and

(E) each amendment, revision, or repeal of the foregoing. . . .

(2) Each agency, in accordance with published rules, shall make available for public inspection and copying—

(A) final opinions, including concurring and dissenting opinions, as well as orders, made in the adjudication of cases;

(B) those statements of policy and interpretations which have been adopted by the agency and are not published in the Federal Register; and

(C) administrative staff manuals and instructions to staff that affect a member of the public. . . .

(3) Except with respect to the records made available under paragraphs (1) and (2) of this subsection, each agency, upon any request for records which (A) reasonably describes such records and (B) is made in accordance with published rules stating the time, place, fees (if any), and procedures to be followed, shall make the records promptly available to any person.

(4)(A) In order to carry out the provisions of this section, each agency shall promulgate regulations, pursuant to notice and receipt of public comment, specifying a uniform schedule of fees applicable to all constituent units of such agency. Such fees shall be limited to reasonable standard charges for document search and duplication and provide for recovery of only the direct costs of such search and duplication. Documents shall be furnished without charge or at a reduced charge where the agency determines that waiver or reduction of the fee is in the public interest because furnishing the information can be considered as primarily benefiting the general public. . . .

This section does not apply to matters that are—

(1)(A) specifically authorized under criteria established by an Executive order to be kept secret in the interest of national defense or foreign policy and (B) are in fact properly classified pursuant to such Executive order;

(2) related solely to the internal personnel rules and practices of an agency;

(3) specifically exempted from disclosure by statute (other than section 552b of this title), provided that such statute (A) requires that the matters be withheld from the public in such a manner as to leave no discretion on the issue, or (B) establishes particular criteria for withholding or refers to particular types of matters to be withheld;

(4) trade secrets and commercial or financial information obtained from a person and privileged or confidential;

(5) inter-agency or intra-agency memorandums or letters which would not be available by law to a party other than an agency in litigation with the agency;

(6) personnel and medical files and similar files the disclosure of which would constitute a clearly unwarranted invasion of personal privacy;

(7) investigatory records compiled for law enforcement purposes, but only to the extent that the production of such records would (A) interfere with enforcement proceedings, (B) deprive a person of a right to a fair trial or an impartial adjudication, (C) constitute an unwarranted invasion of personal privacy, (D) disclose the identity of a confidential source and, in the case of a record compiled by a criminal law enforcement authority in the course of a criminal investigation, or by an agency conducting a lawful national security intelligence investigation, confidential information furnished only by the confidential source, (E) disclose investigative techniques and procedures, or (F) endanger the life or physical safety of law enforcement personnel;

(8) contained in or related to examination, operating, or condition reports prepared by, on behalf of, or for the use of an agency responsible for the regulation or supervision of financial institutions; or

(9) geological and geophysical information and data, including maps, concerning wells.

Any reasonably segregable portion of a record shall be provided to any person requesting such record after deletion of the portions which are exempt under this subsection. . . .

Core Provisions of the Privacy Act

§552a. Records maintained on individuals . . .

(d) Access to records
Each agency that maintains a system of records shall—

(1) upon request by any individual to gain access to his record or to any information pertaining to him which is contained in the system, permit him and upon his request, a person of his own choosing to accompany him, to review the record and have a copy made of all or any portion thereof in a form comprehensive to him, except that the agency may require the individual to furnish a written statement authorizing discussion of that individual's record in the accompanying person's presence;

(2) permit the individual to request amendment of a record pertaining to him and—

(A) not later than 10 days (excluding Saturdays, Sundays, and legal public holidays) after the date of receipt of such request, acknowledge in writing such receipt; and (B) promptly, either—

(i) make any correction of any portion thereof which the individual believes is not accurate, relevant, timely, or complete; or

(ii) inform the individual of its refusal to amend the record in accordance with his request, the reason for the refusal, the procedures established by the agency for the individual to request a review of that refusal by the head of the agency or an officer designated by the head of the agency, and the name and business address of that official. . . .

(e) Agency requirements
Each agency that maintains a system of records shall—

(1) maintain in its records only such information about an individual as is relevant and necessary to accomplish a purpose of the agency required to be accomplished by statute or by executive order of the President. . . .

(5) maintain all records which are used by the agency in making any determination about any individual with such accuracy, relevance, timeliness, and completeness as is reasonably necessary to assure fairness to the individual in the determination; . . .

(7) maintain no record describing how any individual exercises rights guaranteed by the First Amendment unless expressly authorized by statute or by the individual about whom the record is maintained or unless pertinent to and within the scope of an authorized law enforcement activity; . . .

(10) establish appropriate administrative, technical, and physical safeguards to insure the security and confidentiality of records and to protect against any anticipated threats or hazards to their security or integrity which could result in substantial harm, embarrassment, inconvenience, or unfairness to any individual on whom information is maintained . . .

CASE STUDY: THE 1981 FOIA AMENDMENTS

Does the Freedom of Information Act, as amended in 1974, properly protect sensitive intelligence and law enforcement records against disclosure? Many in the executive branch and Congress think not, but the present law has strong support in the media, among civil liberties interest groups, and in the law schools.

FBI director William Webster has worried publicly about the identities of Bureau informants being discovered as a result of FOIA disclosures. In some cases the request for documents have come from convicted organized crime figures!

The CIA director, William J. Casey, has stressed the fears of intelligence services of other countries. He argues that friendly countries will not entrust us with sensitive, secret information unless they have faith in our ability to protect it from disclosure. It is the FOIA, and especially the 1974 amendments, that has shaken that faith. To restore it, Casey maintains, there must be clear exemption for intelligence materials.

William H. Taft, IV, General Counsel of the Defense Department, testified that "significant costs to the taxpayer are being imposed by those who were not intended to be the beneficiaries of the act." Taft explained that since 1975 only 20 percent of the FOIA requests received by the Defense Department came from private individuals, while 55 percent came from business concerns, law firms, lobbyists, and other commercial interests seeking lists of names for mailing purposes. Concern also has been voiced over the number of simple mistakes that are bound to occur as FOIA examiners in various agencies review millions of pages. If something is incorrectly released (an informer's identity or a piece of properly classified information), it is not clear the government has any authority to retrieve it.

Defenders of the FOIA argued that the dangers were being overstated and that the existing exemptions protect everything that should be protected. As to the expense of reviewing files to determine what might safely be released and what might not, Katherine A. Meyer, director of the Freedom of Information Clearinghouse, called it "the cost of carrying out democratic government."

Not surprisingly, the incoming Reagan administration was persuaded that the FOIA needed tightening. The administration's proposals "surfaced" on October 15, 1981, and were later incorporated in bills introduced into both the House and Senate. It was another bill, however, S. 1730, introduced by Senator Orrin G. Hatch, Republican of Utah, that received the most attention in the 97th Congress. It had administration support and would have given the attorney general broad powers to exempt all materials relating to terrorism, organized crime, and foreign counterintelligence. The Hatch bill also would have paved the way for the CIA to seek court injunctions against the disclosure of material that might reveal sources or methods of intelligence collection, and it increased the protection of information that businesses were required to submit to the federal government and might be sought by competitors for commercial advantage.

Lobbying against S. 1730 was as intense as the executive branch pressure for it. A coordinating body, the Joint Media Committee, was set up by a variety of press interest groups, and the Reports Committee for Freedom of the Press took the point position as most radical critic of Hatch's proposals. As Tonda Rush of the Reporters Committee put it, there was a "good-cop, bad-cop" routine working in which the major media organizations bargained politely with Hatch's staff for changes in the bill, while the "bad-cop" Reporters Committee excoriated Hatch and his supporters. While changes were being negotiated, for example, Jack Landau, executive director of the Reporters Committee, sent a letter to all editors, broadcasters, and publishers in Utah, marked "URGENT." The letter asked the recipients' help "to save the federal Freedom of Information Act" which was under "severe attack ... led and coordinated by Senator Orrin Hatch." With the Senator facing a tough reelection campaign in the fall, his staff in Washington smarted as several of the state's newspapers, including the largest, the *Salt Lake City Tribune,* editorialized against S. 1730.

On May 20, 1982, the Senate Judiciary Committee reported out a compromise version of S. 1730. This contained access limitations for organized crime information and materials that dealt with the use of informants or Secret Service protective operations. Gone were the added protections for files on terrorism and foreign counterintelligence—in response to fears such secrecy could be used to hide law enforcement abuses. Gone also was the wider shield for business records that critics objected might hamper the works of consumer advocates.

The compromise was carefully carpentered but all for naught. With the fall, 1982, elections heightening interest in adjournment, Senator Patrick J. Leahy, Democrat of Vermont, warned that he might undertake a filibuster if the bill reached the Senate floor. In the House, where the Democrats controlled, Representative Glenn English, Democrat of Oklahoma and chairman of the Information Subcommittee of the Government Operations Committee, announced: "We've waited on the Senate ... the House-side, we didn't see the pressing need to make major changes that Senator Hatch and the Reagan administration saw."

It remains to be seen whether a durable compromise can be hammered out. In the 98th Congress in the spring of 1983 a new intelligence information bill was proposed, which did not altogether exempt the CIA from the General disclosure requirements of the FOIA, but provided a broadened exemption for the Agency by which all "operational files" were protected. The ACLU, while denying that it had made any "deal" with the CIA to weaken the FOIA, signaled that it would not "reflexively oppose" the bill. A dispute quickly developed over the question of whether the Agency's determination of what was an "operational file" should be reviewable by a federal judge. (Senator

Leahy thought it should; Director of Central Intelligence Casey wasn't so sure.) It appears at this writing that the bill still has a chance, but in the politics of the Freedom of Information Act, it is always a mistake to be confident. The professional civil libertarian establishment was further alienated from the Reagan administration in the summer of 1983 by a proposal drafted in the Justice Department to subject publications by former government officials to prescreening for security breaches. This vastly unpopular suggestion was withdrawn (at least temporarily) in early 1984, but it probably had the effect of narrowing the margin for compromise on information policy between the administration and its critics.

PART II

FREEDOM OF RELIGION

DISPUTES over the relationship between religion and the public order divided America in its beginnings and continue to vex us into the late twentieth century. In fact, issues of religious freedom are perhaps the oldest type of civil liberties issue. Well before the eighteenth century conflict in Britain over freedom of speech, before the nineteenth century battles over the right to vote, and before the twentieth century struggles over racial and sexual equality, questions of church-state relations and freedom of worship headed the agenda of politicians, publicists, and philosophers in Britain and in the American colonies.

The sixteenth century had seen the religious unity of England shattered by the Protestant reformation. Roman Catholics found themselves rather suddenly a minority and on the defensive as church lands were confiscated and the new "Anglican" state religion of the 39 Articles was established throughout the realm. However, the civil peace brought by the so-called Elizabethan Settlement was only temporary. On England's northern border was Scotland, a religiously divided kingdom with a Catholic queen, Mary, and a form of radically dissenting Protestantism emerging under John Knox. Mary, in fact, had a strong claim of succession to the throne of England. Her cousin, Elizabeth Tudor, finally eliminated the threat of Mary Stuart by sending her to the block in 1587 after Mary had been forced by a Protestant insurrection to flee from Scotland into England.

But the guerrilla warfare between Anglican, Roman Catholic, Puritan (English Protestants who regarded the Anglican establishment as insufficiently reformed), and Scottish Presbyterian was only forestalled by Elizabeth, not abated. Mary Stuart's son, James VI of Scotland, nominally an Anglican Protestant, acceded to the throne of England as James I in 1603. This began the Stuart dynasty in which the crowns of Scotland and England were united. The attachment of the Stuarts to Roman Catholicism, however, remained so strong as to trouble many Anglicans, and James' sponsorship of an authorized Anglican version of the Bible (the "King James Version") alienated both Puritans and Catholics.

James' son succeeded him in 1625 as Charles I. Charles immediately offended his Protestant subjects by marrying a Roman Catholic—a sister of Louis XIII of France to boot. By this time the House of Commons, and many in the House of Lords, were strongly in sympathy with the Puritans. Charles I staked out a strong position as a defender of the established Anglican Church and through the agency of Archbishop William Laud bore down heavily on Puritans in England and Covenanters (the radical Presbyterians) in Scotland. Significant emigrations of both dissenting Protestants and Catholics to the American colonies took place. Tensions rose in both England and Scotland and the stage was set for the violent revolution. Puritans under Oliver Cromwell and Covenanters under the Duke of Argyll drew their swords against Charles and defeated his forces in crucial battles in 1644 and 1645.

However, the Commonwealth created under Oliver Cromwell had no permanent cure for the religious strife that ravaged seventeenth century Britain. The strict Puritan principles of Cromwell and his followers soon began to bear heavily on Englishmen. In Scotland the victorious Covenanters moved to restore the Stuart dynasty in the form of the second son of the executed King. In 1660 this new Charles was restored (as Charles II) to preside over a strongly Anglican Parliament and a restored episcopacy in England. But again the pendulum swung, and the King's leaning toward Roman Catholicism and relaxing the disabilities of English Catholics gave rise to new Protestant opposition.

Antagonism toward Catholics flared again in response to the lies of the demagogue Titus Oates about a "Popish Plot" to recover England and Scotland for Rome. When Charles II died in 1685 his crypto-Catholic brother ascended the throne peacefully as James II, despite an effort in Parliament to exclude him from the succession. The peace was quickly broken by an uprising led by the Duke of Monmouth. James put down the rebellion bloodily, and the severe reprisals taken sowed the seeds of further intolerance. James was given to autocratic methods and sought to further lighten the civil disabilities imposed by law on English Catholics.

In the so-called Glorious Revolution of 1688, James II was forced to flee to France, and Protestant William of Orange and his Queen Mary acceded to the throne jointly. From this point forward British history was one of developing religious tolerance. But the minds of an entire nation of people had been seared by the religiously motivated conflicts of the seventeenth century. The philosopher, Thomas Hobbes, who had tutored Charles II in his youth and observed with horror the unfolding drama of revolution, regicide, Commonwealth, and counterrevolution, concluded that social peace could only be achieved through separation of the temporal and spiritual authorities.

In his great work of political theory, *Leviathan,* published in 1651, Hobbes rejected the doctrine of the divine right of kings as the basis for the authority of the state. In Hobbes' hard-bitten view, men must create the state by contracting to surrender their natural rights and submit themselves to the authority of the sovereign. Today, most political philosophers recoil from Hobbes' vision of an authoritarian state, but the real importance of his thought lies in Hobbes' sharp break with the past. The past had seen the authority of the state necessarily resting on divine investiture. If governmental authority were derived from God, then every change or nuance of religious doctrine had implications for who should properly hold state power. Religious conflict inevitably begat political revolution. The significant point of Hobbes's vision of the state is not that it was authoritarian, but that is was *secular.*

The importance of this point was underscored toward the end of the religiously riven seventeenth century by John Locke. In his *Two Treatises on Government,* published in 1690, Locke justified the Glorious Revolution of 1688 and further developed the secular or contract theory of the state. For Locke, as for Hobbes, the authority of the state derived not from God but from men agreeing to an implicit social contract for the creation of government. In sharp contrast to Hobbes, however, Locke saw men as able to create a limited state in which the individual would surrender only that increment of liberty necessary to allow the state to protect the lives and property of all.

This notion of a secular state, created by the volition of its subjects, with sufficient power over them to protect one from another while allowing for the retention of substantial personal liberties, is the essence of what became known in the West as *liberalism.* This new liberalism, distinctly a product of sixteenth and seventeenth century religious political turmoil, made rapid gains in the British colonies in North America in the decades preceding the American Revolution.

But what were the implications of liberalism for the relations between religion and the public order? One clear implication suggested toleration of religious diversity by those holding governmental power. But contrary to persistent mythology, little religious tolerance was displayed by the early American colonists. The most extreme example, of course, was Massachusetts Bay, in which the Puritan settlers established something approaching a theocracy with the authorities of church and state intimately intertwined. To the South, conditions were better, but established churches were the rule and the tentative experiments with toleration in Maryland and Pennsylvania were just that. The brightest spot in the colonies was Rhode Island, where, under the leadership of Roger Williams, who earlier had been expelled from Massachusetts Bay for deviating from the Puritan orthodoxy, there was at least a policy of tolerating all Protestant Christian persuasions.

By the beginning of the eighteenth century, however, secularization and toleration (liberalism) had made considerable inroads in the colonies. Even in Massachusetts the instrumentalities of the secular state, the town and the

General Court (the colonial legislature), had assumed a separate existence quite distinct from the Congregationalist establishment. With the coming of the Revolution, the colonial governors were replaced by indigenous, secular, republican regimes in the former colonies, but this was not thought incompatible with the continued existence of established churches. While American republicanism of the revolutionary period clearly rejected any fusing of the authorities of church and state, the use of tax monies to support majority denomination continued to be accepted generally through the eighteenth and into the early nineteenth centuries, as it is accepted today in the United Kingdom.

The kind of separation of church and state implied by the English liberal tradition, as understood by the newly independent Americans, was a separation of the authorities of the state and the church, not the prohibition of supportive arrangements between them. There was, perhaps, a practical tension between the growth of religious toleration and the perpetuation of single state supported denominations in the newly independent colonies. There also was a question of the appropriate posture of the new central government in the matter of religion and the public order. It is against this background that the framing of the religion clauses of the First Amendment of the Constitution to the United States must be understood.

SELECTED READINGS

Gianella, Donald A., ed. *Religion and the Public Order.* These were annual volumes, edited by the late Professor Gianella at his Institute of Church and State of the Villanova University Law School. They were published by the University of Chicago Press for 1963, 1964, and 1965, and are an excellent source of secondary material.

Greene, Evarts B. *Religion and the State: The Making and Testing of an American Tradition* (New York: New York University Press, 1941). Especially helpful on the colonial period. Reprinted in paperback by Great Seal Books (of the Cornell University Press) in 1959.

Howe, Mark DeWolfe. *The Garden and the Wilderness: Religion and Government in American History* (Chicago: University of Chicago Press, 1965). A sensitive exploration of the meanings of the religion clauses by one of the most literate of American constitutional lawyers.

Kurland, Philip B. *Religion and the Law: Of Church and State and the Supreme Court* (Chicago: Aldine, 1962). A lucid analysis of some of the contradictions and difficulties inhering in the Court's exposition of the religion clauses.

Malbin, Michael J. *The Supreme Court and the Definition of Religion* (unpublished doctoral dissertation, Cornell University, 1973). A detailed study of the intent of the framers of religion clauses of the First Amendment.

————. *Religion and Politics: The Intentions of the Authors of the First Amendment* (Washington, D.C.: American Enterprise Institute, 1978). An abbreviated but easily available version of Malbin's larger work.

Morgan, Richard E. *The Supreme Court and Religion* (New York: The Free Press, 1972). A survey of the interpretation by the Court of the religion clauses. Somewhat dated, but still useful.

Pfeffer, Leo. *God, Caesar and the Constitution* (Boston: Beacon Press, 1975). A passionate statement by the leading protagonist of strict separation of church and state.

Stokes, Anson Phelps. *Church and State in the United States,* 3 vols. (New York: Harper, 1950). An excellent scholarly survey of the variegated American tradition in the relationship of religion to the public order.

Stout, Cushing. *The New Heavens and New Earth* (New York: Harper and Row, 1974). Argues that religious development in America reinforced the development of liberal democracy.

Weber, Paul J. and Gilbert, Dennis A. *Private Churches and Public Monies: Church State Fiscal Relations* (Westport, Conn.: Greenwood Press, 1981). A sophisticated study of the complex interrelations of church-related institutions and government in contemporary America.

CHAPTER · 9

GOVERNMENT AND THE CHURCHES—THE PROBLEM OF "ESTABLISHMENT"

" ... CONGRESS shall make no law respecting an establishment of religion, or prohibiting the free exercise thereof." What did the framers of the First Amendment intend by this somewhat opaque language? The Congress was forbidden to make laws "respecting an establishment of religion," but the words are far from self-defining. Only by understanding them in the late eighteenth century American political context, and by analyzing the surviving record of congressional debates and actions leading up to the proposal of the First Amendment, can trustworthy conclusions be reached.

The most reliable work on the framing of the religion clauses has been done by political scientist Michael J. Malbin. Malbin argues that there are three views held by contemporary scholars about the meaning of the establishment clause, and that each of these views claims to be based on the intention of the framers of the First Amendment.

The first interpretation, adopted as we shall see by the Supreme Court of the United States, holds that the establishment clause prohibits not only the establishment of a national church, or laws which discriminate between religious sects, but also prohibits nondiscriminatory cooperative relations between government and the institutional structures of the churches—schools, hospitals, relief agencies, and so on.

A second interpretation of the establishment clause disagrees fundamentally with the historical analysis on which the first interpretation is based. According to this view, the clause is a prohibition only of those forms of governmental aid to religion that discriminate between sects or establish a national church.

The third interpretation, closely related to the second, holds that the establishment clause was designed to secure two purposes: to separate church and state in the sense of precluding the establishment of a national church, and, equally important, to preclude interference by the newly established national government with the existing religious establishments in several of the states.

Malbin's meticulous exposition of the development of the language of the establishment clause in the First Congress reveals a historical foundation that supports both the second and third theories of the meaning of establishment, but not the first. Supporters of the first theory, including the majority of Supreme Court justices who have considered the problem over the years, find historical support for their position not in the actual framing of the First Amendment language in Congress, but rather in the politics of one state, Virginia.

The Declaration of Rights of the Virginia Constitution, adopted in 1776, contains a broad affirmation of the right of free exercise of religious conscience, consistent with the good order of society. During the revolutionary years, required tithes for the support of Anglican clergymen were first suspended and then abolished. In 1784, however, substantial sentiment had developed in the Virginia Assembly, spearheaded by Patrick Henry, to provide state support to churches and to shore up the position of the newly organized Episcopal Church (the successor to the old Anglican establishment). Two bills were introduced: The Incorporation Bill would have accorded special legal status to the Episcopal Church. The General Assessment Bill would have established Christianity as the official religion of the state and assessed citizens for the support of some church or other (if no choice were recorded by a citizen, the assessment went to support seminaries within Virginia).

James Madison opposed both bills and succeeded in getting them postponed to the following year. In the interim Patrick Henry was elected Governor and there were other changes in the membership of the Assembly. In July of 1785, before the Assembly met, Madison drafted his famous *Memorial and Remonstrance.* This was a petition, opposing the establishment of the Christian faith and the assessments for maintenance of churches, which circulated in Virginia receiving hundreds of signatures. When the Assembly was reconvened the Incorporation Bill was passed. But when the General Assessment Bill was taken up, Madison had the votes to defeat it.

It is clear that Madison himself opposed any state support for churches, even on a nondiscriminatory basis. But the meaning of the vote in the Assembly is not as clear. The combination of the Incorporation Bill and the General Assessment Bill may have struck non-Episcopalians (Baptists and Presbyterians) as constituting not a plural establishment, but a de facto establishment of the Episcopal church. This special status of the Episcopal church, and not non-discriminatory aid, may have been what was defeated.

Overall, the important point is that there is ample evidence that other framers of the First Amendment did not share Madison's hostility to nondis-criminatory governmental support of religious institutions. Nor did the struggle for disestablishment in Virginia turn on such hostility. That successive Supreme Court majorities since 1947 have adopted a Madisonian position led the distinguished constitutional lawyer Mark DeWolf Howe, of the Harvard Law School, to conclude that "the Supreme Court has gone astray in its interpretations of American history."

In the cases that follow, you will see the evolution of the Court's strict separationist position with reference to the participation of church-related schools in various programs of general educational enrichment.

Everson v. *Board of Education*
330 U.S 1, 67 S.Ct. 504, 91 L.Ed. 711 (1947)

Everson was the beginning of the contemporary constitutional conflict over the meaning of the establishment clause. Through most of our national history, the strictures of the First Amendment had not been understood to apply to the states, and the national government had not been involved in the kind of activities (education, health services, and so on) that would involve it in cooperative relations with the churches. In *Everson* the majority assumed the religious clauses applied to the states. The facts were simple. A 1941 New Jersey statute authorized towns to reimburse the cost of transportation of children to school on regularly scheduled buses. The towns could decide for themselves whether to include children attending church related schools in this program. Ewing did include them and was challenged by a plaintiff, who was ultimately supported by *amicis* briefs from the ACLU and Americans United. Note that Justice Black's opinion for the Court divides sharply into two parts. The first part announces a theory of strict separation between church and state; the second part sets forth Black's view of the facts in *Everson*. The dissents were all from Black's construction of the facts of *Everson*. There was no dissent from the theory at that time. The next year, in *McCollum* v. *Board of Education*, 333 U.S. 203 (1948), Justice Reed did repudiate the strict separationist theory, but this gets ahead of our story.

Mr. Justice Black delivered the opinion of the Court.

A New Jersey statute authorizes its local school districts to make rules and contracts for the transportation of children to and from schools. The appellee, a township board of education, acting pursuant to this statute authorized reimbursement to parents of money expended by them for the bus transportation system. Part of this money was for the payment of transportation of some children in the community to Catholic parochial schools, . . .

. . . .

The New Jersey statute is challenged as a "law respecting an establishment of religion." The First Amendment, as made applicable to the states by the Fourteenth, . . . commands that a state "shall make no law respecting an establishment of religion, or prohibiting the free exercise thereof." . . . Whether this New Jersey law is one respecting the "establishment of religion" requires an understanding of the meaning of that language, particularly with respect to the imposition of taxes. . . .

. . . .

The "establishment of religion" clause of the First Amendment means at least this: Neither a state nor the Federal Government can set up a church. Neither can pass laws which aid one religion, aid all religions, or prefer one religion over another. Neither can force nor influence a person to go to or to remain away from church against his will or force him to profess a belief or disbelief in any religion. No person can be punished for entertaining or professing religious beliefs or disbeliefs, for church attendance or nonattendance. No tax in any amount, large or small, can be levied to support any religious activities or institutions, whatever they may be called, or whatever form they may adopt to teach or practice religion. Neither a state nor the Federal Government can, openly or secretly, participate in the affairs of any religious organizations or groups and vice versa. In the words of Jefferson, the clause against establishment of religion by law was intended to erect "a wall of separation between Church and State. . . . "

We must consider the New Jersey statute in accordance with the foregoing limitations imposed by the First Amendment. But we must not strike that state statute down if it is within the state's constitutional power even though it approaches the verge of that power. . . . New Jersey cannot consistently with the "establishment of religion" clause of the First Amendment contribute tax-raised funds to the support of an institution which teaches the tenets and faith of any church. On the other hand, other language of the amendment commands that New Jersey cannot hamper its citizens in the free exercise of their own religion. Consequently, it cannot exclude individual Catholics, Lutherans, Mohammedans, Baptists, Jews, Methodists, Non-believers, Presbyterians, or the members of any other faith, *because of their faith, or lack of it,* from receiving the benefits of public welfare legislation. While we do not mean to intimate that a state could not provide transportation only to children attending public schools, we must be careful, in protecting the citizens of New Jersey against state-established churches, to be sure that we do not inadvertently prohibit New Jersey from extending its general State law benefits to all its citizens without regard to their religious belief.

Measured by these standards, we cannot say that the First Amendment prohibits New Jersey from spending tax-raised funds to pay the bus fares of parochial school pupils as a part of a general program under which it pays the fares of pupils attending public and other schools. It is undoubtedly true that children are helped to get to church schools. There is even a possibility that some of the children might not be sent to the church schools if the parents were compelled to pay their children's bus fares out of their own pockets when transportation to a public school would have been paid for by the State. The same possibility exists where the state requires a local transit company to provide reduced fares to school children including those attending parochial schools, or where a municipally owned transportation system undertakes to carry all school children free of charge. Moreover, state-paid policemen, detailed to protect children going to and from church schools from the very real hazards of traffic, would serve much the same purpose and accomplish much the same result as state provisions intended to guarantee free transportation of a kind which the state deems to be best for the school children's welfare. And parents might refuse to risk their children to the serious danger of traffic accidents going to and from parochial schools, the approaches to which were not protected by policemen. Similarly, parents might be reluctant to permit their children to attend schools which the state had cut off from such general government services as ordinary police and fire protection, connections for sewage disposal, public highways and sidewalks. Of course, cutting off church schools from these services, so separate and so indisputably marked off from the religious function, would make it far more difficult for the schools to operate. But such is obviously not the purpose of the First Amendment. That Amendment requires the state to be a neutral in its relations with groups of religious believers and non-believers; it does not require the state to be their adversary. State power is no more to be used so as to handicap religions, than it is to favor them. . . .

. . . .

The First Amendment has erected a wall between church and state. That wall must be kept high and impregnable. We could not approve the slightest breach. New Jersey has not breached it here

Affirmed.

Mr. Justice Jackson [with whom Mr. Justice Frankfurter joined], dissenting.

The Court's opinion marshals every argument in favor of state aid and puts the case in its most favorable light, but much of its reasoning confirms my conclusions that there are no good grounds upon which to support the present legislation. In fact, the undertones of the opinion, advocating complete and un-compromising separation of Church from State, seem utterly discordant with its conclusion yielding support to their commingling in educational matters. The case which irresistibly comes to mind as the most fitting precedent is that of Julia who, according to Byron's reports, "whispering 'I will ne'er consent,'—consented." . . .

Mr. Justice Rutledge, with whom Mr. Justice Frankfurter, Mr. Justice Jackson and Mr. Justice Burton, agree, dissenting.

This case forces us to determine squarely for the first time what was "an establishment of religion" in the First Amendment's conception; and by that measure to decide whether New Jersey's action violates its command. . . .

The Amendment's purpose was not to strike merely at the official establishment of a single sect, creed or religion, outlawing only a formal relation such as had prevailed in England and some of the colonies. Necessarily it was to uproot all such relationships. But the object was broader than separating church and state in this narrow sense. It was to create a complete and permanent separation of the spheres of religious activity and civil authority by comprehensively forbidding every form of public aid or support for religion. . . .

Does New Jersey's action furnish support for religion by use of the taxing power? Certainly it does, if the test remains undiluted as Jefferson and Madison made it, that money taken by taxation from one is not to be used or given to support another's religious training or belief, or indeed one's own. . . .

The judgment should be reversed.

Board of Education v. Allen
392 U.S. 236, 88 S.Ct. 1923, 20 L.Ed.2d. 1060 (1968)

By the mid-1960s politicians in a number of states with large parochial school systems were casting about for ways of aiding this increasingly straited sector. Governor Nelson A. Rockefeller took the lead in securing passage by the New York legislature in 1965 of a bill requiring local school boards to furnish textbooks from the state-approved lists to all nonprofit private schools in their districts. The books, technically, remained the property of the public school district, but once "loaned," they remained in the private schools until written off for fair wear and tear. The New York Civil Liberties Union took the lead in seeking a court challenge to the program. The plaintiff was a school board seeking to enjoin the New York Commissioner of Education from requiring it to participate in the program. A group of Catholic parents intervened to support the program, and they were represented by Porter Chandler of Davis, Polk—a prestigious Wall Street law firm that had a way of turning up in church-state cases in which the Roman Catholic Archdiocese of New York had an interest. New York courts upheld the textbook arrangement, and in that configuration the matter came to the U.S. Supreme Court.

Mr. Justice White delivered the opinion of the Court.

A law of the State of New York requires local public school authorities to lend textbooks free of charge to all students in grades seven through 12; students attending private schools are included. This case presents the question whether this statute is a "law respecting the establishment of religion or prohibiting the free exercise thereof," and so in conflict with the First and Fourteenth Amendments to the Constitution, because it authorizes the loan of textbooks to students attending parochial schools. We hold that the law is not in violation of the Constitution. . . .

Everson v. *Board of Education*, 330 U.S. 1 (1947), is the case decided by this Court that is most nearly in point for today's problem. . . . As with public provision of police and fire protection, sewage facilities, and streets and sidewalks, payment of bus fares was of some value to the religious school, but was nevertheless not such support of a religious institution as to be a prohibited establishment of religion within the meaning of the First Amendment.

Everson and later cases have shown that the line between state neutrality to religion and state support of religion is not easy to locate. "The constitutional standard is the separation of Church and State. The problem, like many problems in constitutional law, is one of degree.". . . *Abington School District* v. *Schempp*, 374 U.S. 203 (1963), fashioned a test ascribed to by eight Justices for distinguishing between forbidden involvements of the State with religion and those contacts which the Establishment Clause permits:"The test may be stated as follows: what are the purpose and the primary effect of the enactment? If either is the advancement or inhibition of religion then the enactment exceeds the scope of legislative power as circumscribed by the Constitution. That is to say that to withstand the strictures of the Establishment Clause there must be a secular legislative purpose and a primary effect that neither advances nor inhibits religion. *Everson* v. *Board of Education*." ...

This test is not easy to apply, but the citation of *Everson* by the *Schempp* Court to support its general standard made clear how the *Schempp* rule would be applied to the facts of *Everson*. The statute upheld in *Everson* would be considered a law having "a secular legislative purpose and a primary effect that neither advances nor inhibits religion." We reach the same result with respect to the New York law requiring school books to be loaned free of charge to all students in specified grades. ...

Of course books are different from buses. Most bus rides have no inherent religious significance, while religious books are common. However, [the New York law] does not authorize the loan of religious books, and the State claims no right to distribute religious literature. Although the books loaned are those required by the parochial school for use in specific courses, each book loaned must be approved by the public school authorities; only secular books may receive approval. The law was construed by the Court of Appeals of New York as "merely making available secular textbooks at the request of the individual student," and the record contains no suggestion that religious books have been loaned. Absent evidence we cannot assume that school authorities, who constantly face the same problem in selecting textbooks for use in the public schools, are unable to distinguish between secular and religious books or that they will not honestly discharge their duties under the law. In judging the validity of the statute on this record we must proceed on the assumption that books loaned to students are books that are not unsuitable for use in the public schools because of religious content. ...

....

Underlying these cases, and underlying also the legislative judgments that have preceded the court decisions, has been a recognition that private education has played and is playing a significant and valuable role in raising national levels of knowledge, competence, and experience. Americans care about the quality of the secular education available to their children. ... Considering this attitude, the continued willingness to rely on private school systems, including parochial systems, strongly suggests that a wide segment of informed opinion, legislative and otherwise, has found that those schools do an acceptable job of providing secular education to their students. This judgment is further evidence that parochial schools are performing, in addition to their sectarian function, the task of secular education.

Against this background of judgment and experience, unchallenged in the meager record before us in this case, we cannot agree with appellants either that all teaching in a sectarian school is religious or that the processes of secular and religious training are so intertwined that secular textbooks furnished to students by the public are in fact instrumental in the teaching of religion.

The judgment is affirmed.

Mr. Justice Harlan, concurring.

Although I join the opinion and judgment of the Court, I wish to emphasize certain of the principles which I believe to be central to the determination of this case, and which I think are implicit in the Court's decision. ... I would hold that where the contested governmental activity is calculated to achieve nonreligious purposes otherwise within the competence of the State, and where the activity does not involve the State "so significantly and directly in the realm of the sectarian as to give rise to . . . divisive influences and inhibitions of freedom," it is not forbidden by the religious clauses of the First Amendment.

In my opinion, [the contested provision] of the Education Law of New York does not employ religion as its standard for action or inaction, and is not otherwise inconsistent with these principles.

Mr. Justice Black, dissenting.

[Everson] plainly interpret[s] the First and Fourteenth Amendments as protecting the taxpayers of a State from being compelled to pay taxes to their government to support the agencies of private religious organizations the taxpayers oppose. To authorize a State to tax its residents for such church purposes is to put the State squarely in the religious activities of certain religious groups that happen to be strong enough politically to write their own religious preferences and prejudices into the laws. This links state and churches together in controlling the lives and destinies of our citizenship—a citizenship composed of people of myriad religious faiths, some of them bitterly hostile to and completely intolerant of the others. It was to escape laws precisely like this that a large part of the Nation's early immigrants fled to this country. It was also to escape such laws and such consequences that the First Amendment was written in language strong and clear barring passage of any law "respecting establishment of religion." . . .

Mr. Justice Douglas, dissenting.

The statute on its face empowers each parochial school to determine for itself which textbooks will be eligible for loans to its students, for the Act provides that the only text which the State may provide is "a book which a pupil is required to use as a text for a semester or more in a particular class in the school he legally attends." . . . This initial and crucial selection is undoubtedly made by the parochial school's principal or its individual instructors, who are, in the case of Roman Catholic schools, normally priests or nuns. . . .

The role of the local public school board is to decide whether to veto the selection made by the parochial school. This is done by determining first whether the text has been or should be "approved" for use in public schools and second whether the text is "secular," "non-religious," or "non-sectarian." The local boards apparently have broad discretion in exercising this veto power.

Thus the statutory system provides that the parochial school will ask for the books that it wants. Can there be the slightest doubt that the head of the parochial school will select the book or books that best promote its sectarian creed?

If the board of education supinely submits by approving and supplying the sectarian or sectarian-oriented textbooks, the struggle to keep church and state separate has been lost. If the board resists, then the battleline between church and state will have been drawn and the contest will be on to keep the school board independent or to put it under church domination and control.

Mr. Justice Fortas, dissenting.

. . . .

This case is not within the principle of *Everson* v. *Board of Education*, 330 U.S. 1 (1947). Apart from the differences between textbooks and bus rides, the present statute does not call for extending to children attending sectarian schools the same service or facility extended to children in public schools. This statute calls for furnishing special, separate, and particular books, specially, separately, and particularly chosen by religious sects or their representatives for use in their sectarian schools. This is the infirmity, in my opinion. This is the feature that makes it impossible, in my view, to reach any conclusion other than that this statute is an unconstitutional use of public funds to support an establishment of religion. . . .

Lemon v. Kurtzman
403 U.S. 602, 91 S.Ct. 2105, 29 L.Ed.2d. 745 (1971)

The decision in *Allen* encouraged and emboldened those who favored accommodation between government and the church-related schools. Following what they thought was the lead of Justice White's opinion, legislatures in several states enacted "purchase of service" programs. These were efforts to support the salaries of teachers in secular subjects in independent schools (most of which were church-related). *Lemon* involved Pennsylvania's program. It was decided along with *Robinson* v. *Di Censo,* which involved a similar Rhode Island program. Instructional budgets—teachers' salaries—grew rapidly during the 1960s and were the most acute of the financial difficulties besetting parochial schools. But the Court's answer this time was a ringing "no." Only Justice White, the author of *Allen,* evinced some willingness to accept the purchase of service concept. He would have sustained the Rhode Island program against the attack that it was unconstitutional on its face and concurred in the result in *Lemon* only on technical grounds. Decided on the same day as *Lemon,* however, was *Tilton* v. *Richardson,* 403 U.S. 672 (1971), in which the Court approved aid for church-related colleges and universities, which it would not allow for elementary and secondary schools. Chief Justice Burger, the author of *Lemon,* concluded in *Tilton* that college students were more mature and less open to proselytizing than their juniors.

Mr. Chief Justice Burger delivered the opinion of the Court.

These two appeals raise questions as to Pennsylvania and Rhode Island statutes providing state aid to church-related elementary and secondary schools. . . .

The Rhode Island Salary Supplement Act [of 1969] . . . authorizes state officials to supplement the salaries of teachers of secular subjects in nonpublic elementary schools by paying directly to a teacher an amount not in excess of 15% of his current annual salary. As supplemented, however, a nonpublic school teacher's salary cannot exceed the maximum paid to teachers in the State's public schools, and the recipient must be certified by the state board of education in substantially the same manner as public school teachers. . . .

. . . .

The Act also requires that teachers eligible for salary supplement must teach only those subjects that are offered in the State's public schools. They must use "only teaching materials which are used in the public schools." Finally, any teacher applying for a salary supplement must first agree in writing "not to teach a course in religion for so long as or during such time as he or she receives any salary supplements" under the Act. . . .

. . . .

. . . The Pennsylvania Nonpublic Elementary and Secondary Education Act was passed in 1968 in response to a crisis that the Pennsylvania legislature found existed in the State's nonpublic schools due to rapidly rising costs. The statute affirmatively reflects the legislative conclusion that the State's educational goals could appropriately be fulfilled by government support of "those purely secular educational objectives achieved through nonpublic education. . . ."

The statute authorizes appellee state Superintendent of Public Instruction to "purchase" specified "secular educational services" from nonpublic schools. Under the "contracts" authorized by the statute, the State directly reimburses nonpublic schools solely for their actual expenditures for teachers' salaries, textbooks, and instructional materials. A school seeking reimbursement must maintain prescribed accounting procedures that identify the "separate" cost of the "secular educational service." These accounts are subject to state audit. . . .

There are several significant statutory restrictions on state aid. Reimbursement is limited to courses "presented in the curricula of the public schools." It is further limited "solely" to courses in the following "secular" subjects: mathematics, modern foreign languages, physical science, and physical education. Textbooks and instructional materials included in the program must be approved by the state Superintendent of Public Instruction. Finally, the statute prohibits reimbursement for any course that contains "any subject matter expressing religious teaching, or the morals or forms of worship of any sect." . . .

Our prior holdings do not call for total separation between church and state; total separation is not possible in an absolute sense. Some relationship between government and religious organizations is inevitable. . . .

In order to determine whether the government entanglement with religion is excessive, we must examine the character and purposes of the institutions which are benefited, the nature of the aid that the State provides, and the resulting relationship between the government and the religious authority. . . . Here we find that both statutes foster an impermissible degree of entanglement. . . .

. . . .

In *Allen* the Court refused to make assumptions, on a meager record, about the religious content of the textbooks that the State would be asked to provide. We cannot, however, refuse here to recognize that teachers have a substantially different ideological character than books. In terms of potential for involving some aspect of faith or morals in secular subjects, a textbook's content is ascertainable, but a teacher's handling of a subject is not. We cannot ignore the dangers that a teacher under religious control and discipline poses to the separation of the religious from the purely secular aspects of precollege education. The conflict of functions inheres in the situation. . . .

. . . .

We need not and do not assume that teachers in parochial schools will be guilty of bad faith or any conscious design to evade the limitations imposed by the statute and the First Amendment. We simply recognize that a dedicated religious person, teaching in a school affiliated with his or her faith and operated to inculcate its tenets, will inevitably experience great difficulty in remaining religiously neutral. Doctrines and faith are not inculcated or advanced by neutrals. . . .

A broader base of entanglement of yet a different character is presented by the divisive political potential of these state programs. In a community where such a large number of pupils are served by church-related schools, it can be assumed that state assistance will entail considerable political activity. Partisans of parochial schools, understandably concerned with rising costs and sincerely dedicated to both the religious and secular educational missions of their schools, will inevitably champion this cause and promote political action to achieve their goals. Those who oppose state aid, whether for constitutional, religious, or fiscal reasons, will inevitably respond and employ all of the usual political campaign techniques to prevail. Candidates will be forced to declare and voters to choose. It would be unrealistic to ignore the fact that many people confronted with issues of this kind will find their votes aligned with their faith.

Ordinarily political debate and division, however vigorous or even partisan, are normal and healthy manifestations of our democratric system of government, but political division along religious lines was one of the principal evils against which the First Amendment was intended to protect. Freund, *Comment: Public Aid to Parochial Schools*, 82 Harv.L.Rev. 1680, 1692 (1969). The potential divisiveness of such conflict is a threat to the normal political process. . . . It conflicts with our whole history and tradition to permit questions of the Religion Clauses to assume such importance in our legislatures and in our elections that they could divert attention from the myriad issues and problems which confront every level of government. . . .

The decision of the Rhode Island District Court in [*DiCenso*] is affirmed. The decision of the Pennsylvania District Court in [*Lemon*] is reversed, and the case is remanded for further proceedings consistent with this opinion.

Mr. Justice Douglas, whom Mr. Justice Black joins, concurring.

A history class, a literature class, a science class in a parochial school is not a separate institute; it is part of the organic whole which the State subsidizes. The funds are used in these cases to pay or help pay the salaries of teachers in parochial schools; and the presence of teachers is critical to the essential purpose of the parochial school, viz. to advance the religious endeavors of the particular church. It matters not that the teacher receiving taxpayers' money only teaches religion a fraction of the time. Nor does it matter that he or she teaches no religion. The school is an organism living on one budget. What the taxpayers give for salaries of those who teach only the humanities or science without any trace of proselytizing enables the school to use all of its own funds for religious training. . . .

In my view the taxpayers' forced contribution to the parochial schools in the present cases violates the First Amendment.

Mr. Justice Marshall took no part in the consideration or decision of [*Lemon*]. . . . He concurs in Mr. Justice Douglas' opinion covering [*DiCenso*].

[Separate opinions of Justices White and Brennan in *Tilton* apply as well to the Pennsylvania and Rhode Island cases.]

Committee for Public Education and Religious Liberty v. *Regan*
444 U.S. 646, 100 S.Ct. 840, 63 L.Ed.2d 94 (1980)

Committee v. *Regan* is one of a series of cases decided since *Lemon* in which the Court has wrestled with the question of aid to church-related schools. If textbooks are acceptable and salary supplements are not, what about other things? In *Levitt* v. *Committee for Public Education,* 413 U.S. 472 (1972), the Court struck down state reimbursement of private schools for the cost of preparing, administering, and scoring certain teacher-prepared tests necessary to determine whether students would be advanced in grade. Considering a Pennsylvania statute in *Meek* v. *Pittinger,* 421 U.S. 349 (1975), a badly divided Court upheld textbooks laws (again), but disallowed loans of instructional materials and equipment, such as tapes and films. Also disallowed were certain "auxiliary services"—counseling, speech therapy, and so on— which were to be made available on private school premises. In 1977, considering an Ohio statute in *Wolman* v. *Walter,* 433 U.S. 229, the Court again sustained books and disallowed instructional materials and equipment. On auxiliary services, however, those of a diagnostic nature could be provided on private school premises; remedial and therapeutic services could be provided, but only off private school premises—say, by mobile units. Also approved was the provision of standardized tests used in public schools with no private school teachers involved in drafting or scoring. Finally, in *Regan* the Court was faced with reimbursement of expenses for *administering* and *scoring* state-required standardized tests. This was allowed despite the best efforts of Leo Pfeffer for the "Committee," which was actually a coalition of interest groups favoring strict separation. In *Lemon* v. *Kurtzman* Chief Justice Burger referred to the line between permissible and impermissible aid to church-related schools as a "blurred, indistinct, and variable barrier." That "barrier" now twists between books and filmstrips and between teacher prepared tests and standardized tests.

Mr. Justice White delivered the opinion of the Court.

The issue in this case is the constitutionality [of] a New York statute authorizing the use of public funds to reimburse church-sponsored and secular nonpublic schools for performing various testing and reporting services mandated by state law. The District Court sustained the statute.

In 1970 the New York Legislature appropriated public funds to reimburse both church-sponsored and secular nonpublic schools for performing various services mandated by the State. The most expensive of these services was the "administration, grading and the compiling and reporting of the results of tests and examinations." Covered tests included both state-prepared examinations and the more common and traditional teacher-prepared tests. Although the legislature stipulated that "[n]othing contained in this act shall be construed to authorize the making of any payment [for] religious worship or instruction," the statute did not provide for any state audit of school financial records that would ensure that public funds were used only for secular purposes. In *Levitt* v. *Committee for Public Education* ... the Court struck down this enactment as violative of the Establishment Clause. The majority focused its concern on the statute's reimbursement of funds spent by schools on traditional teacher-prepared tests. The Court was troubled that, "despite the obviously integral role of such testing in the total teaching process, no attempt is made under the statute, and no means are available, to assure that internally prepared tests are free of religious instruction." It was not assumed that nonpublic school teachers would attempt in bad faith to evade constitutional requirements. Rather, the Court simply observed that "the potential for conflict 'inheres in the situation,' and because of that the State is constitutionally compelled to assure that the state-supported activity is not being used for religious indoctrination." Because the State failed to provide the required assurance, the challenged statute was deemed to constitute an impermissible aid to religion. ...

Almost immediately the New York Legislature attempted to eliminate these defects from its statutory scheme. A new statute was enacted in 1974, and it directed New York's Commissioner of Education to apportion and to pay to nonpublic schools the actual costs incurred as a result of compliance with certain state-mandated requirements, including "the requirements of the state's pupil evaluation program, the basic educational data system, regents examinations, the statewide evaluation plan, the uniform procedure for pupil attendance reporting, and other similar state prepared examinations and reporting procedures." Of signal interest and importance in light of *Levitt*, the new scheme does not reimburse nonpublic schools for the preparation, administration, or grading of teacher-prepared tests. Further, the 1974 statute, unlike the 1970 version struck down in Levitt, provides a means by which payments of state funds are audited, thus ensuring that only the actual costs incurred in providing the covered secular services are reimbursed out of state funds. ...

   . . . .

The New York statute ... provides for direct cash reimbursement to the nonpublic school for administering the state-prescribed examinations and for grading two of them. We agree with the District Court that such reimbursement does not invalidate the New York statute. If the State furnished state-prepared tests, thereby relieving the nonpublic schools of the expense of preparing their own examinations, but left the grading of the tests to the schools, and if the grading procedures could be used to further the religious mission of the school, serious Establishment Clause problems would be posed under the Court's cases, for by furnishing the tests it might be concluded that the State was directly aiding religious education. But as we have already concluded, grading the secular tests furnished by the State in this case is a function that has a secular purpose and primarily a secular effect. This conclusion is not changed simply because the State pays the school for performing the grading function. As the District Court observed, "[p]utting aside the question of whether direct financial aid can be administered without excessive entanglement by the State in the affairs of a sectarian institution, there does not appear to be any reason why payments to sectarian schools to cover the cost of specified activities would have the impermissible effect of advancing religion if the same activities performed by sectarian school personnel without reimbursement but with State-furnished materials have no such effect."

A contrary view would insist on drawing a constitutional distinction between paying the nonpublic school to do the grading and paying state employees or some independent service to perform that task, even though the grading function is the same regardless of who performs it and would not have the primary effect of aiding religion whether or not performed by nonpublic school personnel. In either event, the nonpublic school is being relieved of the cost of grading state-required, state-furnished examinations. We decline to embrace a formalistic dichotomy that bears so little relationship either to common sense or to the realities of school finance. . . .

This is not to say that this case, any more than past cases, will furnish a litmus-paper test to distinguish permissible from impermissible aid to religiously oriented schools. But Establishment Clause cases are not easy; they stir deep feelings; and we are divided among ourselves, perhaps reflecting the different views on this subject of the people of this country. What is certain is that our decisions have tended to avoid categorical imperatives and absolutist approaches at either end of the range of possible outcomes. This course sacrifices clarity and predictability for flexibility, but this promises to be the case until the continuing interaction between the courts and the States—the former charged with interpreting and upholding the Constitution and the latter seeking to provide education for their youth—produces a single, more encompassing construction of the Establishment Clause.

The judgment of the District Court is

Affirmed.

Mr. Justice Blackmun, with whom Mr. Justice Brennan and Mr. Justice Marshall join, dissenting.

The Court in this case, I fear, takes a long step backwards in the inevitable controversy that emerges when a state legislature continues to insist on providing public aid to parochial schools.

I thought that the Court's judgments in *Meek* v. *Pittenger* and in *Wolman* v. *Walter* . . . at last had fixed the line betweeen that which is constitutionally appropriate public aid and that which is not. The line necessarily was not a straight one. It could not be, when this Court, on the one hand, in *Everson* v. *Board of Education,* . . . by a 5-4 vote, decided that there was no barrier under the First and Fourteenth Amendments to parental reimbursement of the cost of fares for the transportation of children attending parochial schools, and in *Board of Education* v. *Allen,* . . . by a 6-3 vote, ruled that New York's lending of approved textbooks to students in private secondary schools was not violative of those Amendments, and yet, on the other hand, in *Lemon* v. *Kurtzman* . . . struck down, as violative of the Religion Clauses, statutes that, respectively, would have supplemented nonpublic school teachers' salaries and would have authorized the "purchase" of certain "secular educational services" from nonpublic schools, and also in *Levitt* v. *Committee for Public Education,* ... struck down New York's previous attempt to reimburse nonpublic schools for the expenses of tests and examinations. ...

But, I repeat, the line, wavering though it may be, was indeed drawn in *Meek* and in *Wolman,* albeit with different combinations of Justices, those who perceive no barrier under the First and Fourteenth Amendments and who would rule in favor of almost any aid a state legislature saw fit to provide, on the one hand, and those who perceive a broad barrier and would rule against aid of almost any kind, on the other hand, in turn joining Justices in the center on these issues, to make order and a consensus out of the earlier decisions. Now, some of those who joined in *Lemon, Levitt, Meek,* and *Wolman* in invalidating, depart and validate. I am able to attribute this defection only to a concern about the continuing and emotional controversy and to a persuasion that a good-faith attempt on the part of a state legislature is worth a nod of approval. ...

Mr. Justice Stevens, dissenting.

Although I agree with Mr. Justice Blackmun's demonstration of why today's holding is not compelled by precedent, my vote also rests on a more fundamental disagreement with the Court. The Court's approval of a direct subsidy to sectarian schools to reimburse them for staff time spent in taking attendance and grading standardized tests is but another in a long line of cases making largely ad hoc decisions about what payments may or may not be constitutionally made to nonpublic schools. In groping for a rationale to support today's decision, the Court has taken a position that could equally be used to support a subsidy to pay for staff time attributable to conducting fire drills or even for constructing and maintaining fireproof premises in which to conduct classes. Though such subsidies might represent expedient fiscal policy, I firmly believe they would violate the Establishment Clause of the First Amendment.

The Court's adoption of such a position confirms my view, expressed in *Wolman* v. *Walter* ... that the entire enterprise of trying to justify various types of subsidies to nonpublic schools should be abandoned. Rather than continuing with the sisyphean task of trying to patch together the "blurred, indistinct, and variable barrier" described in *Lemon* v. *Kurtzman,* ... I would resurrect the "high and impregnable" wall between church and state constructed by the Framers of the First Amendment. See *Everson* v. *Board of Education."* ...

CASE STUDY: SENATOR MOYNIHAN AGAINST THE COURT

Finding constitutional ways of aiding private schools, including church-related schools, has been an issue at the national as well as the state level. In 1968 and 1972, Richard Nixon included pledges of concern for parochial schools in his campaigns, and in 1980 Ronald Reagan promised, if elected, to introduce legislation providing federal income tax credits for parents paying private school tuitions for their children.

Indeed, the device of the tax credit has been the favored approach in Washington among those seeking to help private schools. In both the 96th and 97th Congresses (1976–1982), Senators Daniel Patrick Moynihan, Democrat of New York, and Bob Packwood, Republican of Oregon, proposed a "Tuition Tax Relief Act." This legislation sought to support the "diversity and pluralism that constitute important strengths of education in America" by a credit against federal taxes owed of up to $1,000 per year for tuition paid during the taxable year.

The Moynihan-Packwood proposal had difficulty attracting support on Capitol Hill, in part because of doubts about its constitutionality. In a post-*Lemon* case, the Supreme Court already had ruled against aid to private schools involving state income tax relief. In *Committee for Public Education* v. *Nyquist,* 413 U.S. 756 (1973), the justices considered a New York program that included tax credits for parochial school tuitions. The Chief Justice, Justice White, and Justice Rehnquist would have approved this on the grounds that it was aid to individuals and only indirectly aid to the schools. But Justice Powell, for the majority, held the credits would have "the effect of advancing religion" and thus were banned by the establishment clause.

Moynihan and Packwood continued to believe the Court was wrong, and that a clear expression of congressional sentiment to that effect (plus, perhaps, some new justices), would lead the Court to change its collective mind. Their bill in the 97th Congress, S.550, declared that while "the Congress recognizes that the Supreme Court is ultimately responsible for determining the constitutionality of provisions of law, the Congress finds that this assistance can appropriately be provided through the income tax structure. . . . " And in the fall, 1979, in an issue of the neo-conservative journal, *The Public Interest,* Senator Moynihan published an article titled "What Do You Do When the Supreme Court is Wrong?"

The Senator, a former Harvard Professor of Government, quarreled not just with *Nyquist,* but identified the roots of the Court's "error" in *Everson* and the efforts of groups such as the ACLU and Americans for Democratic Action "to maintain the *Everson* doctrine in as strict a form as possible." The result "has been an intellectual shambles: one confused and convoluted decision requiring a yet more confused and convoluted explanation or modification." *Debate, litigate,* and *legislate* was Moynihan's answer to the question posed in his article.

On April 15, 1982, Moynihan, Packwood, and their supporters received some heavyweight help in their effort to legislate. President Reagan, keeping his campaign commitment, sent to the Hill legislation providing tax credits for private elementary and secondary school tuitions. But it was too late for the 97th Congress. A conflict was raging over budget deficits and the administration was about to stake its prestige on a measure to *increase* tax revenues. As Senator Packwood put it, "the administration has waited so long to make its intentions known that it may prove to be impossible for this Congress to deal with this issue."

In the spring of 1983, however, the campaign to find some constitutional way of aiding church-related schools received its most important boost. On April 18, the Supreme court decided *Mueller* v. *Allen,* an establishment-clause challenge to a Minnesota program whereby parents could take state income tax deductions for certain expenses incurred in educating their children. Among the allowable items were books and materials, transportation, and *tuition* up to specified limits. These deductions were available whether the children attended public or private schools—including church-related institutions. Justice Rehnquist, speaking for a Court divided 5-4, upheld Minnesota. He distinguished *Mueller* from *Committee* v. *Nyquist* on the grounds that in the New York program the aid had gone only to private-school parents; also, since the deductions were a function of actual expenditures, as opposed to tax credits, they were a more attenuated form of benefit to church-related schools. As might be expected, dissent was sharp, with Justice Marshall, writing for Brennan, Blackmun, and Stevens, arguing that there were no differences between the *Mueller* and *Nyquist* situations sufficient to distinguish the cases. Among politicians, as the presidential campaign gathered momentum, the hopefuls again began to sort themselves out on the issue of aid to independent schools. Democratic candidate Ernest F. "Fritz" Hollings, of South Carolina, took the first clear position in opposition to tax relief for private school parents, declaring that "the public school teaches the American way as no other school can teach it." And on November 16, 1983, the Senate defeated President Reagan's tax credit proposal. Whether Senator Moynihan and his supporters in Congress can take advantage of the *Mueller* decision in a future Congress will depend very much on the 1984 presidential outcome.

CHAPTER · 10

CONFLICTS OVER CRÈCHES— THE PROBLEM OF CIVIL RELIGION

IN Chapter 9 we examined the ways in which the Supreme Court's interpretation of the establishment clause of the First Amendment bore on the problem of government aid to church-related schools. In this chapter we shall see that the Court's interpretation of the same clause is crucial to another continuing controversy—the dispute over religious invocations, references, and imagery as part of public ceremonies, especially as part of the ritual of the public schools.

Are nondenominational invocations of the Diety, when made as part of public ceremonies, acts "respecting an establishment of religion" forbidden to the national government by the First Amendment and to the states by the due process clause of the Fourteenth? On this question there is little evidence as to the intention of the framers. The records of the First Congress tell us much more about the "establishment" language than what was meant by "free exercise." There is, however, a rich record of traditional practice that may not be irrelevant to the question of the framers' intent. Invocations of the Diety were part of the ritual of the Congress which proposed the "free exercise" language, and the state legislatures which ratified it. Writing about the state constitutions (all of which included guarantees of religious liberty), Thomas N. Cooley noted in his influential *Constitutional Limitations* that "while . . . careful to establish, protect, and defend religious freedom and equality, the American constitutions contain no provisions which prohibit the authorities from such solemn recognition of a superintending Providence in public transactions and exercises as the general religious sentiment of mankind inspires." This is a fair portrayal of the general state of informed American opinion not only in 1790–91, but right through the nineteenth century. Until the middle of the twentieth century, in fact, deference to a kind of "civil religion" was part of the ritual of public ceremony in America.

This was a very broad, watered down Protestant Christianity which, while it undoubtedly discomfited Jews and some Roman Catholics, enjoyed wide popular support.

Against this background it is difficult to argue that it was the intention of the framers of the free exercise clause to extirpate religious observances and references from the ceremonial life of the nation.

It is certainly true that in their personal views (as distinct from what they could persuade the national Congress and the Virginia Assembly to endorse) both Madison and Jefferson regarded governmental religious references and ceremonies as suspect. The very phrase "separation of church and state," so often thought to be part of the Constitution, was given currency by Thomas Jefferson in 1802. As President, Jefferson refused to issue the Thanksgiving Day proclamation that had become routine under his predecessors (and would become routine again under his successors). The President was applauded for this initiative by the Baptist Association of Danbury, Connecticut, which, as a result of their experience as a persecuted minority sect in some of the former colonies, developed a theory of strict separation. In his letter to Baptists responding to their congratulations, Jefferson asserted that the establishment clause of the First Amendment had been intended to "erect a wall of separation between church and state." Today this is widely accepted as an authoritative gloss, but to do so disregards other evidence as to what the framing generation thought they were about.

As to the specific issue of religious observances in the public schools, the historical record on this point is necessarily silent. The institution of the public school did not develop until well into the nineteenth century. The private schools and academies of the early nineteenth century, of course, regarded religious ceremonies as an integral part of their activity. And when local governments began to contribute to private academies, gradually taking them over as "common schools," the place of religious exercises in the life of the schools remained essentially unchanged. Since the First Amendment to the Federal Constitutions was not then understood to apply to the states, challenges to these religious practices through the first century and a half of our history were based on state constitutional provisions. The outcomes in these cases are mixed, but one point must be borne in mind. The early challenges were to the *compulsory* nature of participation in the religious exercises. Sometimes the nonconforming plaintiffs won on state constitutional grounds and in other instances they lost. But there was no suggestion that the states were violating their own constitutional provisions by maintaining religious exercises as part of the school ritual. Until the middle of the twentieth century the issue was whether or not participation could be compelled.

In the cases below you will see what happened when the Supreme Court of the United States entered the field in the 1960s on the basis of the establishment clause of the First Amendment. The issue in these cases was not compulsion, but whether the observance itself by agencies of the state (the schools) were acts constituting an establishment of religion.

McCollum v. Board of Education
333 U.S. 203, 68 S.Ct. 461, 92 L.Ed. 649 (1948)

Zorach v. Clauson
343 U.S. 306, 72 S.Ct. 679, 96 L.Ed. 954 (1952)

In the late 1940s and early 1950s "released time" programs enjoyed a considerable vogue in American school systems. This was a period of increasing church membership and activity, and many communities became persuaded that their public schools should cooperate with local churches by setting aside school time during which, should a student's parents so choose, the student would receive religious instruction from a priest, minister, or rabbi of the parents' choice. The program in Champaign, Illinois, at issue in *McCollum* was typical. Time and space in the school building was set aside. At the appointed hour, students would go from their regular classrooms to meet with the religious counselor of their parents' choice. Nonparticipating students remained in their regular classrooms. Writing for the Court, a year after *Everson,* Justice Black found the Champaign system violated the establishment clause. The extent of state support of religion was impermissible. But Black stressed particularly the use of the physical facilities of the school, and this left a doctrinal door ajar. Only Justice Stanley Reed dissented, rejecting the broad theory of separation that the majority endorsed, and maintaining that the establishment clause only forbade a state church, denominational preferences, or direct subsidy of the religious program of a church. Government efforts to accommodate religion, generally, were not precluded. In the New York released time program that came before the Court in *Zorach,* four years later, the students *left* the school premises to receive their instruction. This, for Justice Douglas, made all the difference.

Mr. Justice Douglas delivered the opinion of the Court.

New York City has a program which permits its public schools to release students during the school day so that they may leave the school buildings and school grounds and go to religious centers for religious instruction or devotional exercises. A student is released on written request of his parents. Those not released stay in the classrooms. The churches make weekly reports to the schools, sending a list of children who have been released from public school but who have not reported for religious instruction.

This "released time" program involves neither religious instruction in public school classrooms nor the expenditure of public funds. All costs, including the application blanks, are paid by the religious organizations. The case is therefore unlike *McCollum* v. *Board of Education,* ... which involved a "released time" program from Illinois. In that case the classrooms were turned over to religious instructors. We accordingly held that the program violated the First Amendment. ...

... [W]e do not see how New York by this type of "released time" program has made a law respecting an establishment of religion within the meaning of the First Amendment. [There] cannot be the slightest doubt that the First Amendment reflects the philosophy that Church and State should be separated [and] within the scope of its coverage permits no exception; the prohibition is absolute. The First Amendment, however, does not say that in every and all respects there shall be a separation of Church and State. Rather, it studiously defines the manner, the specific ways, in which there shall be no concert or union or dependency one on the other. That is the common sense of the matter. Otherwise the state and religions would be aliens to each other—hostile, suspicious, and even unfriendly. Churches could not be required to pay even property taxes. Municipalities would not be permitted to render police or fire protection to religious groups. Policemen who helped parishioners into their places of worship would violate the Constitution. Prayers in our legislative halls; the appeals to the Almighty in the messages of the Chief Executive; the proclamations making Thanksgiving Day a holiday; "so help me God" in our courtroom oaths—these and all other references to the Almighty that run through our laws, our public rituals, our ceremonies would be flouting the First Amendment. A fastidious atheist or agnostic could even object to the supplication with which the Court opens each session; "God save the United States and this Honorable Court."

We would have to press the concept of separation of Church and State to these extremes to condemn the present law on constitutional grounds. . . .

We are a religious people whose institutions presuppose a Supreme Being. We guarantee the freedom to worship as one chooses. [We] sponsor an attitude on the part of government that shows no partiality to any one group and that lets each flourish according to the zeal of its adherents and the appeal of its dogma. When the state encourages religious instruction or cooperates with religious authorities by adjusting the schedule of public events to sectarian needs, it follows the best of our traditions. For it then respects the religious nature of our people and accommodates the public service to their spiritual needs. To hold that it may not would be to find in the Constitution a requirement that the government show a callous indifference to religious groups. That would be preferring those who believe in no religion over those who do believe. . . .

In the McCollum case the classrooms were used for religious instruction and the force of the public school was used to promote that instruction. Here, [the] public schools do no more than accommodate their schedules to a program of outside religious instructions. We follow [McCollum]. But we cannot expand it to cover the present released time program unless separation of Church and State means that public institutions can make no adjustments of their schedules to accommodate the religious needs of the people. We cannot read into the Bill of Rights such a philosophy of hostility to religion.

Affirmed.

Justice Black, the author of *McCollum,* dissented bitterly. He claimed that the prior case rested not only on the use of publicly owned facilities, but equally on the cooperation of the state, which compels school attendance, in an essentially religious enterprise. Justices Jackson and Frankfurter also dissented on similar grounds.

Engel v. *Vitale*
370 U.S. 421, 82 S.CT 1261, 8 L.Ed.2d. 601 (1962)

In an attempt to defuse the increasingly controversial issue of religious exercises in the classroom, the Board of Regents of the State of New York authorized a short prayer for recitation in schools: "Almighty God, we acknowledge our dependence upon Thee, and beg Thy blessings upon us, our teachers, and our country." Schools did not have to use the prayer, and if they did, no child was required to repeat it. But if there was to be prayer in a New York classroom, it had to be this one. The prayer was challenged as an establishment of religion, and Justice Hugo Black wrote for the Court.

Mr. Justice Black delivered the opinion of the Court.

We think that by using its public school system to encourage recitation of the Regents' prayer, the State of New York has adopted a practice wholly inconsistent with the Establishment Clause. There can, of course, be no doubt that New York's program of daily classroom invocation of God's blessings as prescribed in the Regents' prayer is a religious activity. It is a solemn avowal of divine faith and application for the blessings of the Almighty. . . .

. . . .

There can be no doubt that New York's state prayer program officially established the religious beliefs embodied in the Regents' prayer. . . . Neither the fact that the prayer may be denominationally neutral, nor the fact that its observance on the part of the students is voluntary can serve to free it from the limitations of the Establishment Clause, as it might from the Free Exercise Clause, of the First Amendment, both of which are operative against the States by virtue of the Fourteenth Amendment. Although these two clauses may in certain instances overlap, they forbid two quite different kinds of governmental encroachment upon religious freedom. The Establishment Clause, unlike the Free Exercise Clause, does not depend upon any showing of direct governmental compulsion and is violated by the enactment of laws which establish an official religion whether those laws operate directly to coerce nonobserving individuals or not. This is not to say, of course, that laws officially prescribing a particular form of religious worship do not involve coercion of such individuals. When the power, prestige and financial support of government is placed behind a particular religious belief, the indirect coercive pressure upon religious minorities to conform to the prevailing officially approved religion is plain. But the purposes underlying the Establishment Clause go much further than that. Its first and most immediate purpose rested on the belief that a union of government and religion tends to destroy government and to degrade religion. . . .

. . . It is neither sacreligious nor antireligious to say that each separate government in this country should stay out of the business of writing or sanctioning official prayers and leave that purely religious function to the people themselves and to those the people choose to look to for religious guidance. . . .

Reversed and remanded.

Mr. Justice Frankfurter took no part in the decision of this case.
Mr. Justice White took no part in the consideration or decision of this case.

Justice William O. Douglas concurred. He concluded that while the prayer did not establish religion "in the strictly historic meaning of these words," it had the potential for divisiveness that the framers of the free exercise clause had sought to avoid.

Only Justice Potter Stewart dissented. He argued that "the Court had misapplied a great constitutional principle." Stewart could not see how a voluntary prayer could be held to constitute state adoption of an official religion. For him, this was the authentic meaning of, "establishment of religion." He noted that invocations of the diety in public ceremonies of all sorts had been a feature of our national life from its outset.

Sunday Closing Cases
(Establishment Clause Dimension)

From the beginning of the Republic, and antedating it in the colonial period, states have maintained "Blue Laws" prohibiting certain kinds of commercial activity on Sunday. By the middle of the twentieth century, with more and more Americans wishing to shop on Sunday, and with merchants ready to cater to this, Sunday closing laws appeared to some as arbitrary and anachronistic. This impression was not improved by the crazy-quilt patterns of coverage that had evolved as state legislatures revised and made exceptions to their laws over the years. In New York, for instance, one could buy toothpaste, but not a toothbrush; in Massachusetts, a merchant could sell fish but not meat! Hoping that the Supreme court was now committed to a strict separationist line in establishment clause cases, it was an obvious step for opponents to attack the constitutionality of the Blue Laws. Chief Justice Earl Warren considered the issue for the Court and found that, through the passage of time, Sunday closing laws had come to rest on a purely secular foundation.

On May 29, 1961, the Supreme Court decided four cases involving the application of such statutes in Maryland, Pennsylvania, and Massachusetts. In two of the cases, *McGowan* v. *Maryland,* 366 U.S. 420 (1961), arising in Maryland, and *Two Guys from Harrison-Allentown* v. *McGinley,* 366 U.S. 582 (1961), arising in Pennsylvania, the parties complaining of the legislation proved only the economic injury resulting from being compelled to close their business on Sunday. The other two cases, *Braunfeld* v. *Brown,* 366 U.S. 599 (1961), also from Pennsylvania, and *Gallagher* v. *Crown Kosher Super Market,* 366 U.S. 617 (1961) from Massachusetts, involved Orthodox Jews who argued that because the tenets of their religion prevented them from doing business on Saturday, Sunday closing subjected them to a special burden not imposed on persons of other faiths. These cases presented a free exercise issue as well as an establishment issue, and we will touch on this in the next chapter. The establishment clause question was dealt with in *McGowan*. The Chief Justice wrote that:

> It would seem that a legislature could reasonably find that the Sunday sale of the exempted commodities was necessary either for the health of the populace or for the enhancement of the recreational atmosphere of the day— that a family which takes a Sunday ride into the country will need gasoline for the automobile and may find pleasant a soft drink or fresh fruit; that those who go to the beach may wish ice cream or some other item normally sold there; that some people will prefer alcoholic beverages or games of chance to add to their relaxation; that newspapers and drug products should always be available to the public.

And Warren concluded that:

> In the light of the evolution of our Sunday Closing Laws through the centuries, and of their more or less recent emphasis upon secular considerations, it is not difficult to discern that as presently written and administered, most of them, at least, are of a secular rather than of a religious character, and that presently they bear no relationship to the establishment of religion as those words are used in the Constitution of the United States. . . . To say that the states cannot prescribe Sunday as the day of rest for these [secular] purposes solely because centuries ago such laws had their genesis in religion would give a constitutional interpretation of hostility to the public welfare rather that one of mere separation of church and state.

This, for Warren, disposed of the establishment clause dimension of all four cases.

Abington School District v. *Schempp*
374 U.S. 203, 83 S.Ct. 1560, 10 L.Ed. 2d. 844 (1963)

Pennsylvania required that at least ten verses from the Holy Bible be read, without comment, at the opening of each public school day. A student might be excused from this exercise upon the written request of parents or guardian. In *Engel* the prayer in question was written by state officials. The question in *Schempp* was whether this made a difference—there being no claim that Pennsylvania was implicated in the authorship of holy scripture. Justice Tom C. Clark concluded that the Pennsylvania exercise suffered from establishment clause infirmity every bit as grave as that affecting the New York's Regents' Prayer. Clark's opinion in *Schempp* was the first strict separationist opinion of the Court not written by Justice Hugo Black, and Clark formulated a test for establishment clause validity with a precision that had eluded his Brother. A state program touching upon religion or religious institutions must have a valid secular purpose and have the primary effect of neither advancing nor inhibiting religion. *Schempp,* along with *Murray* v. *Carlett,* a Maryland case involving the recitation of the Lord's prayer that was decided at the same time, settled whatever lingering question there might have been about the constitutionality of religious exercises in public schools.

Mr. Justice Clark delivered the opinion of the Court.

... As we have indicated, the Establishment Clause has been directly considered by this Court eight times in the past score of years and, with only one Justice dissenting on the point, it has consistently held that the clause withdrew all legislative power respecting religious belief or the expression thereof. The test may be stated as follows: what are the purpose and the primary effect of the enactment? If either is the advancement or inhibition of religion then the enactment exceeds the scope of legislative power as circumscribed by the Constitution. That is to say that to withstand the strictures of the Establishment Clause there must be a secular legislative purpose and a primary effect that neither advances nor inhibits religion. ...

Applying the Establishment Clause principles to the cases at bar we find that the States are requiring the selection and reading at the opening of the school day of verses from the Holy Bible and the recitation of the Lord's Prayer by the students in unison. These exercises are prescribed as part of the curricular activities of students who are required by law to attend school. They are held in the school buildings under the supervision and with the participation of teachers employed in those schools. None of these factors, other than compulsory school attendance, was present in the program upheld in *Zorach* v. *Clauson.* ...

. . . .

The conclusion follows that in both cases the laws require religious exercises and such exercises are being conducted in direct violation of the rights of the appellees and petitioners. Nor are these required exercises mitigated by the fact that individual students may absent themselves upon parental request, for that fact furnishes no defense to a claim of unconstitutionality under the Establishment Clause. See *Engel* v. *Vitale.* Further, it is no defense to urge that the religious practices here may be relatively minor encroachments on the First Amendment. The breach of neutrality that is today a trickling stream may all too soon become a raging torrent and, in the words of Madison, "it is proper to take alarm at the first experiment on our liberties." *Memorial and Remonstrance Against Religious Assessments.*

It is insisted that unless these religious exercises are permitted a "religion of secularism" is established in the schools. We agree of course that the State may not establish a "religion of secularism" in the sense of affirmatively opposing or showing hostility to religion, thus "preferring those who believe in no religion over those who do believe." We do not agree, however, that this decision in any sense has that effect. In addition, it might well be said that one's education is not complete without a study of comparative religion or the history of religion and its relationship to the advancement of civilization. It certainly may be said that the Bible is worthy of study for its literary and historic qualities. Nothing we have said here indicates that such study of the Bible or of religion, when presented objectively as part of a secular program of education, may not be effected consistent with the First Amendment. But the exercises here do not fall into those categories. They are religious exercises, required by the States in violation of the command of the First Amendment that the Government maintain strict neutrality, neither aiding nor opposing religion.

Finally, we cannot accept that the concept of neutrality, which does not permit a State to require a religious exercise even with the consent of the majority of those affected, collides with the majority's right to free exercise of religion. While the Free Exercise Clause clearly prohibits the use of station action to deny the rights of free exercise to *anyone,* it has never meant that a majority could use the machinery of the State to practice its beliefs. . . .

Justices William O. Douglas and William Brennan concurred separately in opinions reflecting their growing stricter separationism. Justice Arthur Goldberg also filed a brief concurring opinion. Justice Potter Stewart dissented, as he had in *Engel.* As long as the state authority administered the devotions in such a way as to avoid coercion (which would constitute a free exercise problem) Stewart argued that religious exercises as part of public ceremonies were permissible.

Epperson v. *Arkansas*
393 U.S. 97, 89 S.Ct. 266, 21 L.Ed.2d. 228 (1968)

This case represents the high watermark of the strict separationism of the contemporary Supreme Court. An Arkansas statute prohibited teaching in its public schools "that mankind ascended or descended from a lower order of animals." Justice Abe Fortas delivered the opinion of the Court and recalled the Tennessee "Monkey Law," which was the basis for the celebrated Scopes trial in 1927. Fortas concluded that the Arkansas law violated the establishment clause. Leo Pfeffer and Melvin Wulf were on the *amicus* brief urging unconstitutionality, as was Joseph B. Robinson, of the American Jewish Congress. The National Education Association also appeared, *amicus curiae,* opposing the Arkansas law.

Mr. Justice Fortas delivered the opinion of the Court.

This appeal challenges the constitutionality of the "anti-evolution" statute which the State of Arkansas adopted in 1928 to prohibit the teaching in its public schools and universities of the theory that man evolved from other species of life. The statute was a product of the upsurge of "fundamentalist" religious fervor of the twenties. The Arkansas statute was an adaptation of the famous Tennessee "monkey law" which that State adopted in 1925. The constitutionality of the Tennessee law was upheld by the Tennessee Supreme Court in the celebrated *Scopes* case in 1927.

The Arkansas law makes it unlawful for a teacher in any state-supported school or university "to teach the theory or doctrine that mankind ascended or descended from a lower order of animals," or "to adopt or use in any such institution a textbook that teaches" this theory. Violation is a misdemeanor and subjects the violator to dismissal from his position. . . .

There is and can be no doubt that the First Amendment does not permit the State to require that teaching and learning must be tailored to the principles or prohibitions of any religious sect or dogma. In *Everson* v. *Board of Education,* this Court, in upholding a state law to provide free bus service to school children, including those attending parochial schools, said: "Neither [a State nor the Federal Government] can pass laws which aid one religion, aid all religions, or prefer one religion over another." ...

. . . .

... In the present case, there can be no doubt that Arkansas has sought to prevent its teachers from discussing the theory of evolution because it is contrary to the belief of some that the Book of Genesis must be the exclusive source of doctrine as to the origin of man. No suggestion has been made that Arkansas' law may be justified by considerations of state policy other than the religious views of some of its citizens. It is clear that fundamentalist sectarian conviction was and is the law's reason for existence. Its antecedent, Tennessee's "monkey law," candidly stated its purpose: to make it unlawful "to teach any theory that denies the story of the Divine Creation of man as taught in the Bible, and to teach instead that man has descended from a lower order of animals." Perhaps the sensational publicity attendant upon the *Scopes* trial induced Arkansas to adopt less explicit language. It eliminated Tennessee's reference to "the story of the Divine Creation of man" as taught in the Bible, but there is no doubt that the motivation for the law was the same: to suppress the teaching of a theory which, it was thought, "denied" the divine creation of man.

Arkansas' law cannot be defended as an act of religious neutrality. Arkansas did not seek to excise from the curricula of its schools and universities all discussion of the origin of man. The law's effort was confined to an attempt to blot out a particular theory because of its supposed conflict with the Biblical account, literally read. Plainly, the law is contrary to the mandate of the First, and in violation of the Fourteenth, Amendment to the Constitution.

The judgment of the Supreme Court of Arkansas is

Reversed.

Justice Black concurred in the conclusion that Arkansas' statute violated the establishment clause, and Justice Stewart concurred in a very brief opinion, which rested essentially on free speech grounds.

CASE STUDY: "KEEP GOD IN SCHOOL!"

Criticism of the Supreme Court's decision in *Engel, Schempp,* and *Murray* has risen and slackened and risen again over the years, but it has never died out. In the weeks after *Engel,* in 1961, one could find "Keep God in school!" scrawled on New York City subway cars and blazened on billboards in the midwest. At that time Francis Cardinal Spellman, head of the Roman Catholic Archdiocese of New York, and Senator Everett McKinley Dirkson, Protestant Republican of Illinois, were the leaders of the movement to "reverse" the Supreme Court by amending the Constitution to permit voluntary school prayer. While this initial push for an amendment failed, many school districts informally reversed the Court by continuing classroom observances—see the excellent study by William K. Muir, Jr., *Prayer in the Public Schools* (Chicago: University of Chicago Press, 1967).

With the upswing in visibility and influence of "New Right" groups and with the election of Ronald Reagan in 1980, the stage was set for a new effort to restore school prayer. The President was as committed on this issue as he was on aid to private school parents, and so was Senator Jesse Helms, Republican of North Carolina.

In the 97th Congress (1978–1980) Senator Helms introduced legislation that would have stripped the federal courts of their appellate jurisdiction over school prayer cases. This failed. But Helms succeeded, over the filibuster attempt by Senator Lowell P. Weicker, Jr., Republican of Connecticut, in attaching a rider to a 1982 appropriations bill prohibiting the Justice Department from expending any funds in entering suits against voluntary school prayer. The Department was not doing this, so the significance of the maneuver was purely symbolic, but Washington is a city that feeds on symbols and signals.

On May 17, 1982, President Reagan sent to Congress his own proposal for a voluntary school prayer amendment. However, the fate of this initiative is uncertain. While Helms thrashed Weicker in the early going, John Shattuck, director of the Washington Office of the ACLU, was confident of victory. "The New Right has been forced to start defending a lot of proposals in public," he argued, adding that "they came to Congress thinking they would be able to sign up scared members who would not stand in their way. I think when they got here, they found that 10–15 percent of Congress was with them." The majority of members, Shattuck concluded, "wish these issues would go away. They don't want to vote on them."

There was special basis for Shattuck's confidence in the organization of the 98th Congress. The Democrats enjoyed firm control of the House, and however prayer amendments might fare in the Republican controlled Senate Judiciary Committee, the House Judiciary Committee enjoyed a history of success in bottling up conservative social legislation. A long-time chairman of that committee, the late Emanuel Celler, Democrat of New York, was once asked where he stood on school prayer. "I don't stand on it," Celler shot back, "I sit on it." Celler's successor, Congressman Peter W. Radino, Jr., Democrat of New Jersey, has proved as ample as his predecessor in this regard.

Meanwhile, with the 1984 election approaching, conservative pressure on the White House to produce results on Capital Hill on social issues such as school prayer and abortion increased (see Chapter 22). In early March of 1984, the Supreme Court decided the case of *Lynch* v. *Donnelly*, which involved the constitutionality of Christmas crèches on government property. While not dealing with prayer, the issue was closely related. And when the Court (divided 5-4) upheld Pawtucket, Rhode Island's display (which included a crèche along with candy-striped poles, a Christmas tree, and the familiar banal banner announcing "Seasons Greetings") supporters of school prayer were encouraged that some senators might regard this as a significant constitutional signal. Two weeks later, however, such hopes were dashed when the Senate vote fell eleven short of the two-thirds required to approve President Reagan's proposed constitutional amendment.

Senator Weicker and John Shattuck proved shrewd vote counters and tacticians, while the Reverend Mr. Jerry Falwell and the New Right vowed to fight another day. Polls before the Senate vote indicated that 80 percent of the people favored some form of organized school prayer, but Reagan's amendment was opposed by most "mainline" Protestant denominations (Methodist, Presbyterian, Episcopalian, and Lutheran) and by Jewish groups. It was a fascinating configuration of political forces, especially because the fundamentalist and evangelical sectors of American protestantism which support school prayer are growing sectors, while the establishment denominations which oppose it are either not growing or not growing nearly as rapidly. So twenty-three years after *Engel* v. *Vitale,* the only thing that seems clear is that the controversy over the Court's initiative will continue.

CHAPTER · 11

GOD AND CAESAR—
THE PROBLEM OF
"FREE EXERCISE"

TO what extent should religiously motivated acts that otherwise violate the law be protected by the First Amendment? As we saw in Chapter 10, records of the First Congress are less clear with respect to the free exercise clause than with respect to the establishment clause. But the direction of the American tradition up to 1789 is clear. Toleration of diverse religious opinion was widely accepted by late eighteenth century American intellectuals and statesmen.

In 1776, in drafting the provisions of the Virginia Declaration of Rights dealing with religious freedom, George Mason used the phrase "toleration in the exercise of religion." The young James Madison felt that term was inadequate because it implied an act of grace by the state in accepting differences among individuals. Madison successfully urged the replacement of toleration by a right of "free exercise" of religion, which all persons possessed equally.

It is clear that Mason and Madison, and the entire generation of Virginians who debated the place of religion in the public order in 1780, sought to protect the freedom of religious opinion. The question that vexes us today, however, is whether the free exercise clause of the First Amendment should be interpreted to protect religiously motivated behavior, when that behavior conflicts with otherwise valid secular law. It appears that Mason and Madison differed in their answers to this question in 1776. Mason was content to safeguard beliefs and acts not in violation of law. Madison sought something more and would have protected religiously motivated acts up to the point where these *"manifestly endangered"* the existence of the state. The Convention adopted Madison's "free exercise" language but stuck with Mason on the issue of protecting only belief and lawful behavior. Malbin makes the point that Virginia's church-state policy, as reflected in the thought of Madison and Jefferson (and there were probably differences between the two), constituted the most separationist and libertarian position on the spectrum of church-state policy in the formative period. And there is nothing to suggest that Congress, in adopting the free exercise language, intended to go any further than Virginia had gone in the Bill for Establishing Religious Freedom. This was enacted in 1785, after the conflict over the Incorporation Bill and the General Assessment Bills. The Bill was based on a draft by Thomas Jefferson, originally written in 1779.

Jefferson's views on the matter of religiously motivated nonconformity to law were better worked out than Madison's. In his 1779 version, Jefferson inveighed against intrusions by the civil magistrate into the field of religious opinions, but emphasized that when religious principles "break out into overt acts against peace and good order" government could move to restrain even religiously motivated behavior. The bill actually passed by the Virginia assembly in 1785 went even further. While all of Jefferson's language about the inviolability of religious opinion was retained, the assembly gave no protection at all to persons who acted on the basis of religious motivation if their action "in the judgment of government officials" was against peace and good order. Protection was bestowed on religious worship as such; protection was limited to worship that was the pure expression of religious opinion. Activities undertaken sincerely by an individual, in the belief that they were required of him by his creator, could still be punishable under the legislated rules of civil society.

Again, it is likely that Madison himself desired more protection of religiously motivated behavior than Virginia had been willing to afford, but it is very difficult to argue that when Fisher Ames of Massachusetts introduced the free exercise language into an early draft of the First Amendment, and when successive congressional majorities and state legislatures voted to approve that formulation, they were somehow endorsing Madison's expansive notion rather than the more limited position of Jefferson and the Virginia assembly.

In the cases that follow you will see the Supreme Court in the nineteenth century adopting an interpretation of free exercise based on freedom of belief. In *Reynolds* v. *U.S.*, Chief Justice Morrison Waite emphasized that the First Amendment protected belief absolutely but stressed that action of persons were absolutely regulable by civil law.

By the middle of the twentieth century, however, this interpretation was increasingly called into question. In *Cantwell* v. *Connecticut,* Justice Owen Roberts generalized that both religious belief and religious action were protected; in the former case, the protection was absolute, in the latter case it could not be. Restrictions on religiously motivated behavior, Roberts suggested, could be justified by significant state interests.

In the 1960s and 1970s the Supreme Court shifted away from the traditional standard of protecting belief and, in cases such as *Sherbert* v. *Verner* and *Wisconsin* v. *Yoder,* bestowed free exercise protection on nonconforming action.

Reynolds v. United States
98 U.S. 145, 25 L.Ed. 244 (1878)

The "Mormons," followers of the prophet Joseph Smith and organized as the Church of Jesus Christ of the Latter-Day Saints, were an unpopular bunch in the late nineteenth century. Moving further and further west to escape the hostility of scandalized neighbors, a strong community was organized finally under the leadership of Brigham Young around the Great Salt Lake in what was then the Utah Territory. In 1853 Young had announced the doctrine of polygamy. Lurid tales of the goings-on in Utah found their way into the press in the 1870s, and Congress, which governs territories directly, made polygamy a crime. George Reynolds was duly convicted. He defended himself with the argument that punishment for an act required of him by religious doctrine constituted a denial of free exercise (since this was an act of Congress, the First Amendment applied directly).

Mr. Chief Justice Waite delivered the opinion of the court.

> On the trial ... the accused, proved that at the time of his alleged second marriage he was, and for many years before had been, a member of the Church of Jesus Christ of Latter-Day Saints, commonly called the Mormon Church, and a believer in its doctrines; that it was an accepted doctrine of that church "that it was the duty of male members of said church, circumstances permitting, to practice polygamy; ... that this duty was enjoined by different books which the members of said church believed to be of divine origin, and among others the Holy Bible, and also that the members of the church believed that the practice of polygamy was directly enjoined upon the male members thereof by the Almighty God, in a revelation to Joseph Smith, the founder and prophet of said church; that the failing or refusing to practice polygamy by such male members of said church, when circumstances would admit, would be punished, and that the penalty for such failure and refusal would be damnation in the life to come." He also proved "that he had received permission from the recognized authorities in said church to enter into polygamous marriage; ... that Daniel H. Wells, one having authority in said church to perform the marriage ceremony, married the said defendant on or about the time the crime is alleged to have been committed, to some woman by the name of Schofield, and that such marriage ceremony was performed under and pursuant to the doctrines of said church." ...
>
> . . . .
>
> ... The inquiry is not as to the power of Congress to prescribe criminal laws for the Territories, but as to the guilt of one who knowingly violates a law which has been properly enacted, if he entertains a religious belief that the law is wrong.
>
> Congress cannot pass a law for the government of the Territories which shall prohibit the free exercise of religion. The first amendment to the Constitution expressly forbids such legislation. Religious freedom is guaranteed everywhere throughout the United States, so far as congressional interference is concerned.

The question to be determined is, whether the law now under consideration comes within this prohibition.

The word "religion" is not defined in the Constitution. We must go elsewhere, therefore, to ascertain its meaning, and nowhere more appropriately, we think, than to the history of the times in the midst of which the provision was adopted. The precise point of the inquiry is, what is the religious freedom which has been guaranteed.

Before the adoption of the Constitution, attempts were made in some of the colonies and States to legislate not only in respect to the establishment of religion, but in respect to its doctrines and precepts as well. The people were taxed, against their will, for the support of religion, and sometimes for the support of particular sects to whose tenets they could not and did not subscribe. Punishments were prescribed for a failure to attend upon public worship, and sometimes for entertaining heretical opinions. The controversy upon this general subject was animated in many of the States, but seemed at last to culminate in Virginia. In 1784, the House of Delegates of that State having under consideration "a bill establishing provision for teachers of the Christian religion," postponed it until the next session, and directed that the bill should be published and distributed, and that the people be requested "to signify their opinion respecting the adoption of such a bill at the next session of assembly."

This brought out a determined opposition. Amongst others, Mr. Madison prepared a "Memorial and Remonstrance," which was widely circulated and signed, and in which he demonstrated "that religion, or the duty we owe the Creator," was not within the cognizance of civil government. . . . At the next session the proposed bill was not only defeated, but another, "for establishing religious freedom," drafted by Mr. Jefferson, was passed. 1 Jeff. Works, 45; 2 Howison, Hist. of Va. 298. In the preamble of this net (12 Hening's Stat. 84) religious freedom is defined; and after a recital "that to suffer the civil magistrate to intrude his powers into the field of opinion, and to restrain the profession or propagation of principles on supposition of their ill tendency, is a dangerous fallacy which at once destroys all religious liberty," it is declared "that it is time enough for the rightful purposes of civil government for its officers to interfere when principles break out into overt acts against peace and good order." In these two sentences is found the true distinction between what properly belongs to the church and what to the state. . . .

. . . .

. . . Congress was deprived of all legislative power over mere opinion, but was left free to reach actions which were in violation of social duties or subversive of good order.

Polygamy has always been odious among the northern and western nations of Europe, and, until the establishment of the Mormon Church, was almost exclusively a feature of the life of Asiatic and of African people. At common law, the second marriage was always void . . . and from the earliest history of England polygamy has been treated as an offence against society. After the establishment of the ecclesiastical courts, and until the time of James I., it was punished through the instrumentality of those tribunals, not merely because ecclesiastical rights had been violated, but because upon the separation of the ecclesiastical courts from the civil the ecclesiastical were supposed to be the most appropriate for the trial of matrimonial causes and offences against the rights of marriage, just as they were for testamentary causes and the settlement of the estates of deceased persons. . . .

Professor [Francis] Lieber says, polygamy leads to the patriarchal principle, and which, when applied to large communities, fetters the people in stationary despotism, while that principle cannot long exist in connection with monogamy. . . .

In our opinion, the statute immediately under consideration is within the legislative power of Congress. It is constitutional and valid as prescribing a rule of action for all those residing in the Territories, and in places over which the United States have exclusive control. This being so, the only question which remains is, whether those who make polygamy a part of their religion are excepted from the operation of the statute. . . .

Laws are made for the government of actions, and while they cannot interfere with mere religious belief and opinions, they may with practices. Suppose one believed that human sacrifices were a necessary part of religious worship, would it be seriously contended that the civil government under which he lived could not interfere to prevent a sacrifice? Or if a wife religiously believed it was her duty to burn herself upon the funeral pile of her dead husband, would it be beyond the power of the civil government to prevent her carrying her belief into practice?

Upon a careful consideration of the whole case, we are satisfied that no error was committed by the court below.

Judgment affirmed.

Cantwell v. Connecticut
310 U.S. 296, 60 S.Ct. 900, 84 L.Ed. 1213 (1940)

Newton Cantwell and his sons, Jesse and Russell, were arrested in New Haven, Connecticut. As Jehovah's Witnesses, they considered themselves ministers of the gospel to the "gentiles" and were engaged in street solicitation. They distributed pamphlets, made statements critical of the Roman Catholic Church, and offered to play for passers-by a phonograph record that included an attack on Catholicism. All three Cantwells were convicted of violating a Connecticut statute prohibiting persons from soliciting money for any cause without a certificate issued by the State Secretary of the state public welfare council. Justice Owen J. Roberts delivered the opinion of a unanimous Court. He concluded that the certificate requirement infringed upon the free exercise of religion of those who would go forth on the streets to proselytize and raise funds.

Justice Roberts made clear that the free exercise clause of the First Amendment applied to the states through the due process clause of the Fourteenth Amendment, and that in contrast to the doctrine of *Reynolds* v. *United States,* the free exercise clause protected not only beliefs but actions. The protection of belief was absolute, Roberts wrote, but the protection of action was not—it must give way to legitimate regulation undertaken by government for the protection of society. Hayden Covington was there to argue for the Cantwells, and "Judge" Rutherford was with him in the brief.

Mr. Justice Roberts delivered the opinion of the Court.

. . . .

The statute under which the appellants were charged provides:

"No person shall solicit money, services, subscriptions or any valuable thing for any alleged religious, charitable or philanthropic cause, from other than a member of the organization for whose benefit such person is soliciting or within the county in which such person or organization is located unless such cause shall have been approved by the secretary of the public welfare council. Upon application of any person in behalf of such cause, the secretary shall determine whether such cause is a religious one or is a bona fide object of charity or philanthropy and conforms to reasonable standards of efficiency and integrity, and, if he shall so find, shall approve the same and issue to the authority in charge a certificate to that effect. Such certificate may be revoked at any time. Any person violating any provision of this section shall be fined not more than one hundred dollars or imprisoned not more than thirty days or both." . . .

. . . .

. . . We hold that the statute, as construed and applied to the appellants, deprives them of their liberty without due process of law in contravention of the Fourteenth Amendment. The fundamental concept of liberty embodied in that Amendment embraces the liberties guaranteed by the First Amendment. The First Amendment declares that Congress shall make no law respecting an establishment of religion or prohibiting the free exercise thereof. The Fourteenth Amendment has rendered the legislatures of the states as incompetent as Congress to enact such laws. The constitutional inhibition of legislation on the subject of religion has a double aspect. On the one hand, it forestalls compulsion by law of the acceptance of any creed or the practice of any form of worship. Freedom of conscience and freedom to adhere to such religious organization or form of worship as the individual may choose cannot be restricted by law. On the other hand, it safeguards the free exercise of the chosen form of religion. Thus the Amendment embraces two concepts,—freedom to believe and freedom to act. The first is absolute but, in the nature of things, the second cannot be. Conduct remains subject to regulation for the protection of society. The freedom to act must have appropriate definition to preserve the enforcement of that protection. In every case the power to regulate must be so exercised as not, in attaining a permissible end, unduly to infringe the protected freedom. No one would contest the proposition that a State may not, by statute, wholly deny the right to preach or to disseminate religious views. Plainly such a previous and absolute restraint would violate the terms of the guarantee. It is equally clear that a State may by general and non-discriminatory legislation regulate the times, the places, and the manner of soliciting upon its streets, and of holding meetings thereon; and may in other respects safeguard the peace, good order and comfort of the community, without unconstitutionally invading the liberties protected by the Fourteenth

Amendment. The appellants are right in their insistence that the Act in question is not such a regulation. If a certificate is procured, solicitation is permitted without restraint but, in the absence of a certificate, solicitation is altogether prohibited.

The [Cantwells] urge that to require them to obtain a certificate as a condition of soliciting support for their views amounts to a prior restraint on the exercise of their religion within the meaning of the Constitution. The State insists that the Act, as construed by the Supreme Court of Connecticut, imposes no previous restraint upon the dissemination of religious views or teaching but merely safeguards against the perpetration of frauds under the cloak of religion. Conceding that this is so, the question remains whether the method adopted by Connecticut to that end transgresses the liberty safeguarded by the Constitution.

The general regulation, in the public interest, of solicitation, which does not involve any religious test and does not unreasonably obstruct or delay the collection of funds, is not open to any constitutional objection, even though the collection be for a religious purpose. Such regulation would not constitute a prohibited previous restraint on the free exercise of religion or interpose an inadmissible obstacle to its exercise.

It will be noted, however, that the Act requires an application to the secretary of the public welfare council of the State; that he is empowered to determine whether the cause is a religious one, and that the issue of a certificate depends upon his affirmative action. If he finds that the cause is not that of religion, to solicit for it becomes a crime. He is not to issue a certificate as a matter of course. His decision to issue or refuse it involves appraisal of facts, the exercise of judgment, and the formation of an opinion. He is authorized to withhold his approval if he determines that the cause is not a religious one. Such a censorship of religion as the means of determining its right to survive is a denial of liberty protected by the First Amendment and included in the liberty which is within the protection of the Fourteenth. . . .

Reversed.

Sunday Closing Cases
(Free Exercise Dimension)

In the preceding chapter, we touched upon the establishment dimension of the Sunday closing cases. It remains to examine the free exercise dimension. Recall that two of the four cases, *Braunfeld* and *Crown Kosher,* involved Orthodox Jewish merchants. In addition to arguing that the choice of Sunday as a state imposed day of rest constituted an establishment of religion (the argument Chief Justice Warren rejected in *McGowan*), they argued that because they closed another day of the week as a matter of religious conviction, their states were required to exempt them from the general Sunday closing requirement. To fail to do so would result in the states forcing individual merchants to choose between the requirements of their religious practices and the economic disadvantage of being closed *two* days a week. This, it was asserted, was a choice the state could not force upon a person, given the free exercise clause. It was for the Justices to decide whether to follow the *Reynolds* approach (belief protected, but action must conform to law) or the *Cantwell* approach (action protected to some extent). Chief Justice Warren addressed the free exercise question for the Court in *Braunfeld* (covering *Crown Kosher,* as well), and leaned toward *Reynolds:*

> To strike down, without the most critical scrutiny, legislation which imposes only an indirect burden on the exercise of religion, i.e. legislation which does not make unlawful the religious practice itself, would radically restrict the operating latitude of the legislature. Statutes which tax income and limit the amount which may be deducted for religious contributions impose an indirect economic burden on the observance of the religion of the citizen whose religion requires him to donate a greater amount to his church; statutes which require the courts to be closed on Saturday and Sunday impose a similar indirect burden on the observance of the religion of the trial lawyer whose religion requires him to rest on a weekday. The list of legislation of this nature is nearly limitless.

Justice Frankfurter concurred, with Justice Harlan joining him. But Justice Brennan, with Justice Stewart joining him, dissented sharply. He would have followed and even extended the *Cantwell* approach to hold that religiously motivated behavior is entitled (as a matter of First Amendment free exercise of religion) to exemption from otherwise valid laws unless the state can show a *compelling interest* in enforcing the law uniformly:

> What, then, is the compelling state interest which impels the Commonwealth of Pennsylvania to impede appellant's freedom of worship?
>   ... It is not even the interest in seeing that everyone rest one day a week, for appellant's religion requires that they take such rest. It is the mere convenience of having everyone rest on the same day. It is to defend this interest that the Court holds that a State need not follow the alternative route of granting an exemption for those who in good faith observe a day of rest other than Sunday.
>   It is true, I suppose, that the granting of such an exemption would make Sundays a little noisier, and the task of police and prosecutor a little more difficult. It is also true that a majority—21—of the 34 states which have general Sunday regulations have exemptions of this kind. We are not told that those states are significantly noisier, or that their police are significantly more burdened, than Pennsylvania's. Even England, not under the compulsion of a written constitution, but simply influenced by considerations of fairness, has such an exemption for some activities.

Quite soon Justice Brennan was to have the chance to write his "compelling interest" test for religious exemptions into a majority opinion for the Court.

Sherbert v. *Verner*
374 U.S. 398, 83 S.Ct. 1790, 10 L.Ed.2d. 965 (1963)

In *Braunfeld* Justice Brennan filed a dissent urging an exemption for Sabbatarians (those who observed Saturday, the seventh day of the week, as holy) from the Sunday closing laws on free exercise grounds. Now Brennan incorporated the reasoning of that dissent into an opinion for the Court. Mrs. Sherbert was a Seventh Day Adventist and as such did not work on Saturday as a matter of religious conscience. She was employed in the textile industry in the Spartanburg area of South Carolina but lost her job when the mill began to require work on Saturday.

Mrs. Sherbert filed for unemployment compensation under the South Carolina program, which required as a condition for continued eligibility that the claimant must be "available for work." After a time, Mrs. Sherbert was referred to a job but declined it because of a Saturday work requirement. Under South Carolina's rules, declining proffered employment meant one was no longer available for work and hence no longer eligible for unemployment compensation.

Justice Brennan concluded that the disqualification for benefits imposed a burden on Mrs. Sherbert's free exercise of religion. Free exercise protected not only belief but observance, and while Brennan conceded that it was not the purpose of South Carolina to impede observance, even the incidental burden here could only be justified if the state could show a compelling interest in not granting such exception.

Mr. Justice Brennan delivered the opinion of the Court.

> Appellant, a member of the Seventh-day Adventist Church was discharged by her South Carolina employer because she would not work on Saturday, the Sabbath Day of her faith. When she was unable to obtain other employment because from conscientious scruples she would not take Saturday work, she filed a claim for unemployment compensation benefits under the South Carolina Unemployment Compensation Act. . . . The appellee Employment Security Commission, in administrative proceedings under the statute, found that appellant's restriction upon her availability for Saturday work brought her within the provision disqualifying for benefits insured workers who fail, without good cause, to accept "suitable work when offered . . . by the employment office or the employer. . . ."
>
> We turn first to the question whether the disqualification for benefits imposes any burden on the free exercise of appellant's religion. We think it is clear that it does. In a sense the consequences of such a disqualification to religious principles and practices may be only an indirect result of welfare legislation within the State's general competence to enact; it is true that no criminal sanctions directly compel appellant to work a six-day week. But this is only the beginning, not the end, of our inquiry. . . . Here not only is it apparent that appellant's declared ineligibility for benefits derives solely from the practice of her religion, but the pressure upon her to forego that practice is unmistakable. The ruling forces her

to choose between following the precepts of her religion and forfeiting benefits, on the one hand, and abandoning one of the precepts of her religion in order to accept work, on the other hand. Governmental imposition of such a choice puts the same kind of burden upon the free exercise of religion as would a fine imposed against appellant for her Saturday worship. . . .

We must next consider whether some compelling state interest enforced in the eligibility provisions of the South Carolina statute justifies the substantial infringement of appellant's First Amendment right. It is basic that no showing merely of a rational relationship to some colorable state interest would suffice; in this highly sensitive constitutional area, "[o]nly the gravest abuses, endangering paramount interests, give occasion for permissible limitation," *Thomas* v. *Collins*, 323 U.S. 516, 530. No such abuse or danger has been advanced in the present case. The appellees suggest no more than a possibility that the filing of fraudulent claims by unsrupulous claimants feigning religious objections to Saturday work might not only dilute the unemployment compensation fund but also hinder the scheduling by employers of necessary Saturday work. But that possibility is not apposite here because no such objection appears to have been made before the South Carolina Supreme Court, and we are unwilling to assess the importance of an asserted state interest without the views of the state court. Nor, if the contention had been made below, would the record appear to sustain it; there is no proof whatever to warrant such fears of malingering or deceit as those which the respondents now advance. Even if consideration of such evidence is not foreclosed by the prohibition against judicial inquiry into the truth or falsity of religious beliefs, *United States* v. *Ballard*, 322 U.S. 78—a question as to which we intimate no view since it is not before us—it is highly doubtful whether such evidence would be sufficient to warrant a substantial infringement of religious liberties. For even if the possibility of spurious claims did threaten to dilute the fund and disrupt the scheduling of work, it would plainly be incumbent upon the appellees to demonstrate that no alternative forms of regulation would combat such abuses without infringing First Amendment rights.

In these respects, then, the state interest asserted in the present case is wholly dissimilar to the interests which were found to justify the less direct burden upon religious practices in *Braunfeld* v. *Brown, supra.* The Court recognized that the Sunday closing law which that decision sustained undoubtedly served "to make the practice of [the Orthodox Jewish merchants'] . . . religious beliefs more expensive," 366 U.S., at 605. But the statute was nevertheless saved by a countervailing factor which finds no equivalent in the instant case—a strong state interest in providing one uniform day of rest for all workers. That secular objective could be achieved, the Court found, only by declaring Sunday to be that day of rest. Requiring exemptions for Sabbatarians, while theoretically possible, appeared to present an administrative problem of such magnitude, or to afford the exempted class so great a competitive advantage, that such a requirement would have rendered the entire statutory scheme unworkable. In the present case no such justifications underlie the determination of the state court that appellant's religion makes her ineligible to receive benefits.

In holding as we do, plainly we are not fostering the "establishment" of the Seventh-day Adventist religion in South Carolina, for the extension of unemployment benefits to Sabbatarians in common with Sunday worshippers reflects nothing more than the governmental obligation of neutrality in the face of religious differences, and does not represent that involvement of religious with secular institutions which it is the object of the Establishment Clause to forestall. ...

The judgment of the South Carolina Supreme Court is reversed and the case is remanded for further proceedings not inconsistent with this opinion.

Justice Douglas concurred in an opinion that rejected the older, *Reynolds* approach out of hand. Douglas noted that the approach had been affirmed in *Braunfeld,* but recalled that he had dissented in the case and was perfectly comfortable with its reversal *sub silentio.*

Justice Stewart concurred only in the result, disassociating himself from Brennan's reasoning. What bothered him was the contradiction he perceived between the Court's interpretation of the free exercise and establishment clauses. In some free-exercise cases, Stewart argued, we grant exemptions from otherwise valid laws and thus prefer religious people over nonreligious. In establishment clause cases, however, we forbid any governmental action that has the effect of advancing religion. While content with religious exemptions to secular regulations in certain instances, Stewart would have had the Court adopt an equally flexible attitude in establishment clause cases.

Justice Harlan, joined by Justice White, dissented. Harlan stressed the "disturbing" extent to which Brennan's opinion rejected existing precedent (especially *Braunfeld*). He was concerned with the implications of the principle implied in Brennan's opinion. For him, the constitutional compulsion to "carve out an exception" based on religious conviction was a very dangerous one. Special treatment on account of religion not only was not commanded by the First Amendment, it was contrary to its intention and spirit.

Wisconsin v. *Yoder*
406 U.S 205, 92 S.Ct. 1526, 32 L.Ed.2d. 15 (1972)

What was a departure in *Sherbert* v. *Verner* became a doctrinal trend in *Yoder.* Wisconsin's compulsory school attendance law required that children attend school until the age of sixteen. Members of the Old Order Amish Religion declined, as a matter of religious conscience, to send their children to organized schools after they had successfully completed the eighth grade. Instead, the Amish provided continuing vocational training in their own communities designed to fit their children for the rural life their religion mandated. Thus, Freida Yoder, age fifteen, after graduating from the eighth grade, failed to appear for the ninth. Wisconsin chose to force the issue, and Yoder's counsel replied that while the requirement may be valid as to others, the free exercise clause of the First Amendment required exemption in the case of the Amish. The Yoders went to federal court and won. Wisconsin took the case to the U.S. Supreme Court. William Ball argued the case for Freida Yoder and the other "respondents" (they had won below and Wisconsin was the moving party at this stage of the litigation). Ball had support in the form of *amici* briefs from some who were usually his antagonists, including William S. Ellis for the National Council of Churches and Leo Pfeiffer for the Synagogue Council of America, whose strict separationist organizations regarded Wisconsin's law as unduly restricting the liberty of a particular denomination.

Mr. Chief Justice Burger delivered the opinion of the Court.

The essence of all that has been said and written on the subject is that only those interests of the highest order and those not otherwise served can overbalance legitimate claims to the free exercise of religion. We can accept it as settled, therefore, that however strong the State's interest in universal compulsory education, it is by no means absolute to the exclusion or subordination of all other interests. . . .

We come then to the quality of the claims of the respondents concerning the alleged encroachment of Wisconsin's compulsory school attendance statute on their rights and the rights of their children to the free exercise of the religious beliefs they and their forebears have adhered to for almost three centuries. In evaluating those claims we must be careful to determine whether the Amish religious faith and their mode of life are, as they claim, inseparable and inter-dependent. A way of life, however virtuous and admirable, may not be interposed as a barrier to reasonable state regulation of education if it is based on purely secular considerations; to have the protection of the Religion Clauses, the claims must be rooted in religious belief. Although a determination of what is a "religious" belief or practice entitled to constitutional protection may present a most delicate question, the very concept of ordered liberty precludes allowing every person to make his own standards on matters of conduct in which society as a whole has important interests. Thus, if the Amish asserted their claims because of their subjective evaluation and rejection of the contemporary secular values accepted by the majority, much as Thoreau rejected the social values of his time and isolated himself at Walden Pond, their claim would not rest on a religious basis. Thoreau's choice was philosophical and personal rather that religious, and such belief does not rise to the demands of the Religion Clause.

Giving no weight to such secular considerations, however, we see that the record in this case abundantly supports the claim that the traditional way of life of the Amish is not merely a matter of personal preference, but one of deep religious conviction, shared by an organized group, and intimately related to daily living. That the Old Order Amish daily life and religious practice stems from their faith is shown by the fact that it is in response to their literal interpretation of the Biblical injunction from the Epistle of Paul to the Romans, "Be not conformed to this world. . . ." This command is fundamental to the Amish faith. Moreover, for the Old Order Amish, religion is not simply a matter of theocratic belief. As the expert witnesses explained, the Old Order Amish religion pervades and determines virtually their entire way of life, regulating it with the detail of the Talmudic diet through the strictly enforced rules of the church community. . . .

So long as compulsory education laws were confined to eight grades of elementary basic education imparted in a nearby rural schoolhouse, with a large proportion of students of the Amish faith, the Old Order Amish had little basis to fear that school attendance would expose their children to the worldly influence they reject. But modern compulsory secondary education in rural areas is now largely carried on in a consolidated school, often remote from the student's home and alien to his daily home life. . . . The conclusion is inescapable that secondary schooling, by exposing Amish children to worldly influences in terms of attitudes, goals and values contrary to beliefs, and by substantially interfering with the religious development of the Amish child and his integration into the way of life of the Amish faith community at the crucial adolescent state of development, contravenes the basic religious tenets and practice of the Amish faith, both as to the parent and the child. . . .

In sum, the unchallenged testimony of acknowledged experts in education and religious history, almost 300 years of consistent practice, and strong evidence of a sustained faith pervading and regulating respondents' entire mode of life support the claim that enforcement of the State's requirement of compulsory formal education after the eighth grade would gravely endanger if not destroy the free exercise of respondents' religious beliefs.

Neither the findings of the trial court nor the Amish claims as to the nature of their faith are challenged in this Court by the State of Wisconsin. Its position is that the State's interest in universal compulsory formal secondary education to age 16 is so great that it is paramount to the undisputed claim of respondents that their mode of preparing their youth for Amish life, after the traditional elementary education, is an essential part of their religious belief and practice. Nor does the State undertake to meet the claim that the Amish mode of life and education is inseparable from and a part of the basic tenets of their religion— indeed, as much a part of their religious belief and practices as baptism, the confessional, or a sabbath may be for others. . . .

The State advances two primary arguments in support of its system of compulsory education. It notes, as Thomas Jefferson pointed out early in our history, that some degree of education is necessary to prepare citizens to participate effectively and intelligently in our open political system if we are to preserve freedom and independence. Further, education prepares individuals to be self-reliant and self-sufficient participants in society. We accept these proportions.

However, the evidence adduced by the Amish in this case is persuasively to the effect that an additional one or two years of formal high school for Amish children in place of their long established program of informal vocational education would do little to serve those interests. Respondents' experts testified at trial, without challenge, that the value of all education must be assessed in terms of its capacity to prepare the child for life. It is one thing to say that compulsory education for a year or two beyond the eighth grade may be necessary when its goal is the preparation of the child for life in modern society as the majority live, but it is quite another if the goal of education be viewed as the preparation of the child for life in the separated agrarian community that is the keystone of the Amish faith. . . .

Whatever their idiosyncrasies as seen by the majority, this record strongly shows that the Amish community has been a highly successful social unit within our society even if apart from the conventional "main-stream." Its members are productive and very law-abiding members of society; they reject public welfare in any of its usual modern forms. The Congress itself recognized their self-sufficiency by authorizing exemption of such groups as the Amish from the obligation to pay social security taxes. . . .

. . . .

In these terms, Wisconsin's interest in compelling the school attendance of Amish children to age 16 emerges as somewhat less substantial than requiring such attendance for children generally. For, while agricultural employment is not totally outside the legitimate concerns of the child labor laws, employment of children under parental guidance and on the family farm from age 14 to age 16 is an ancient tradition which lies at the periphery of the objectives of such laws. There is no intimation that the Amish employment of their children on family farms is in any way deleterious to their health or that Amish parents exploit children at tender years. Any such inference would be contrary to the record before us. Moreover, employment of Amish children on the family farm does not present the undesirable economic aspects of eliminating jobs which might otherwise be held by adults. . . .

Contrary to the suggestion of the dissenting opinion of Mr. Justice Douglas, our holding today in no degree depends on the assertion of the religious interest of the child as contrasted with that of the parents. It is the parents who are subject to prosecution here for failing to cause their children to attend school, and it is their right of free exercise, not that of their children, that must determine Wisconsin's power to impose criminal penalties on the parent. . . .

Our holding in no way determines the proper resolution of possible competing interests of parents, children, and the State in an appropriate state court proceeding in which the power of the State is asserted on the theory that Amish parents are preventing their minor children from attending high school despite their expressed desire to the contrary. Recognition of the claim of the State in such a proceeding would, of course, call into question traditional concepts of parental control over the religious upbringing and education of their minor children recognized in this Court's past decisions. It is clear that such an intrusion by a State into family decisions in the area of religious training would give rise to grave questions of religious freedom comparable to those raised here and those presented in *Pierce* v. *Society of Sisters*. On this record we neither reach nor decide those issues. . . .

For the reasons stated we hold, with the Supreme Court of Wisconsin, that the First and Fourteenth Amendments prevent the State from compelling respondents to cause their children to attend formal high school to age 16. Our disposition of this case, however, in no way alters our recognition of the obvious fact that courts are not school boards or legislatures, and are ill-equipped to determine the "necessity" of discrete aspects of a State's program of compulsory education. . . .

Nothing we hold is intended to undermine the general applicability of the State's compulsory school attendance statutes or to limit the power of the State to promulgate reasonable standards that, while not impairing the free exercise of religion, provide for continuing agricultural vocational education under parental and church guidance by the Old Order Amish or others similarly situated. The States have had a long history of amicable and effective relationships with church-sponsored schools, and there is no basis for assuming that, in this related context, reasonable standards cannot be established concerning the content of the continuing vocational education of Amish children under parental guidance, provided always that the state regulations are not inconsistent with what we have said in this opinion.

Affirmed.

Mr. Justice Powell and Mr. Justice Rehnquist took no part in the consideration or decision of this case.

Justice White filed a concurring opinion, which Justices Brennan and Stewart joined. White found the issue in *Yoder* much harder than Burger. White pointed out that many Amish children left the religious fold upon attaining their majority and had to make their way in the larger world just like everybody else. Did not Wisconsin have a powerful state interest in protecting these persons? Mr. Justice Douglas dissented in part. He thought Frieda Yoder's personal feelings and desires should be determinative, not her parents' views or religious beliefs. Justice Stewart, joined by Justice Brennan, filed a brief concurrence that took issue with Douglas on this point, and noted there was nothing to indicate that Frieda's beliefs differed in any way from those of her parents.

CASE STUDY: OF GOD AND TANK TURRETS

In the late 1970s Eddie C. Thomas, a Jehovah's Witness, worked for the Blau-Knox Foundry and Machinery Company in Indiana, where he fabricated sheet steel for a variety of industrial uses. Blau-Knox closed the foundry, and Eddie was transferred to a department that made turrets for military tanks. Eddie asserted that his religious beliefs prevented him from participating in the production of weapons. Blau-Knox's other operating departments were all engaged in direct production of some weapons parts, so Eddie quit and applied for unemployment compensation.

The Indiana Compensation Security Act provided that someone who voluntarily quit a job was eligible for relief only if the voluntary termination was based on "good cause [arising] in connection with [the] work." After an administrative hearing in Eddie's case, the hearing referee found that while Eddie had quit for religious reasons, he was not entitled to unemployment compensation because his leaving was not based on "good cause" arising in connection with his work, as the statute required. The Indiana courts agreed.

Eddie's case was carried to the Supreme Court of the United States by Blanc Bianchi de la Torre, a rising star among activist lawyers. There were supportive amicis briefs by Nathan Dershowitz for the American Jewish Congress, Judith Levin for the ACLU, and Leo Pfeiffer for the Jewish Peace Fellowship.

Chief Justice Burger, the proud author of *Yoder,* wrote for the majority. See *Thomas* v. *Review Board of the Indiana Employment Security Division,*

450 U.S.707 (1981). Holding that Eddie's reasons for quitting Blau-Knox were religious, the Chief Justice went on to conclude that for Indiana to decline to pay him unemployment compensation was to unconstitutionally abridge his free exercise of religion. The case was, in short, "on all fours" with *Sherbert* v. *Verner,* and while it involved specially favorable treatment of people who did things for religious reasons, there was no tension with the establishment clause.

Justice Blackmun concurred in all but the last part of Burger's opinion, which asserted that there was no tension between the reading being given by the Court to the free exercise and establishment clauses. Justice Rehnquist alone dissented, commenting that "the decision of today adds mud to the already muddied waters of First Amendment jurisprudence."

There are several points of interest about *Thomas.* First, it does represent a significant doctrinal step beyond *Sherbert* v. *Verner* and *Yoder.* In those cases the basis of the individual's religiously motivated action was a clear and long-standing tenet of faith, and a tenet held in common by all or most of the religious group to which the individual belonged. In Eddie's case, his view was not common to Jehovah's Witnesses— some share it, and some do not. In fact, another Jehovah's Witness working in the tank turret department at Blau-Knox had tried to persuade Eddie that working on weapons parts was not "unscriptural." Eddie, however, was not able to "rest with" this view, and concluded that it was based upon a less strict reading of Witness' principles than his own. Thus essentially personal religious views and interpretations may now be asserted as the basis for free exercise exceptions to otherwise valid laws.

A second point of significance is that *Thomas* coincided precisely with the rise of a significant pacifist movement within many American churches. The "nuclear freeze" movement attracted great attention in late 1981 and early 1982, and many individual churchmen counseled their followers to consult their consciences about working on weapons. The Roman Catholic Bishop of Amarillo, Texas, for instance, called upon his diocesan flock to quit their jobs at the nearby Pentax plant, where nuclear warheads were assembled, and seek "life-enhancing" rather than "life-destroying" jobs. Similarly, a Lutheran Bishop in Seattle referred to the nearby nuclear submarine maintenance facility at Bremerton, Washington, as similar to having "Dachau in our backyard." The question for the future is what are the limitations, if any, on the *Thomas* logic? Are all persons who decide their employment brings them into too close an association with the implements of war entitled to quit and file for unemployment compensation? Are only those who assert a religious reason (as opposed to a merely "ethical" reason) so enabled? Does there have to be a track record of church membership, as there was in Eddie Thomas's case? Does working on raw materials that will go into weapons count? If a significant swing toward pacifism occurs in America, the Supreme Court will have to supply some answers.

PART III

RIGHTS OF THE ACCUSED

JUSTICE Frankfurter once remarked that "the history of American freedom is, in no small measure, the history of procedure." In this part of the book we will examine those procedures which are constitutionally required in the American criminal justice process. We will be concerned with the guilt or innocence of the criminal defendants involved in the cases only indirectly. At first glance this may appear paradoxical. After all, guilt or innocence is what the whole business is about. But procedures—"technicalities," as they are sometimes called by those who would demean their importance—are, as Frankfurter properly reminded us, crucially important to the quality of society. It is an awful thing for the community to strip an individual of his liberty or even his life; we are properly preoccupied with the ways by which such grave determinations are made. We do not want just to discover the truth, but to discover the truth in a fashion that is reasonably fair and humane.

Today the very complicated and elaborate procedures of the American criminal justice process are the subject of searching inquiry and sometimes bitter controversy. Some argue that the system suffers from "procedural hypertrophy"; that defendants' rights have proliferated to the extent that truth finding and guilt determining ends are submerged and sacrificed in the pursuit of perfect fairness. In fact, the search for balance between the requirements of truth finding and fairness is always an elusive business. Simple procedures directed solely at determining the truth—"did she do it?"—run the risk of arbitrariness and unfairness. More elaborate procedures that protect accused persons from unfairness run the risk that truth will be lost sight of in an excessive preoccupation with procedural niceties.

Societies must have some mechanisms for determining who is guilty of breaking basic rules. In America this truth-finding mechanism is the criminal trial. Today, as we shall see, the criminal trial has become so costly, time consuming, and complicated that it is used only in a small fraction of all criminal cases. Most of these are disposed of through the process of "plea bargaining," which we will discuss in Chapter 18. Nevertheless, the way in which the American criminal trial is presently organized affects the whole of the criminal justice process. Investigation, arrest, and plea bargaining are the way they are because the trial is the way it is. Not all the aspects of a criminal trial are matters of constitutional law, but the Constitution does touch on the trial and other aspects of the criminal justice process at a number of points—and that number has increased dramatically in recent years. Whether the balance is being struck properly in American society today is for you to judge after considering the materials presented here.

Other societies in other times have, of course, used other mechanisms than the criminal trial to answer the question of guilt or innocence. In medieval Europe and in England until the beginning of the thirteenth century or so, the omniscience of God was invoked to settle such questions. Trial by ordeal and trial by combat were thought to give answers beyond the capacity of man to hazard.

By the middle of the thirteenth century, continental Europe had replaced trial by ordeal with a procedure in which human participants sought to determine truth. However, the standard for guilt for serious crimes was set so high that the system proved cumbersome. Only an eyewitness or a confession was considered adequate to sentence a person to the severe penalties of death or physical maiming. One result of this on the continent was the introduction, or resort to, the practice of torture. If circumstances pointed to guilt, but there was neither eyewitness nor confession, the court was forced either to supervise the imposition of torture to secure confession or step back and let the accused go. Since the pressures of society would not allow the court to permit many palpably guilty people to walk away, judicially supervised torture became a standard practice. Professor John H. Langbein, of the University of Chicago Law School, has pointed to this as an example of the kind of pathology that can develop when a society's truth-finding mechanism sets requirements that are too high and seeks to achieve perfect certainty.

In England the situation developed differently. The transition from appeal to God to the use of a human tribunal did not result in the adaptation of a standard of guilt so elevated as to warp the system. Instead, there was increasing use of lay juries—twelve good men and true of visonage—to settle the question of guilt or innocence. Today we think of the jury as necessarily impartial; indeed, that is one of the constitutional requirements for a criminal trial discussed in Chapter 17. Initially, however, the jurors were chosen precisely because of their knowledge of the accused, of local circumstances, and, indeed, of the facts surrounding the crime/events with which the accused was charged.

If one looks at the criminal trial in seventeenth and eighteenth century England—and that was the criminal trial imported into the American colonies— it strikes us as an unfair proceeding. The accused was not always or even usually represented by counsel, the rules of evidence were underdeveloped by contemporary standards, and the whole proceedings went so swiftly that to modern eyes it appears preemptory. This somewhat rough-and-ready criminal trial changed only slowly in America through the nineteenth century; most of us would have found the criminal trial as it existed at the beginning of this century still weighted unfairly in favor of the prosecution and against the defendant. We are all familiar with the old stories of hanging judges and swift justice meted out by legal illiterates on the bench.

Today, by contrast, criminal proceedings are very different. In part the change is the result of interpreting the few provisions of the United States Constitution that bear on the criminal justice process; in part it has been accomplished by Congress and the state legislatures adopting more subtle, complicated, and rigorous codes of criminal procedure. In this chapter we will be concerned principally with the constitutional protections of the accused in the criminal justice process, but we also will have occasion to note some of the statutory protections of individual liberties now built into the trial.

The constitutional protections of the accused are really of two sorts: (1) those considerations of fundamental fairness that inhere in the phrase "due process of law," which occurs in the Fifth and Fourteenth Amendments; and (2) the protections that have been created by the Supreme Court through interpretation of the specific provisions of Amendments Four through Eight— that part of the Bill of Rights which addresses criminal procedure. As we saw in Chapter 2, the provisions regarding search and seizure, the protection against self-incrimination, and so on, which originally applied only to Federal trials, have been extended by the Supreme Court through the due process clause of the Fourteenth Amendment to apply to the states. This process is now virtually complete and is reflected in the summary below. For our purposes we can take the major provisions of Amendments Four through Eight as applying to all levels of government within the United States.

To put that question behind us, however, is merely to arrive at the beginning of the maze. To say that a particular stricture, like the privilege against self-incrimination, applies universally in America does not tell us what the privilege against self-incrimination *is.* In the 1960s and 1970s the Supreme Court not only extended the specifics of the Bill of Rights to the states, it also expanded and reinterpreted these specifics—a process still very much under way. We will concentrate on this process and acquaint you with the debates that rage around what the Court has been doing. As in the preceding sections, we also will touch on the major interest groups involved and indicate how the battle lines are drawn in this area of civil liberties policy.

It may be useful before turning to the particulars of these chapters to review briefly the anatomy of the criminal justice process (see the figure on page 202). At each stage in the process, questions of procedure arise that are the subject of intense conflict today.

The Nationalization of Amendments
Four through Eight

The Fourth Amendment.

Search and Seizure. The Fourth Amendment was applied to the state in *Wolf* v. *Colorado,* 338 U.S. 25 (1949) and the federal rule requiring the exclusion of evidence seized in violation of its strictures was applied in *Mapp* v. *Ohio,* 367 U.S. 643 (1961).

The Fifth Amendment.

Double Jeopardy. In *Benton* v. *Maryland,* 395 U.S. 784 (1969), the Supreme Court held that charges of double jeopardy in state proceedings "must be judged not by the watered-down standard enunciated in Palko, but under this Court's interpretations of the Fifth Amendment double jeopardy provision."

Privilege Against Self-Incrimination. "The Fifth Amendment's exception from compulsory self-incrimination is also protected by the Fourteenth Amendment against abridgment by the States." *Malloy* v. *Hogan,* 378 U.S. 1 (1964).

Taking of Property Without Just Compensation. The "taking" clause has long been held applicable to the states. In *Penn Central Transportation Co.* v. *New York City,* 438 U.S. 104 (1978), the Court said that "of course" the taking clause "is made applicable to the States through the Fourteenth Amendment."

The Sixth Amendment.

Speedy Trial. In *Klopfer* v. *North Carolina,* 386 U.S. 213, 223 (1967), the Court said: "We hold that the right to a speedy trial is as fundamental as any of the rights secured by the Sixth Amendment." The Court reversed an order under a state procedure which permitted the prosecutor to bring a case to trial at any time on his own motion.

Public Trial. In *Estes* v. *Texas,* 381 U.S. 532, 538 (1965), dealing with a state prosecution the Court said: "We start with the proposition that it is a 'public trial' that the Sixth Amendment guarantees to the 'accused'."

Jury Trial. See *Duncan* v. *Louisiana,* 391 U.S. 145 (1968).

Notice of Charge. "No principle of procedural due process is more clearly established than that notice of the specific charge, and a chance to be heard in a trial of the issues raised by that charge, if desired, are among the constitutional rights of every accused in a criminal proceeding in all courts, state or federal." *Cole* v. *Arkansas,* 333 U.S. 196, 201 (1948).

Confrontation of Witnesses. In *Pointer* v. *Texas,* 380 U.S. 400 (1965), the Court reversed a conviction where the transcript of the testimony of a witness whom the defendant had not had a fair opportunity to cross-examine was used at the trial. "We hold today that the Sixth Amendment's right of an accused to confront the witnesses against him is likewise a fundamental right and is made obligatory on the States by the Fourteenth Amendment."

Compulsory Process of Obtaining Witnesses. In *Washington* v. *Texas,* 388 U.S. 14 (1967), the Court held: "The right of an accused to have compulsory process for obtaining witnesses in his favor stands on no lesser footing than the other Sixth Amendment rights that we have previously held applicable to the States."

Right to Counsel. See *Gideon* v. *Wainwright,* 372 U.S. 335 (1963).

The Seventh Amendment.

Civil Juries. *Walker* v. *Sauvinet,* 92 U.S 90 (1876), held that the fourteenth amendment did not require the states to provide a jury in civil cases. This interpretation stands and the states have been left free to construct their own systems for providing jury trial in civil cases.

The Eighth Amendment.

Bail. The question whether the states are under federal constitutional constraints with reference to bail was raised but not decided in *New York* v. *O'Neill,* 359 U.S. 1 (1959). Many judges seem to assume the Eighth Amendment stricture applies.

Cruel and Unusual Punishment. In *Robinson* v. *California,* 370 U.S. 660, 667 (1962), the Court stated that "a state law which imprisons a person (afflicted with the illness of narcotic addition) as a criminal, even though he has never touched any narcotic drug within the State or been guilty of any irregular behavior there inflicts a cruel and unusual punishment in violation of the Fourteenth Amendment," and in *Furman* v. *Georgia,* 408 U.S. 238 (1972), the court held "that the imposition and carrying out of the death penalty in these cases constitutes cruel and unusual punishment in violation of the Eighth and Fourteenth Amendments."

Investigation. What may law enforcement authorities do in seeking to discover violators and in gathering evidence to present to a prosecutor? In Chapter 23, when discussing personal privacy and the problem of government surveillance, we will have more to say about the question of when law enforcement should begin collecting information about people. In considering the criminal justice process here, the most troubling issues that arise during the investigative process are those of physical searches, electronic surveillance, and police interrogation.

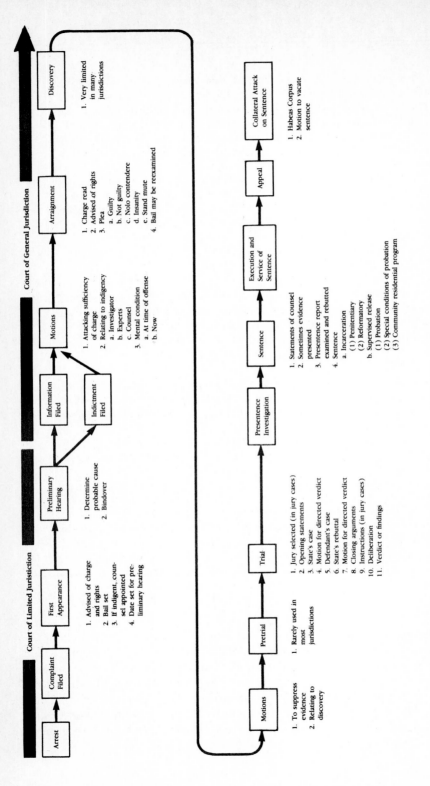

Court of Limited Jurisdiction

Arrest → Complaint Filed → First Appearance → Preliminary Hearing → Information Filed → Indictment Filed

Court of General Jurisdiction

Motions → Arraignment → Discovery

First Appearance
1. Advised of charge and rights
2. Bail set
3. If indigent, counsel appointed
4. Date set for preliminary hearing

Preliminary Hearing
1. Determine probable cause
2. Bindover

Motions
1. Attacking sufficiency of charge
2. Relating to indigency
   a. Investigator
   b. Experts
   c. Counsel
3. Mental condition
   a. At time of offense
   b. Now

Arraignment
1. Charge read
2. Advised of rights
3. Plea
   a. Guilty
   b. Not guilty
   c. Nolo contendere
   d. Insanity
   e. Stand mute
4. Bail may be reexamined

Discovery
1. Very limited in many jurisdictions

Motions → Pretrial → Trial → Presentence Investigation → Sentence → Execution and Service of Sentence → Appeal → Collateral Attack on Sentence

Motions
1. To suppress evidence
2. Relating to discovery

Pretrial
1. Rarely used in most jurisdictions

Trial
1. Jury selected (in jury cases)
2. Opening statements
3. State's case
4. Motion for directed verdict
5. Defendant's case
6. State's rebuttal
7. Motion for directed verdict
8. Closing arguments
9. Instructions (in jury cases)
10. Deliberation
11. Verdict or findings

Sentence
1. Statements of counsel
2. Sometimes evidence presented
3. Presentence report examined and rebutted
4. Sentence
   a. Incarceration
      (1) Penitentiary
      (2) Reformatory
   b. Supervised release
      (1) Probation
      (2) Special conditions of probation
      (3) Community residential program

Collateral Attack on Sentence
1. Habeas Corpus
2. Motion to vacate sentence

Stages in the Criminal Justice Process. From *The Courts: Fulcrum of the Justice System*, H. Ted Rubin, p. 189. Copyright © 1976 by Newbury Awards Records, Inc.; a subsidiary of Random House, Inc. Reprinted by permission of Random House, Inc.

Arrest. How much must the police know before they arrest a suspect and formally deprive him of liberty? The standard is something called "probable" or "reasonable" cause, and we shall see that for such an important standard it is singularly elusive.

Right to counsel. The Sixth Amendment's guarantee of a right to have counsel "cuts in" at the stage of custodial arrest and interrogation. This includes the right to have counsel provided at public expense for indigent persons.

Preliminary hearing. This is usually a relatively simple proceeding in which the accused comes before a magistrate, who determines whether probable cause exists to continue the proceeding or the accused should be discharged. If the decision is made that probable cause exists, the accused may be "bound over" or kept in jail until the matter can be placed before a grand jury, or bail may be set.

Grand jury indictment. Prosecutions of misdemeanors (minor crimes for which the punishment is characteristically less than a year's imprisonment) are usually undertaken on the basis of "information" filed by the prosecuting attorney after he has received a sworn complaint of a victim or some other person with personal knowledge of the facts. Some states allow more serious crimes (felonies) to be prosecuted in the same way. Many states, however, require that serious crimes be submitted to a grand jury. Such a body is usually composed of twenty-three persons and the votes of twelve are necessary to return an indictment—also known as a "true bill." Grand juries have great discretion as to the range of information they desire and the persons they wish to examine. Since it is not itself a criminal proceeding, individuals are not represented by counsel when they are before grand juries, but they are required to answer questions under threat of punishment for contempt of court. They may only decline to answer on the Fifth Amendment grounds of personal self-incrimination. The Fifth Amendment requires a grand jury indictment for serious crimes in federal court, but this is one of the few Bill of Rights provisions not carried through to the states.

Arraignment and plea. This is the point at which the individual appears again before a magistrate, the indictment is read, and the individual enters a plea of guilty or not guilty. In some states for some crimes a plea of *nolo contendere* is also allowed. This has the same practical affect as a plea of guilty but does not constitute a legal admission of guilt.

Pretrial motions. After the formal charge has been launched and the plea made, defense may seek to utilize a variety of motions, either to terminate the prosecutor's case by persuading the judge that the indictment does not really state a criminal charge or by attacking the admissibility of evidence. The defense also may seek "discovery" of what evidence the prosecution tends to introduce.

The trial. We will discuss the various stages of the trial in the introduction to Chapter 17.

Post-conviction remedies. If the individual is convicted, there are several possible avenues of attack open. The defendant, now the appellant, may seek to appeal. If convicted in the state system, the appeal must go up through the stages of the state judicial process to a final determination. When state remedies are exhausted, the Supreme Court of the United States might be asked to review the case. There is also the possibility of "collateral attack." After conviction in a state proceeding in which the defendant believes a substantial error of federal constitutional dimension has been committed, there is no state forum then available in which claim may be heard, so the individual may seek direct relief from a United States district court through a petition for a writ of *habeas corpus*. If that relief is denied, the individual may proceed up through the federal system seeking higher court reversal of the district court's action. With very limited exceptions, only defendants may appeal from a conviction at trial. To allow the prosecution to appeal from a verdict of not guilty is held to violate the Fifth Amendment's prohibition against double jeopardy.

SELECTED READINGS

Dershowitz, Alan M. *The Best Defense.* (New York: Random House, 1982). The reminiscences of one of the most colorful activist law professors. Includes some interesting reflections on the contemporary American criminal trial.

Fellman, David. *The Defendant's Rights Under English Law.* (Madison: University of Wisconsin Press, 1966). A very useful little volume for making comparisons to American procedure.

Fleming, Macklin. *The Price of Perfect Justice.* (New York: Basic Books, 1974). A state criminal court judge elaborates his charge of "procedural hypertrophy" with a variety of examples.

Landynski, Jacob W. *Search and Seizure and the Supreme Court.* (Baltimore, Md.: John Hopkins University Press, 1966). Although now somewhat out of date, this provides good Fourth Amendment background.

Levy, Leonard W. *Origins of the Fifth Amendment: The Right Against Self-Incrimination.* (New York: Oxford University Press, 1968). An excellent study stressing the link between coercion and unreliability of testimony.

Packer, Herbert L, *The Limits of the Criminal Sanction.* (Stanford, California: Stanford University Press, 1968). A very important essay contrasting the requirements of the criminal justice process, the "crime control model," and the "due process model."

Rutland, Robert A. *The Birth of the Bill of Rights, 1776–1791.* (Chapel Hill: University of North Carolina Press, 1955). A good, brief, standard history.

Schwartz, Bernard. *A Statutory History of the United States: Civil Rights.* 2 vols. (New York: Chelsea House, 1970). An important research tool that includes not just texts, but material on legislative history.

Sigler, Jay A. *Double Jeopardy: The Development of a Legal and Social Policy.* (Ithaca, N.Y.: Cornell University Press, 1969). A fine tracing of the evolution of doctrine in this area.

Stephens, Otis H., Jr. *The Supreme Court and Confessions of Guilt.* (Knoxville: University of Tennessee Press, 1973). Excellent treatment of the background of *Miranda.*

CHAPTER · 12

GENERAL PRINCIPLES OF DUE PROCESS

THE phrase "due process of law" in the Fourteenth Amendment has, as we have seen, two distinct constitutional functions with respect to the state judiciaries. First, the phrase embodies certain core notions of fairness, which will be developed below. Second, the phrase has been the vehicle for extending the specifics of Amendments Four through Eight to state proceedings. With regard to the first aspect of due process—the intrinsic procedural significance of the phrase—what is this required core of fairness in criminal proceedings?

Common law tradition must be our first guide, but this is not the place to trace the notion of due process back to the Saxon wood-mote. For our purposes, Justice Joseph Story, in his *Commentaries on the Constitution of the United States,* is sufficiently ancient. "Due process of law in each particular case means such an exercise of the powers of government as the settled maxims of law permit and sanction, ... " Story's work was published in 1833, but over a half century later, Thomas Cooley, in his *Constitutional Limitations,* wrote that the words due process mean "a course of legal proceedings according to those rules and principles which have been established in our systems of jurisprudence for the enforcement and protection of private rights." What is clear from these definitions is that due process was a concept firmly anchored in past practice. The basic protection was against, *irregularity* in court procedure or government action without court procedure where such was traditionally required. It is basic to an understanding of due process, as that phrase was employed in the Fifth and in the Fourteenth Amendments, to grasp that it was not an ambiguous incorporation into law of some notion of natural justice or fairness. Thus in American practice there are certain aspects of criminal procedure which have been so widely observed for so long that for a state to deny them to an individual, even though there is no specific constitutional requirement, would constitute a violation of due process.

This is what is meant by requirements of "core fairness" inherent in the phrase due process as used in the Fifth and Fourteenth Amendments. One of these core concepts of fairness is that it is the responsibility of the state in a criminal proceeding to prove the guilt of the accused beyond reasonable doubt. This "burden of proof" may not be diluted by legislation, nor may it be transferred in any part from the prosecution to the defense. We will examine the issue of burden of proof and the standard of guilt beyond reasonable doubt in the case of *In re Winship.*

Another core aspect of due process fairness is the requirement that criminal statutes not be vague; that is, for criminal sanctions to be imposed, the law must give fairly precise warning to persons of what constitutes criminal behavior. We will consider this aspect of core fairness in the context of the Supreme Court decision in *Village of Hoffman* v. *Flipside.*

In *Mason* v. *Brathwait,* we will see the Court struggling to decide when the procedure for identifying a defendant as the perpetrator of a crime is so tainted by suggestiveness as to violate core due process fairness.

In re Winship
397 U.S. 358, 90 S.Ct. 1068, 25 L.Ed.2d. 368 (1970)

The device of the juvenile court was developed early in this century to provide for dealing with children who had run afoul of the law without trying them as criminals. The ostensible task of the juvenile court is to help and to rehabilitate the child, which often involves a "finding of delinquency." While this is not a criminal conviction, it may result in involuntary institutionalization, and over the years a stigma came to be attached to this status. For these reasons the Supreme Court in *In re Gault,* 387 U.S. 1 (1967), held that *certain* of the procedural safeguards that are constitutionally required in a criminal trial also are required in a juvenile court proceeding. But *which* criminal process safeguards were required? In *Winship* the Court confronted the question of whether the findings of juvenile courts had to be based on the evidentiary standard of "beyond reasonable doubt," or whether such findings could be based on a "preponderance of evidence" standard commonly employed in civil cases and prescribed by New York as the appropriate standard for its juvenile courts. Courts below had decided that the "preponderance of evidence" was adequate, but the Supreme Court reversed. In explaining this holding, Justice Brennan had to answer two questions: Is the "beyond reasonable doubt" standard, in fact, constitutionally mandated for adult criminal trials? And, if it is, should this be one of the adult criminal safeguards required in juvenile proceedings? We are concerned only with the first of these questions, since *Winship* provided the first occasion for the Court to explain why "guilt beyond reasonable doubt" was constitutionally mandated as a matter of core due process fairness. Justice Black, in dissent, opposed the very idea of core due process fairness, taking the very traditional position that "due process" meant only "in accordance with settled and usual procedures."

Mr. Justice Brennan delivered the opinion of the Court.

Constitutional questions decided by this Court concerning the juvenile process have centered on the adjudicatory stage at "which a determination is made as to whether a juvenile is a "delinquent" as a result of alleged misconduct on his part, with the consequence that he may be committed to a state institution." *In re Gault, . . . Gault* decided that, although the Fourteenth Amendment does not require that the hearing at this stage conform with all the requirements of a criminal trial or even of the usual administrative proceeding, the Due Process Clause does require application during the adjudicatory hearing of " 'the essentials of due process and fair treatment.' " . . . This case presents the single, narrow question whether proof beyond a reasonable doubt is among the "essentials of due process and fair treatment" required during the adjudicatory stage when a juvenile is charged with an act which would constitute a crime if committed by an adult.

The requirement that guilt of a criminal charge be established by proof beyond a reasonable doubt dates at least from our early years as a Nation. The "demand for a higher degree of persuasion in criminal cases was recurrently expressed from ancient times, [though] its crystallization into the formula 'beyond a reasonable doubt' seems to have occurred as late as 1798. It is now accepted in common law jurisdictions as the measure of persuasion by which the prosecution must convince the trier of all the essential elements of guilt." . . . Although virtually unanimous adherence to the reasonable-doubt standard in common-law jurisdictions may not conclusively establish it as a requirement of due process, such adherence does "reflect a profound judgment about the way in which law should be enforced and justice administered." . . .

The reasonable-doubt standard plays a vital role in the American scheme of criminal procedure. It is a prime instrument for reducing the risk of convictions resting on factual error. The standard provides concrete substance for the presumption of innocence—that bedrock "axiomatic and elementary" principle whose "enforcement lies at the foundation of the administration of our criminal law." . . .

The requirement of proof beyond a reasonable doubt has this vital role in our criminal procedure for cogent reasons. The accused during a criminal prosecution has at stake interests of immense importance, both because of the possibility that he may lose his liberty upon conviction and because of the certainty that he would be stigmatized by the conviction. . . .

Moreover, use of the reasonable-doubt standard is indispensable to command the respect and confidence of the community in applications of the criminal law. It is critical that the moral force of the criminal law not be diluted by a standard of proof that leaves people in doubt whether innocent men are being condemned. It is also important in our free society that every individual going about his ordinary affairs have confidence that his government cannot adjudge him guilty of a criminal offense without convincing a proper factfinder of his guilt with utmost certainty.

Lest there remain any doubt about the constitutional stature of the reasonable-doubt standard, we explicitly hold that the Due Process Clause protects the accused against conviction except upon proof beyond a reasonable doubt of every fact necessary to constitute the crime with which he is charged. . . .

Reversed.

Justice Harlan concurred and Chief Justice Burger, with whom Justice Stewart joined, dissented on the issue of extending the requirement of guilt beyond reasonable doubt to juvenile proceedings. Justice Black, however, doubted that guilt beyond reasonable doubt was constitutionally mandated at all.

Mr. Justice Black, dissenting.

The majority states that "many opinions of this Court indicate that it has long been assumed that proof of a criminal charge beyond a reasonable doubt is constitutionally required." . . . I have joined in some of those opinions. . . . The Court has never clearly held, however, that proof beyond a reasonable doubt is either expressly or impliedly commanded by any provision of the Constitution. The Bill of Rights, which in my view is made fully applicable to the States by the Fourteenth Amendment, see *Adamson* v. *California,* . . . does by express language provide for, among other things, a right to counsel in criminal trials, a right to indictment, and the right of a defendant to be informed of the nature of the charges against him. And in two places the Constitution provides for trial by jury, but nowhere in that document is there any statement that conviction of crime requires proof of guilt beyond a reasonable doubt. The Constitution thus goes into some detail to spell out what kind of trial a defendant charged with crime should have, and I believe the Court has no power to add to or subtract from the procedures set forth by the Founders. I realize that it is far easier to substitute individual judges' ideas of "fairness" for the fairness prescribed by the Constitution, but I shall not at any time surrender my belief that that document itself should be our guide, not our own concept of what is fair, decent, and right. . . .

. . . .

"Due process of law" was originally used as a shorthand expression for governmental proceedings according to the "law of the land" as it existed at the time of those proceedings. Both phrases are derived from the laws of England and have traditionally been regarded as meaning the same thing. . . .

. . . .

While it is thus unmistakably clear that "due process of law" means according to "the law of the land," this Court has not consistently defined what "the law of the land" means and in my view members of this Court frequently continue to misconceive the correct interpretation of that phrase. . . .

It can be, and has been, argued that when this Court strikes down a legislative act because it offends the idea of "fundamental fairness," it furthers the basic thrust of our Bill of Rights by protecting individual freedom. But that argument ignores the effect of such decisions on perhaps the most fundamental individual liberty of our people—the right of each man to participate in the self-government of his society. Our Federal Government was set up as one of limited powers, but it was also given broad power to do all that was "necessary and proper" to carry out its basic purpose of governing the Nation, so long as those powers were not exercised contrary to the limitations set forth in the Constitution. And the States, to the extent they are not restrained by the provisions in that document, were to be left free to govern themselves in accordance with their own views of fairness and decency. ... I admit a strong, persuasive argument can be made for a standard of proof beyond a reasonable doubt in criminal cases—and the majority has made that argument well—but it is not for me as a judge to say for that reason that Congress or the States are without constitutional power to establish another standard that the Constitution does not otherwise forbid. It is quite true that proof beyond a reasonable doubt has long been required in federal criminal trials. It is also true that this requirement is almost universally found in the governing laws of the States. And as long as a particular jurisdiction requires proof beyond a reasonable doubt, then the Due Process Clause commands that every trial in that jurisdiction must adhere to that standard. ... But when, as here, a State through its duly constituted legislative branch decides to apply a different standard, then that standard, unless it is otherwise unconstitutional, must be applied to insure that persons are treated according to the "law of the land." The State of New York has made such a decision, and in my view nothing in the Due Process Clause invalidates it.

Village of Hoffman Estates v. *Flipside*
455 U.S. 489 (1982)

Another element of core due process fairness involves the specificity of criminal law. A criminal law must be clear enough to allow persons to steer a course between lawful and unlawful conduct. That is, since vague laws may entrap the innocent, fair warning must be given to the community at large as to what is forbidden and what is not. This prohibition of vagueness in criminal law is nowhere spelled out in the Constitution, but has been a constant in our legal tradition, and consistently is required by courts. It has risen to constitutional standing.

This does not mean that ignorance of the law is an excuse. Violators who come to the bar arguing that they "just didn't know" are properly condemned. The point is that we all must have a fair opportunity to know, and this is the value served by the core due process prohibition against vagueness. In this case, a local government required that any business selling items "designed or marketed for use with illegal cannabis or drugs" was required to obtain a municipal license. Guidelines specified that items such as "roach clips" and pipes used to smoke cannabis were the sorts of items for which a license was required. Flipside sold a variety of these items and sued in federal district court to enjoin the enforcement of the law against it, claiming that the ordinance was unconstitutional on two grounds. First, Flipside argued that the ordinance was overbroad and therefore interfered with its First Amendment rights of free speech. Second, Flipside argued that the ordinance was so vague as to violate the due process clause of the Fourteenth Amendment. Flipside prevailed below, and the town brought the case to the Supreme Court. It is with the second argument, involving an element of due process fairness, that we are concerned.

It should be noted that the ordinance enacted by the village of Hoffman Estates was not itself criminal in nature. It was a civil regulation of a particular economic activity within the village. The Court recognized that the due process standard of vagueness is somewhat more flexible with respect to civil regulations than with criminal liability; nonetheless the opinion by Justice Marshall represents the dominant view of the vagueness issue on the contemporary Court.

Justice Marshall delivered the opinion of the Court.

> This case presents a pre-enforcement facial challenge to a drug paraphernalia ordinance on the ground that it is unconstitutionally vague and overbroad. The ordinance in question requires a business to obtain a license if it sells any items that are "designed or marketed for use with illegal cannabis or drugs." . . .
>
> For more than three years prior to May 1, 1978, appellee The Flipside, Hoffman Estates, Inc. (Flipside) sold a variety of merchandise, including phonographic records, smoking accessories, novelty devices and jewelry, in its store located in the village of Hoffman Estates, Illinois (the village). On February 20, 1978, the village enacted an ordinance regulating drug paraphernalia, to be effective May 1, 1978. The ordinance makes it unlawful for any person "to sell any items, effect, paraphernalia, accessory or thing which is designed or marketed for use with illegal cannabis or drugs, as defined by Illinois Revised Statutes, without obtaining a license thereof." The license fee is $150.00. A business must also file affidavits that the licensee and its employees have not been convicted of a drug-related offense. Moreover, the business must keep a record of each sale of a regulated item, including the name and address of the purchaser, to be open to police inspection. No regulated item may be sold to a minor. A violation is subject to a fine of not less than $10.00 and not more than $500.00, and each day that a violation continues gives rise to a separate offense. A series of licensing guidelines prepared by the village attorney define "Paper," "Roach Clips," "Pipes" and "Paraphernalia," the sale of which is required to be licensed. . . .
>
> A law that does not reach constitutionally protected conduct and therefore satisfies the overbreadth test may nevertheless be challenged on its face as unduly vague, in violation of due process. To succeed, however, the complainant must demonstrate that the law is impermissibly vague in all of its applications. Flipside makes no such showing.
>
> The standards for evaluating vagueness were enunciated in *Grayned* v. *City of Rockford* [in 1972].
>
> "Vague laws offend several important values. First, because we assume that man is free to steer between lawful and unlawful conduct, we insist that laws give the person of ordinary intelligence a reasonable opportunity

to know what is prohibited, so that he may act accordingly. Vague laws may trap the innocent by not providing fair warning. Second, if arbitrary and discriminatory enforcement is to be prevented, laws must provide explicit standards for those who apply them. A vague law impermissibly delegates basic policy matters to policemen, judges, and juries for resolution on an *ad hoc* and subjective basis, with the attendant dangers of arbitrary and discriminatory applications."

These standards should not, of course, be mechanically applied. The degree of vagueness that the Constitution tolerates—as well as the relative importance of fair notice and fair enforcement—depend in part on the nature of the enactment. . . .
   . . . .

The ordinance requires Flipside to obtain a license if it sells "any items, effect, paraphernalia, accessory or thing which is designed or marketed for use with illegal cannabis or drugs, as defined by the Illinois Revised Statutes." . . .

The ordinance and guidelines do contain ambiguities. Nevertheless, the "designed for use" standard is sufficiently clear to cover at least some of the items that Flipside sold. The ordinance, through the guidelines, explicitly regulates "roach clips." Flipside's co-operator admitted that the store sold such items, . . . and the village Chief of Police testified that he had never seen a "roach clip" used for any purpose other than to smoke cannabis. . . . The chief also testified that a specially-designed pipe that Flipside marketed is typically used to smoke marijuana. . . . Whether further guidelines, administrative rules, or enforcement policy will clarify the more ambiguous scope of the standard in other respects is of no concern in this facial challenge. . . .

Whatever ambiguities the "designed . . . for use" standard may engender, the alternative "marketed for use" standard is transparently clear: it describes a retailer's intentional display and marketing of merchandise. The guidelines refer to the display of paraphernalia, and to the proximity of covered items to otherwise uncovered items. A retail store therefore must obtain a license if it deliberately displays its wares in a manner that appeals to or encourages illegal drug use. The standard requires scienter, since a retailer could scarcely "market" items "for" a particular use without intending that use.

Under this test, Flipside had ample warning that its marketing activities required a license. Flipside displayed the magazine "High Times" and books entitled "Marijuana Grower's Guide," "Children's Garden of Grass," and "The Pleasures of Cocaine," physically close to pipes and colored rolling papers, in clear violation of the guidelines. As noted above, Flipside's co-operator admitted that his store sold "roach clips," which are principally used for illegal purposes. Finally, in the same section of the store, Flipside had posted the sign, "You must be 18 or older to purchase any head supplies." . . .

Many American communities have recently enacted laws regulating or prohibiting the sale of drug paraphernalia. Whether these laws are wise or effective is not, of course, the province of this Court. We hold only that such legislation is not facially overbroad or vague if it does not reach constitutionally protected conduct and is reasonably clear in its application to the complainant.

Accordingly, the judgment of the Court of Appeals is reversed, and the case is remanded for further proceedings consistent with this opinion.

Justice Stevens took no part in the consideration of the case, and Justice White wrote a brief opinion concurring in the judgement.

Mason v. *Brathwaite*
432 U.S. 98, 97 S.Ct. 2243, 53 L.Ed.2d 140 (1977)

Brathwaite was convicted for selling narcotics on the basis of an eyewitness identification by an undercover police officer. It was argued on appeal that the identification was tainted because the undercover officer had been shown a single photograph of the suspect in the period between initially seeing him and making the eyewitness identification. There was no question that a certain suggestiveness was involved, and the Court of Appeals for the Second Circuit granted Brathwaite's petition for *habeas corpus*. Mason, the Connecticut state Commissioner of Corrections, who was responsible for Brathwaite as a state prisoner, took the case to the Supreme Court. He argued that the petition should not have been granted since there had been no violation of core Fourteenth Amendment due process fairness. The Court, speaking through Mr. Justice Blackmun, agreed. The majority concluded that reliability was the linchpin of fairness and thus of the admissibility of testimony as to identification. The Court rejected the suggestion that testimony as to identification should be excluded, per se, whenever there was any suggestiveness in the identification procedure.

Mr. Justice Blackmun delivered the opinion of the Court.

This case presents the issue as to whether the Due Process Clause of the Fourteenth Amendment compels the exclusion, in a state criminal trial, apart from any consideration of reliability, of pretrial identification evidence obtained by a police procedure that was both suggestive and unnecessary.

Jimmy D. Glover, a full-time trooper of the Connecticut State Police, in 1970 was assigned to the Narcotics Division in an undercover capacity. On May 5 of that year, about 7:45 p.m., e.d.t., and while there was still daylight, Glover and Henry Alton Brown, an informant, went to an apartment building at 201 Westland, in Hartford, for the purpose of purchasing narcotics from "Dickie Boy" Cicero, a known narcotics dealer. Cicero, it was thought, lived on the third floor of that apartment building. ... Glover and Brown entered the building, observed by backup Officers D'Onofrio and Gaffey, and proceeded by stairs to the third floor. Glover knocked at the door of one of the two apartments served by the stairway. The area was illuminated by natural light from a window in the third floor hallway. ... The door was opened 12 to 18 inches in response to the knock. Glover observed a man standing at the door and, behind him, a woman. Brown identified himself. Glover then asked for "two things" of narcotics. ... The man at the door held out his hand, and Glover gave him two $10 bills. The door closed. Soon the man returned and handed Glover two glassine bags. While the door was open, Glover stood within two feet of the person from whom he made the purchase and observed his face. Five to seven minutes elapsed from the time the door first opened until it closed the second time. . . .

Glover and Brown then left the building. This was about eight minutes after their arrival. Glover drove to headquarters where he described the seller to D'Onofrio and Gaffey. Glover at that time did not know the identity of the seller. . . . He described him as being "a colored man, approximately five feet eleven inches tall, dark complexion, black hair, short Afro style, and having high cheekbones, and of heavy build. He was wearing at the time blue pants and a plaid shirt." . . . D'Onofrio, suspecting from this description that respondent [Brathwaite] might be the seller, obtained a photograph of respondent from the Records Division of the Hartford Police Department. He left it at Glover's office. D'Onofrio was not acquainted with respondent personally, but did know him by sight and had seen him "[s]everal times" prior to May 5. . . . Glover, when alone, viewed the photograph for the first time upon his return to headquarters on May 7; he identified the person shown as the one from whom he had purchased the narcotics. . . .

In [this] case the District Court observed that the "sole evidence tying Brathwaite to the possession and sale of the heroin consisted in his identifications by the police undercover agent, Jimmy Glover." . . . On the constitutional issue, the court stated that the first inquiry was whether the police used an impermissibly suggestive procedure in obtaining the out-of-court identification. If so, the second inquiry is whether, under all the circumstances, that suggestive procedure gave rise to a substantial likelihood of irreparable misidentification.

Petitioner [Mason] at the outset acknowledges that "the procedure in the instant case was suggestive [because only one photograph was used] and unnecessary" [because there was no emergency or exigent circumstance]. . . . The respondent . . . proposes a *per se* rule of exclusion that he claims is dictated by the demands of the Fourteenth Amendment's guarantee of due process. . . .

The . . . *per se* approach . . . focuses on the procedures employed and requires exclusion of the out-of-court identification evidence, without regard to reliability, whenever it has been obtained through unnecessarily suggested confrontation procedures. The justifications advanced are the elimination of evidence of uncertain reliability, deterrence of the police and prosecutors, and the stated "fair assurance against the awful risks of misidentification." . . .

The second, or more lenient, approach is one that continues to rely on the totality of the circumstances. It permits the admission of the confrontation evidence if, despite the suggestive aspect, the out-of-court identification possesses certain features of reliability. Its adherents feel that the *per se* approach is not mandated by the Due Process Clause of the Fourteenth Amendment. This second approach, in contrast to the other, is ad hoc and serves to limit the societal costs imposed by a sanction that excludes relevant evidence from consideration and evaluation by the trier of fact.

There are, of course, several interests to be considered and taken into account. . . .

[First,] that the jury not hear eyewitness testimony unless that evidence has aspects of reliability. It must be observed that both approaches before us are responsive to this concern. The *per se* rule, however, goes too far since its application automatically and peremptorily, and without consideration of alleviating factors, keeps evidence from the jury that is reliable and relevant.

The second factor is deterrence. Although the *per se* approach has the more significant deterrent effect, the totality approach also has an influence on police behavior. The police will guard against unnecessarily suggestive procedures under the totality rule, as well as the *per se* one, for fear that their actions will lead to the exclusion of identifications as unreliable.

The third factor is the effect on the administration of justice. Here the *per se* approach suffers serious drawbacks. Since it denies the trier reliable evidence, it may result, on occasion, in the guilty going free. Also, because of its rigidity, the *per se* approach may make error by the trial judge more likely than the totality approach. And in those cases in which the admission of identification evidence is error under the *per se* approach but not under the totality approach— cases in which the identification is reliable despite an unnecessarily suggestive identification procedure—reversal is a Draconian sanction. Certainly, inflexible rules of exclusion that may frustrate rather than promote justice have not been viewed recently by this Court with unlimited enthusiasm. . . .

. . . .

We therefore conclude that reliability is the linchpin in determining the admissibility of identification testimony. . . .

Although identifications arising from single-photograph displays may be viewed in general with suspicion, . . . we find in the instant case little pressure on the witness to acquiesce in the suggestion that such a display entails. D'Onofrio had left the photograph at Glover's office and was not present when Glover first viewed it two days after the event. There thus was little urgency and Glover could view the photograph at his leisure. . . .

. . . .

Of course, it would have been better had D'Onofrio presented Glover with a photographic array including "so far as practicable . . . a reasonable number of persons similar to any person then suspected whose likeness is included in the array." . . . The use of that procedure would have enhanced the force of the identification at trial and would have avoided the risk that the evidence would be excluded as unreliable. But we are not disposed to view D'Onofrio's failure as one of constitutional dimension to be enforced by a rigorous and unbending exclusionary rule. The defect, if there be one, goes to weight and not to substance. . . .

The judgment of the Court of Appeals is reversed.

Justice Stevens wrote a concurring opinion, and Justice Marshall wrote a dissenting opinion, supporting the per se approach, in which Justice Brennan joined.

CASE STUDY: PROSECUTORIAL DISCLOSURE

Linda Agurs accompanied James Sowell to a motel room in the District of Columbia where they engaged in sexual intercourse. Sowell then left the room to go to a bathroom down the hall. When he returned a struggle ensued. Sowell had apparently left the contents of his pockets in disarray on the top of a dresser in the room. Two hours before entering the room Sowell had had $360 on his person and had been carrying two knives, one of them a "Bowie knife." It was with this knife that Sowell was stabbed repeatedly. No trace was found of the money and Linda Agurs was apparently unmarked by the struggle.

Agurs was convicted of second degree murder, but three months later her defense counsel filed a motion for a new trial asserting that he had discovered that Sowell had a prior criminal record including convictions for assault and possession of a deadly weapon. Counsel argued, further, that the prosecution had known of this information and failed to disclose it to the defendant at the time of the trial, and that such information, if offered into evidence, would have supported the theory of self-defense advanced in Agurs' behalf and apparently rejected by the jury. The federal district court denied a motion for a new trial, but the D.C. Circuit Court of Appeals reversed the decision, holding that the nondisclosure of Sowell's criminal record violated core due process fairness. (In this case, the due process guaranteed by the Fifth Amendment to the Constitution.)

The Government carried the case to the Supreme Court, and it was decided in 1976 as *United States* v. *Agurs,* 427 U.S. 97. Justice Stevens delivered the opinion of the Court and held that the *Agurs* case was governed by the Supreme court's prior decision in the case of *Brady* v. *Maryland,* 373 U.S. 84 (1963). Core due process required that the prosecution spontaneously disclose information which, if withheld, would result in fundamental unfairness to the defendant. In a situation such as *Agurs,* where there had been no request by the defense to the prosecution to disclose particular evidence, the proper standard, Stevens argued, was whether the omitted information, if furnished, would have created a reasonable doubt as to the guilt of the defendant where none otherwise existed. If the information was this important, and it had not been disclosed spontaneously by the prosecution, an error of constitutional magnitude had been committed.

Justice Marshall filed a dissenting opinion joined by Justice Brennan. Marshall argued that Stevens and the majority had defined the class of material that prosecutors must spontaneously disclose too narrowly. For Marshall, core due process fairness required that any significant exculpatory material in the possession of the prosecution had to be disclosed or fundamental unfairness resulted.

Both the majority and minority of the Court were agreed that due process fairness does not require the prosecution to turn over every scrap of paper in its files; rather, it must make some judgement as to the relative degree of importance of the material the defense does not know about. The judgement required by the majority—whether the information would create a reasonable doubt where none otherwise existed—is not an easy one, and one can imagine that reasonable prosecutors might well differ as to what this standard requires them to disclose. Neither is this standard of "any exculpatory material" self-implementing. Certainly material might be exculpatory and yet not necessarily create a reasonable doubt in the minds of jurors. Equally clearly, reasonable prosecutors will differ as to what is exculpatory and what is not. The Court has left prosecutors in the interesting position of making an educated guess that determines their obligation toward the defense. The minority would simply insist on a different guess than the majority.

CHAPTER · 13

ARREST

THE contemporary law of arrest in America developed out of English common law understandings, which in turn rested upon traditional custom and usage of courts running back into the Middle Ages. It is important to remember in this connection that organized police forces are a relatively modern development—the first to achieve a high level of professionalization was the London Metropolitan Force, in 1829, under the leadership of Sir Robert Peel. Before that time law enforcement had been effected in a variety of different ways. From medieval times on, the British Crown had appointed sheriffs and constables among whose duties was that of arresting wrongdoers. However, the principal task of arrest fell not on these specialized officers but on citizens generally. Two institutions are particularly interesting—the *posse commitatis* and the hue and cry.

In the event of a serious crime, when there was knowledge or suspicion as to the offender, the hue and cry would be raised, and it was the duty of all persons in the community to seize their weapons and aid in the pursuit, which continued until the offender was captured or escaped. The sheriffs and the constables also could call on ordinary citizens to form a *posse* to assist in making arrests.

The point of all this is that the notion of arrest is based on the legal status of citizenship, not on any special legal status enjoyed by police as an organized force. While most arrests today are effected by professional police, we still have the notion of citizen's arrest and, in fact, the capacity of private persons to make arrests is still theoretically equivalent to that of the police. In order for there to be an arrest, the arresting individual, whether police or civilian, must have "probable cause" or "reasonable cause" to believe that the individual being arrested has committed a serious crime—a felony. Arrests for misdemeanors—minor crimes—may only be made if the offense takes place in one's presence or on the basis of a sworn complaint from someone who did witness the behavior complained of.

The preferred mode of arrest is for a magistrate, having satisfied himself that there is probable cause to believe that a specific felony has been committed, and that a particular person has committed it, to then issue a warrant—a court order—for that person's arrest. The warrant will be executed by sworn law enforcement officers. But when a felony takes place in the presence of citizens, or where law enforcement officers have probable cause to believe that a felony has taken place, arrests without a warrant are permissible.

The key question, obviously, is what constitutes probable cause? What kind of information must a magistrate be furnished with to justify issuing a warrant? And what kind of knowledge must a street cop have to conclude that there is probable cause to arrest someone? Probable cause is, frankly, one of the most frequently invoked and most elusive concepts in American constitutional law. In the cases of *Draper* v. *the United States* and *the United States* v. *Watson,* we will see how the Supreme Court has approached the problem.

In *Terry* v. *Ohio* we will encounter another arrest related problem: May law enforcement officers detain individuals for brief periods, thus technically depriving them of their liberty, without making arrests?

Draper v. *United States*
358 U.S. 307, 79 S.Ct. 329, 3 L.Ed.2d 327 (1959)

What are the elements of "probable cause" (sometimes referred to as reasonable cause) necessary to effect a valid arrest? *Draper* is the classic case on this point, and you should be careful in reading it to note such factors as (1) the track record of the informant for reliability, (2) the detailed nature of the description and other information provided by the informer, and (3) the indications that the informer had considerable first hand knowledge of the particular illegal activity about which he provided information.

Mr. Justice Whittaker delivered the opinion of the court.

Petitioner was convicted of knowingly concealing and transporting narcotic drugs in Denver, Colorado, ... His conviction was based in part on the use in evidence against him of two "envelopes containing [865 grains of] heroin" and a hypodermic syringe that had been taken from his person, following his arrest, by the arresting officer. Before the trial, he moved to suppress that evidence as having been secured through an unlawful search and seizure. After hearing, the District Court found that the arresting officer had probable cause to arrest petitioner without a warrant and that the subsequent search and seizure were therefore incident to a lawful arrest, and overruled the motion to suppress. ... At the subsequent trial, that evidence was offered and, over petitioner's renewed objection, was received in evidence, and the trial resulted, as we have said, in petitioner's conviction. ...

The evidence offered at the hearing on the motion to suppress was not substantially disputed. It established that one Marsh, a federal narcotic agent with 29 years' experience, was stationed at Denver; that one Hereford had been engaged as a "special employee" of the Bureau of Narcotics at Denver for about six months, and from time to time gave information to Marsh regarding violations of the narcotic laws, for which Hereford was paid small sums of money, and that Marsh had always found the information given by Hereford to be accurate and reliable. On September 3, 1956, Hereford told Marsh that James Draper (petitioner) recently had taken up abode at a stated address in Denver and "was peddling narcotics to several addicts" in that city. Four days later, on September 7, Hereford told Marsh "that Draper had gone to Chicago the day before [September 6] by train [and] that he was going to bring back three ounces of heroin [and] that he would return to Denver either on the morning of the 8th of September or the morning of the 9th of September also by train." Hereford also gave Marsh a detailed physical description of Draper and of the clothing he was wearing,* and said that he would be carrying "a tan zipper bag," and that he habitually "walked real fast."

On the morning of September 8, Marsh and a Denver police officer went to the Denver Union Station and kept watch over all incoming trains from Chicago, but they did not see anyone fitting the description that Hereford had given. Repeating the process on the morning of September 9, they saw a person, having the exact physical attributes and wearing the precise clothing described by Hereford, alight from an incoming Chicago train and start walking "fast" toward the exit. He was carrying a tan zipper bag in his right hand and the left was thrust in his raincoat pocket. Marsh, accompanied by the police officer, overtook, stopped and arrested him. They then searched him and found the two "envelopes containing heroin" clutched in his left hand in his raincoat pocket, and found the syringe in the tan zipper bag. Marsh then took him (petitioner) into custody. Hereford died four days after the arrest and therefore did not testify at the hearing on the motion. . . .

The crucial question for us then is whether knowledge of the related facts and circumstances gave Marsh "probable cause" within the meaning of the Fourth Amendment, and "reasonable grounds" within the meaning of § 104(a), supra,† to believe that petitioner had committed or was committing a violation of the narcotic laws. If it did, the arrest, though without a warrant, was lawful and the subsequent search of petitioner's person and the seizure of the found heroin were validly made incident to a lawful arrest, and therefore the motion to suppress was properly overruled and the heroin was competently received in evidence at the trial. . . .

    . . . .

[We cannot agree] . . . that Marsh's information was insufficient to show probable cause and reasonable grounds to believe that petitioner had violated or was violating the narcotic laws and to justify his arrest without a warrant. The information given to narcotic agent Marsh by "special employee" Hereford may

---

* Hereford told Marsh that Draper was a Negro of light brown complexion, 27 years of age, 5 feet 8 inches tall, weighed about 160 pounds, and that he was wearing a light colored raincoat, brown slacks and black shoes.

† The terms "probable cause" as used in the Fourth Amendment and "reasonable grounds" as used in § 104(a) of the Narcotic Control Act, 70 Stat. 570, are substantial equivalents of the same meaning. . . .

have been hearsay to Marsh, but coming from one employed for that purpose and whose information had always been found accurate and reliable, it is clear that Marsh would have been derelict in his duties had he not pursued it. And when, in pursuing that information, he saw a man, having the exact physical attributes and wearing the precise clothing and carrying the tan zipper bag that Hereford had described, alight from one of the very trains from the very place stated by Hereford and start to walk at a "fast" pace toward the station exit, Marsh had personally verified every facet of the information given him by Hereford except whether petitioner had accomplished his mission and had the three ounces of heroin on his person or in his bag. And surely, with every other bit of Hereford's information being thus personally verified, Marsh had "reasonable grounds" to believe that the remaining unverified bit of Hereford's information—that Draper would have the heroin with him—was likewise true.

"In dealing with probable cause, ... as the very name implies, we deal with probabilities. These are not technical; they are the factual and practical considerations of everyday life on which reasonable and prudent men, not legal technicians, act." Brinegar v. United States, supra, at 175. Probable cause exists where "the facts and circumstances within [the arresting officers'] knowledge and of which they had reasonably trustworthy information [are] sufficient in themselves to warrant a man of reasonable caution in the belief that" an offense has been or is being committed. ...

We believe that, under the facts and circumstances here, Marsh had probable cause and reasonable grounds to believe that petitioner was committing a violation of the laws of the United States relating to narcotic drugs at the time he arrested him. The arrest was therefore lawful, and the subsequent search and seizure, having been made incident to that lawful arrest, were likewise valid. It follows that petitioner's motion to suppress was properly denied and that the seized heroin was competent evidence lawfully received at the trial.

Affirmed.

Justice Douglas wrote a dissenting opinion.

United States v. *Watson*
423 U.S. 411, 96 S.Ct. 820, 46 L.Ed.2d 598 (1976)

The *Watson* case represents an application of the criteria for probable cause elaborated in *Draper* to a different set of facts. Did the federal officers have probable cause based on the informer's signal to arrest Watson? The test, remember, is not certainty, or guilty "beyond reasonable doubt" (the standard for criminal conviction), but reasonable probability.

Mr. Justice White delivered the opinion of the Court.

This case presents questions under the Fourth Amendment as to the legality of a warrantless arrest and of an ensuing search of the arrestee's automobile carried out with his purported consent.

The relevant events began on August 17, 1972, when an informant, one Khoury, telephoned a postal inspector informing him that respondent Watson was in possession of a stolen credit card and had asked Khoury to cooperate in using the card to their mutual advantage. On five to 10 previous occasions Khoury had provided the inspector with reliable information on postal inspection matters, some involving Watson. Later that day Khoury delivered the card to the inspector. On learning that Watson had agreed to furnish additional cards, the inspector asked Khoury to arrange to meet with Watson. Khoury did so, a meeting being scheduled for August 22. Watson cancelled that engagement, but at noon on August 23, Khoury met with Watson at a restaurant designated by the latter. Khoury had been instructed that if Watson had additional stolen credit cards, Khoury was to give a designated signal. The signal was given, the officers closed in, and Watson was forthwith arrested. He was removed from the restaurant to the street where he was given the warnings required by Miranda v. Arizona. . . . A search having revealed that Watson had no credit cards on his person, the inspector asked if he could look inside Watson's car, which was standing within view. Watson said, "Go ahead," and repeated these words when the inspector cautioned that "[i]f I find anything, it is going to go against you." Using keys furnished by Watson, the inspector entered the car and found under the floor mat an envelope containing two credit cards in the names of other persons. These cards were the basis for two counts of a four-count indictment charging Watson with possessing stolen mail in violation of [federal law].

. . . .

The cases construing the Fourth Amendment thus reflect the ancient common-law rule that a peace officer was permitted to arrest without a warrant for a misdemeanor or felony committed in his presence as well as for a felony not committed in his presence if there was reasonable grounds for making the arrest. . . . This has also been the prevailing rule under state constitutions and statutes. . . .

The balance struck by the common law in generally authorizing felony arrests on probable cause, but without a warrant, has survived substantially intact. It appears in almost all of the States in the form of express statutory authorization. In 1963, the American Law Institute undertook the task of formulating a model statute governing police powers and practice in criminal law enforcement and related aspects of pretrial procedure. In 1975, after years of discussion, A Model Code of Pre-arraignment Procedure was proposed. Among its provisions was § 120.1 which authorized an officer to take a person into custody if the officer has reasonable cause to believe that the person to be arrested has committed a felony, or has committed a misdemeanor or petty misdemeanor in his presence. The commentary to this section said: "The Code thus adopts the traditional and almost universal standard for arrest without a warrant."

This is the rule Congress has long directed its principal law enforcement officers to follow. Congress has plainly decided against conditioning warrantless arrest power on proof of exigent circumstances. Law enforcement officers may find it wise to seek arrest warrants where practicable to do so, and their judgments about probable cause may be more readily accepted where backed by a warrant issued by a magistrate. . . . But we decline to transform this judicial preference into a constitutional rule when the judgment of the Nation and Congress has for so long been to authorize warrantless public arrests on probable cause rather than to encumber criminal prosecutions with endless litigation with respect to the existence of exigent circumstances, whether it was practicable to get a warrant, whether the suspect was about to flee, and the like.

Watson's arrest did not violate the Fourth Amendment, and the Court of Appeals erred in holding to the contrary.

. . .

In consequence, we reverse the judgment of the Court of Appeals. So ordered.

Justice Powell wrote a concurring opinion. Justice Stewart wrote an opinion concurring in the result. Justice Marshall wrote a dissenting opinion, which Justice Brennan joined.

Terry v. Ohio
392 U.S. 1, 88 S.Ct. 1868, 20 L.Ed.2d 889 (1968)

Until the decision in *Terry,* a legally paradoxical situation had existed in America's streets. As a matter of strict constitutional theory, the police had no right to detain anyone who was passing along the public ways unless they made a formal arrest based on probable cause. Police could request that people stop and respond to questions, and there was occasional judicial reference to a civic duty to assist the police, but that was it. Of course, police, in the everyday conduct of their work, *behaved* as though they had the power to compel people to stop and answer simple questions without making an arrest. And most people complied because they thought the police were right. A further problem arose with respect to the conduct of limited searches by officers in the course of street "stops." As we shall see in Chapter 14, a limited warrantless search is allowed pursuant to a valid arrest. But if there were no arrest, was even a "frisk" (patting down the exterior clothing to determine if a weapon is being carried) constitutional? In *Terry* the Court recognized the practical necessity of some brief detention by the police, and formulated a constitutional guideline—street "stops" and protective frisks were allowed when there was "reasonable suspicion" of a crime.

Chief Justice Warren delivered the opinion of the Court.

This case presents serious questions concerning the role of the Fourth Amendment in the confrontation on the street between the citizen and the policeman investigating suspicious circumstances.

Petitioner Terry was convicted of carrying a concealed weapon and sentenced to the statutorily prescribed term of one to three years in the penitentiary. Following the denial of a pretrial motion to suppress, the prosecution introduced in evidence two revolvers and a number of bullets seized from Terry and a codefendant, Richard Chilton, by Cleveland Police Detective Martin McFadden. At the hearing on the motion to suppress this evidence, Officer McFadden testified that while he was patrolling in plain clothes in downtown Cleveland at approximately

2:30 in the afternoon of October 31, 1963, his attention was attracted by two men, Chilton and Terry, standing on the corner of Huron Road and Euclid Avenue. He had never seen the two men before, and he was unable to say precisely what first drew his eye to them. However, he testified that he had been a policeman for 39 years and a detective for 35 and that he had been assigned to patrol this vicinity of downtown Cleveland for shoplifters and pickpockets for 30 years. He explained that he had developed routine habits of observation over the years and that he would "stand and watch people or walk and watch people at many intervals of the day." He added: "Now, in this case when I looked over they didn't look right to me at the time."

His interest aroused, Officer McFadden took up a post of observation in the entrance to a store 300 to 400 feet away from the two men. "I get more purpose to watch them when I seen their movements," he testified. He saw one of the men leave the other one and walk southwest on Huron Road, past some stores. The man paused for a moment and looked in a store window, then walked on a short distance, turned around and walked back toward the corner, pausing once again to look in the same store window. He rejoined his companion at the corner, and the two conferred briefly. Then the second man went through the same series of motions, strolling down Huron Road, looking in the same window, walking on a short distance, turning back, peering in the store window again, and returning to confer with the first man at the corner. The two men repeated this ritual alternately between five and six times apiece—in all, roughly a dozen trips. At one point, while the two were standing together on the corner, a third man approached them and engaged them briefly in conversation. This man then left the two others and walked west on Euclid Avenue. Chilton and Terry resumed their measured pacing, peering, and conferring. After this had gone on for 10 to 12 minutes, the two men walked off together, heading west on Euclid Avenue, following the path taken earlier by the third man.

By this time Officer McFadden had become thoroughly suspicious. He testified that after observing their elaborately casual and oft-repeated reconnaissance of the store window on Huron Road, he suspected the two men of "casing a job, a stick-up," and that he considered it his duty as a police officer to investigate further. He added that he feared "they may have a gun." Thus, Officer McFadden followed Chilton and Terry and saw them stop in front of Zucker's store to talk to the same man who had conferred with them earlier on the street corner. Deciding that the situation was ripe for direct action, Officer McFadden approached the three men, identified himself as a police officer and asked for their names. At this point his knowledge was confined to what he had observed. He was not acquainted with any of the three men by name or by sight, and he had received no information concerning them from any other source. When the men "mumbled something" in response to his inquiries, Officer McFadden grabbed petitioner Terry, spun him around so that they were facing the other two, with Terry between McFadden and the others, and patted down the outside of his clothing. In the left breast pocket of Terry's overcoat Officer McFadden felt a pistol. He reached inside the overcoat pocket, but was unable to remove the gun. At this point, keeping Terry between himself and the others, the officer ordered all three men to enter Zucker's store. As they went in, he removed Terry's overcoat completely, removed a .38-caliber revolver from the pocket and ordered all three men to face the wall with their hands raised. Officer McFadden proceeded to pat down the outer clothing of Chilton and the third man, Katz. He discovered another revolver in the outer pocket of Chilton's overcoat, but no weapons were found on Katz. The officer testified that he only patted the men down to see whether they had weapons, and that he did not put his hands beneath the outer garments of either Terry or Chilton until he felt their guns. So far as appears from the record, he never placed his hands beneath Katz' outer garments. Officer McFadden seized Chilton's gun, asked the proprietor of the store to call a police wagon, and took all three men to the station, where Chilton and Terry were formally charged with carrying concealed weapons.

On the motion to suppress the guns the prosecution took the position that they had been seized following a search incident to a lawful arrest. The trial court rejected this theory, stating that it "would be stretching the facts beyond reasonable comprehension" to find that Officer McFadden had had probable cause to arrest the men before he patted them down for weapons. However, the court denied the defendants' motion on the ground that Officer McFadden, on the basis of his experience, "had reasonable cause to believe . . . that the defendants were conducting themselves suspiciously, and some interrogation should be made of their action." Purely for his own protection, the court held, the officer had the right to pat down the outer clothing of these men, who he had reasonable cause to believe might be armed. The court distinguished between an investigatory "stop" and an arrest, and between a "frisk" of the outer clothing for weapons and a full-blown search for evidence of crime. The frisk, it held, was essential to the proper performance of the officer's investigatory duties, for without it "the answer to the police officer may be a bullet, and a loaded pistol discovered during the frisk is admissible."

After the court denied their motion to suppress, Chilton and Terry waived jury trial and pleaded not guilty. The court adjudged them guilty. . . . We affirm the conviction.

The Fourth Amendment provides that "the right of the people to be secure in their persons, houses, papers, and effects, against unreasonable searches and seizures, shall not be violated. . . ." This inestimable right of personal security belongs as much to the citizen on the streets of our cities as to the homeowner closeted in his study to dispose of his secret affairs. . . . We have recently held that "the Fourth Amendment protects people, not places," *Katz* v. *United States*, . . . and wherever an individual may harbor a reasonable "expectation of privacy," . . . he is entitled to be free from unreasonable governmental intrusion. . . . The question is whether in all the circumstances of this on-the-street encounter, his right to personal security was violated by an unreasonable search and seizure.

We would be less than candid if we did not acknowledge that this question thrusts to the fore difficult and troublesome issues regarding a sensitive area of police activity—issues which have never before been squarely presented to this Court. Reflective of the tensions involved are the practical and constitutional arguments pressed with great vigor on both sides of the public debate over the power of the police to "stop and frisk"—as it is sometimes euphemistically termed—suspicious persons.

On the one hand, it is frequently argued that in dealing with the rapidly unfolding and often dangerous situations on city streets the police are in need of an escalating set of flexible responses, graduated in relation to the amount of information they possess. For this purpose it is urged that distinctions should be made between a "stop" and an "arrest" (or a "seizure" of a person), and between a "frisk" and a "search". Thus, it is argued, the police should be allowed to "stop" a person and detain him briefly for questioning upon suspicion that he may be connected with criminal activity. Upon suspicion that the person may be armed, the police should have the power to "frisk" him for weapons. If the "stop" and the "frisk" give rise to probable cause to believe that the suspect has committed a crime, then the police should be empowered to make a formal "arrest," and a full incident "search" of the person. This scheme is justified in part upon the notion that a "stop" and a "frisk" amount to a mere "minor inconvenience and petty indignity," which can properly be imposed upon the citizen in the interest of effective law enforcement on the basis of a police officer's suspicion.

On the other side the argument is made that the authority of the police must be strictly circumscribed by the law of arrest and search as it has developed to date in the traditional jurisprudence of the Fourth Amendment. It is contended with some force that there is not—and cannot be—a variety of police activity which does not depend solely upon the voluntary cooperation of the citizen and yet which stops short of an arrest based upon probable cause to make such an arrest. The heart of the Fourth Amendment, the argument runs, is a severe requirement of specific justification for any intrusion upon protected personal security, coupled with a highly developed system of judicial controls to enforce upon the agents of the State the commands of the Constitution. Acquiescence by the courts in the compulsion inherent in the field interrogation practices at issue here, it is urged, would constitute an abdication of judicial control over, and indeed an encouragement of, substantial interference with liberty and personal security by police officers whose judgment is necessarily colored by their primary involvement in "the often competitive enterprise of ferreting out crime." . . . This, it is argued, can only serve to exacerbate police-community tensions in the crowded centers of our Nation's cities. . . .

. . . .

If this case involved police conduct subject to the Warrant Clause of the Fourth Amendment, we would have to ascertain whether "probable clause" existed to justify the search and seizure which took place. However, that is not the case. We do not retreat from our holdings that the police must, whenever practicable, obtain advance judicial approval of searches and seizures through the warrant procedure . . . or that in most instances failure to comply with the warrant re-quirement can only be excused by exigent circumstances. . . . But we deal here with an entire rubric of police conduct—necessarily swift action predicated upon the on-the-spot observations of the officer on the beat—which historically has not been, and as a practical matter could not be, subjected to the warrant procedure. Instead, the conduct involved in this case must be tested by the Fourth Amendment's general proscription against unreasonable searches and seizures.

Nonetheless, the notions which underlie both the warrant procedure and the requirement of probable cause remain fully relevant in this context. In order to assess the reasonableness of Officer McFadden's conduct as a general proposition, it is necessary "first to focus upon the governmental interest which allegedly justifies official intrusion upon the constitutionally protected interests of the private citizen," for there is "no ready test for determining reasonableness other than by balancing the need to search [or seize] against the invasion which the search [or seizure] entails." ... And in justifying the particular intrusion the police officer must be able to point to specific and articulable facts which, taken together with rational inferences from those facts, reasonably warrant that intrusion. The scheme of the Fourth Amendment becomes meaningful only when it is assured that at some point the conduct of those charged with enforcing the laws can be subjected to the more detached, neutral scrutiny of a judge who must evaluate the reasonableness of a particular search or seizure in light of the particular circumstances. And in making that assessment it is imperative that the facts be judged against an objective standard: would the facts available to the officer at the moment of the seizure or the search "warrant a man of reasonable caution in the belief" that the action taken was appropriate? ... Anything less would invite intrusions upon constitutionally guaranteed rights based on nothing more substantial than inarticulate hunches, a result this Court has consistently refused to sanction. ... And simple " 'good faith on the part of the arresting officer is not enough.' ... If subjective good faith alone were the test, the protections of the Fourth Amendment would evaporate, and the people would be 'secure in their persons, houses, papers, and effects,' only in the discretion of the police." ...

. . . .

We conclude that the revolver seized from Terry was properly admitted in evidence against him. At the time he seized petitioner and searched him for weapons, Officer McFadden had reasonable grounds to believe that petitioner was armed and dangerous, and it was necessary for the protection of himself and others to take swift measures to discover the true facts and neutralize the threat of harm if it materialized. The policeman carefully restricted his search to what was appropriate to the discovery of the particular items which he sought. Such a search is a reasonable search under the Fourth Amendment, and any weapons seized may properly be introduced in evidence against the person from whom they were taken.

Affirmed.

Mr. Justice Black concurs in the judgment and the opinion except where the opinion quotes from and relies upon this Court's opinion in *Katz* v. *United States* and the concurring opinion in *Warden* v. *Hayden.* [Decisions from which Black had dissented.]

Mr. Justice Harlan, concurring.

While I unreservedly agree with the Court's ultimate holding in this case, I am constrained to fill in a few gaps, as I see them, in its opinion. I do this because what is said by this Court today will serve as initial guidelines for law enforcement authorities and courts throughout the land as this important new field of law develops.

A police officer's right to make an on-the-street "stop" and an accompanying "frisk" for weapons is of course bounded by the protections afforded by the Fourth and Fourteenth Amendments. The Court holds, and I agree, that while the right does not depend upon possession by the officer of a valid warrant, nor upon the existence of probable cause, such activities must be reasonable under the circumstances as the officer credibly relates them in court. Since the question in this and most cases is whether evidence produced by a frisk is admissible, the problem is to determine what makes a frisk reasonable. ...

. . . .

I would affirm this conviction for what I believe to be the same reasons the Court relies on. I would, however, make explicit what I think is implicit in affirmance on the present facts. Officer McFadden's right to interrupt Terry's freedom of movement and invade his privacy arose only because circumstances warranted forcing an encounter with Terry in an effort to prevent or investigate a crime. Once that forced encounter was justified, however, the officer's right to take suitable measures for his own safety followed automatically.

Upon the foregoing premises, I join the opinion of the Court.

Mr. Justice White, concurring.

I join the opinion of the Court, reserving judgment, however, on some of the Court's general remarks about the scope and purpose of the exclusionary rule which the Court has fashioned in the process of enforcing the Fourth Amendment. ...

Mr. Justice Douglas, dissenting.

I agree that petitioner was "seized" within the meaning of the Fourth Amendment. I also agree that frisking petitioner and his companions for guns was a "search." But it is a mystery how that "search" and that "seizure" can be constitutional by Fourth Amendment standards, unless there was "probable cause" to believe that (1) a crime had been committed or (2) a crime was in the process of being committed or (3) a crime was about to be committed.

The opinion of the Court disclaims the existence of "probable cause." If loitering were in issue and that was the offense charged, there would be "probable cause" shown. But the crime here is carrying concealed weapons; and there is no basis for concluding that the officer had "probable cause" for believing that that crime was being committed. Had a warrant been sought, a magistrate would, therefore, have been unauthorized to issue one, for he can act if there is a showing of "probable cause." We hold today that the police have greater authority to make a "seizure" and conduct a "search" than a judge has to authorize such action. We have said precisely the opposite over and over again.

In other words, police officers up to today have been permitted to effect arrests or searches without warrants only when the facts within their personal knowledge would satisfy the constitutional standard of *probable cause*. At the time of their "seizure" without a warrant they must possess facts concerning the person arrested that would have satisfied a magistrate that "probable cause" was indeed present. The term "probable cause" rings a bell of certainty that is not sounded by phrases such as "reasonable suspicion." ...

. . . .

The infringement on personal liberty of any "seizure" of a person can only be "reasonable" under the Fourth Amendment if we require the police to possess "probable cause" before they seize him. Only that line draws a meaningful distinction between an officer's mere inkling and the presence of facts within the officer's personal knowledge which would convince a reasonable man that the person seized has committed, is committing, or is about to commit a particular crime. "In dealing with probable cause, ... as the very name implies, we deal with probabilities. These are not technical; they are the factual and practical considerations of everyday life on which reasonable and prudent men, not legal technicians, act." ...

To give the police greater power than a magistrate is to take a long step down the totalitarian path. Perhaps such a step is desirable to cope with modern forms of lawlessness. But if it is taken, it should be the deliberate choice of the people through a constitutional amendment. ...

CASE STUDY: USE OF FORCE IN ARRESTS

What degree of force may law enforcement officers use in effecting arrests? When, if ever, may police employ deadly force to preclude the escape of a fleeing felon when neither their lives nor those of civilian bystanders are immediately endangered? And under what circumstances, if any, is it legitimate for civilians to use force against officers who seek to take them into custody?

There is sharp controversy within the American legal community today over the answers to these questions. Present law is a mixture of ancient common law understandings, state statutory law, and constitutional law. In fact, the closer one looks, the more it becomes apparent that the law of arrest in America is singularly ambiguous and unsatisfactory. The reason for this lies in the accidental nature of the law in this area. The basic understandings of the law of arrest grew up to govern the relationship between *private persons* proceeding against one another. Thus if A thought a serious crime had been committed by B, A would lay forceful hands upon B and bring him before a magistrate. The magistrate would usually commit the putative felon to an extremely unpleasant jail to await trial. If, on the other hand, B correctly believed that A was mistaken, he was justified in resisting the arrest because it was not an arrest at all, but an assault on his person. Just as in a civil suit, the business of effecting a criminal arrest involves private parties in risks. Specifically, a suit for assault or false arrest if he was wrong; B risked commiting a crime if he resisted when A was right. Furthermore, if A used excessive force in arresting B, even though A had probable cause to believe that B had comitted a felony, B might resort to whatever increment of force was necessary to discourage A from using too much force in the first place!

Today, the law governing the relationships between private parties is superimposed on the activities of a uniformed, disciplined, and (one hopes and supposes) professional police force. While state legislatures have made some statutory modifications in the common law of arrests, some commentators urge fundamental rethinking of the ground rules governing contemporary police-citizen encounters. One wonders, for instance, how many people would defend the ancient common law right to use force in resisting arrest if you believe the arrest to be unlawful. Surely the better rule is that no force may be used against law enforcement officers effecting an arrest, with the legalities being sorted out in court. In the past, arrest by a private citizen might receive only a cursory review by a magistrate and result in a considerable period of incarceration under vile conditions. In such a situation a right of resistance to what is perceived as a false arrest made sense. Today, when judicial testing of probable cause is almost immediate, the risk of unjustified incarceration is relatively low. A similar argument for a new balance, struck in the light of the existence of professional police forces, can be made with respect to the excessive force. While the use of excessive force by police continues as a problem in our times, it is hard to see how that problem is anything but exacerbated by licensing counterforce.

Perhaps the most difficult question regarding the use of force in arrests involves deadly force. Minority groups, especially Blacks and Hispanics, perceive that police officers use their guns disproportionately on minority subjects. And while the traditional rule, still followed by most states, allows police officers to use all necessary means to effect the arrest of a fleeing felon, controversial police shootings are frequent throughout America and are a major block to improving police-community relations.

Consider the case of *Mattis* v. *Schnarr,* decided by the Court of Appeals of the Eighth Circuit in 1976 (547 F.2d 1007). Here Michael Mattis, age eighteen, along with a companion, age seventeen, were discovered in the office of a golf driving range at 1:30 in the morning by police officer Richard Schnarr. The boys climbed out through the back window and Schnarr shouted at them to halt. He then twice shouted, "Halt or I'll shoot." When the boys failed to stop he fired one shot in the air and one at Mattis's companion, missing him. Meanwhile a backup officer, Robert Mareck, who had arrived on the scene, ran to intercept the boys, colliding with Mattis as he came around the corner of a building. Both men fell to the pavement and a brief scuffle ensued. Mattis broke away from Marek and, as Marek was losing ground in the chase he shouted, "Stop or I'll shoot." Mattis did not stop and Marek, believing that his action was necessary to prevent Mattis' escape, fired one shot killing him. There was no question that under the law of the jurisdiction, Missouri, the action was warranted.

Circuit Judge Heaney, however, writing for a majority of the Eighth Circuit, held that the Missouri law in question was unconstitutional. For a person to be deprived of his life when this was not necessary to save the life of another, or to prevent grievous bodily harm to another, constituted a denial of that due process protected against state action by the Fourteenth Amendment.

Circuit Judge Gibson, in a vigorous dissent, joined by two other members of the Eighth Circuit (which sat *en banc* in this case), argued that such a conclusion was without foundation in American constitutional law or history and represented judicial legislation.

The U.S. Supreme Court subsequently vacated the judgment of the Eighth Circuit in *Ashcroft* v. *Mattis,* 431 U.S. 171 (1977). Nonetheless, Judge Heaney's position is one that commands increasing assent among civil libertarians. Others respond, however, that to restrict police use of their guns to self-protection will send a powerful signal to law breakers that the option of fleeing is costless. We can expect continuing and mounting controversy over the substantive policy of states with respect to deadly force, and over the question of whether the issue should be constitutionalized and thereby transferred from the authority of the state legislatures to the authority of the courts.

CHAPTER · 14

SEARCH AND SEIZURE

IN English history searches of dwellings by the King's men were considered particularly obnoxious when undertaken in connection with licensing laws for printers and tax laws of various sorts. In order to enforce these statutes, Parliament granted broad powers to enter premises in search of contraband such as illegal printing presses or smuggled goods—things people did not have a right to possess. By the late seventeenth and early eighteenth century this rather free wheeling search and seizure was provoking a strong reaction. In 1679 Parliament failed to renew the Printing Act, which provided for the licensing of printing presses, when it expired. And in 1763, when Parliament was considering the enforcement aspects of a proposed tax law, William Pitt the Elder argued that "the poorest man may in his cottage bid defiance to all the force of the Crown. It may be frail; its roof may shake; the wind may blow through it; the storm may enter; the rain may enter—but the King of England cannot enter; all his forces dare not cross the threshold of that ruined tentament."

It was also in the 1760s that "writs of assistance" were becoming increasingly troublesome to the American colonists. These writs were general authorizations to search, issued by the King's officers in America, usually in connection with enforcing the laws against smuggling. Under these orders custom inspectors could enter places they chose and search any property or papers that interested them. Since smuggling, especially in New England, was a popular cottage industry, engaged in by urban merchant and upright yeoman farmer alike, the outcry against the writs was considerable. On February 24, 1761, James Otis, representing sixty-three Boston merchants, made an argument in a Boston court that urged judges to deny applications for writs of assistance. Otis' argument is a classic formulation of the concern that underlay the framing of the Fourth Amendment to the Constitution. To be legal, warrants must be specific both as to place and what is supposed to be there. "A man in his home," Otis argued, "must be as secure as a prince in his castle. A law which violates that privacy is an instrument of slavery and villany." John Adams later commented of Otis' argument that "then and there the child of independence was born."

Thus the essential elements of the Fourth Amendment—the right of the people to be secure in their persons, houses, papers; the right against unreasonable searches and seizures; and the requirement that warrants for searches should issue from a neutral judicial magistrate only upon probable cause— had their origins in a long English and colonial history of opposition to general authorizations, whether from executive officers or from judicial officers, to enter premises and search for broad categories of material. What is prohibited is an *unreasonable search;* what makes a search reasonable is the existence of probable cause and the issuance, where practical, of a warrant. We have already explored some of the subtleties of the concept of probable cause in connection with arrests in the preceding chapter. Here we will use the case *Illinois* v. *Gates* to explore the notion of probable cause for the issuance of a search warrant.

But not all reasonable searches have to be warranted. While there is a powerful constitutional presumption in favor of securing a warrant from a magistrate, there are limited classes of specialized searches that may be undertaken by a law enforcement officer in a tight spot when there is probable cause.

One of the most common kinds of warrantless searches is the search incident to an arrest, and we shall examine that type of search in connection with the case of *Chimel* v. *California.* Another controversial class of warrantless searches involves automobiles, and we will examine this through the case of *Chambers* v. *Maroney.* Finally, a variety of "exigent circumstances" justify warrantless searches. The most common such circumstance is fresh pursuit of a fleeing felon by a law enforcement officer. In the case of *Warden* v. *Hayden*, we will encounter the debate over this type of warrantless search.

Illinois v. Gates
51 LW 4709 (1983)

The showing of probable cause necessary for the issuance of a search warrant is similar to the showing of probable cause required for an arrest warrant, which we examined in the preceding chapter in the context of *Draper* v. *U.S..* As in the case of a warrant for an arrest, a search warrant must be based upon a specified felony and further specification of what is to be searched for and why it is supposed to be at the place to be searched. This tracks the requirements of specificity and particularity developed by the court in *Draper* for arrest warrants. A further problem arises with respect to search warrants and the use of informants by the police. If the affidavit of the officer seeking a search warrant is based on information obtained from an informant, how much must be disclosed to the magistrate concerning the character and reliability of the informant? In *Spinelli* v. *U.S.,* 393 U.S. 410 (1969), Justice Harlan, speaking for the Court, harked back to the Court's previous decision in the case of *Aguilar* v. *Texas,* 378 U.S. 108 (1964), and emphasized that that case had established a two-pronged test for the issuance of the search warrant based on an informant's information. First, the officers' affidavit must set forth enough of the underlying circumstances of the case to enable the magistrate to make an independent judgment as to the validity of the informant's conclusions about what is to be searched for and where. Second, the officers seeking the warrant must support their claim that the informant is credible and the information reliable. For over a decade it was thought by most lawyers and scholars that these prongs of the *Aguilar/Spinelli* test were independent requirements—that each had to be separately satisfied for a warrant to issue properly. In *Illinois* v. *Gates,* however, the Court abandoned the formalistic *Aguilar/Spinelli* in favor of a more flexible "totality of circumstances" approach to assessing the reliability of informants.

Justice Rehnquist delivered the opinion of the Court.

Respondents Lance and Susan Gates were indicted for violation of state drug laws after police officers, executing a search warrant, discovered marijuana and other contraband in their automobile and home. Prior to trial the Gates' moved to suppress evidence seized during this search. The Illinois Supreme Court affirmed the decisions of lower state courts granting the motion. It held that the affidavit submitted in support of the State's application for a warrant to search the Gates' property was inadequate under this Court's decisions in *Aguilar* v. *Texas,* . . . and *Spinelli* v. *United States.* . . .

Bloomingdale, Ill., is a suburb of Chicago located in DuPage County. On May 3, 1978, the Bloomingdale Police Department received by mail an anonymous handwritten letter which read as follows:

"This letter is to inform you that you have a couple in your town who strictly make their living on selling drugs. They are Sue and Lance Gates, they live on Greenway, off Bloomingdale Rd. in the condominiums. Most of their buys are done in Florida. Sue his wife drives their car to Florida, where she leaves it to be loaded up with drugs, then Lance flys down and drives it back. Sue flys back after she drops the car off in Florida. May 3 she is driving down there again and Lance will be flying down in a few days to drive it back. At the time Lance drives the car back he has the trunk loaded with over $100,000.00 in drugs. Presently they have over $100,000.00 worth of drugs in their basement.

They brag about the fact they never have to work, and make their entire living on pushers.

I guarentee if you watch them carefully you will make a big catch. They are friends with some big drugs dealers, who visit their house often. Lance & Susan Gates
Greenway
in Condominiums"

The letter was referred by the Chief of Police of the Bloomingdale Police Department to Detective Mader, who decided to pursue the tip. Mader learned, from the office of the Illinois Secretary of State, that an Illinois driver's license had been issued to one Lance Gates, residing at a stated address in Bloomingdale. He contacted a confidential informant, whose examination of certain financial records revealed a more recent address for the Gates, and he also learned from a police officer assigned to O'Hare Airport that "L. Gates" had made a reservation on Eastern Airlines flight 245 to West Palm Beach, Fla., scheduled to depart from Chicago on May 5 at 4:15 p.m.

Mader then made arrangements with an agent of the Drug Enforcement Administration for surveillance of the May 5 Eastern Airlines flight. The agent later reported to Mader that Gates had boarded the flight, and that federal agents in Florida had observed him arrive in West Palm Beach and take a taxi to the nearby Holiday Inn. They also reported that Gates went to a room registered to one Susan Gates and that, at 7:00 a.m. the next morning, Gates and an unidentified woman left the motel in a Mercury bearing Illinois license plates and drove northbound on an interstate frequently used by travelers to the Chicago area. In addition, the DEA agent informed Mader that the license plate number on the Mercury was registered to a Hornet station wagon owned by Gates. The agent also advised Mader that the driving time between West Palm Beach and Bloomingdale was approximately 22 to 24 hours.

Mader signed an affidavit setting forth the foregoing facts, and submitted it to a judge of the Circuit Court of DuPage County, together with a copy of the anonymous letter. The judge of that court thereupon issued a search warrant for the Gates' residence and for their automobile.

At 5:15 a.m. on March 7th, only 36 hours after he had flown out of Chicago, Lance Gates, and his wife, returned to their home in Bloomingdale, driving the car in which they had left West Palm Beach some 22 hours earlier. The Bloomingdale police were awaiting them, searched the trunk of the Mercury, and uncovered approximately 350 pounds of marijuana. A search of the Gates' home revealed marijuana, weapons, and other contraband. The Illinois Circuit Court ordered suppression of all these items, on the ground that the affidavit submitted to the Circuit Judge failed to support the necessary determination of probable cause to believe that the Gates' automobile and home contained the contraband in question. This decision was affirmed in turn by the Illinois Appellate Court and by a divided vote of the Supreme Court of Illinois. In holding that the affidavit in fact did not contain sufficient additional information to sustain a determination of probable cause, the Illinois court applied a "two-pronged test," derived from our decision in *Spinelli* v. *United States*. ... The Illinois Supreme Court, like some others, apparently understood *Spinelli* as requiring that the anonymous letter satisfy each of two independent requirements before it could be relied on. ... According to this view, the letter, as supplemented by Mader's affidavit, first had to adequately reveal the "basis of knowledge" of the letter writer—the particular means by which he came by the information given in his report. Second, it had to provide facts sufficiently establishing either the "veracity" of the affiant's informant, or, alternatively, the "reliability" of the informant's report in this particular case.

We agree with the Illinois Supreme Court that an informant's "veracity," "reliability" and "basis of knowledge" are all highly relevant in determining the value of his report. We do not agree, however, that these elements should be understood as entirely separate and independent requirements to be rigidly exacted in every case, which the opinion of the Supreme Court of Illinois would imply. Rather ... they should be understood simply as closely intertwined issues that may usefully illuminate the commonsense, practical question whether there is "probable cause" to believe that contraband or evidence is located in a particular place.

This totality of the circumstances approach is far more consistent with our prior treatment of probable cause than is any rigid demand that specific "tests" be satisfied by every informant's tip. Perhaps the central teaching of our decisions bearing on the probable cause standard is that it is a "practical, nontechnical conception." ...

As these comments illustrate, probable cause is a fluid concept—turning on the assessment of probabilities in particular factual contexts—not readily, or even usefully, reduced to a neat set of legal rules. Informants' tips doubtless come in many shapes and sizes from many different types of persons. ...

Moreover, the "two-pronged test" directs analysis into two largely independent channels—the informant's "veracity" or "reliability" and his "basis of knowledge." ... There are persuasive arguments against according these two elements such independent status. Instead, they are better understood as relevant considerations in the totality of circumstances analysis that traditionally has guided probable cause determinations: a deficiency in one may be compensated for, in determining the overall reliability of a tip, by a strong showing as to the other, or by some other indicia of reliability. ...

Finally, the direction taken by decisions following *Spinelli* poorly serves "the most basic function of any government": "to provide for the security of the individual and of his property." ... The strictures that inevitably accompany the "two-pronged test" cannot avoid seriously impeding the task of law enforcement. ... If, as the Illinois Supreme Court apparently thought, that test must be rigorously applied in every case, anonymous tips seldom would be of greatly diminished value in police work. Ordinary citizens, like ordinary witnesses ... generally do not provide extensive recitations of the basis of their everyday observations. Likewise, as the Illinois Supreme Court observed in this case, the veracity of persons supplying anonymous tips is by hypothesis largely unknown, and unknowable. As a result, anonymous tips seldom could survive a rigorous application of either of the *Spinelli* prongs. Yet, such tips, particularly when supplemented by independent police investigation, frequently contribute to the solution of otherwise "perfect crimes." While a conscientious assessment of the basis for crediting such tips is required by the Fourth Amendment, a standard that leaves virtually no place for anonymous citizen informants is not.

For all these reasons, we conclude that it is wiser to abandon the "two-pronged test" established by our decisions in *Aguilar* and *Spinelli*. In its place we reaffirm the totality of the circumstances analysis that traditionally has informed probable cause determinations. ...

Justice Brennan, with whom Justice Marshall joins, dissenting.

Although I join Justice Stevens' dissenting opinion and agree with him that the warrant is invalid even under the Court's newly announced "totality of the circumstances" test, see *post*, at 4–5, and n. 8, I write separately to dissent from the Court's unjustified and ill-advised rejection of the two-prong test for evaluating the validity of a warrant based on hearsay announced in *Aguilar* v. *Texas* . . . and refined in *Spinelli* v. *United States*. . . .

In rejecting the *Aguilar-Spinelli* standards, the Court suggests that a "totality of the circumstances approach is far more consistent with our prior treatment of probable cause than is any rigid demand that specific 'tests' be satisfied by every informant's tip." . . .

At the heart of the Court's decision to abandon *Aguilar* and *Spinelli* appears to be its belief that "the direction taken by decisions following *Spinelli* poorly serves 'the most basic function of any government: to provide for the security of the individual and of his property.' " . . . This conclusion rests on the judgment that *Aguilar* and *Spinelli* "seriously imped[e] the task of law enforcement," . . . and render anonymous tips valueless in police work. . . . Surely, the Court overstates its case. . . . But of particular concern to all Americans must be that the Court gives virtually no consideration to the value of insuring that findings of probable cause are based on information that a magistrate can reasonably say has been obtained in a reliable way by an honest or credible person. I share Justice White's fear that the Court's rejection of *Aguilar* and *Spinelli* and its adoption of a new totality of the circumstances test, . . . "may foretell an evisceration of the probable cause standard. . . ." *Ante,* at 27 (White, J., concurring in the judgment).

The Court's complete failure to provide any persuasive reason for rejecting *Aguilar* and *Spinelli* doubtlessly reflects impatience with what it perceives to be "overly technical" rules governing searches and seizures under the Fourth Amendment. Words such as "practical," "nontechnical," and "commonsense," as used in the Court's opinion, are but code words for an overly permissive attitude towards police practices in derogation of the rights secured by the Fourth Amendment. . . . By replacing *Aguilar* and *Spinelli* with a test that provides no assurance that magistrates, rather than the police, or informants, will make determinations of probable cause; imposes no structure on magistrates' probable cause inquiries; and invites the possibility that intrusions may be justified on less than reliable information from an honest or credible person, today's decision threatens to "obliterate one of the most fundamental distinctions between our form of government, where officers are under the law, and the police-state where they are the law." . . .

Justice White wrote an opinion concurring in the judgment of the Court, and Justice Stevens wrote a dissenting opinion, which Justice Brennan joined.

Chimel v. *California*
395 U.S. 752, 89 S.Ct. 2034, 23 L.Ed.2d 637 (1969)

Perhaps the most important type of warrantless search is that "incident to a valid arrest." The arrest itself must, of course, be based on probable cause, but may be made with or without a judicial warrant. In either case, officers effecting the arrest are entitled to search the person of the arrestee and the area within his or her immediate control. In 1950 the Court had decided the case of *U.S.* v. *Rabinowitz,* 339 U.S. 56, in which federal officers arrested a forger in his one-room place of business. Incident to that arrest the officers had conducted a thorough search of the entire room including a desk, a safe, and file cabinets. *Rabinowitz* came to stand for the proposition that a search incident to a lawful arrest might extend to an area considered to be in the possession, or under the legal control, of the person arrested— Rabinowitz rented the one-room office in which he was arrested. *Chimel* v. *California* considerably narrowed the scope of a warrantless search incident to arrest, and Mr. Justice Stewart's opinion makes clear that the area within the control of the person arrested means the area of physical control. The rationale for this limited search is to protect the arresting officer by discovering any weapons that the arrestee might reach and to secure any evidence that the arrestee might reach and physically destroy if it were not sequestered. Since it is unlikely that an arrestee in custody could reach inside a locked safe or a locked cabinet, either to get a weapon or to destroy evidence, a search that wide ranging is no longer considered reasonable by the Court.

Mr. Justice Stewart delivered the opinion of the Court.

This case raises basic questions concerning the permissible scope under the Fourth Amendment of a search incident to a lawful arrest.

The relevant facts are essentially undisputed. Late in the afternoon of September 13, 1965, three police officers arrived at the Santa Ana, California, home of the petitioner with a warrant authorizing his arrest for the burglary of a coin shop. The officers knocked on the door, identified themselves to the petitioner's wife, and asked if they might come inside. She ushered them into the house, where they waited 10 or 15 minutes until the petitioner returned home from work. When the petitioner entered the house, one of the officers handed him the arrest warrant and asked for permission to "look around." The petitioner objected, but was advised that "on the basis of the lawful arrest," the officers would nonetheless conduct a search. No search warrant had been issued.

Accompanied by the petitioner's wife, the officers then looked through the entire three-bedroom house, including the attic, the garage, and a small workshop. In some rooms the search was relatively cursory. In the master bedroom and sewing room, however, the officers directed the petitioner's wife to open drawers and "to physically move contents of the drawers from side to side so that [they] might view any items that would have come from [the] burglary." After completing the search, they seized numerous items—primarily coins, but also several medals, tokens, and a few other objects. The entire search took between 45 minutes and an hour. . . .

Without deciding the question, we proceed on the hypothesis that the California courts were correct in holding that the arrest of the petitioner was valid under the Constitution. This brings us directly to the question whether the warrantless search of the petitioner's entire house can be constitutionally justified as incident to that arrest. . . .

In 1950 . . . came *United States* v. *Rabinowitz,* 339 U.S. 56, the decision upon which California primarily relies in the case now before us. In *Rabinowitz*, federal authorities had been informed that the defendant was dealing in stamps bearing forged overprints. On the basis of that information they secured a warrant for his arrest, which they executed at his one-room business office. At the time of the arrest, the officers "searched the desk, safe, and file cabinets in the office for about an hour and a half," . . . and seized 573 stamps with forged overprints. The stamps were admitted into evidence at the defendant's trial, and this Court affirmed his conviction, rejecting the contention that the warrantless search had been unlawful. The Court held that the search in its entirety fell within the principle giving law enforcement authorities "[t]he right 'to search the place where the arrest is made in order to find and seize things connected with the crime. . . .' "

Rabinowitz has come to stand for the proposition, *inter alia,* that a warrantless search "incident to a lawful arrest" may generally extend to the area that is considered to be in the "possession" or under the "control" of the person arrested. And it was on the basis of that proposition that the California courts upheld the search of the petitioner's entire house in this case. That doctrine, however, at least in the broad sense in which it was applied by the California courts in this case, can withstand neither historical nor rational analysis.

Even limited to its own facts, the *Rabinowitz* decision was . . . hardly founded on an unimpeachable line of authority. . . .

Nor is the rationale by which the State seeks here to sustain the search of the petitioner's house supported by a reasoned view of the background and purpose of the Fourth Amendment. Mr. Justice Frankfurter wisely pointed out in his *Rabinowitz* dissent that the Amendment's proscription of "unreasonable searches and seizures" must be read in light of "the history that gave rise to the words"— a history of "abuses so deeply felt by the Colonies as to be one of the potent causes of the Revolution. . . ." The Amendment was in large part a reaction to the general warrants and warrantless searches that had so alienated the colonists and had helped speed the movement for independence. In the scheme of the Amendment, therefore, the requirement that "no Warrants shall issue, but upon probable cause," plays a crucial part. . . .

Only last Term in *Terry* v. *Ohio*, 392 U.S. 1, we emphasized that "the police must, whenever practicable, obtain advance judicial approval of searches and seizures through the warrant procedure," . . . and that "[t]he scope of [a] search must be 'strictly tied to and justified by' the circumstances which rendered its initiation permissible." . . . The search undertaken by the officer in that "stop and frisk" case was sustained under that test, because it was no more than a "protective . . . search for weapons." . . .

. . . .

There is no comparable justification, however, for routinely searching any room other than that in which an arrest occurs—or, for that matter, for searching through all the desk drawers or other closed or concealed areas in that room itself. Such searches, in the absence of well-recognized exceptions, may be made only under the authority of a search warrant. The "adherence to judicial processes" mandated by the Fourth Amendment requires no less. . . .

Application of sound Fourth Amendment principles to the facts of this case produces a clear result. The search here went far beyond the petitioner's person and the area from within which he might have obtained either a weapon or something that could have been used as evidence against him. There was no constitutional justification, in the absence of a search warrant, for extending the search beyond that area. The scope of the search was, therefore, "unreasonable" under the Fourth and Fourteenth Amendments, and the petitioner's conviction cannot stand.

Reversed.

Chambers v. Maroney
399 U.S. 42, 90 S.Ct. 1975, 26 L.Ed.2d. 419 (1970)

The arrival of the mass-produced automobile on the American scene in the years after World War I resulted in dislocations of many sorts in American society. Even the Fourth Amendment law of search and seizure was modified to respond to the novel aspects of this new American habitat. Americans were spending a great deal of time in cars. In one sense, the car was like a house. It was a personal environment in which individuals could hide things, conduct private conversations, and be secure by locking up against the outside world. But the fact that automobiles moved rapidly from place to place made them distinctly unlike houses. They were not fixed to the ground and anyone with a key or a rudimentary knowledge of auto mechanics could move one in seconds. Many criminals used cars to their advantage, especially in transporting contraband. In *Carroll v. U.S.,* 267 U.S. 132 (1925), the Supreme Court held that automobiles could be searched without a warrant in circumstances that would not justify a warrantless search of a house or an office. Officers searching a car, however, did have to have probable cause to believe that it contained articles they were entitled to search for. Ever since *Carroll,* this "automobile exception" to the general warrant requirement has troubled the Court. Questions continue to recur as to the kind of knowledge and degree of suspicion that law enforcement officers must have to stop and search all or parts of moving vehicles. In *Chambers* we see the Court wrestling with just such a problem: Did the police officers know enough to stop the auto in question and affect a warrantless search? Did they have probable cause?

Mr. Justice White delivered the opinion of the Court.

During the night of May 20, 1963, a Gulf service station in North Braddock, Pennsylvania, was robbed by two men each of whom carried and displayed a gun. The robbers took the currency from the cash register; the service station attendant, one Stephen Kovacich, was directed to place the coins in his right hand glove, which was then taken by the robbers. Two teen-agers, who had earlier noticed a blue compact station wagon circling the block in the vicinity of the Gulf station, then saw the station wagon speed away from a parking lot close to the Gulf station. About the same time, they learned that the Gulf station had been robbed. They reported to police, who arrived immediately, that four men were in the station wagon and one was wearing a green sweater. Kovacich told the police that one of the men who robbed him was wearing a green sweater and the other was wearing a trench coat. A description of the car and the two robbers was broadcast over the police radio. Within an hour, a light blue compact station wagon answering the description and carrying four men was stopped by the police about two miles from the Gulf station. Petitioner was one of the men in the station wagon. He was wearing a green sweater and there was a trench coat in the car. The occupants were arrested and the car was driven to the police station. In the course of a thorough search of the car at the station, the police found concealed in a compartment under the dashboard two .38-caliber revolvers (one loaded with dumdum bullets), a right-hand glove containing small change, and certain cards bearing the name of Raymond Havicon, the attendant at a Boron service station in McKeesport, Pennsylvania, who had been robbed at gunpoint on May 13, 1963. In the course of a warrant-authorized search of petitioner's home the day after petitioner's arrest, police found and seized certain .38-caliber ammunition, including some dumdum bullets similar to those found in one of the guns taken from the station wagon.

Petitioner was indicted for both robberies. His first trial ended in a mistrial but he was convicted of both robberies at the second trial. Both Kovacich and Havicon identified petitioner as one of the robbers. The materials taken from the station wagon were introduced into evidence, Kovacich identifying his glove and Havicon the cards taken in the May 13 robbery. The bullets seized at petitioner's house were also introduced over objections of petitioner's counsel. Petitioner was sentenced to a term of four to eight years' imprisonment for the May 13 robbery and to a term of two to seven years' imprisonment for the May 20 robbery, the sentences to run consecutively. . . .

As the state courts correctly held, there was probable cause to arrest the occupants of the station wagon that the officers stopped; just as obviously was there probable cause to search the car for guns and stolen money.

In terms of the circumstances justifying a warrantless search, the Court has long distinguished between an automobile and a home or office. In *Carroll* v. *United States*, 267 U.S. 132 (1925), the issue was the admissibility in evidence of contraband liquor seized in a warrantless search of a car on the highway. After surveying the law from the time of the adoption of the Fourth Amendment onward, the Court held that automobiles and other conveyances may be searched without a warrant in circumstances that would not justify the search without a warrant of a house or an office, provided that there is probable cause to believe that the car contains articles that the officers are entitled to seize. . . .

 . . . .

In enforcing the Fourth Amendment's prohibition against unreasonable searches and seizures, the Court has insisted upon probable cause as a minimum requirement for a reasonable search permitted by the Constitution. As a general rule, it has also required the judgment of a magistrate on the probable-cause issue and the issuance of a warrant before a search is made. Only in exigent circumstances will the judgment of the police as to probable cause serve as a sufficient authorization for a search. *Carroll,* supra, holds a search warrant unnecessary where there is probable cause to search an automobile stopped on the highway; the car is movable, the occupants are alerted, and the car's contents may never be found again if a warrant must be obtained. Hence an immediate search is constitutionally permissible.

Arguably, because of the preference for a magistrate's judgment, only the immobilization of the car should be permitted until a search warrant is obtained; arguably, only the "lesser" intrusion is permissible until the magistrate authorizes the "greater." But which is the "greater" and which the "lesser" intrusion is itself a debatable question and the answer may depend on a variety of circumstances. For constitutional purposes, we see no difference between on the one hand seizing and holding a car before presenting the probable cause issue to a magistrate and on the other hand carrying out an immediate search without a warrant. Given probable cause to search, either course is reasonable under the Fourth Amendment.

On the facts before us, the blue station wagon could have been searched on the spot when it was stopped since there was probable cause to search and it was a fleeting target for a search. The probable cause factor still obtained at the station house and so did the mobility of the car unless the Fourth Amendment permits a warrantless seizure of the car and the denial of its use to anyone until a warrant is secured. In that event there is little to choose in terms of practical consequences between an immediate search without a warrant and the car's immobilization until a warrant is obtained. The same consequences may not follow where there is unforeseeable cause to search a house.

Affirmed.

Warden v. Hayden
387 U.S. 294, 87 S.Ct. 1642, 18 L.Ed.2d. 782 (1967)

One of the exceptions to the general requirement that a warrant is necessary to a search involves the presence of "exigent circumstances." Thus in a situation where the police find themselves hard pressed—where human life or important evidence is reasonably thought to hang in the balance—a warrantless entry of premises and a search may be effected. In *Warden* v. *Hayden* we examine a situation in which the police were in fresh pursuit of a felony suspect. Holding up the pursuit outside of the house while a warrant was sought would have provided an opportunity not only for evidence to be destroyed but possibly for physical harm to be inflicted on those caught inside the premises with an armed and potentially dangerous suspect.

Mr. Justice Brennan delivered the opinion of the Court.

About 8 a.m. on March 17, 1962, an armed robber entered the business premises of the Diamond Cab Company in Baltimore, Maryland. He took some $363 and ran. Two cab drivers in the vicinity, attracted by shouts of "Holdup," followed the man to 2111 Cocoa Lane. One driver notified the company dispatcher by radio that the man was a Negro about 5'8" tall, wearing a light cap and dark jacket, and that he had entered the house on Cocoa Lane. The dispatcher relayed the information to police who were proceeding to the scene of the robbery. Within minutes, police arrived at the house in a number of patrol cars. An officer knocked and announced their presence. Mrs. Hayden answered, and the officers told her they believed that a robber had entered the house, and asked to search the house. She offered no objection.

The officers spread out through the first and second floors and the cellar in search of the robber. Hayden was found in an upstairs bedroom feigning sleep. He was arrested when the officers on the first floor and in the cellar reported that no other man was in the house. Meanwhile an officer was attracted to an adjoining bathroom by the noise of running water, and discovered a shotgun and a pistol in a flush tank; another officer who, according to the District Court, "was searching the cellar for a man or the money" found in a washing machine a jacket and trousers of the type the fleeing man was said to have worn. A clip of ammunition for the pistol and a cap were found under the mattress of Hayden's bed, and ammunition for the shotgun was found in a bureau drawer in Hayden's room. All these items of evidence were introduced against respondent at his trial.

We agree with the Court of Appeals that neither the entry without warrant to search for the robber, nor the search for him without warrant was invalid. Under the circumstances of this case, "the exigencies of the situation made that course imperative." . . . The police were informed that an armed robbery had taken place, and that the suspect had entered 2111 Cocoa Lane less than five minutes before they reached it. They acted reasonably when they entered the house and began to search for a man of the description they had been given and for weapons which he had used in the robbery or might use against them. The Fourth Amendment does not require police officers to delay in the course of an investigation if to do so would gravely endanger their lives or the lives of others. Speed here was essential, and only a thorough search of the house for persons and weapons could have insured that Hayden was the only man present and that the police had control of all weapons which could be used against them or to effect an escape. . . .

The permissible scope of search must, therefore, at the least, be as broad as may reasonably be necessary to prevent the dangers that the suspect at large in the house may resist or escape.

It is argued that, while the weapons, ammunition, and cap may have been seized in the course of a search for weapons, the officer who seized the clothing was searching neither for the suspect nor for weapons when he looked into the washing machine in which he found the clothing. But even if we assume, although we do not decide, that the exigent circumstances in this case made lawful a search without warrant only for the suspect or his weapons, it cannot be said on this record that the officer who found the clothes in the washing machine was not searching for weapons. He testified that he was searching for the man or the money, but his failure to state explicitly that he was searching for weapons, in the absence of a specific question to that effect, can hardly be accorded controlling weight. He knew that the robber was armed and he did not know that some weapons had been found at the time he opened the machine. In these circumstances the inference that he was in fact also looking for weapons is fully justified.

The judgment of the Court of Appeals is

Reversed.

CASE STUDY: *MAPP* v. *OHIO* AND THE EXCLUSIONARY RULE

Under what circumstances, if any, should evidence obtained as the result of an unconstitutional search be admitted into evidence? This question has become the focus of intense and often bitter controversy within the Supreme Court and within the legal community generally. Unlike the product of a coerced confession, there is nothing intrinsically unreliable about evidence seized illegally. If the basic purpose of the criminal trial is to achieve a reliable determination of guilt, surely reliable evidence always furthers this end. But it is also important to create disincentives for policemen to violate constitutional rules. If the product of a search that violates the Fourth Amendment may be introduced as evidence, will this not tempt the police to excesses? Is there a middle way? Are there ways that pressure can be kept on law enforcement officers to abide by Fourth Amendment strictures while avoiding, at least to some extent, the cost to society of excluding reliable evidence?

The contemporary "exclusionary rule," about which controversy swells, had its origins in the Supreme Court in cases where the Fourth and Fifth Amendments flowed "almost into each other." See *Boyd* v. *U.S.,* 116 U.S. 616 (1886). To explain, early exclusions by the Supreme Court of reliable evidence had to do with illegal searches that resulted in the seizure of papers—letters, journals, or business records. Such material was "testimentary" in nature, since it involved the subject's own thoughts expressed in words and numbers. Using testimentary papers to convict someone of a crime exacerbated the Fourth Amendment violation by adding a dimension of self-incrimination proscribed by the Fifth Amendment. In 1914, in *Weeks* v. *U.S.,* 232 U.S. 383, the Court, again dealing with a case involving the seizure of papers, widened the exclusionary rule to ban all evidence seized in violation of the Fourth Amendment reasonableness requirement. This became established practice within the federal courts.

In 1949 in *Wolf* v. *Colorado,* 383 U.S. 25, the Supreme Court held the Fourth Amendment applicable to the states through the due process clause of the Fourteenth Amendment. The Court declined, however, to extend to state trials the exclusionary rule that had operated in the federal context since *Weeks.* Speaking for the Court in *Wolf,* Justice Felix Frankfurter argued that the exclusionary rule was not part of the Fourth Amendment protection against unreasonable searches and seizures but was a prudential rule, adopted by the federal courts as a matter of policy, for insuring First Amendment compliance by federal officers. It was for the states, Frankfurter argued, to decide for themselves how best to assure compliance by their officers with the Fourth Amendment.

This decision was the subject of continuing criticism for over a decade, and in 1961 in the case of *Mapp* v. *Ohio,* 364 U.S. 643, the Court, speaking through Justice Tom Clark, did extend the federal exclusionary rule to the states. But in contrast to Frankfurter in *Wolf,* Clark wrote of the exclusionary rule as inhering in the Fourth Amendment—as being part and parcel of the protection of privacy afforded by the Constitution, rather than as a matter of policy for securing compliance by police.

Since 1961, the operative constitutional law of the United States has been that any evidence seized in violation of Fourth Amendment reasonableness requirements may not be admitted into evidence. But by the late 1960s criticism of the blanket exclusionary rule was growing. It was urged by some that many police infractions (and even judicial infractions in the issuance of warrants) were innocent and of technical significance only. Supporters of the blanket exclusionary approach of *Mapp* countered that any relaxation would signal the police that wholesale invasion of Fourth Amendment rights would meet with passive official approval.

It was in 1971, in the case of *Bivens* v. *Six Unknown Federal Agents,* 403 U.S. 388, that significant opposition to the exclusionary rule within the Court resurfaced. The Court had held that the victim of a warrantless search could bring suit against the federal government for violation of Fourth Amendment rights, even though Congress had never created such a cause of action or provided any civil remedies. Dissenting from this, Chief Justice Burger first objected to the usurpation by the Court of the role of Congress in providing civil remedies against the federal government. But Burger went on to review the exclusionary rule and took the occasion to ask pointedly whether the exclusionary rule really had the deterrent effect on police misconduct that was claimed for it. If it did not, the Chief Justice suggested, then it could no longer be justified. Burger did not question "the need for some remedy to give meaning" to the constitutional guarantees against unlawful conduct by government officials, but wondered whether it was valid policy to use the exclusionary rule in the absence of "emperical evidence to support the claim that the rule actually deters." Burger wrote that Congress might take the lead in seeking "reasonable and effective substitutes" by enacting a tort remedy for a violation of Fourth Amendment rights by federal agents. Perhaps the states would follow such a lead, and the Court could withdraw from the mechanical application of the exclusionary rule.

Chief Justice Burger simply ignored the conclusion of Justice Clark, in *Mapp* v. *Ohio,* that the exclusionary rule was constitutionally mandated. He assumed, rather, the older Frankfurtarian view of exclusion as a rule of judicial policy.

In *U.S.* v. *Peltier,* 422 U.S. 531 (1977), Justice Rehnquist, writing for the majority, suggested that the exclusionary rule might be modified to allow the admission of evidence which was seized in technical violation of the Fourth Amendment if the law enforcement officers "reasonably believed that the evidence they had seized was admissible." In other words, exclusion would turn on whether the law enforcement officers operated with a good faith understanding that they were within Fourth Amendment boundaries. Defenders of the exclusionary rule, such as Mr. Justice Brennan, have rallied to argue that the rule is part and parcel of the constitutional requirement of the Fourth Amendment (so the Court can't change it even if it thinks it is bad policy). They further argue that even if the deterrence rationale is weak, it demeans courts to entertain evidence seized in violation of the Constitution.

Early in the 1982 term of Court, in a previously argued case involving a narcotics seizure in Illinois, the Court ordered reargument on the question of whether the exclusionary rule "should to any extent be modified." The reargument took place on March 1, 1983. But when *Illinois* v. *Gates* came down on June 8, it was decided on a different point (see the excerpt from the case earlier in this chapter). We shall have a further wait on the fate of the *Mapp* exclusionary rule as the battle within the Court continues.

It is interesting to note, however, how other legal systems deal with the problem of illegally seized evidence. In England, and throughout the British Commonwealth generally, the illegality of a seizure does not bar the admission of the evidence. But in Scotland a flexible exclusionary rule has been developed. A totality of circumstances approach is taken to the question of whether illegally seized evidence should be admitted in particular cases. In this way, Scottish courts seek to strike a balance between the interest of the citizen in being protected from illegal invasions of his liberties and the interest of the community in securing evidence bearing on the commission of crime.

CHAPTER · 15

ELECTRONIC EAVESDROPPING

THE Fourth Amendment strictly regulates entering homes and other places for physical searches. But what happens when a new technology comes into existence that allows information to be gathered from within a home or office without any physical entry onto the premises? This was precisely the problem presented to the Supreme Court in the middle twentieth century with the development of the telephone and then of increasingly sophisticated "bugging" devices.

The initial response of the Court was to maintain the traditional model of the Fourth Amendment in which a search was something that required physical trespass onto premises. In 1928, in the case of *Olmstead* v. *U.S.,* the justices were presented with a situation in which federal agents enforcing prohibition had placed a tap on Olmstead's telephone line at some distance from his residence. Olmstead had no property interest in the telephone line, and the tap was placed with permission of the telephone company. Chief Justice William Howard Taft, speaking for the Court, concluded that no Fourth Amendment violation had taken place. Without a trespass there was no search, and without a search there was nothing that the Court needed to test for reasonableness.

Thus telephone tapping was placed beyond the pale of the Fourth Amendment.* Electronic eavesdropping devices ("bugs") were treated differently by the Court in the 1940s and 1950s. If the placing of the device required the entry upon premises owned or occupied by the subject—premises in which he or she had a property interest—this was considered a search under the Fourteenth Amendment and governed by the reasonableness and warrant

---

* A statutory provision, section 605 of the Federal Communications Act of 1934, did make the interception and divulging of the contents of an electronic communication a crime. But this is another story.

requirements. But if the microphone could be placed without trespass, there was no search. This distinction could be quite fine—indeed, almost paper thin. In the case of *Silverman* v. *U.S.,* in 1961, a "spike mike" had been driven into the party wall separating two row houses in Washington, D.C. Since the point of the spike passed beyond the midpoint of the party wall, the Supreme Court held that a search had taken place, and because a warrant had not been obtained the evidence obtained was not usable. In another case, a microphone of high sensitivity was placed against a wall on one side and picked up conversations taking place in the office beyond the partition. Since no physical penetration of the premises next door was involved, this was not considered a search. The fruits of the eavesdrop were admissible. *Goldman* v. *U.S.,* 316 U.S. 129 (1942).

As the technology of eavesdropping was perfected, it became easier and easier to overhear conversations from outside premises and even from some distance away. While microphones concealed in olives in martinis were more popular with novelists than with law enforcement officers, the development of the parabolic microphone was fraught with implications for the traditional Fourth Amendment interpretation. If the core value of the Fourth Amendment was protection of the privacy of the home, and if that privacy could be penetrated with impunity from outside, then perhaps a kind of technological nullification of the Fourth Amendment had taken place?

The Supreme Court finally responded to the challenge, as we shall see in the case of *Katz* v. *United States.* In *U.S.* v. *White,* we shall examine the problems presented for Fourth Amendment analysis when one party consents to an electronic "overhearing" without the knowledge of the other party to the conversations. Finally, through *Hoffa* v. *U.S.,* we shall see how the Court has distinguished overhearing by a live informant from overhearing by covert electronic means.

Katz v. United States
389 U.S. 347, 88 S.Ct. 507, 19 L.Ed.2d. 576 (1967)

The year before *Katz,* in *Berger* v. *New York,* 388 U.S. 41, a majority of the Supreme Court had signaled strongly that it was finally prepared to jettison the *Olmstead* or physical trespass theory of Fourth Amendment violations. Certainly the framers of the Fourth Amendment had thought in terms of physical intrusion into premises, but technological development had created a situation in which the same sort of invasions of a person's private space, which had been possible in the framers' day only through physical trespass, could now be accomplished by electronic means. In *Katz,* special agents of the Federal Bureau of Investigation had placed a listening device in a telephone booth regularly used by the suspect (Katz) in a gambling case. Katz had no property interest in the telephone booth. Nevertheless, the Court, in the words of Justice Harlan's concurring opinion, concluded that it was a place in which a person enjoyed "a reasonable expectation of privacy" and therefore was constitutionally protected space—protected from electronic as well as physical intrusion.

Mr. Justice Stewart delivered the opinion of the Court.

The petitioner was convicted in the District Court for the Southern District of California under an eight-count indictment charging him with transmitting wagering information by telephone from Los Angeles to Miami and Boston, in violation of a federal statute. At trial the Government was permitted, over the petitioner's objection, to introduce evidence of the petitioner's end of telephone conversations, overheard by FBI agents who had attached an electronic listening and recording device to the outside of the public telephone booth from which he had placed his calls. In affirming his conviction, the Court of Appeals rejected the contention that the recordings had been obtained in violation of the Fourth Amendment, because "[t]here was no physical entrance into the area occupied by [the petitioner]." We granted certiorari in order to consider the constitutional questions thus presented.

The petitioner has phrased those questions as follows:

"A. Whether a public telephone booth is a constitutionally protected area so that evidence obtained by attaching an electronic listening recording device to the top of such a booth is obtained in violation of the right to privacy of the user of the booth.

"B. Whether physical penetration of a constitutionally protected area is necessary before a search and seizure can be said to be violative of the Fourth Amendment to the United States Constitution."

We decline to adopt this formulation of the issues. In the first place, the correct solution of Fourth Amendment problems is not necessarily promoted by incantation of the phrase "constitutionally protected area." Secondly, the Fourth Amendment cannot be translated into a general constitutional "right to privacy." That Amendment protects individual privacy against certain kinds of governmental intrusion, but its protections go further, and often have nothing to do with privacy at all. Other provisions of the Constitution protect personal privacy from other forms of governmental invasion. But the protection of a person's *general* right to privacy—his right to be let alone by other people—is, like the protection of his property and of his very life, left largely to the law of the individual States.

Because of the misleading way the issues have been formulated, the parties have attached great significance to the characterization of the telephone booth from which the petitioner placed his calls. The petitioner has strenuously argued that the booth was a "constitutionally protected area." The Government has maintained with equal vigor that it was not. But this effort to decide whether or not a given "area," viewed in the abstract, is "constitutionally protected" deflects attention from the problem presented by this case. For the Fourth Amendment protects people, not places. What a person knowingly exposes to the public, even in his own home or office, is not a subject of Fourth Amendment protection. . . .

The Government stresses the fact that the telephone booth from which the petitioner made his calls was constructed partly of glass, so that he was as visible after he entered it as he would have been if he had remained outside. But what he sought to exclude when he entered the booth was not the intruding eye—it was the uninvited ear. He did not shed his right to do so simply because he made his calls from a place where he might be seen. No less than an individual in a business office, in a friend's apartment, or in a taxicab, a person in a telephone booth may rely upon the protection of the Fourth Amendment. One who occupies it, shuts the door behind him, and pays the toll that permits him to place a call is surely entitled to assume that the words he utters into the mouthpiece will not be broadcast to the world. To read the Constitution more narrowly is to ignore the vital role that the public telephone has come to play in private communication.

The Government contends, however, that the activities of its agents in this case should not be tested by Fourth Amendment requirements, for the surveillance technique they employed involved no physical penetration of the telephone booth from which the petitioner placed his calls. It is true that the absence of such penetration was at one time thought to foreclose further Fourth Amendment inquiry. Olmstead v. United States, ...

We conclude that the underpinnings of *Olmstead* . . . have been so eroded by our subsequent decisions that the "trespass" doctrine there enunciated can no longer be regarded as controlling. The Government's activities in electronically listening to and recording the petitioner's words violated the privacy upon which he justifiably relied while using the telephone booth and thus constituted a "search and seizure" within the meaning of the Fourth Amendment. The fact that the electronic device employed to achieve that end did not happen to penetrate the wall of the booth can have no constitutional significance. . . .

. . . .

Wherever a man may be, he is entitled to know that he will remain free from unreasonable searches and seizures. The government agents here ignored "the procedure of antecedent justification . . . that is central to the Fourth Amendment," a procedure that we hold to be a constitutional precondition of the kind of electronic surveillance involved in this case. Because the surveillance here failed to meet that condition, and because it led to the petitioner's conviction, the judgment must be reversed.

Mr. Justice Harlan, concurring.

I join the opinion of the Court, which I read to hold only (a) that an enclosed telephone booth is an area where, like a home, . . . a person has a constitutionally protected reasonable expectation of privacy; (b) that electronic as well as physical intrusion into a place that is in this sense private may constitute a violation of the Fourth Amendment; and (c) that the invasion of a constitutionally protected area by federal authorities is, as the Court has long held, presumptively unreasonable in the absence of a search warrant.

As the Court's opinion states, "the Fourth Amendment protects people, not places." The question, however, is what protection it affords to those people. Generally, as here, the answer to that question requires reference to a "place." My understanding of the rule that has emerged from prior decisions is that there is a twofold requirement, first that a person have exhibited an actual (subjective) expectation of privacy and, second, that the expectation be one that society is prepared to recognize as "reasonable." Thus a man's home is, for most purposes, a place where he expects privacy, but objects, activities, or statements that he exposes to the "plain view" of outsiders are not "protected" because no intention to keep them to himself has been exhibited. ...

Justice Douglas wrote a concurring opinion, which Justice Brennan joined. Justice White also concurred and Justice Black dissented.

United States v. White
401 U.S. 745, 91 S.Ct. 1122, 28 L.Ed.2d. 453 (1971)

Katz established that a Fourth Amendment warrant was necessary in order for government to invade the expectation of privacy that parties had in what was perceived as a secure electronic communication. But what if one party to an electronic communication consents to it being overheard by a third party, while the second party remains ignorant? As we shall see in the *Hoffa* case, the Court has held that the testimony of an informer as to things told him in confidence by a criminal defendant does not violate the Fourth Amendment. This holding was left intact by the Court's decision in *Katz*. The question in *U.S.* v. *White* was whether the simultaneous transmission and recording of a conversation engaged in by an informant, without the knowledge of the individual who eventually became the subject of prosecution, is more like the electronic eavesdropping that *Katz* held to be subject to the Fourth Amendment's warrant requirement, or is governed by the *Hoffa* doctrine that we all take our chances in what we disclose to other persons. The question of third party electronic eavesdropping has proved extremely vexing to the Court, and the Justices are deeply divided about it. In *U.S.* v. *White* there is no opinion for the Court. Justice White delivered a plurality opinion.

Mr. Justice White announced the judgment of the Court and an opinion in which the Chief Justice, Mr. Justice Stewart, and Mr. Justice Blackmun join.

In 1966, respondent James A. White was tried and convicted under two consolidated indictments charging various illegal transactions in narcotics. ... The issue before us is whether the Fourth Amendment bars from evidence the testimony of governmental agents who related certain conversations which had occurred between defendant White and a government informant, Harvey Jackson, and which the agents overheard by monitoring the frequency of a radio transmitter carried by Jackson and concealed on his person. On four occasions the conversations took place in Jackson's home; each of these conversations was overheard by an agent concealed in a kitchen closet with Jackson's consent and by a second agent outside the house using a radio receiver. Four other conversations—one in respondent's home, one in a restaurant, and two in Jackson's car—were overheard by the use of radio equipment. ...

Katz v. United States ... finally swept away doctrines that electronic eavesdropping is permissible under the Fourth Amendment unless physical invasion of a constitutionally protected area produced the challenged evidence. In that case government agents, without petitioner's consent or knowledge, attached a listening device to the outside of a public telephone booth and recorded the defendant's end of his telephone conversations. In declaring the recordings inadmissible in evidence in the absence of a warrant authorizing the surveillance, the Court overruled *Olmstead* . . . and held that the absence of physical intrusion into the telephone booth did not justify using electronic devices in listening to and recording Katz' words, thereby violating the privacy on which he justifiably relied while using the telephone in those circumstances. . . .

Hoffa v. United States . . . which was left undisturbed by *Katz,* held that however strongly a defendant may trust an apparent colleague, his expectations in this respect are not protected by the Fourth Amendment when it turns out that the colleague is a government agent regularly communicating with the authorities. In these circumstances, "no interest legitimately protected by the Fourth Amendment is involved," for that amendment affords no protection to "a wrongdoer's misplaced belief that a person to whom he voluntarily confides his wrongdoing will not reveal it." . . .

Conceding that *Hoffa* . . . remained unaffected by *Katz,* the Court of Appeals nevertheless read both *Katz* and the Fourth Amendment to require a different result if the agent not only records his conversations with the defendant but instantaneously transmits them electronically to other agents equipped with radio receivers. Where this occurs, the Court of Appeals held, the Fourth Amendment is violated and the testimony of the listening agents must be excluded from evidence.

To reach this result it was necessary for the Court of Appeals to hold that On *Lee* v. *United States*, 343 U.S. 747 (1952), was no longer good law. In that case, which involved facts very similar to the case before us, the Court first rejected claims of a Fourth Amendment violation because the informer had not trespassed when he entered the defendant's premises and conversed with him. To this extent the Court's rationale cannot survive *Katz*. But the Court announced a second and independent ground for its decision; for it went on to say that overruling *Olmstead* . . . would be of no aid to On Lee since he "was talking confidentially and indiscreetly with one he trusted, and he was overheard. . . . It would be a dubious service to the genuine liberties protected by the Fourth Amendment to make them bedfellows with spurious liberties improvised by farfetched analogies which would liken eavesdropping on a conversation, with the connivance of one of the parties, to an unreasonable search or seizure. We find no violation of the Fourth Amendment here." . . . We see no indication in *Katz* that the Court meant to disturb that understanding of the Fourth Amendment or to disturb the result reached in the *On Lee* case, nor are we now inclined to overturn this view of the Fourth Amendment.

. . . .

Our problem is not what the privacy expectations of particular defendants in particular situations may be or the extent to which they may in fact have relied on the discretion of their companions. Very probably, individual defendants neither know nor suspect that their colleagues have gone or will go to the police or are carrying recorders or transmitters. Otherwise, conversation would cease and our problem with these encounters would be nonexistent or far different from those now before us. Our problem, in terms of the principles announced in *Katz,* is what expectations of privacy are constitutionally "justifiable"—what expectations the Fourth Amendment will protect in the absence of a warrant. So far, the law permits the frustration of actual expectations of privacy by permitting authorities to use the testimony of those associates who for one reason or another have determined to turn to the police, as well as by authorizing the use of informants in the manner exemplified by *Hoffa*. . . . If the law gives no protection to the wrongdoer whose trusted accomplice is or becomes a police agent, neither should it protect him when that same agent has recorded or transmitted the conversations which are later offered in evidence to prove the State's case. . . .

The judgment of the Court of Appeals is reversed.

Justice Brennan and Justice Black concurred in the result. Justices Harlan, Douglas, and Marshall wrote dissenting opinions.

Hoffa v. *United States*
385 U.S. 293, 87 S.Ct. 408, 17 L.Ed.2d. 374 (1966)

The problem of a "wired informer," which was examined in *White*, was only difficult because the use of informants, per se, is not governed by the Fourth Amendment. In *Hoffa*, a divided court adopted the theory of "assumption of the risk," and held that we all must take our chances in confiding to other individuals. Confiding is a voluntary act we undertake with open eyes and is, therefore, qualitatively different from the unconsented overhearing through a telephone tap or by an electronic device covertly placed.

Mr. Justice Stewart delivered the opinion of the Court.

Over a period of several weeks in the late autumn of 1962 there took place in a federal court in Nashville, Tennessee, a trial by jury in which James Hoffa was charged with violating a provision of the Taft-Hartley Act. That trial, known in the present record as the Test Fleet trial, ended with a hung jury. The petitioners now before us—James Hoffa, Thomas Parks, Larry Campbell, and Ewing King— were tried and convicted in 1964 for endeavoring to bribe members of that jury. The convictions were affirmed by the Court of Appeals. A substantial element in the Government's proof that led to the convictions of these four petitioners was contributed by a witness named Edward Partin, who testified to several incriminating statements which he said petitioners Hoffa and King had made in his presence during the course of the Test Fleet trial. Our grant of certiorari was limited to the single issue of whether the Government's use in this case of evidence supplied by Partin operated to invalidate these convictions.

It is contended that only by violating the petitioner's rights under the Fourth Amendment was Partin able to hear the petitioner's incriminating statements in the hotel suite, and that Partin's testimony was therefore inadmissible under the exclusionary rule of *Weeks* v. *United States*, 232 U.S. 383. The argument is that Partin's failure to disclose his role as a government informer vitiated the consent that the petitioner gave to Partin's repeated entries into the suite, and that by listening to the petitioner's statements Partin conducted an illegal "search" for verbal evidence. . . .

Where the argument falls is in its misapprehension of the fundamental nature and scope of Fourth Amendment protection. What the Fourth Amendment protects is the security a man relies upon when he places himself or his property within a constitutionally protected area, be it his home or his office, his hotel room or his automobile. There he is protected from unwarranted governmental intrusion. And when he puts something in his filing cabinet, in his desk drawer, or in his pocket, he has the right to know it will be secure from an unreasonable search or an unreasonable seizure. . . .

In the present case, however, it is evident that no interest legitimately protected by the Fourth Amendment is involved. It is obvious that the petitioner was not relying on the security of his hotel suite when he made the incriminating statements to Partin or in Partin's presence. Partin did not enter the suite by force or by stealth. He was not a surreptitious eavesdropper. Partin was in the suite by invitation, and every conversation which he heard was either directed to him or knowingly carried on in his presence. The petitioner, in a word, was not relying on the security of the hotel room; he was relying upon his misplaced confidence that Partin would not reveal his wrongdoing. As counsel for the petitioner himself points out, some of the communications with Partin did not take place in the suite at all, but in the "hall of the hotel," in the "Andrew Jackson Hotel lobby," and "at the courthouse."

Neither this Court nor any member of it has ever expressed the view that the Fourth Amendment protects a wrongdoer's misplaced belief that a person to whom he voluntarily confides his wrongdoing will not reveal it. . . .

Adhering to these views, we hold that no right protected by the Fourth Amendment was violated in the present case.

Chief Justice Warren wrote a dissenting opinion. Justices Douglas and Clark also dissented.

CASE STUDY: INFORMING IS A DIRTY BUSINESS

We learned from the *Hoffa* case that the use of informers, per se, is not governed by the Fourth Amendment. But this does not end the matter. For the use of informants ("running informers," in the argot of the trade) is a business which, while necessary, is deeply problematical. Informants come in all shapes and sizes. Sometimes they are people who "walk in" to a law enforcement agency and volunteer to furnish information. Such walk-ins can be motivated by ideology, a desire for personal revenge, or by anticipation of reward from the officials with which they deal. Or an informant may be an obliging bartender at a watering place frequented by persons in whom the police have an interest. Alternatively, law enforcement officers may take the initiative in seeking to penetrate a particular group or network of associations by recruiting an informer. In these cases, the inducement is typically financial, although in some context, notably the enforcement of the drug laws, recruitment may be affected by a threat of arrest and prosecution if the target does not agree to become an informer.

The most reliable technique for penetration is to employ a trained undercover officer. This, however, is always expensive and in many instances altogether impossible—the law enforcement agency may have no one available with the proper age or ethnic characteristics, and penetration may only be achieved in certain circumstances by persons with a long "track record" in the particular line of illegal activity being investigated.

In most cases, when police do use informants, this involves people who are professionally and legally committed to the rule of law in deals with persons who are unstable, venial, and highly likely to be deceptive and difficult to control. There is an indisposition to the use of informants in this way which runs deeply in the Anglo-American legal tradition. But simply to renounce the use of informants altogether would cripple law enforcement in specialized areas such as organized crime, narcotics dealing, and political terrorism.

An excellent example of the dangers of the use of informants occurs in David J. Gallo's study of *The FBI and Martin Luther King, Jr.* (New York, Norton, 1981). A Soviet double agent run by the FBI in a counter-intelligence operation triggered concern within the Bureau over the influence of an American Communist within Dr. Martin Luther King, Jr.'s immediate entourage. How was the Bureau to discover whether the influence was apparent or real? Obviously, the most efficient way was to cultivate informants within the Southern Christian Leadership Conference, which King headed. This was done, in addition to extensive surveillance of King through microphones and other electronic devices. The problem was that the interest in Dr. King, driven in part by the racism of J. Edgar Hoover, the Director of the FBI, resulted in an investigation of such scope that the immediate justification for its undertaking, the possibility of Communist intervention in the civil rights movement, was lost sight of. Tactics of blackmail and disinformation were used against King which, while they might conceivably be justified in combating the activities of a foreign intelligence service within the United States, were altogether out of place in dealing with a major domestic political figure. In short, the King investigation got completely out of hand, and the development of informants within a domestic political group, on which millions of Americans fixed their legitimate aspirations, was scandalous.

Professor Anthony Amsterdam of the New York University Law School has been one of a number of commentators to argue that the use of informants by law enforcement should be brought within the scope of Fourth Amendment protection. In an influential article, "Perspectives on the Fourth Amendment," 58 *Minnesota Law Review* 349 (1974), Amsterdam asked why the invasion of privacy by a hidden microphone was any more severe or obnoxious than the invasion of privacy that took place when an informant, paid and directed by law enforcement, insinuated himself into the bosom of a group and reported on intimate conversations and doings.

The point has force, but the difficulties with Amsterdam's suggestion are considerable. Who is an informant? Would the Fourth Amendment requirement cover walk-ins? Would it cover persons who casually volunteered evidence without specific inducement? Is it realistic to suppose that informants, a notoriously shy species, would come forward to volunteer their services if Fourth Amendment warrant requirements were extended to them (with the attendant records available to be consulted by clerks and lawyers)?

The Supreme Court may be right in not requiring warrants, but there is no question that the practical difficulties of using informants will continue to plague the courts and the police into the future.

CHAPTER · 16

RIGHT TO COUNSEL AND PROTECTION AGAINST SELF-INCRIMINATION

IN Chapter 1 we discussed Anthony Lewis' influential book, *Gideon's Trumpet,* on the case of *Gideon* v. *Wainwright.* This was the story of the ways in which the Supreme Court extended the Sixth Amendment's requirement of counsel—interpreted as court-appointed counsel if the defendant could not afford one—to the states. This requirement of court-appointed counsel now obtains at all levels of government for all serious crimes, meaning any crime where incarceration may result from a conviction. The requirement of court-appointed counsel also obtains for all parts of the criminal prosecution. This includes appearances such as a preliminary hearing, and, as we shall see, it includes the provision of counsel immediately after arrest and before interrogation.

In this immediate post-arrest context the right to counsel is intimately interrelated with the Fifth Amendment's privilege against self-incrimination, which was extended to the states in 1964. In the wake of this, however, a gray area existed with respect to questioning by the police of suspects who had been taken into custody. The right of self-incrimination was understood to apply in the detective squadroom, but must the suspect be told he need not say anything? And was this coupled with a Sixth Amendment right of court-appointed counsel to advise the suspect?

Of course, it was understood that any statement to the police that was not given voluntarily was in violation of the Fifth Amendment, and the Supreme Court traditionally used a "totality of circumstances" approach in determining whether a statement was voluntary. Not only would physical coercion render a statement involuntary and hence inadmissible, but psychological pressure also was recognized as capable of overcoming the will. The Court examined factors such as the age of the defendant, the complexity of the charge, the length of the time the subject had been held, the mental and physical state of the defendant, and so on, in determining whether a statement was voluntary.

But it was not necessary under this approach that the individual be explicitly informed that he or she had a right to remain silent.

In the cases that follow *Gideon* v. *Wainwright*, *Ross* v. *Moffitt* is involved with the question of how far the Sixth Amendment right to counsel continues after the conviction of a defendant at trial. *Miranda* v. *Arizona*, in 1966, marks the watershed with respect to both the privilege against self-incrimination and the right to counsel as they obtain in the immediate post-arrest context. In that case, the Court held that the individual must be informed of his or her right to remain silent and of the right to have a court-appointed counsel. In the final case of *Brewer* v. *Williams*, we will examine a controversial application of the so-called *Miranda* rule, which resulted in an incriminating statement to the police being excluded as evidence.

Gideon v. *Wainwright*
372 U.S. 335, 83 S.Ct. 792, 9 L.Ed.2d. 799 (1963)

The story of this case was briefly told in Chapter 1, and we noted the significance of Anthony Lewis' popular book about it. Here we need only to emphasize the issue actually before the Court. In the case of *Betts* v. *Brady*, in 1942, the Court had held that a defendant's federal constitutional right to counsel under the due process clause of the Fourteenth Amendment depended on the circumstances of the particular case. Whether or not a defendant had been denied due process by the refusal of the court to appoint free counsel depended on whether the charge was especially complex, whether the defendant was reasonably intelligent or retarded, whether there was a language barrier to be overcome, and whether the case was tried under circumstances of community hostility to the defendant. In short, a "totality of circumstances" approach was followed. The question was whether the refusal to appoint free counsel for an indigent defendant rendered the proceedings fundamentally unfair to the defendant. In *Gideon,* the Court was urged to abandon the fundamental fairness approach to counsel under the Fourteenth Amendment, and simply to extend to the states, via the due process clause, the Sixth Amendment's guarantee (operative in federal forums) of counsel in all serious criminal cases. A majority of the Court was persuaded. The selective approach of *Betts* v. *Brady* was abandoned in favor of a blanket requirement of court-appointed counsel for all indigent defendants charged with serious crimes.

Mr. Justice Black delivered the opinion of the Court.

Petitioner was charged in a Florida state court with having broken and entered a poolroom with intent to commit a misdemeanor. This offense is a felony under Florida law. Appearing in court without funds and without a lawyer, petitioner asked the court to appoint counsel for him, whereupon the following colloquy took place:

"The Court: Mr. Gideon, I am sorry, but I cannot appoint Counsel to represent you in this case. Under the laws of the State of Florida, the only time the Court can appoint Counsel to represent a Defendant is when that person is charged with a capital offense. I am sorry, but I will have to deny your request to appoint Counsel to defend you in this case.

"The Defendant: The United States Supreme Court says I am entitled to be represented by Counsel." [Not so, but Gideon's declaration proved prophetic.] Put to trial before a jury, Gideon conducted his defense about as well as could be expected from a layman. He made an opening statement to the jury, cross-examined the State's witnesses, presented witnesses in his own defense, declined to testify himself, and made a short argument "emphasizing his innocence to the charge contained in the Information filed in this case." The jury returned a verdict of guilty, and petitioner was sentenced to serve five years in the state prison. . . . Since Gideon was proceeding *in forma pauperis,* we appointed counsel to represent him and requested both sides to discuss in their briefs and oral arguments the following: "Should this Court's holding in *Betts* v. *Brady,* 316 U.S. 455, be reconsidered?" . . .

The Sixth Amendment provides, "In all criminal prosecutions, the accused shall enjoy the right . . . to have the Assistance of Counsel for his defence." We have construed this to mean that in federal courts counsel must be provided for defendants unable to employ counsel unless the right is competently and intelligently waived. Betts argued that this right is extended to indigent defendants in state courts by the Fourteenth Amendment. In response the Court stated that, while the Sixth Amendment laid down "no rule for the conduct of the States, the question recurs whether the constraint laid by the Amendment upon the national courts expresses a rule so fundamental and essential to a fair trial, and so, to due process of law, that it is made obligatory upon the States by the Fourteenth Amendment." . . . In order to decide whether the Sixth Amendment's guarantee of counsel is of this fundamental nature, the Court in *Betts* set out and considered "[r]elevant data on the subject . . . afforded by constitutional and statutory provisions subsisting in the colonies and the States prior to the inclusion of the Bill of Rights in the national Constitution, and in the constitutional, legislative, and judicial history of the States to the present date." . . . On the basis of this historical data the Court concluded that "appointment of counsel is not a fundamental right, essential to a fair trial." . . . It was for this reason the *Betts* Court refused to accept the contention that the Sixth Amendment's guarantee of counsel for indigent federal defendants was extended to or, in the words of that Court, "made obligatory upon the States by the Fourteenth Amendment." Plainly, had the Court concluded that appointment of counsel for an indigent criminal defendant was "a fundamental right, essential to a fair trial," it would have held that the Fourteenth Amendment requires appointment of counsel in a state court, just as the Sixth Amendment requires in a federal court.

We accept *Betts* v. *Brady's* assumption, based as it was on our prior cases, that a provision of the Bill of Rights which is "fundamental and essential to a fair trial" is made obligatory upon the States by the Fourteenth Amendment. We think the Court in *Betts* was wrong, however, in concluding that the Sixth Amendment's guarantee of counsel is not one of these fundamental rights. . . .

[R]eason and reflection require us to recognize that in our adversary system of criminal justice, any person haled into court, who is too poor to hire a lawyer, cannot be assured a fair trial unless counsel is provided for him. This seems to us to be an obvious truth. Governments, both state and federal, quite properly spend vast sums of money to establish machinery to try defendants accused of crime. Lawyers to prosecute are everywhere deemed essential to protect the public's interest in an orderly society. Similarly, there are few defendants charged with crime, few indeed, who fail to hire the best lawyers they can get to prepare and present their defenses. That government hires lawyers to prosecute and defendants who have the money hire lawyers to defend are the strongest indications of the widespread belief that lawyers in criminal courts are necessities, not luxuries. The right of one charged with crime to counsel may not be deemed fundamental and essential to fair trials in some countries, but it is in ours. From the very beginning, our state and national constitutions and laws have laid great emphasis on procedural and substantive safeguards designed to assure fair trials before impartial tribunals in which every defendant stands equal before the law. This noble ideal cannot be realized if the poor man charged with crime has to face his accusers without a lawyer to assist him. . . .

The judgment is reversed and the cause is remanded to the Supreme Court of Florida for further action not inconsistent with this opinion.

Reversed.

Justice Douglas wrote a brief separate opinion. Justice Clark wrote an opinion concurring in the result, while Justice Harlan wrote a concurring opinion.

Ross v. Moffitt
417 U.S. 600, 94 S.Ct. 2437, 41 L.Ed.2d. 341 (1974)

The Court, in *Gideon* v. *Wainwright,* held that free, court-appointed counsel to those who cannot afford to retain counsel themselves is required in all serious criminal cases. Given this decision, the question was bound to arise, what about counsel on appeal? In 1963, in *Douglas* v. *California,* 372 U.S. 353, the Supreme Court held that states must provide counsel for indigent defendants for the first level of appeal beyond the trial court. Such first level appeals are usually appeals "as of right"; that is, the first level appellate court is bound by law to review the appeal made by a convicted defendant. Beyond this first level, however, higher state courts and the Supreme Court have discretion over whether to review cases or not. Appeals are screened for merit before they are considered. *Ross* v. *Moffitt* raises the question of whether a state should be required to provide free counsel to indigent defendants for discretionary appeals to the state supreme court and for the seeking of review by the Supreme Court of the United States. Justice Rehnquist wrote for the majority that discretionary appeals were sufficiently different from first level appeals as of right so that counsel was not required.

Mr. Justice Rehnquist delivered the opinion of the Court.

We are asked in this case to decide whether *Douglas* v. *California*, 372 U.S. 353 (1963), which requires appointment of counsel for indigent state defendants on their first appeal as of right, should be extended to require counsel for discretionary state appeals and for applications for review in this Court. . . .

We do not believe that the Due Process Clause requires North Carolina to provide respondent with counsel on his discretionary appeal to the State Supreme Court. At the trial stage of a criminal proceeding, the right of an indigent defendant to counsel at his trial is fundamental and binding upon the States by virtue of the Sixth and Fourteenth Amendments. *Gideon* v. *Wainwright*, 372 U.S. 335 (1963). But there are significant differences between the trial and appellate stages of a criminal proceeding. The purpose of the trial stage from the State's point of view is to convert a criminal defendant from a person presumed innocent to one found guilty beyond a reasonable doubt. To accomplish this purpose, the State employs a prosecuting attorney who presents evidence to the court, challenges any witnesses offered by the defendant, argues rulings of the court, and makes direct arguments to the court or jury seeking to persuade them of the defendant's guilt. Under these circumstances ". . . reason and reflection require us to recognize that in our adversary system of criminal justice, any person haled into court, who is too poor to hire a lawyer, cannot be assured a fair trial unless counsel is provided for him." *Gideon* v. *Wainwright*, 372 U.S., at 344.

By contrast, it is ordinarily the defendant, rather than the State, who initiates the appellate process, seeking not to fend off the efforts of the State's prosecutor but rather to overturn a finding of guilt made by a judge or jury below. The defendant needs an attorney on appeal not as a shield to protect him against being "haled into court" by the State and stripped of his presumption of innocence, but rather as a sword to upset the prior determination of guilt. This difference is significant for, while no one would agree that the State may simply dispense with the trial stage of proceedings without a criminal defendant's consent, it is clear that the State need not provide any appeal at all. . . . The fact that an appeal *has* been provided does not automatically mean that a State then acts unfairly by refusing to provide counsel to indigent defendants at every stage of the way. . . . Unfairness results only if indigents are singled out by the State and denied meaningful access to that system because of their poverty. . . .

This is not to say, of course, that a skilled lawyer, particularly one trained in the somewhat arcane art of preparing petitions for discretionary review, would not prove helpful to any litigant able to employ him. An indigent defendant seeking review in the Supreme Court of North Carolina is therefore somewhat handicapped in comparison with a wealthy defendant who has counsel assisting him in every conceivable manner at every stage in the proceeding. But both the opportunity to have counsel prepare an initial brief in the Court of Appeals [where appeal in North Carolina is "as of right"] and the nature of discretionary review in the Supreme Court of North Carolina make this relative handicap far less than the handicap borne by the indigent defendant denied counsel on his initial appeal as of right in *Douglas*. And the fact that a particular service might be of benefit to an indigent defendant does not mean that the service is constitutionally required. The duty of the State under our cases is not to duplicate the legal arsenal that may be privately retained by a criminal defendant in a continuing effort to reverse his conviction, but only to assure the indigent defendant an adequate opportunity to present his claims fairly in the context of the State's appellate process. We think respondent was given that opportunity under the existing North Carolina system.

Much of the discussion [above] . . . is equally relevant to the question of whether a State must provide counsel for a defendant seeking review of his conviction in this Court. North Carolina will have provided counsel for a convicted defendant's only appeal as of right, and the brief prepared by that counsel together with one and perhaps two North Carolina appellate opinions will be available to this Court in order that it may decide whether or not to grant certiorari. This Court's review, much like that of the Supreme Court of North Carolina, is discretionary and depends on numerous factors other than the perceived correctness of the judgment we are asked to review. . . .

. . . .

The suggestion that a State is responsible for providing counsel to one petitioning this Court simply because it initiated the prosecution which led to the judgment sought to be reviewed is unsupported by either reason or authority. . . .

The judgment of the Court of Appeals' holding to the contrary is

Reversed.

Justice Douglas dissented, joined by Justices Brennan and Marshall.

Miranda v. *Arizona*
384 U.S. 436, 86 S.Ct. 1602, 16 L.Ed.2d. 694 (1966)

Even more insistent than the questions about court-appointed counsel on appeal, which were raised in the mid-60s after *Gideon* v. *Wainright,* were the questions asked during the same period about the right to counsel before trial. Specifically, the writings of Professor Yale Kamizar, of the University of Michigan Law School, and other civil libertarians focused attention on the interrogation of criminal suspects whom police had taken into custody. The Court had long recognized that a confession could be admitted into evidence only when it was voluntary. Physical or even psychological coercion overbore the will of the defendant, introduced an element of unreliability into the statement, and disqualified it as evidence. In cases before *Miranda* v. *Arizona* involving confessions by detainees to the police, the Court examined the "totality of circumstances" surrounding the making of the statement to determine if it was "voluntary." The problem, according to Kamizar and his fellows, was that detained suspects might make statements that were voluntary, in the sense of being uncoerced, which they would not make if it were clear to them that they were under no obligation whatever to respond to questions by the police. It should be clearly understood, it was argued, that the Fifth Amendment's protection against self-incrimination applied not only in court proceedings, but from the moment that a subject was taken into custodial detention. If it were clearly understood that the Fifth Amendment protection applied in the detective squadroom as well as the courtroom, then it followed, according to this argument, that the subject must be informed that he or she had an absolute Fifth Amendment right, made applicable to the states by the due process clause of the Fourteenth Amendment, to decline to respond to any questions put by the police. Furthermore, to protect the exercise of this right—to make sure that individuals understood it and were perfectly free to assert it—the Sixth Amendment's requirement of court-appointed counsel for indigent persons must be extended to the detective squadroom. This argument was adopted by a Court divided 5-4 in *Miranda.* From the date of this decision forward, the question with respect to a confession made to the police became not whether it was voluntary, but whether the subject had been appropriately warned of all of his constitutional rights before making the statement, and whether the police had borne their burden of proof of showing that the individual had voluntarily waived the right to remain silent.

Mr. Chief Justice Warren delivered the opinion of the Court.

The cases before us raise questions which go to the roots of our concepts of American criminal jurisprudence: the restraints society must observe consistent with the Federal Constitution in prosecuting individuals for crime. More specifically, we deal with the admissibility of statements obtained from an individual who is subjected to custodial police interrogation and the necessity for procedures which assure that the individual is accorded his privilege under the Fifth Amendment to the Constitution not to be compelled to incriminate himself. . . .

Our holding will be spelled out with some specificity in the pages which follow but briefly stated it is this: the prosecution may not use statements, whether exculpatory or inculpatory, stemming from custodial interrogation of the defendant unless it demonstrates the use of procedural safeguards effective to secure the privilege against self-incrimination. By custodial interrogation, we mean questioning initiated by law enforcement officers after a person has been taken into custody or otherwise deprived of his freedom of action in any significant way. As for the procedural safeguards to be employed, unless other fully effective means are devised to inform accused persons of their right of silence and to assure a continuous opportunity to exercise it, the following measures are required. Prior to any questioning, the person must be warned that he has a right to remain silent, that any statement he does make may be used as evidence against him, and that he has a right to the presence of an attorney, either retained or appointed. The defendant may waive effectuation of these rights, provided the waiver is made voluntarily, knowingly and intelligently. If, however, he indicates in any manner and at any stage of the process that he wishes to consult with an attorney before speaking there can be no questioning. Likewise, if the individual is alone and indicates in any manner that he does not wish to be interrogated, the police may not question him. The mere fact that he may have answered some questions or volunteered some statements on his own does not deprive him of the right to refrain from answering any further inquiries until he has consulted with an attorney and thereafter consents to be questioned. . . .

. . . .

We sometimes forget how long it has taken to establish the privilege against self-incrimination, the sources from which it came and the fervor with which it was defended. Its roots go back into ancient times. . . .

The question in these cases is whether the privilege is fully applicable during a period of custodial interrogation. In this Court, the privilege has consistently been accorded a liberal construction. . . . We are satisfied that all the principles embodied in the privilege apply to informal compulsion exerted by law-enforcement officers during in-custody questioning. An individual swept from familiar surroundings into police custody, surrounded by antagonistic forces, and subjected to the techniques of persuasion described above cannot be otherwise than under compulsion to speak. As a practical matter, the compulsion to speak in the isolated setting of the police station may well be greater than in courts or other official investigations, where there are often impartial observers to guard against intimidation or trickery. . . .

Today, then, there can be no doubt that the Fifth Amendment privilege is available outside of criminal court proceedings and serves to protect persons in all settings in which their freedom of action is curtailed in any significant way from being compelled to incriminate themselves. We have concluded that without proper safeguards the process of in-custody interrogation of persons suspected or accused of crime contains inherently compelling pressures which work to undermine the individual's will to resist and to compel him to speak where he would not otherwise do so freely. In order to combat these pressures and to permit a full opportunity to exercise the privilege against self-incrimination, the accused must be adequately and effectively apprised of his rights and the exercise of those rights must be fully honored. . . .

. . . .

The warning of the right to remain silent must be accompanied by the explanation that anything said can and will be used against the individual in court. This warning is needed in order to make him aware not only of the privilege, but also of the consequences of forgoing it. It is only through an awareness of these consequences that there can be any assurance of real understanding and intelligent exercise of the privilege. Moreover, this warning may serve to make the individual more acutely aware that he is faced with a phase of the adversary system—that he is not in the presence of persons acting solely in his interest. . . .

. . . .

The presence of counsel at the interrogation may serve several significant subsidiary functions as well. If the accused decides to talk to his interrogators, the assistance of counsel can mitigate the dangers of untrustworthiness. With a lawyer present the likelihood that the police will practice coercion is reduced, and if coercion is nevertheless exercised the lawyer can testify to it in court.

The presence of a lawyer can also help to guarantee that the accused gives a fully accurate statement to the police and that the statement is rightly reported by the prosecution at trial. . . .

. . . .

Accordingly we hold that an individual held for interrogation must be clearly informed that he has the right to consult with a lawyer and to have the lawyer with him during interrogation under the system for protecting the privilege we delineate today. . . .

. . . .

In order fully to apprise a person interrogated of the extent of his rights under this system then, it is necessary to warn him not only that he has the right to consult with an attorney, but also that if he is indigent a lawyer will he appointed to represent him. Without this additional warning, the admonition of the right to consult with counsel would often be understood as meaning only that he can consult with a lawyer if he has one or has the funds to obtain one. The warning of a right to counsel would be hollow if not couched in terms that would convey to the indigent—the person most often subjected to interrogation—the knowledge that he too has a right to have counsel present. As with the warnings of the right to remain silent and of the general right to counsel, only by effective and express explanation to the indigent of this right can there be assurance that he was truly in a position to exercise it.

Once warnings have been given, the subsequent procedure is clear. If the individual indicates in any manner, at any time prior to or during questioning, that he wishes to remain silent, the interrogation must cease. At this point he has shown that he intends to exercise his Fifth Amendment privilege; any statement taken after the person invokes his privilege cannot be other than the product of compulsion, subtle or otherwise. Without the right to cut off questioning, the setting of in-custody interrogation operates on the individual to overcome free choice in producing a statement after the privilege has been once invoked. If the individual states that he wants an attorney, the interrogation must cease until an attorney is present. At that time, the individual must have an opportunity to confer with the attorney and to have him present during any subsequent questioning. If the individual cannot obtain an attorney and he indicates that he wants one before speaking to police, they must respect his decision to remain silent. . . .

An express statement that the individual is willing to make a statement and does not want an attorney followed closely by a statement could constitute a waiver. But a valid waiver will not be presumed simply from the silence of the accused after warnings are given or simply from the fact that a confession was in fact eventually obtained. . . .

The warnings required and the waiver necessary in accordance with our opinion today are, in the absence of a fully effective equivalent, prerequisites to the admissibility of any statement made by a defendant. . . .

. . . .

Therefore, in accordance with the . . . foregoing, the judgments of the Supreme Court of Arizona [is] . . . reversed.

Justice Clark dissented in *Miranda*, and Justice Harlan wrote a dissenting opinion in which Justices Stewart and White joined.

Mr. Justice Harlan, whom Mr. Justice Stewart and Mr. Justice White join, dissenting.

I believe the decision of the Court represents poor constitutional law and entails harmful consequences for the country at large. How serious these consequences may prove to be only time can tell. But the basic flaws in the Court's justification seem to me readily apparent now once all sides of the problem are considered. . . .

I believe that reasoned examination will show that the Due Process Clauses provide an adequate tool for coping with confessions and that, even if the Fifth Amendment privilege against self-incrimination be invoked, its precedents taken as a whole do not sustain the present rules. Viewed as a choice based on pure policy, these new rules prove to be a highly debatable, if not one-sided, appraisal of the competing interests, imposed over widespread objection, at the very time when judicial restraint is most called for by the circumstances. . . .

There are several relevant lessons to be drawn from this constitutional history. The first is that with over 25 years of precedent the Court has developed an elaborate, sophisticated, and sensitive approach to admissibility of confessions. [The "totality-of-circumstances" approach to determining whether a statement was voluntary.] It is "judicial" in its treatment of one case at a time, . . . flexible in its ability to respond to the endless mutations of fact presented, and ever more familiar to the lower courts. Of course, strict certainty is not obtained in this developing process, but this is often so with constitutional principles, and disagreement is usually confined to that borderland of close cases where it matters least. . . .

I turn now to the Court's asserted reliance on the fifth Amendment, an approach which I frankly regard as a *trompe l'oeil.* The Court's opinion in my view reveals no adequate basis for extending the Fifth Amendment's privilege against self-incrimination to the police station. Far more important, it fails to show that the Court's new rules are well supported, let alone compelled, by Fifth Amendment precedents. Instead, the new rules actually derive from quotation and analogy drawn from precedents under the Sixth Amendment, which should properly have no bearing on police interrogation. . . .

Examined as an expression of public policy, the Court's new regime proves so dubious that there can be no due compensation for its weakness in constitutional law. The foregoing discussion has shown, I think, how mistaken is the Court in implying that the Constitution has struck the balance in favor of the approach the Court takes. . . . Rather, precedent reveals that the Fourteenth Amendment in practice has been construed to strike a different balance, that the Fifth Amendment gives the Court little solid support in this context, and that the Sixth Amendment should have no bearing at all. Legal history has been stretched before to satisfy deep needs of society. In this instance, however, the Court has not and cannot make the powerful showing that its new rules are plainly desirable in the context of our society, something which is surely demanded before those rules are engrafted onto the Constitution and imposed on every State and county in the land. . . .

. . . .

It is no secret that concern has been expressed lest long-range and lasting reforms be frustrated by this Court's too rapid departure from existing constitutional standards. Despite the Court's disclaimer, the practical effect of the decision made today must inevitably be to handicap seriously sound efforts at reform, not least by removing options necessary to a just compromise of competing interests. Of course legislative reform is rarely speedy or unanimous, though this Court has been more patient in the past. But the legislative reforms when they come would have the vast advantage of empirical data and comprehensive study, they would allow experimentation and use of solutions not to open to the courts, and they would restore the initiative in criminal law reform to those forums where it truly belongs. . . .

Nothing in the letter or the spirit of the Constitution or in the precedents squares with the heavy-handed and one-sided action that is so precipitously taken by the Court in the name of fulfilling its constitutional responsibilities. . . .

Justice White also wrote a dissenting opinion in which Justices Harlan and Stewart joined.

Brewer v. *Williams*
430 U.S. 387, 97 S.Ct. 1232, 51 L.Ed.2d. 424 (1977)

How strictly was *Miranda* to be applied? And what constituted "interrogation"? Does interrogation include any verbal exchange with police by a suspect in custodial detention? Under what circumstances, after the appropriate *Miranda* warning has been given, can it be concluded that the subject has voluntarily decided to waive the right to remain silent, to waive the presence of counsel, and to make a statement? *Brewer* v. *Williams,* the "Christian burial case," raises all of these questions. A bare majority of the Court, speaking through Justice Stewart, found that *Miranda* had been violated in this case, but the dissent by the Chief Justice was spirited.

Mr. Justice Stewart delivered the opinion of the Court.

On the afternoon of December 24, 1968, a 10-year-old girl named Pamela Powers went with her family to the YMCA in Des Moines, Iowa, to watch a wrestling tournament in which her brother was participating. When she failed to return from a trip to the washroom, a search for her began. The search was unsuccessful.

Robert Williams, who had recently escaped from a mental hospital, was a resident of the YMCA. Soon after the girl's disappearance Williams was seen in the YMCA lobby carrying some clothing and a large bundle wrapped in a blanket. He obtained help from a 14-year-old boy in opening the street door of the YMCA and the door to his automobile parked outside. When Williams placed the bundle in the front seat of his car the boy "saw two legs in it and they were skinny and white." Before anyone could see what was in the bundle Williams drove away. His abandoned car was found the following day in Davenport, Iowa, roughly 160 miles east of Des Moines. A warrant was then issued in Des Moines for his arrest on a charge of abduction.

On the morning of December 26, a Des Moines lawyer named Henry McKnight went to the Des Moines police station and informed the officers present that he had just received a long distance call from Williams, and that he had advised Williams to turn himself in to the Davenport police. Williams did surrender that morning to the police in Davenport, and they booked him on the charge specified in the arrest warrant and gave him the warnings required by Miranda v. Arizona, 384 U.S. 436. The Davenport police then telephoned their counterparts in Des Moines to inform them that Williams had surrendered. McKnight, the lawyer, was still at the Des Moines police headquarters, and Williams conversed with McKnight on the telephone. In the presence of the Des Moines chief of police and a police detective named Leaming, McKnight advised Williams that Des Moines police officers would be driving to Davenport to pick him up, that the officers would not interrogate him or mistreat him, and that Williams was not to talk to the officers about Pamela Powers until after consulting with McKnight upon his return to Des Moines. As a result of these conversations, it was agreed between McKnight and the Des Moines police officials that Detective Leaming and a fellow officer would drive to Davenport to pick up Williams, that they would bring him directly back to Des Moines, and that they would not question him during the trip.

In the meantime Williams was arraigned before a judge in Davenport on the outstanding arrest warrant. The judge advised him of his *Miranda* rights and committed him to jail. Before leaving the courtroom, Williams conferred with a lawyer named Kelly, who advised him not to make any statements until consulting with McKnight back in Des Moines.

Detective Leaming and his fellow officer arrived in Davenport about noon to pick up Williams and return him to Des Moines. Soon after their arrival they met with Williams and Kelly, who, they understood, was acting as Williams' lawyer. Detective Leaming repeated the *Miranda* warnings, and told Williams:

"[W]e both know that you're being represented here by Mr. Kelly and you're being represented by Mr. McKnight in Des Moines, and . . . I want you to remember this because we'll be visiting between here and Des Moines." . . .

The two detectives, with Williams in their charge, then set out on the 160-mile drive. At no time during the trip did Williams express a willingness to be interrogated in the absence of an attorney. Instead, he stated several times that "[w]hen I get to Des Moines and see Mr. McKnight, I am going to tell you the whole story." Detective Leaming knew that Williams was a former mental patient, and knew also that he was deeply religious.

The detective and his prisoner soon embarked on a wide-ranging conversation covering a variety of topics, including the subject of religion. Then, not long after leaving Davenport and reaching the interstate highway, Detective Leaming delivered what has been referred to in the briefs and oral arguments as the "Christian burial speech." Addressing Williams as "Reverend," the detective said:

"I want to give you something to think about while we're traveling down the road. . . . Number one, I want you to observe the weather conditions, it's raining, it's sleeting, it's freezing, driving is very treacherous, visibility is poor, it's going to be dark early this evening. They are predicting several inches of snow for tonight, and I feel that you yourself are the only person that knows where this little girl's body is, that you yourself have only been there once, and if you get a snow on top of it you yourself may be unable to find it. And, since we will be going right past the area on the way into Des Moines, I feel that we could stop and locate the body, that the parents of this little girl should be entitled to a Christian burial for the little girl who was snatched away from them on Christmas [E]ve and murdered. And I feel we should stop and locate it on the way in rather than waiting until morning and trying to come back out after a snow storm and possibly not being able to find it at all."

Williams asked Detective Leaming why he thought their route to Des Moines would be taking them past the girl's body, and Leaming responded that he knew the body was in the area of Mitchellville—a town they would be passing on the way to Des Moines. Leaming then stated: "I do not want you to answer me. I don't want to discuss it any further. Just think about it as we're riding down the road."

As the car approached Grinnell, a town approximately 100 miles west of Davenport, Williams asked whether the police had found the victim's shoes. When Detective Leaming replied that he was unsure, Williams directed the officers to a service station where he said he had left the shoes; a search for them proved unsuccessful. As they continued towards Des Moines, Williams asked whether the police had found the blanket, and directed the officers to a rest area where he said he had disposed of the blanket. Nothing was found. The car continued towards Des Moines, and as it approached Mitchellville, Williams said that he would show the officers where the body was. He then directed the police to the body of Pamela Powers.

Williams was indicted for first-degree murder. Before trial, his counsel moved to suppress all evidence relating to or resulting from any statements Williams had made during the automobile ride from Davenport to Des Moines. . . .

The evidence in question was introduced over counsel's continuing objection at the subsequent trial. The jury found Williams guilty of murder, and the judgment of conviction was affirmed by the Iowa Supreme Court, a bare majority of whose members agreed with the trial court that Williams had "waived his right to the presence of his counsel" on the automobile ride from Davenport to Des Moines. . . .

. . . .

There can be no doubt in the present case that judicial proceedings had been initiated against Williams before the start of the automobile ride from Davenport to Des Moines. A warrant had been issued for his arrest, he had been arraigned on that warrant before a judge in a Davenport courtroom, and he had been committed by the court to confinement in jail. The State does not contend otherwise.

There can be no serious doubt, either, that Detective Leaming deliberately and designedly set out to elicit information from Williams just as surely as—and perhaps more effectively than—if he had formally interrogated him. Detective Leaming was fully aware before departing for Des Moines that Williams was being represented in Davenport by Kelly and in Des Moines by McKnight. Yet he purposely sought during Williams' isolation from his lawyers to obtain as much incriminating information as possible. Indeed, Detective Leaming conceded as much when he testified at Williams' trial. . . .

The Iowa courts recognized that Williams had been denied the constitutional right to the assistance of counsel. They held, however, that he had waived that right during the course of the automobile trip from Davenport to Des Moines. The state trial court explained its determination of waiver as follows:

"The time element involved on the trip, the general circumstances of it, and more importantly the absence on the Defendant's part of any assertion of his right or desire not to give information absent the presence of his attorney, are the main foundations for the Court's conclusion that he voluntarily waived such right."

In its lengthy opinion affirming this determination, the Iowa Supreme Court applied "the totality-of-circumstances test for a showing of waiver of constitutionally-protected rights in the absence of an express waiver," and concluded that "evidence of the time element involved on the trip, the general circumstances of it, and the absence of any request or expressed desire for the aid of counsel before or at the time of giving information, were sufficient to sustain a conclusion that defendant did waive his constitutional rights as alleged." . . .

In the federal habeas corpus proceeding the District Court, believing that the issue of waiver was not one of fact but of federal law, held that the Iowa courts had "applied the wrong constitutional standards" in ruling that Williams had waived the protections that were his under the Constitution. . . .

. . . In the face of this evidence, the State has produced no affirmative evidence whatsoever to support its claim of waiver, and, a fortiori, it cannot be said that the State has met its 'heavy burden' of showing a knowing and intelligent waiver. . . .

The crime of which Williams was convicted was senseless and brutal, calling for swift and energetic action by the police to apprehend the perpetrator and gather evidence with which he could be convicted. No mission of law enforcement officials is more important. Yet "[d]isinterested zeal for the public good does not assure either wisdom or right in the methods it pursues." . . . Although we do not lightly affirm the issuance of a writ of habeas corpus in this case, so clear a violation of the Sixth and Fourteenth Amendments as here occurred cannot be condoned. The pressures on state executive and judicial officers charged with the administration of the criminal law are great, especially when the crime is murder and the victim a small child. But it is precisely the predictability of those pressures that makes imperative a resolute loyalty to the guarantees that the Constitution extends to us all.

The judgment of the Court of Appeals is affirmed. [The Court of Appeals had upheld the Federal District Court's conclusion that the contested evidence had been improperly admitted.]

Justices Marshall, Powell, and Stevens wrote concurring opinions. Justice White wrote a dissenting opinion in which Justices Blackmun and Rehnquist joined, and Justice Blackmun wrote a dissenting opinion in which Justices White and Rehnquist joined. Chief Justice Burger dissented alone:

Mr. Chief Justice Burger, dissenting.

The result in this case ought to be intolerable in any society which purports to call itself an organized society. It continues the Court—by the narrowest margin—on the much-criticized course of punishing the public for the mistakes and misdeeds of law enforcement officers, instead of punishing the officer directly, if in fact he is guilty of wrongdoing. It mechanically and blindly keeps reliable evidence from juries whether the claimed constitutional violation involves gross police misconduct or honest human error.

Williams is guilty of the savage murder of a small child; no member of the Court contends he is not. While in custody, and after no fewer than *five* warnings of his rights to silence and to counsel, he led police to the concealed body of his victim. The Court concedes Williams was not threatened or coerced and that he spoke and acted voluntarily and with full awareness of his constitutional rights. In the face of all this, the Court now holds that because Williams was prompted by the detective's statement—not interrogation but a statement—the jury must not be told how the police found the body.

Today's holding fulfills Judge (later Mr. Justice) Cardozo's grim prophecy that someday some court might carry the exclusionary rule to the absurd extent that its operative effect would exclude evidence relating to the body of a murder victim because of the means by which it was found.* In so ruling the Court regresses to playing a grisly game of "hide and seek," once more exalting the sporting theory of criminal justice which has been experiencing a decline in our jurisprudence. With Justices White, Blackmun, and Rehnquist, I categorically reject the remarkable notion that the police in this case were guilty of unconstitutional misconduct, or any conduct justifying the bizarre result reached by the Court. Apart from a brief comment on the merits, however, I wish to focus on the irrationality of applying the increasingly discredited exclusionary rule to this case.

Under well-settled precedents which the Court freely acknowledges, it is very clear that Williams had made a valid waiver of his Fifth Amendment right to silence and his Sixth Amendment right to counsel when he led police to the child's body. Indeed, even under the Court's analysis I do not understand how a contrary conclusion is possible.

The Court purports to apply as the appropriate constitutional waiver standard the familiar "intentional relinquishment or abandonment of a known right or privilege" test. . . .

The Court assumes, without deciding, that Williams' conduct and statements were voluntary. It concedes, as it must, . . . that Williams had been informed of and fully understood his constitutional rights and the consequences of their waiver. Then, having either assumed or found every element necessary to make out a valid waiver under its own test, the Court reaches the astonishing conclusion that no valid waiver has been demonstrated.

---

* "The criminal is to go free because the constable has blundered. . . . A room is searched against the law, and the body of a murdered man is found. . . . The privacy of the home has been infringed, and the murderer goes free." *People* v. *Defore,* 242 N.Y. 13, 21, 23–24, 150 N.E. 585, 587, 588 (1926). . . .

This remarkable result is compounded by the Court's failure to define what evidentiary showing the State failed to make. . . .

The evidence is uncontradicted that Williams had abundant knowledge of his right to have counsel present and of his right to silence. Since the Court does not question his mental competence, it boggles the mind to suggest that Williams could not understand that leading police to the child's body would have other than the most serious consequences. All of the elements necessary to make out a valid waiver are shown by the record and acknowledged by the Court; we thus are left to guess how the Court reached its holding.

One plausible but unarticulated basis for the result reached is that once a suspect has asserted his right not to talk without the presence of an attorney, it becomes legally impossible for him to waive that right until he has seen an attorney. But constitutional rights are *personal,* and an otherwise valid waiver should not be brushed aside by judges simply because an attorney was not present.
. . .

In his concurring opinion Mr. Justice Powell suggests that the result in this case turns on whether Detective Leaming's remarks constituted "interrogation," as he views them, or whether they were "statements" intended to prick the conscience of the accused. I find it most remarkable that a murder case should turn on judicial interpretation that a statement becomes a question simply because it is followed by an incriminating disclosure from the suspect. The Court seems to be saying that since Williams said he would "tell the whole story" at Des Moines, the police should have been content and waited; of course, that would have been the wiser course, especially in light of the nuances of constitutional jurisprudence applied by the Court, but a murder case ought not turn on such tenuous strands. . . .

CASE STUDY: HENRY FRIENDLY AND FIFTH AMENDMENT REVISION

In the wake of the Court's decision in *Miranda* v. *Arizona,* there was considerable concern that the balance in the police investigative process had been tipped too far in favor of the criminal suspect and against the interests of society in identifying malefactors. Perhaps the most distinguished exponent of this view was Judge Henry J. Friendly of the United States Circuit Court of Appeals for the Second Circuit. In a famous law review article ("The Fifth Amendment Tomorrow: The Case for Constitutional Change," 37 *Cincinnati Law Review* 671) in 1968, Friendly wrote that it was "necessary to vindicate the rights of society against what in my view has become a kind of obsession which has stretched the privilege beyond not only its language and history but any justification in policy".

Judge Friendly stressed that the privilege against self-incrimination had its origins in the abhorrence of torture and of star chamber practices; that is, placing individuals at criminal risk in trial type situations where they must either confess or have their silence construed as evidence of guilt. While recognizing the continuing importance of the privilege against self-incrimination at the stage of the criminal trial, Friendly insisted that there was nothing in its history or its function within the judicial process that necessitated its extension through the investigative process "before the formal criminal process had begun."

Noting that "until a few years ago it was widely believed that the self-incrimination clause did not apply at this stage," he argued that the problem of police bullying was adequately dealt with by the prohibition against the admission of involuntary confessions. While recognizing the criticism made by Yale Kamizar and others of the "voluntariness approach," Friendly maintained that while the process had been slow, the state courts, by the time of *Miranda*, were increasingly taking the initiative to insure that they were not lied to by the police about what occurred in the station house. That is, the voluntariness approach was proving a success at the very time of its demise.

Judge Friendly went on to propose a remedy by constitutional amendment:

> The clause of the Fifth Amendment to the Constitution of the United States, "nor shall be compelled in any criminal case to be a witness against himself," shall not be construed to prohibit:
>
> (1) interrogating any person or requesting him to furnish goods or chattels, including books, papers and other writings, without warning that he is not obliged to comply, unless such person has been taken into custody because of, or has been charged with, a crime to which the interrogation or request relates. . . .

The first thing to be noted about Judge Friendly's proposal is that it would not overrule *Miranda.* Rather, Friendly's language seeks to replace the "significant deprivation of liberty" trigger for the *Miranda* warning with the trigger of formal arrest. Beyond that, Judge Friendly's amendment would have had the affect of precluding future judicial *extension* of the *Miranda* warning to the questioning of persons who were only suspects—persons for whom there was no probable cause sufficient to justify an arrest. What Friendly sought was some leeway, early in the investigative process, where the police would be free to question without the requirement of the privilege against self-incrimination and the counsel requirement to protect it.

Criticism of Friendly's proposal was quick in coming. In 1969, Douglas G. Thompson (38 *Cincinnati Law Review* 488) relied on some early empirical studies of the affect of *Miranda* to argue that it had not significantly reduced the number of incriminating statements made to the police. Furthermore, Thompson suggested, uncounseled prearrest questioning by the police would create an incentive for the police to defer arrest beyond the point where probable cause existed in order to continue questioning without a warning.

Judge Friendly's proposal failed to generate widespread support, and in the almost two decades since *Miranda* there still has been no clear empirical evidence as to precise impact of the decision on law enforcement. Indeed, since what is at issue are nonevents—statements to the police that are not made—and since it is notoriously difficult to count nonevents, the search for empirical evidence may be futile. In the years since Friendly's article, the focus of concern over the *Miranda* warning has shifted from the possibility of changing it or delaying it, to the question of whether incriminating statements made after an imperfect *Miranda* warning must necessarily be excluded—even if the mistake by the police was minor or made without bad faith.

Among the items recommended by President Reagan's task force on violent crime, in its 1981 report, was the admission of "*Miranda* imperfect" statements into evidence where there was no bad faith on the part of the law enforcement officers involved. Civil liberties groups, led by the ACLU, executed a prompt counterattack on the task force report, and nothing has come of it. But the matter will continue to fester because for many types of crimes a confession is often the only sort of hard evidence that can put the prosecution in a position to go to trial.

CHAPTER · 17

FAIR TRIAL

THE Sixth Amendment, made applicable to the states, guarantees the accused a speedy trial. Many states have statutes limiting the time between criminal charge and trial, and the prosecution is obliged to meet these deadlines unless the delay is occasioned by the defense. Criminal trials in federal courts are governed by the Speedy Trial Act of 1974, which fixes short time periods within which trials must begin.

Again, as a matter of Sixth Amendment requirement, a person accused of a "serious crime"—one for which there may be incarceration for six months or more—is entitled to trial by a jury. In some instances, however, the defendant may waive the right of trial by jury and be tried before a judge alone.

In the introduction to Part III, we saw how the jury evolved in medieval England and was exported to the American colonies. Originally made up of persons assumed to have knowledge of the accused and the offense, the mechanism of the jury was perfected over time so that the Sixth Amendment requires an impartial jury as a matter of constitutional law. Where there is a trial by jury, the jury determines what are the facts of the case. The judge, however, serves as something more than an umpire or referee. He decides what testimony or evidence is legally admissible and thus may be heard or considered by the jury. It remains to the jury, however, to decide what evidence it believes and what it disbelieves.

Jury selection is an important stage of the trial. The judge is seeking the impartial jury required by the Sixth Amendment, while the prosecution and defense are concerned about the disposition of prospective jurors toward the accused. Clarence Darrow, the famous defense lawyer of the early twentieth century and an ACLU volunteer counsel, claimed that he automatically challenged Presbyterians and accepted Jews as jurymen on the grounds that the former were almost always hostile to criminals and the latter were lenient. Prospective jurors may be challenged either for cause or by a peremptory challenge. In most jurisdictions defense and prosecution have a certain number of these peremptory challenges by which they may simply exclude a prospective juror.

Once the jury is selected the prosecution and defense make opening statements that outline what each side intends to argue. These are followed by the full presentation of the prosecution's case—testimony and physical evidence. As a representative of the government, the prosecuting attorney bears the burden of proving the state's case "beyond reasonable doubt" as a matter of core due process fairness (touched on in Chapter 12). If, when the prosecution has finished its case, the judge concludes that reasonable jurors can not, on the basis of the prosecution's presentation, reach a verdict of guilty, he may "direct a verdict" of not guilty. The accused goes free just the same as if the jury had heard the entire case and found "not guilty."

In the event there is not a directed verdict, the defense proceeds with its case. Each side has an opportunity to make closing arguments, and the judge then instructs the jury as to its duties and responsibilities, the law of the case, and precisely what it is that the jurors must be sure of in order to reach a verdict of guilty. This is a crucial phase in the trial, and the way in which judges explain legal standards to jurors is often the subject of appellate review.

There is a continuing controversy over what is required by the Constitution for jury verdicts. Traditionally, verdicts in federal courts were required to be unanimous. But many states allowed plurality verdicts, say ten guilty votes out of twelve. When the Sixth Amendment's jury trial guarantee was extended to the states it was unclear whether the unanimity practice of federal courts went along with it. We shall examine the controversy in this chapter.

Whatever verdict is reached by the jury, it is final. No matter how good the judge believes the prosecution's case to have been, or how weak the defense, if the jury returns a verdict of not guilty, there is nothing the court, the prosecutor, or any other authority can do. If the verdict is guilty, though, the former defendant may pursue one or another of those "post-conviction remedies" discussed in the introduction to Part III. In the event an appellate court should discover that there was some defect, constitutional or otherwise, in the trial of the convict, a new trial will be ordered. At this point, it is up to the prosecutor to decide whether to go forward with another trial or to drop the case.

In the cases that follow we will examine the speedy trial requirements in the context of *Barker* v. *Wingo*. The requirement of an impartial jury will be touched on in connection with the case of *Sheppard v. Maxwell*. The number of persons required to constitute a jury will be examined in *Williams* v. *Florida*, and less than unanimous jury verdicts are examined in *Apodaca* v. *Oregon*.

Barker v. *Wingo*
407 U.S. 514, 92 S.Ct. 2182, 33 L.Ed.2d. 101 (1972)

The Sixth Amendment guarantees to defendants in federal cases "the right to a speedy and public trial," and this right was extended to the states through the due process clause of the Fourteenth Amendment in *Klopfer* v. *North Carolina*, 386 U.S. 231 (1967). In *Barker* v. *Wingo*, the Court, speaking through Justice Powell, faces the question of what delays in trial, under what circumstances, constitute denial of the federally protected right. In contrast to the course taken by the majority in *Miranda* v. *Arizona*, where a flexible ("totality of circumstances") approach was abandoned and a hard and fast rule (warning and proof of waiver) was substituted in its place, Powell eschews a hard rule in this area and argues for the necessity of a balancing or totality of circumstances approach.

Mr. Justice Powell delivered the opinion of the Court.

Although a speedy trial is guaranteed the accused by the Sixth Amendment to the Constitution, this Court has dealt with that right on infrequent occasions. ... [I]n none of these cases have we attempted to set out the criteria by which the speedy trial right is to be judged. ... This case compels us to make such an attempt.

On July 20, 1958, in Christian County, Kentucky, an elderly couple was beaten to death by intruders wielding an iron tire tool. Two suspects, Silas Manning and Willie Barker, the petitioner, were arrested shortly thereafter. The grand jury indicted them on September 15. Counsel was appointed on September 17, and Barker's trial was set for October 21. The Commonwealth had a stronger case against Manning, and it believed that Barker could not be convicted unless Manning testified against him. Manning was naturally unwilling to incriminate himself. Accordingly, on October 23, the day Silas Manning was brought to trial, the Commonwealth sought and obtained the first of what was to be a series of 16 continuances of Barker's trial. Barker made no objection. By first convicting Manning, the Commonwealth would remove possible problems of self-incrimination and would be able to assure his testimony against Barker.

The Commonwealth encountered more than a few difficulties in its prosecution of Manning. The first trial ended in a hung jury. A second trial resulted in a conviction, but the Kentucky Court of Appeals reversed because of the admission of evidence obtained by an illegal search. ... At his third trial, Manning was again convicted, and the Court of Appeals again reversed because the trial court had not granted a change of venue. ... A fourth trial resulted in a hung jury. Finally, after five trials, Manning was convicted, in March 1962, of murdering one victim, and after a sixth trial, in December 1962, he was convicted of murdering the other.

The Christian County Circuit Court holds three terms each year—in February, June, and September. Barker's initial trial was to take place in the September term of 1958. The first continuance postponed it until the February 1959 term. The second continuance was granted for one month only. Every term thereafter for as long as the Manning prosecutions were in process, the Commonwealth routinely moved to continue Barker's case to the next term. When the case was continued from the June 1959 term until the following September, Barker, having spent 10 months in jail, obtained his release by posting a $5,000 bond. He thereafter remained free in the community until his trial. Barker made no objection, through his counsel, to the first 11 continuances.

When on February 12, 1962, the Commonwealth moved for the twelfth time to continue the case until the following term, Barker's counsel filed a motion to dismiss the indictment. The motion to dismiss was denied two weeks later, and the Commonwealth's motion for a continuance was granted. The Commonwealth was granted further continuances in June 1962 and September 1962, to which Barker did not object.

In February 1963, the first term of court following Manning's final conviction, the Commonwealth moved to set Barker's trial for March 19. But on the day scheduled for trial, it again moved for a continuance until the June term. It gave as its reason the illness of the ex-sheriff who was the chief investigating officer in the case. To this continuance, Barker objected unsuccessfully.

The witness was still unable to testify in June, and the trial, which had been set for June 19, was continued again until the September term over Barker's objection. This time the court announced that the case would be dismissed for lack of prosecution if it were not tried during the next term. The final trial date was set for October 9, 1963. On that date, Barker again moved to dismiss the indictment, and this time specified that his right to a speedy trial had been violated. The motion was denied; the trial commenced with Manning as the chief prosecution witness; Barker was convicted and given a life sentence. . . .

The right to a speedy trial is generically different from any of the other rights enshrined in the Constitution for the protection of the accused. In addition to the general concern that all accused persons be treated according to decent and fair procedures, there is a societal interest in providing a speedy trial which exists separate from, and at times in opposition to, the interests of the accused. The inability of courts to provide a prompt trial has contributed to a large backlog of cases in urban courts which, among other things, enables defendants to negotiate more effectively for pleas of guilty to lesser offenses and otherwise manipulate the system. In addition, persons released on bond for lengthy periods awaiting trial have an opportunity to commit other crimes. It must be of little comfort to the residents of Christian County, Kentucky, to know that Barker was at large on bail for over four years while accused of a vicious and brutal murder of which he was ultimately convicted. Moreover, the longer an accused is free awaiting trial, the more tempting becomes his opportunity to jump bail and escape. Finally, delay between arrest and punishment may have a detrimental effect on rehabilitation.

If an accused cannot make bail, he is generally confined, as was Barker for 10 months, in a local jail. This contributes to the overcrowding and generally deplorable state of those institutions. Lengthy exposure to these conditions "has a destructive effect on human character and makes the rehabilitation of the individual offender much more difficult." At times the result may even be violent rioting. Finally, lengthy pretrial detention is costly. The cost of maintaining a prisoner in jail varies from $3 to $9 per day, and this amounts to millions across the Nation. In addition, society loses wages which might have been earned, and it must often support families of incarcerated breadwinners.

A second difference between the right to speedy trial and the accused's other constitutional rights is that deprivation of the right may work to the accused's advantage. Delay is not an uncommon defense tactic. As the time between the commission of the crime and trial lengthens, witnesses may become unavailable or their memories may fade. If the witnesses support the prosecution, its case will be weakened, sometimes seriously so. And it is the prosecution which carries the burden of proof. Thus, unlike the right to counsel or the right to be free from compelled self-incrimination, deprivation of the right to speedy trial does not *per se* prejudice the accused's ability to defend himself.

Finally, and perhaps most importantly, the right to speedy trial is a more vague concept than other procedural rights. It is, for example, impossible to determine with precision when the right has been denied. We cannot definitely say how long is too long in a system where justice is supposed to be swift but deliberate. As a consequence, there is no fixed point in the criminal process when the State can put the defendant to the choice of either exercising or waiving the right to a speedy trial. If, for example, the State moves for a 60-day continuance, granting that continuance is not a violation of the right to speedy trial unless the circumstances of the case are such that further delay would endanger the values the right protects. It is impossible to do more than generalize about when those circumstances exist. There is nothing comparable to the point in the process when a defendant exercises or waives his right to counsel or his right to a jury trial.

Perhaps because the speedy trial right is so slippery, two rigid approaches are urged upon us as ways of eliminating some of the uncertainty which courts experience in protecting the right. The first suggestion is that we hold that the Constitution requires a criminal defendant to be offered a trial within a specified time period. ...

But such a result would require this Court to engage in legislative or rulemaking activity, rather than in the adjudicative process to which we should confine our efforts. We do not establish procedural rules for the States, except when mandated by the Constitution. We find no constitutional basis for holding that the speedy trial right can be quantified into a specified number of days or months. The States, of course, are free to prescribe a reasonable period consistent with constitutional standards, but our approach must be less precise.

The second suggested alternative would restrict consideration of the right to those cases in which the accused has demanded a speedy trial. Most States have recognized what is loosely referred to as the "demand rule," although eight States reject it. It is not clear, however, precisely what is meant by that term. Although every federal court of appeals that has considered the question has endorsed some kind of demand rule, some have regarded the rule within the concept of waiver, whereas others have viewed it as a factor to be weighed in assessing whether there has been a deprivation of the speedy trial right. We shall refer to the former approach as the demand-waiver doctrine. The demand-waiver doctrine provides that a defendant waives any consideration of his right to speedy trial for any period prior to which he has not demanded a trial. Under this rigid approach, a prior demand is a necessary condition to the consideration of the speedy trial right. ...

  . . . .

It is also noteworthy that such a rigid view of the demand-waiver rule places defense counsel in an awkward position. Unless he demands a trial early and often, he is in danger of frustrating his client's right. If counsel is willing to tolerate some delay because he finds it reasonable and helpful in preparing his own case, he may be unable to obtain a speedy trial for his client at the end of that time. Since under the demand-waiver rule no time runs until the demand is made, the government will have whatever time is otherwise reasonable to bring the defendant to trial after a demand has been made. Thus, if the first demand is made three months after arrest in a jurisdiction which prescribes a six-month rule, the prosecution will have a total of nine months—which may be wholly unreasonable under the circumstances. The result in practice is likely to be either an automatic, *pro forma* demand made immediately after appointment of counsel or delays which, but for the demand-waiver rule, would not be tolerated. Such a result is not consistent with the interests of defendants, society, or the Constitution.

We reject, therefore, the rule that a defendant who fails to demand a speedy trial forever waives his right. This does not mean, however, that the defendant has no responsibility to assert his right. We think the better rule is that the defendant's assertion of or failure to assert his right to a speedy trial is one of the factors to be considered in an inquiry into the deprivation of the right. Such a formulation avoids the rigidities of the demand-waiver rule and the resulting possible unfairness in its application. It allows the trial court to exercise a judicial discretion based on the circumstances, including due consideration of any applicable formal procedural rule. . . .

. . . .

The difficulty of the task of balancing these factors is illustrated by this case, which we consider to be close. It is clear that the length of delay between arrest and trial—well over five years—was extraordinary. Only seven months of that period can be attributed to a strong excuse, the illness of the ex-sheriff who was in charge of the investigation. Perhaps some delay would have been permissible under ordinary circumstances, so that Manning could be utilized as a witness in Barker's trial, but more than four years was too long a period, particularly since a good part of that period was attributable to the Commonwealth's failure or inability to try Manning under circumstances that comported with due process.

Two counterbalancing factors, however, outweigh these deficiencies. The first is that prejudice was minimal. Of course, Barker was prejudiced to some extent by living for over four years under a cloud of suspicion and anxiety. Moreover, although he was released on bond for most of the period, he did spend 10 months in jail before trial. But there is no claim that any of Barker's witnesses died or otherwise became unavailable owing to the delay. The trial transcript indicates only two very minor lapses of memory—one on the part of a prosecution witness—which were in no way significant to the outcome.

More important than the absence of serious prejudice, is the fact that Barker did not want a speedy trial. Counsel was appointed for Barker immediately after his indictment and represented him throughout the period. No question is raised as to the competency of such counsel. Despite the fact that counsel had notice of the motions for continuances, the record shows no action whatever taken between October 21, 1958, and February 12, 1962, that could be construed as the assertion of the speedy trial right. On the latter date, in response to another motion for continuance, Barker moved to dismiss the indictment. The record does not show on what ground this motion was based, although it is clear that no alternative motion was made for an immediate trial. Instead the record strongly suggests that while he hoped to take advantage of the delay in which he had acquiesced, and thereby obtain a dismissal of the charges, he definitely did not want to be tried. Counsel conceded as much at oral argument. . . . The probable reason for Barker's attitude was that he was gambling on Manning's acquittal. The evidence was not very strong against Manning, as the reversals and hung juries suggest, and Barker undoubtedly thought that if Manning were acquitted, he would never be tried. Counsel also conceded this. . . .

That Barker was gambling on Manning's acquittal is also suggested by his failure, following the *pro forma* motion to dismiss filed in February 1962, to object to the Commonwealth's next two motions for continuances. Indeed, it was not until March 1963, after Manning's convictions were final, that Barker, having lost his gamble, began to object to further continuances. At that time, the Commonwealth's excuse was the illness of the ex-sheriff, which Barker has conceded justified the further delay.

We do not hold that there may never be a situation in which an indictment may be dismissed on speedy trial grounds where the defendant has failed to object to continuances. There may be a situation in which the defendant was represented by incompetent counsel, was severely prejudiced, or even cases in which the continuances were granted *ex parte.* But barring extraordinary circumstances, we would be reluctant indeed to rule that a defendant was denied this constitutional right on a record that strongly indicates, as does this one, that the defendant did not want a speedy trial. We hold, therefore, that Barker was not deprived of his due process right to a speedy trial.

The judgment of the Court of Appeals is

Affirmed.

Justice White concurred in an opinion in which Justice Brennan joined.

Sheppard v. *Maxwell*
384 U.S. 333, 86 S.Ct. 1507, 16 L.Ed.2d. 600 (1966)

Also applicable in state trials is the Sixth Amendment's requirement that trial be by an *impartial* jury. By this is meant a jury composed of persons who are capable of deciding the case before them strictly on the basis of the evidence admitted and presented to them. There can be no reference to outside knowledge of the case in jury deliberations. But what if the crime for which the defendant stands accused is a sensational one, which was widely covered by the news media? Can jurors decide purely in terms of the evidence adduced in court after they have been exposed to extensive media coverage adverse to the defendant? The trial of Dr. Sam Sheppard for the murder of his wife Marilyn posed this question in a particularly stark form. Not only the local press but the national media fixed onto the case of the prosperous doctor, whom it was alleged had killed his wife in order to continue his relationship with his beautiful receptionist, Susan Hayes. The newspapers portrayed Sheppard as a wealthy Lothario and named a number of other women with whom he was allegedly involved sexually. The testimony at the trial, however, never implicated Sheppard in illicit relationships other than the one with Susan Hayes. Headlines such as "Doctor Baulks At Lie Test," and "Why No Inquest?" and "Quit Stalling—Bring Him In" only partially convey the circus atmosphere in which Sheppard was tried. While it was never established that any particular juror in the Sheppard case was specifically influenced by the publicity, the Supreme Court, speaking through Justice Clark, held that the pervasiveness of the publicity made it so likely that prejudice existed that Sheppard had been denied his Sixth Amendment right. In the course of his opinion, Justice Clark grappled with the trade-off between a free press and an impartial jury, which we examined in the First Amendment context in Chapter 7.

Mr. Justice Clark delivered the opinion of the Court.

This federal habeas corpus application involves the question whether Sheppard was deprived of a fair trial in his state conviction for the second-degree murder of his wife because of the trial judge's failure to protect Sheppard sufficiently from the massive, pervasive and prejudicial publicity that attended his prosecution. . . .

There can be no question about the nature of the publicity which surrounded Sheppard's trial. We agree, as did the Court of Appeals, with the findings in Judge Bell's opinion for the Ohio Supreme Court:

"Murder and mystery, society, sex and suspense were combined in this case in such a manner as to intrigue and captivate the public fancy to a degree perhaps unparalleled in recent annals. Throughout the preindictment investigation, the subsequent legal skirmishes and the nine-week trial, circulation-conscious editors catered to the insatiable interest of the American public in the bizarre. . . . In this atmosphere of a 'Roman holiday' for the news media, Sam Sheppard stood trial for his life." . . .

Indeed, every court that has considered this case, save the court that tried it, has deplored the manner in which the news media inflamed and prejudiced the public. . . .

. . . .

Nor is there doubt that this deluge of publicity reached at least some of the jury. On the only occasion that the jury was queried, two jurors admitted in open court to hearing the highly inflammatory charge that a prison inmate claimed Sheppard as the father of her illegitimate child. Despite the extent and nature of the publicity to which the jury was exposed during trial, the judge refused defense counsel's other requests that the jurors be asked whether they had read or heard specific prejudicial comment about the case, including the incidents we have previously summarized. In these circumstances, we can assume that some of this material reached members of the jury. . . .

The court's fundamental error is compounded by the holding that it lacked power to control the publicity about the trial. From the very inception of the proceedings the judge announced that neither he nor anyone else could restrict prejudicial news accounts. And he reiterated this view on numerous occasions.

Since he viewed the news media as his target, the judge never considered other means that are often utilized to reduce the appearance of prejudicial material and to protect the jury from outside influence. We conclude that these procedures would have been sufficient to guarantee Sheppard a fair trial and so do not consider what sanctions might be available against a recalcitrant press nor the charges of bias now made against the state trial judge. . . .

The carnival atmosphere at trial could easily have been avoided since the courtroom and courthouse premises are subject to the control of the court. . . . Bearing in mind the massive pretrial publicity, the judge should have adopted stricter rules governing the use of the courtroom by newsmen, as Sheppard's counsel requested. The number of reporters in the courtroom itself could have been limited at the first sign that their presence would disrupt the trial. They certainly should not have been placed inside the bar. Furthermore, the judge should have more closely regulated the conduct of newsmen in the courtroom. For instance, the judge belatedly asked them not to handle and photograph trial exhibits lying on the counsel table during recesses.

Secondly, the court should have insulated the witnesses. All of the newspapers and radio stations apparently interviewed prospective witnesses at will, and in many instances disclosed their testimony. A typical example was the publication of numerous statements by Susan Hayes, before her appearance in court, regarding her love affair with Sheppard. Although the witnesses were barred from the courtroom during the trial the full verbatim testimony was available to them in the press. This completely nullified the judge's imposition of the rule. . . .

Thirdly, the court should have made some effort to control the release of leads, information, and gossip to the press by police officers, witnesses, and the counsel for both sides. Much of the information thus disclosed was inaccurate, leading to groundless rumors and confusion. . . .

More specifically, the trial court might well have proscribed extrajudicial statements by any lawyer, party, witness, or court official which divulged prejudicial matters, such as the refusal of Sheppard to submit to interrogation or take any lie detector tests; any statement made by Sheppard to officials; the identity of prospective witnesses or their probable testimony; any belief in guilt or innocence; or like statements concerning the merits of the case. . . .

From the cases coming here we note that unfair and prejudicial news comment on pending trials has become increasingly prevalent. Due process requires that the accused receive a trial by an impartial jury free from outside influences. Given the pervasiveness of modern communications and the difficulty of effacing prejudicial publicity from the minds of the jurors, the trial courts must take strong measures to ensure that the balance is never weighed against the accused. . . .

Since the state trial judge did not fulfill his duty to protect Sheppard from the inherently prejudicial publicity which saturated the community and to control disruptive influences in the courtroom, we must reverse the denial of the habeas petition. The case is remanded to the District Court with instructions to issue the writ and order that Sheppard be released from custody unless the State puts him to its charges again within a reasonable time.

It is so ordered.

Justice Black dissented.

Williams v. Florida
399 U.S. 78, 90 S.Ct. 1893, 26 L.Ed.2d. 446 (1973)

In 1968, in *Duncan* v. *Louisiana,* 391 U.S. 145, a divided Supreme Court extended the Sixth Amendment's guarantee of trial by jury in all criminal cases to the states through the due process clause of the Fourteenth Amendment. In its prior application in the federal context, it had been assumed that the Sixth Amendment jury trial requirement implied a twelve person jury. But extended to the states, where juries of less than twelve were common for many sorts of trials, was the twelve person expectation to be insisted upon? In *Williams* v. *Florida,* the majority, speaking through Justice White, decided to the contrary, but Mr. Justice Harlan, in concurring, decried what he viewed as a dilution of the original Sixth Amendment requirement.

Mr. Justice White delivered the opinion of the Court.

In *Duncan* v. *Louisiana,* 391 U.S. 145 (1968), we held that the Fourteenth Amendment guarantees a right to trial by jury in all criminal cases that—were they to be tried in a federal court—would come within the Sixth Amendment's guarantee. Petitioner's trial for robbery on July 3, 1968, clearly falls within the scope of that holding. ... The question in this case then is whether the constitutional guarantee of a trial by "jury" necessarily requires trial by exactly 12 persons, rather than some lesser number—in this case six. We hold that the 12-man panel is not a necessary ingredient of "trial by jury," and that respondent's refusal to impanel more than the six members provided for by Florida law did not violate petitioner's Sixth Amendment rights as applied to the States through the Fourteenth. ...

We do not pretend to be able to divine precisely what the word "jury" imported to the Framers, the First Congress, or the States in 1789. It may well be that the usual expectation was that the jury would consist of 12, and that hence, the most likely conclusion to be drawn is simply that little thought was actually given to the specific question we face today. But there is absolutely no indication in "the intent of the Framers" of an explicit decision to equate the constitutional and common-law characteristics of the jury. Nothing in this history suggests, then, that we do violence to the letter of the Constitution by turning to other than purely historical considerations to determine which features of the jury system, as it existed at common law, were preserved in the Constitution. The relevant inquiry, as we see it, must be the function that the particular feature performs and its relation to the purposes of the jury trial. Measured by this standard, the 12-man requirement cannot be regarded as an indispensable component of the Sixth Amendment. ...

It might be suggested that the 12-man jury gives a defendant a greater advantage since he has more "chances" of finding a juror who will insist on acquittal and thus prevent conviction. But the advantage might just as easily belong to the State, which also needs only one juror out of twelve insisting on guilt to prevent acquittal. What few experiments have occurred—usually in the civil area—indicate that there is no discernible difference between the results reached by the two different-sized juries. In short, neither currently available evidence nor theory suggests that the 12-man jury is necessarily more advantageous to the defendant than a jury composed of fewer members. . . .

The judgment of the Florida District Court of Appeal is

Affirmed.

Apodaca v. *Oregon*
406 U.S. 404, 92 S.Ct. 1628, 32 L.Ed.2d. 184 (1972)

Apodaca represents another piece of fallout from the extension of the Sixth Amendment's jury trial requirements to the states in *Duncan* v. *Louisiana.* In federal courts it had been assumed that the Sixth Amendment jury trial requirement included an expectation that jury verdicts in criminal cases be unanimous. Many states, however, allowed nonunanimous jury verdicts under certain circumstances. Here a majority of the court accepts nonunanimous verdicts as satisfying the Sixth through Fourteenth Amendment requirements. There is no majority opinion.

Mr. Justice White announced the judgment of the Court and an opinion in which The Chief Justice, Mr. Justice Blackmun, and Mr. Justice Rehnquist joined.

Robert Apodaca, Henry Morgan Cooper, Jr., and James Arnold Madden were convicted respectively of assault with a deadly weapon, burglary in a dwelling, and grand larceny before separate Oregon juries, all of which returned less-than-unanimous verdicts. The vote in the cases of Apodaca and Madden was 11−1, while the vote in the case of Cooper was 10−2, the minimum requisite vote under Oregon law for sustaining a conviction.

In *Williams* v. *Florida* . . . we had occasion to consider a related issue: whether the Sixth Amendment's right to trial by jury requires that all juries consist of 12 men. After considering the history of the 12-man requirement and the functions it performs in contemporary society, we concluded that it was not of constitutional stature. We reach the same conclusion today with regard to the requirement of unanimity.

Like the requirement that juries consist of 12 men, the requirement of unanimity arose during the Middle Ages and had become an accepted feature of the common-law jury by the 18th century. But, as we observed in *Williams,* "the relevant constitutional history casts considerable doubt on the easy assumption . . . that if a given feature existed in a jury at common law in 1789, then it was necessarily preserved in the Constitution." . . . The most salient fact in the scanty history of the Sixth Amendment, which we reviewed in full in *Williams,* is that, as it was introduced by James Madison in the House of Representatives, the proposed Amendment provided for trial

"by an impartial jury of freeholders of the vicinage, with the requisite of unanimity for conviction, of the right of challenge, and other accustomed requisites. ...." 1 Annals of Cong. 435 (1789).

Although it passed the House with little alteration, this proposal ran into considerable opposition in the Senate, particularly with regard to the vicinage requirement of the House version. The draft of the proposed Amendment was returned to the House in considerably altered form, and a conference committee was appointed. That committee refused to accept not only the original House language but also an alternate suggestion by the House conferees that juries be defined as possessing "the accustomed requisites." ... Instead, the Amendment that ultimately emerged from the committee and then from Congress and the States provided only for trial

"by an impartial jury of the State and district wherein the crime shall have been committed, which district shall have been previously ascertained by law. ...."

As we observed in *Williams,* one can draw conflicting inferences from this legislative history. One possible inference is that Congress eliminated references to unanimity and to the other "accustomed requisites" of the jury because those requisites were thought already to be implicit in the very concept of jury. A contrary explanation, which we found in *Williams* to be the more plausible, is that the deletion was intended to have some substantive effect. ... Surely one fact that is absolutely clear from this history is that, after a proposal had been made to specify precisely which of the common-law requisites of the jury were to be preserved by the Constitution, the Framers explicitly rejected the proposal and instead left such specification to the future. ...

Our inquiry must focus upon the function served by the jury in contemporary society. ... As we said in *Duncan,* the purpose of trial by jury is to prevent oppression by the Government by providing a "safeguard against the corrupt or overzealous prosecutor and against the compliant, biased, or eccentric judge." ... "Given this purpose, the essential feature of a jury obviously lies in the interposition between the accused and his accuser of the commonsense judgment of a group of laymen. ...." A requirement of unanimity, however, does not materially contribute to the exercise of this commonsense judgment. As we said in *Williams,* a jury will come to such a judgment as long as it consists of a group of laymen representative of a cross section of the community who have the duty and the opportunity to deliberate, free from outside attempts at intimidation, on the question of a defendant's guilt. In terms of this function we perceive no difference between juries required to act unanimously and those permitted to convict or acquit by votes of 10 to two or 11 to one. Requiring unanimity would obviously produce hung juries in some situations where nonunanimous juries will convict or acquit. But in either case, the interest of the defendant in having the judgment of his peers interposed between himself and the officers of the State who prosecute and judge him is equally well served. ...

We accordingly affirm the judgment of the Court of Appeals of Oregon.

To compound confusion, Justice Blackmun wrote a concurring opinion. Justice Powell wrote an opinion concurring in the judgment. Justice Douglas wrote a dissenting opinion in which Justices Brennan and Marshall joined, and Justice Brennan wrote a dissenting opinion in which Justice Marshall joined. And, wait for it, Justice Stewart wrote a dissenting opinion, which Justice Brennan and Justice Marshall joined. Justice Marshall wrote a dissenting opinion in which Justice Brennan joined.

CASE STUDY: THE SOCIOLOGY OF JURIES

In *Sheppard* v. *Maxwell* we noted the difficulties inhering in the concept of "an impartial jury." One threat to impartiality is the impact on prospective jurors of highly dramatic or highly colored accounts of the case broadcast in the media. But there is a more profound and troubling question which lurks in the constitutional concept of impartiality.

In English law a defendant was entitled to a trial by a jury of one's "peers." This was straight-forward enough in a society formally divided into persons of different legal characters, namely, where there were royalty, peers of the realm, and commoners. It was a privilege of a peer of the realm to be tried (remember the Alec Guiness film, *Kind Hearts and Coronets*) by a jury of peers; if necessary, by the House of Lords. "Peer," in this sense, has no application in the American context. But ours *is* a nation of differing races, religions, and national backgrounds, and a nation of considerable socio-economic differences. Is it really possible that a jury radically different in racial, cultural, or economic background from the defendant can be altogether impartial?

Arguments that juries must be socio-economically, culturally, or racially "compatible" with defendants usually are rebuffed by courts and legislatures. But in 1975, in *Taylor* v. *Louisiana,* 419 U.S. 522, the Supreme Court did hold that Sixth Amendment impartiality included "the right to a jury selected from a fair cross section of the community." This requirement of sociological "representativeness" applied to the pool of persons called for jury duty (veniremen) from which actual trial jury panels are drawn. As to the selection of actual trial juries, traditionally viewed as part of the adversary struggle between the prosecutor and defense counsel, the Court has been hesitant to create restrictions.

In 1965, in *Swain* v. *Alabama,* 380 U.S. 202, the Court held that it was not a denial of that equal protection of the laws guaranteed by the Fourteenth Amendment for a prosecutor to use the peremptory challenges available under state laws to "strike" every black venireman from the jury panel. At the time, the Sixth Amendment's impartiality guarantee was not applied to the states. That innovation came in *Duncan* v. *Louisiana,* 391 U.S. 145 (1968). Today it is at least possible to argue that the use of the peremptory challenge in a systematic fashion to exclude members of particular ethnic groups, while not a violation of equal protection, should be considered a denial of impartiality. Indeed, several states (Massachusetts and California) have taken steps to constrain their prosecutors' use of peremptory challenges to achieve ethnic exclusion from jury panels.

However, in *Ristanio* v. *Ross,* 424 U.S. 559 (1976), the Supreme Court divided over the constitutionality of a trial judge denying the request of a defendant that a question specifically directed to the racial prejudice of prospective jurors be asked during their examination for suitability to sit. Justice Powell delivered the opinion of the Court, concluding that the defendant was not entitled, as a matter of Sixth Amendment jury impartiality, to have questions concerning racial prejudice included: "The Constitution does not always entitle a defendant to have questions posed during voir dire specifically directed to matters that might conceivably prejudice veniremen against him."

Did the *Ristanio* majority draw back because to enter the realm of "constructive sociological impartiality" might be to open a Pandora's Box? And what should our response be when some defense counsel uses the techniques of social and psychological modeling to select jurors sympathetic to their clients? Is this a modern version of Clarence Darrow's old rule of thumb about challenging Presbyterians but not Jews, or is it something more sinister? The answers are elusive.

In a relatively homogeneous country such as England at the time the jury evolved, there was little need to worry about jury "representativeness." In America of the late twentieth century it is increasingly a matter of concern to legal theorists.

CHAPTER 18

BAIL, GUILTY PLEAS, DOUBLE JEOPARDY, AND CRUEL AND UNUSUAL PUNISHMENT

THIS chapter is something of a potpourri, but each of the subjects is an important issue area of constitutional law bearing on the rights of the criminal defendant.

In the case of bail, the Eighth Amendment provides that "excessive bail shall not be required." The traditional interpretation is that bail is a mechanism properly used only to insure that the defendant appears for trial. In fact, bail is commonly employed by judges to insure that persons whom they believe dangerous to the public are not at liberty in the period between arraignment and trial. We will examine the controversy surrounding the bail requirement in the case of *Stack* v. *Boyle.*

In the introduction to Part II, we noted the importance of the guilty plea in the American criminal justice process today. The trial—our truth determining mechanism—has become so complicated, time consuming, cumbersome, and expensive that most serious criminal charges are settled through the process of plea bargaining. This process is not, however, without constitutional restraint, and we will approach this through the case of *Brady* v. *U.S.*

The Fifth Amendment provides that no person shall "be subject for the same offense to be twice put in jeopardy of life or limbs. . . . " This "prohibition of double jeopardy" now applies to all levels of the American system and is not without controversy and ambiguity, as we shall see in *Ashe* v. *Swensen.*

Finally, we will begin our consideration of the Eighth Amendment's prohibition of cruel and unusual punishments with the case of *Gregg v. Georgia.*

Stack v. *Boyle*
342 U.S. 1, 72 S.Ct. 1, 96 L.Ed. 3 (1951)

The purpose of bail is to insure that the accused person will be present for trial and not flee the jurisdiction of the court. The Eighth Amendment provides that excessive bail shall not be required, and there has been a traditional assumption that persons should be admitted to bail for noncapital offenses. This once was specifically recognized in federal law. However, with the decline in the number of capital crimes (where the death penalty is abolished altogether or for particular offenses) the problem of what to do with a potentially dangerous defendant—one who may commit further crimes and predations on the community if released on bail—has become more acute. It is possible to argue, of course, that a potentially dangerous defendant is also one whose flight is highly likely, and that this justifies a high bail, which is calculated to keep that person in confinement until trial. The court's decision in *Stack* v. *Boyle* reminds us that the Eighth Amendment's guarantee against excessive bail requires that the amount of bail be tailored to the likelihood of flight and to no other characteristic of the defendant. Whether states and the federal government should adopt some form of preventive detention law to take care of those potentially dangerous defendants who cannot be restrained by bail based on likelihood of flight is a continuing controversy. Would such a preventive detention arrangement be constitutional at all? And if so, how are judges to identify those who are potentially dangerous but unlikely to flee the jurisdiction?

Mr. Chief Justice Vinson delivered the opinion of the Court.

Indictments have been returned in the Southern District of California charging the twelve petitioners with conspiring to violate the Smith Act ... [B]ail was fixed in the District Court for the Southern District of California in the uniform amount of $50,000 for each petitioner.

Petitioners moved to reduce bail on the ground that bail as fixed was excessive under the Eighth Amendment. In support of their motion, petitioners submitted statements as to their financial resources, family relationships, health, prior criminal records, and other information. The only evidence offered by the Government was a certified record showing that four persons previously convicted under the Smith Act in the Southern District of New York had forfeited bail. No evidence was produced relating those four persons to the petitioners in this case. At a hearing on the motion, petitioners were examined by the District Judge and cross-examined by an attorney for the Government. Petitioners' factual statements stand uncontroverted.

From the passage of the Judiciary Act of 1789 ... to the present ... federal law has unequivocally provided that a person arrested for a non-capital offense *shall* be admitted to bail. This traditional right to freedom before conviction permits the unhampered preparation of a defense, and serves to prevent the infliction of punishment prior to conviction. ...

Since the function of bail is limited, the fixing of bail for any individual defendant must be based upon standards relevant to the purpose of assuring the presence of that defendant. The traditional standards as expressed in the Federal Rules of Criminal Procedure are to be applied in each case to each defendant. In this case petitioners are charged with offenses under the Smith Act and, if found guilty, their convictions are subject to review with the scrupulous care demanded by our Constitution. *Dennis* v. *United States*, 341 U.S. 494, 516 (1951). Upon final judgment of conviction, petitioners face imprisonment of not more than five years and a fine of not more than $10,000. It is not denied that bail for each petitioner has been fixed in a sum much higher than that usually imposed for offenses with like penalties and yet there has been no factual showing to justify such action in this case. The Government asks the courts to depart from the norm by assuming, without the introduction of evidence, that each petitioner is a pawn in a conspiracy and will, in obedience to a superior, flee the jurisdiction. To infer from the fact of indictment alone a need for bail in an unusually high amount is an arbitrary act. Such conduct would inject into our own system of government the very principles of totalitarianism which Congress was seeking to guard against in passing the statute under which petitioners have been indicted.

If bail in an amount greater than that usually fixed for serious charges of crimes is required in the case of any of the petitioners, that is a matter to which evidence should be directed in a hearing so that the constitutional rights of each petitioner may be preserved. In the absence of such a showing, we are of the opinion that the fixing of bail before trial in these cases cannot be squared with the statutory and constitutional standards for admission to bail. . . .

The Court concludes that bail has not been fixed by proper methods in this case and that petitioners' remedy is by motion to reduce bail, with right of appeal to the Court of Appeals. Accordingly, the judgment of the Court of Appeals is vacated and the case is remanded to the District Court with directions to vacate its order denying petitioners' applications for writs of habeas corpus and to dismiss the applications without prejudice. Petitioners may move for reduction of bail in the criminal proceeding so that a hearing may be held for the purpose of fixing reasonable bail for each petitioner.

Justice Jackson wrote a concurring opinion in which Justice Frankfurter joined.

Brady v. *United States*
397 U.S. 436, 90 S.Ct. 1463, 25 L.Ed.2d. 747 (1970)

Professor John H. Langbein, of the University of Chicago Law School, is only one of a number of experts who have recently called attention to the major but unintended role that the guilty plea has come to play in American criminal justice. "In our day," Langbein writes, "jury trial continues to occupy its central place both in the formal law and in the mythology of the law. The Constitution has not changed. . . . In truth, criminal jury trial has largely disappeared in America. The criminal justice system now disposes of virtually all cases of serious crime through plea bargaining." ("Torture and Plea Bargaining," *The Public Interest,* Winter, 1980, p. 48.) This has come about in part because of the growth in complexity and expense of the criminal trial, which we noted in the introduction to this chapter.

A major national debate is developing over the plea bargaining. Critics argue that the practice sacrifices both the interest of the accused and the interest of society. Others respond that there is no alternative—that the criminal trial must be reserved for the extraordinary case, while the ordinary flow of business is dealt with through less costly negotiated pleas. The complexities and nuances of this debate are beyond us here, but it is important to note the constitutional guarantee of voluntariness with respect to guilty pleas. It is the teaching of *Brady* v. *U.S.* that a plea can be constitutionally "voluntary" even though, as a practical matter, the defendant is under some practical pressure to "cop out." It is well that this is so, for if the constitutional requirement of voluntariness were more strict, our criminal justice system might cease to function altogether.

Mr. Justice White delivered the opinion of the Court.

In 1959, petitioner was charged with kidnapping. . . . Since the indictment charged that the victim of the kidnapping was not liberated unharmed, petitioner faced a maximum penalty of death if the verdict of the jury should so recommend. Petitioner, represented by competent counsel throughout, first elected to plead not guilty. . . . Upon learning that his codefendant, who had confessed to the authorities, would plead guilty and be available to testify against him, petitioner changed his plea to guilty. His plea was accepted after the trial judge twice questioned him as to the voluntariness of his plea. Petitioner was sentenced to 50 years' imprisonment, later reduced to 30.

In 1967, petitioner sought relief [in a habeas corpus petition] claiming that his plea of guilty was not voluntarily given because . . . his counsel exerted impermissable pressure upon him, and because his plea was induced by representations with respect to reduction of sentence and clemency. . . .

The trial judge in 1959 found the plea voluntary before accepting it; the District Court in 1968, after an evidentiary hearing, found that the plea was voluntarily made; the Court of Appeals specifically approved the finding of voluntariness. We see no reason on this record to disturb the judgment of those courts. Petitioner, advised by competent counsel, tendered his plea after his codefendant, who had already given a confession, determined to plead guilty and became available to testify against petitioner. It was this development that the District Court found to have triggered Brady's guilty plea.

The voluntariness of Brady's plea can be determined only by considering all of the relevant circumstances surrounding it. . . . One of these circumstances was the possibility of a heavier sentence following a guilty verdict after a trial. It may be that Brady, faced with a strong case against him and recognizing that his chances for acquittal were slight, preferred to plead guilty and thus limit the penalty to life imprisonment rather than to elect a jury trial which could result in a death penalty. But even if we assume that Brady would not have pleaded guilty except for the death penalty provision [in federal law] this assumption merely identifies the penalty provision as a "but for" cause of his plea. That the statute caused the plea in this sense does not necessarily prove that the plea was coerced and invalid as an involuntary act. . . .

The record before us also supports the conclusion that Brady's plea was intelligently made. He was advised by competent counsel, he was made aware of the nature of the charge against him, and there was nothing to indicate that he was incompetent or otherwise not in control of his mental faculties; once his confederate had pleaded guilty and became available to testify, he chose to plead guilty, perhaps to ensure that he would face no more than life imprisonment or a term of years. Brady was aware of precisely what he was doing when he admitted that he had kidnapped the victim and had not released her unharmed. . . .

Often the decision to plead guilty is heavily influenced by the defendant's appraisal of the prosecution's case against him and by the apparent likelihood of securing leniency should a guilty plea be offered and accepted. Considerations like these frequently present imponderable questions for which there are no certain answers; judgments may be made that in the light of later events seem improvident, although they were perfectly sensible at the time. The rule that a plea must be intelligently made to be valid does not require that a plea be vulnerable to later attack if the defendant did not correctly assess every relevant factor entering into his decision. A defendant is not entitled to withdraw his plea merely because he discovered long after the plea has been accepted that his calculus misapprehended the quality of the State's case or the likely penalties attached to alternative courses of action.

Although Brady's plea of guilty may well have been motivated in part by a desire to avoid a possible death penalty, we are convinced that his plea was voluntarily and intelligently made and we have no reason to doubt that his solemn admission of guilt was truthful.

Affirmed.

Justice Black wrote a concurring opinion. Justice Brennan wrote an opinion concurring only in the result, which Justices Douglas and Marshall joined.

Ashe v. *Swenson*
397 U.S. 436, 90 S.Ct. 1189, 21 L.Ed.2d. 469 (1970)

Opposition to the idea of successive prosecutions for essentially the same crime is deeply rooted in the Anglo-American legal tradition. But this does not make any less complex and teasing the sorts of questions that arise under the Fifth Amendment's guarantee against double jeopardy. What constitutes a "single crime"? And when is the evidence put before the jury and tested for believability sufficiently different from one case to another to allow multiple prosecutions? In *Ashe,* Justice Stewart, speaking for the majority, reaffirmed the "same evidence" approach to double jeopardy, which is the traditional approach used in English and American courts. By this reasoning, if a trial for a separate crime after a previous acquittal involves testing before the jury essentially the same evidence that was tested (and apparently found wanting) in the earlier trial, the second trial is procluded by the double jeopardy ban. Three members of the court thought the "same evidence" approach did not go far enough, and one member thought it already went too far.

Mr. Justice Stewart delivered the opinion of the Court.

   . . . [T]he Fifth Amendment guarantee against double jeopardy is enforceable against the States through the Fourteenth Amendment. The question in this case is whether the State of Missouri violated that guarantee when it prosecuted the petitioner a second time for armed robbery in the circumstances here presented.
   Sometime in the early hours of the morning of January 10, 1960, six men were engaged in a poker game in the basement of the home of John Gladson at Lee's Summit, Missouri. Suddenly three or four masked men, armed with a shotgun and pistols, broke into the basement and robbed each of the poker players of money and various articles of personal property. The robbers—and it has never been clear whether there were three or four of them—then fled in a car belonging to one of the victims of the robbery. Shortly thereafter the stolen car was discovered in a field, and later that morning three men were arrested by a state trooper while they were walking on a highway not far from where the abandoned car had been found. The petitioner was arrested by another officer some distance away.
   The four were subsequently charged with seven separate offenses—the armed robbery of each of the six poker players and the theft of the car. In May 1960 the petitioner went to trial on the charge of robbing Donald Knight, one of the participants in the poker game. At the trial the State called Knight and three of his fellow poker players as prosecution witnesses. Each of them described the circumstances of the holdup and itemized his own individual losses. The proof that an armed robbery had occurred and that personal property had been taken from Knight as well as from each of the others was unassailable. The testimony of the four victims in this regard was consistent both internally and with that of the others. But the State's evidence that the petitioner had been one of the robbers was weak. Two of the witnesses thought that there had been only three robbers altogether, and could not identify the petitioner as one of them. Another of the victims, who was the petitioner's uncle by marriage, said that at the "patrol station" he had positively identified each of the other three men accused of the holdup, but could say only that the petitioner's voice "sounded very much like" that of one of the robbers. The fourth participant in the poker game did identify the petitioner, but only by his "size and height, and his actions."
   The cross-examination of these witnesses was brief, and it was aimed primarily at exposing the weakness of their identification testimony. . . .
   The question is not whether Missouri could validly charge the petitioner with six separate offenses for the robbery of the six poker players. It is not whether he could have received a total of six punishments if he had been convicted in a single trial of robbing the six victims. It is simply whether, after a jury determined by its verdict that the petitioner was not one of the robbers, the State could constitutionally hale him before a new jury to litigate that issue again.
   After the first jury had acquitted the petitioner of robbing Knight, Missouri

could certainly not have brought him to trial again upon that charge. Once a jury had determined upon conflicting testimony that there was at least a reasonable doubt that the petitioner was one of the robbers, the State could not present the same or different identification evidence in a second prosecution for the robbery of Knight in the hope that a different jury might find that evidence more convincing. The situation is constitutionally no different here, even though the second trial related to another victim of the same robbery. For the name of the victim, in the circumstances of this case, had no bearing whatever upon the issue of whether the petitioner was one of the robbers.

In this case the State in its brief has frankly conceded that following the petitioner's acquittal, it treated the first trial as no more than a dry run for the second prosecution: "No doubt the prosecutor felt the state had a provable case on the first charge and, when he lost, he did what every good attorney would do—he refined his presentation in light of the turn of events at the first trial." But this is precisely what the constitutional guarantee forbids.

The judgment is reversed, and the case is remanded to the Court of Appeals for the Eighth District Circuit for further proceedings consistent with this opinion.

Justices Black and Harlan wrote concurring opinions. Justice Brennan wrote a concurring opinion in which Justice Douglas and Justice Marshall joined. He rejected the "same evidence" test for double jeopardy as inadequate protection. Instead, Brennan argued that the government should be obligated "to join at one trial all the charges against a defendant that grow out of a single criminal act, occurence, episode, or transaction." Even if multiple crimes had been committed in the course of a "transaction," and even if somewhat different bodies of evidence bore on the separate crimes, multiple prosecution would be forbidden.

Chief Justice Burger dissented. He would have allowed separate prosecutions for separate crimes even if there was great similarity in the evidence tested each time. He rejected Justice Brennan's single transaction argument as a "single frolic" theory, stressing that in *Ashe* multiple offenses had been committed against six separate persons.

Gregg v. *Georgia*
428 U.S. 153, 96 S.Ct. 2909, 49 L.Ed.2d. 859 (1976)

One of the longest and most dramatic campaigns in recent American constitutional politics is that involving the effort by some civil libertarians to persuade a majority of the Supreme Court that the death penalty constitutes a cruel and unusual punishment in violation of the Eighth Amendment and made applicable to the states by the Fourteenth. In *Furman* v. *Georgia,* 408 U.S. 238 (1972), a majority of the court declines to find the death penalty cruel or unusual per se. Four justices thought that it was not, and two justices thought that it was, while three justices left the question open; these three concluded that the particular state death penalty provisions before the Court in *Furman* were defective in failing to specify with precision when the death penalty was authorized and when it was not. The holding of *Furman* was that the death penalty could not be administered in a capricious and unpredictable way. Rather, states were required to define precisely what sorts of offenses merited capital punishment. In the wake of *Furman* a majority of the states did revise their death penalty statutes by identifying particular categories of crimes (e.g., the murder of a prison guard in the course of attempted escape) for which the death penalty was warranted. The plurality opinion of Justice Stewart in *Gregg* relied heavily on this greater specificity in concluding that the death penalty was still approved by substantial numbers of Americans and, therefore, could not be viewed as cruel and unusual.

Judgment of the Court, and opinion of Mr. Justice Stewart, Mr. Justice Powell, and Mr. Justice Stevens, annnounced by Mr. Justice Stewart.

The issue in this case is whether the imposition of the sentence of death for the crime of murder under the law of Georgia violates the Eighth and Fourteenth Amendments. . . .

We address initially the basic contention that the punishment of death for the crime of murder is, under all circumstances, "cruel and unusual" in violation of the Eighth and Fourteenth Amendments of the Constitution. . . .

The Court on a number of occasions has both assumed and asserted the constitutionality of capital punishment. In several cases that assumption provided a necessary foundation for the decision, as the Court was asked to decide whether a particular method of carrying out a capital sentence would be allowed to stand under the Eighth Amendment. But until *Furman* v. *Georgia* . . . the Court never confronted squarely the fundamental claim that the punishment of death always, regardless of the enormity of the offense or the procedure followed in imposing the sentence, is cruel and unusual punishment in violation of the Constitution. Although this issue was presented and addressed in *Furman,* it was not resolved by the Court. Four Justices would have held that capital punishment is not unconstituitional *per se;* two Justices would have reached the opposite conclusion; and three justices, while agreeing that the statutes then before the Court were invalid as applied, left open the question whether such punishment may ever be imposed. We now hold that the punishment of death does not invariably violate the Constitution.

The history of the prohibition of "cruel and unusual" punishment already has been reviewed by this Court at length. The phrase first appeared in the English Bill of Rights of 1689, which was drafted by Parliament at the accession of William and Mary. . . . The English version appears to have been directed against punishments unauthorized by statute and beyond the jurisdiction of the sentencing court, as well as those disproportionate to the offense involved. . . . The American draftsmen, who adopted the English phrasing in drafting the Eighth Amendment, were primarily concerned, however, with proscribing "tortures" and other "barbarous" methods of punishment. . . .

In the earliest cases raising Eighth Amendment claims, the Court focused on particular methods of execution to determine whether they were too cruel to pass constitutional muster. The constitutionality of the sentence of death itself was not at issue, and the criterion used to evaluate the mode of execution was its similarity to "torture" and other "barbarous" methods. . . .

But the Court has not confined the prohibition embodied in the Eighth Amendment to "barbarous" methods that were generally outlawed in the 18th century. Instead, the Amendment has been interpreted in a flexible and dynamic manner. The Court early recognized that "a principle to be vital must be capable of wider application than the mischief which gave it birth." . . . Thus the clause forbidding "cruel and unusual" punishments is not fastened to the obsolete but may acquire meaning as public opinion becomes enlightened by a humane justice." . . .

Of course, the requirements of the Eighth Amendment must be applied with an awareness of the limited role to be played by the courts. This does not mean that judges have no role to play, for the Eighth Amendment is a restraint upon the exercise of legislative power. . . .

But, while we have an obligation to insure that constitutional bounds are not overreached, we may not act as judges as we might as legislators. . . .

Therefore, in assessing a punishment selected by a democratically elected legislature against the constitutional measure, we presume its validity. We may not require the legislature to select the least severe penalty possible so long as the penalty selected is not cruelly inhumane or disproportionate to the crime involved. And a heavy burden rests on those who would attack the judgment of the representatives of the people.

This is true in part because the constitutional test is intertwined with an assessment of contemporary standards and the legislative judgment weighs heavily in ascertaining such standards. . . .

In the discussion to this point we have sought to identify the principles and considerations that guide a court in addressing an Eighth Amendment claim. We now consider specifically whether the sentence of death for the crime of murder is a *per se* violation of the Eighth and Fourteenth Amendments to the Constitution. We note first that history and precedent strongly support a negative answer to this question.

The imposition of the death penalty for the crime of murder has a long history of acceptance both in the United States and in England. The common-law rule imposed a mandatory death sentence on all convicted murderers. . . . And the penalty continued to be used into the 20th century by most American States, although the breadth of the common-law rule was diminished, initially by narrowing the class of murders to be punished by death and subsequently by widespread adoption of laws expressly granting juries the discretion to recommend mercy. . . .

It is apparent from the text of the Constitution itself that the existence of capital punishment was accepted by the Framers. At the time the Eighth Amendment was ratified, capital punishment was a common sanction in every State. . . . And the Fourteenth Amendment, adopted over three-quarters of a century later, similarly contemplates the existence of the capital sanction in providing that no State shall deprive any person of "life, liberty, or property" without due process of law.

For nearly two centuries, this Court, repeatedly and often expressly, has recognized that capital punishment is not invalid *per se*. . . .

Four years ago, the petitioners in *Furman* and its companion cases predicated their argument primarily upon the asserted proposition that standards of decency had evolved to the point where capital punishment no longer could be tolerated. The petitioners in those cases said, in effect, that the evolutionary process had come to an end, and that standards of decency required that the Eighth Amendment be construed finally as prohibiting capital punishment for any crime regardless of its depravity and impact on society. This view was accepted by two Justices. Three other Justices were unwilling to go so far; focusing on the procedures by which convicted defendants were selected for the death penalty rather than on the actual punishment inflicted, they joined in the conclusion that the statutes before the Court were constitutionally invalid.

The petitioners in the capital cases before the Court today renew the "standards of decency" argument, but developments during the four years since *Furman* have undercut substantially the assumptions upon which their argument rested. Despite the continuing debate, dating back to the 19th century, over the morality and utility of capital punishment, it is now evident that a large proportion of American society continues to regard it as an appropriate and necessary criminal sanction.

The most marked indication of society's endorsement of the death penalty for murder is the legislative response to *Furman*. The legislatures of at least 35 States have enacted new statutes that provide for the death penalty for at least some crimes that result in the death of another person. And the Congress of the United States, in 1974, enacted a statute providing the death penalty for aircraft piracy that results in death. These recently adopted statutes have attempted to address the concerns expressed by the Court in *Furman* primarily (i) by specifying the factors to be weighed and the procedures to be followed in deciding when to impose a capital sentence, or (ii) by making the death penalty mandatory for specified crimes. But all of the post-*Furman* statutes make clear that capital punishment itself has not been rejected by the elected representatives of the people. . . .

We hold that the death penalty is not a form of punishment that may never be imposed, regardless of the circumstances of the offense, regardless of the character of the offender, and regardless of the procedure followed in reaching the decision to impose it.

. . . [T]he statutory system under which Gregg was sentenced to death does not violate the Constitution. Accordingly, the judgment of the Georgia Supreme Court is affirmed.

Justice White, with whom Chief Justice Burger and Justice Rehnquist joined, concurred in the judgment. They agreed, however, that the death penalty was not cruel and unusual. Justice Blackmun also concurred in the judgement. Justice Brennan dissented.

CASE STUDY: JUDICIAL SUPERVISION OF PRISON CONDITIONS

Over the last fifteen years, the cruel and unusual punishments clause of the Eighth Amendment has been used as a vehicle for the involvement of courts, particularly federal courts, with conditions in prisons and jails. In 1970, in *Holt* v. *Sarver*, 302 F. Supp. 362, a federal district court held that the entire prison system of the state of Arkansas violated the Eighth Amendment, and this decision was upheld by the Eighth Circuit Court of Appeals. The Supreme Court has not, thus far, specifically upheld a ruling quite as broad as this, but in *Hutto* v. *Finney*, 437 U.S. 678 (1978), some particulars of the *Holt* decision were upheld. Judicial involvement with prison administration was further accelerated by the passage in 1980 of the federal Civil Rights of Institutionalized Persons Act. This empowered the Attorney General of the United States to initiate suit in federal court inviting judges to find constitutional violations in state or local institutions.

The use of the cruel and unusual punishment clause to reach prison conditions is a novel modern extension of the Eighth Amendment and in some respects is difficult to justify within the framework of traditional constitutional analysis.

One stream of prison condition cases has to do with discreet adjudications involving specific acts and practices. For instance, in *Estelle* v. *Gamble*, 429 U.S. 97 (1976), the Supreme Court held that the provision of medical care in prisons will not be found constitutionally wanting without proof of specific "acts or omissions" that are sufficiently harmful to inmates to constitute evidence of "deliberate indifference" to their medical needs. Similar cases focusing on discreet acts, practices, and intentions of prison personnel have involved disciplinary procedures. For instance, in *Wolff* v. *McDonnell*, 418 U.S. 539 (1974), the Court asked whether a particular disciplinary procedure is reasonably related to the security needs of the prison. Such cases, with specific fact situations and challenges to the good faith or reasonableness of what prison officials do, are relatively easy to accomodate within the framework of traditional constitutional analysis.

The second stream of prison condition cases, however, is more problematical. In these cases the challenge is not to particular practices but to the character of the institution or system itself. Thus in *Pugh* v. *Locke*, 408 F. Supp. 318 (1976), federal District Judge Frank Johnson in Alabama referred to the "rampant violence and jungle atmosphere" which he found to prevail in Alabama prisons. Rather than dealing with a specific practice, this type of suit seeks to probe what the editors of the *Harvard Law Review* called the "background of the institution or system" ("Complex Enforcement: Unconstitutional Prison Conditions," 94 *Harvard Law Review* 626 (1981)). But the background of an institution or system has to do with such things as the age and configuration of the physical facilities, plus the number and training of guards and prison administrators. In a case involving a discreet fact situation, a court can order a discreet remedy. The remedy may cost money, but typically this will be in modest amounts and might be found by reallocation of resources within the institution or system.

Remedies for systematic constitutional deficiencies are of an altogether different order of magnitude. Here the court must order the hiring of new guards, the creation of new facilities, or the appointment of new administrators with higher educational and professional qualifications from those they replace. Such a remedial order puts the jurisdiction (the state, the county, or the municipality) in the position of requiring considerable new expenditures. Courts, of course, do not have the power to compel jurisdictions to increase taxes, nor, thus far, have courts undertaken to monitor the range of resource allocation decisions made by state and local government. Thus the effect of a sweeping, systematic prison condition order is to say in effect to local authorities, "Find the dollars somehow or close it down."

But if the key to what constitutes cruel and unusual punishment is evolving community standards (c.f., *Gregg* v. *Georgia*), and if the community, through repeated allocative decisions of its elected representatives concludes that a given level of prison conditions is adequate, how firm is the ground on which the court stands in declaring this level of conditions cruel and unusual? And is it appropriate, in any case, for judges to become involved in the details of prison administration, passing on matters of guard training, disciplinary procedures, and diet?

Certainly American views of what constitutes acceptable conditions of life with dignity have changed since millions of men spent chilled nights in uninsulated World War II barracks and breakfasted on fried spam seven times a week. And it is not written in the sky that the soldier-per-toilet ratio of the World War II troopship should govern minimum standards in a county jail today. But the respective roles of courts and legislatures in taking account of evolving community sensibilities will be a rich source of controversy into the future.

PART IV

EQUALITY BEFORE THE LAW

GENERAL Robert E. Lee's surrender at Appomattox settled a fundamental constitutional issue that had troubled the nation since its birth. Member states might not opt out of the Union. The American Republic was, in the words of Chief Justice Salmon Portland Chase in *Texas* v. *White,* 7 Wallace 700 (1869), "an indestructible Union, composed of indestructible states." But the Civil War and the Reconstruction period following gave rise to a whole new set of constitutional questions, and ushered in a decade of constitutional and statutory innovation, which was to be as consequential for the future rights and liberties of Americans as the original constitutional convention of 1787.

Of first importance was the status of newly freed black people in the states of the former Confederacy, the "freedmen". Southern legislatures moved quickly to settle this question on their own terms. In a series of statutes that became known as the Black Codes, southern states decreed that Negroes, while no longer property, were not citizens of the states. Like children or the insane, they were considered without ordinary legal capacities such as the ability to own real property, enter into binding contracts, sue in courts of law, and make legal wills disposing of their property. The national Congress responded to the Black Codes with a statute of its own—the Civil Rights Act of 1866. This provided that states could not deny to persons on grounds of race the ordinary legal capacities the Black Code had sought to deny the freedmen. But did Congress have the power to enact such legislation?

The Thirteenth Amendment, ratified in 1865, had provided a retrospective constitutional foundation for Lincoln's Emancipation Proclamation of 1862, but did it empower Congress to intervene in the internal legal affairs of states to the extent that it had done in the Civil Rights Act? Whatever doubt there may have been was settled by the ratification in 1868 of the Fourteenth Amendment.

This made a number of things clear. Citizenship was unambiguously defined: All persons born or naturalized in the United States were citizens of the state in which they resided. And states were forbidden, among other things, to deny persons within their borders the equal protection of their laws. Congress was empowered to enforce the Fourteenth Amendment by appropriate legislation, and this was quite adequate retrospective authority for the Civil Rights Act of 1866.

But what else did the Fourteenth Amendment do? It provided that no state might deprive a person of life, liberty, or property without due process of law. This phrase was taken from the Fifth Amendment. In Part III, we explored its procedural significances. As to the provision concerning equal protection of the laws, how broadly was it to be construed? It is clear that the immediate intention of the framers of the equal protection language was to protect newly freed blacks in the south; more particularly, to legitimize the federal requirements imposed on state governments by the 1866 Act. But the framers had spoken in general terms. Equal protection was provided not just for blacks but for persons who might be unequal before the law in other ways.

On the other hand, it is also clear that the framers of the Fourteenth Amendment did not mean to forbid the states to make any discriminations between persons in the application of their laws. Ordinary state laws, in both the north and the south, set up classifications based on age, sex, mental competence, felony convictions, and a variety of other criteria. That all legal rights and capacities were not safeguarded by the equal protection language is made clear by the fact that the Congress felt it necessary to follow the Fourteenth Amendment with the Fifteenth, specifically forbidding discrimination in voting on grounds of race. Thus it remained to ask: What kinds of classifications or discriminations in the application of its laws were forbidden to the states by the equal protection command beyond those of race? The answers would be slow in coming but of great consequence for the structure of our public law today. It is not too much to say that the Fourteenth Amendment came to constitute a second Bill of Rights.

In interpreting the equal protection clause the contemporary Supreme Court employs a two-track approach. The justices will subject governmental initiative to especially searching scrutiny and demand extraordinary justification by the authorities when the measure (1) involves the use of some "suspect classification" for discriminating among people or (2) where the measure places a burden on the exercise of some "fundamental right." This two-track approach has only emerged within the last twenty-five years, and its evolving contours are far from clearly visible. Race is the paradigmatic suspect classification, and voting is the paradigmatic fundamental right. In Chapter 19 we shall examine the Supreme Court's treatment of race. In Chapter 20 we shall note congressional action both in the area of race relations and voting rights. In Chapter 21 we shall trace the Court's efforts to explain the implications of the equal protection clause for laws that distinguish between female and male persons. And in Chapter 22 we shall consider further the matter of the two-track equal protection.*

SELECTED READINGS

Abernathy, Charles F. *Civil Rights: Cases and Materials.* (St. Paul, Minn.: West, 1980). A law school case book, but a very good one indeed—especially strong on statutory civil rights.

Bardolph, Richard. *The Civil Rights Record: Black Americans and the Law, 1849–1970.* (New York: Crowell, 1970). While not as richly textured as Higginbotham's history, this is a useful companion volume.

Berger, Raoul. *Government by Judiciary: The Transformation of the Fourteenth Amendment.* (Cambridge: Harvard University Press, 1977). Argues that the Supreme Court has departed radically and in an essentially illegitimate fashion from the intentions of the framers of the Fourteenth Amendment.

Glazer, Nathan. *Affirmative Discrimination: Ethnic Inequality and Public Policy.* (New York: Basic Books, 1978). A searching criticism of the theory and practice of affirmative action.

Graglia, Lino A. *Disaster by Decree: The Supreme Court and Decisions on Race and the Schools.* (Ithaca: Cornell University Press, 1976). An attack on judicial activism in the school desegregation cases.

Higginbotham, A. Leon, Jr. *In the Matter of Color: Race and the American Legal Process.* (New York: Oxford University Press, 1978). This volume covers the colonial period.

Kluger, Richard. *Simple Justice: The History of* Brown v. Board of Education *and Black America's Struggle for Equality.* (N.Y.: Knopf, 1976). A highly readable account.

Livingston, John C. *Fair Game: Inequality and Affirmative Action.* (San Francisco: W. H. Freeman, 1979). A defense of affirmative action as a legitimate tool of governmentally managed social change.

Sindler, Allan P. *Bakke, DeFunis and Minority Admissions: The Quest for Equal Opportunity.* (New York: Longman, 1978). Analysis of these issues in "reverse discrimination" by a political scientist.

Wilkinson, J. Harvie, III. *From* Brown *to* Bakke: *The Supreme Court and School Integration, 1954–1978.* (New York: Oxford University Press, 1979). A very useful short history.

---

* The equal protection clause of the Fourteenth Amendment is directed, as we have seen, to the states. The Fifth Amendment provides that the national government may not deprive persons of life, liberty, or property without due process of law (in this respect it was the prototype for the Fourteenth); but it contains no equal protection language. As a body of new constitutional restrictions was created by the Court on the basis of the equal protection clause of the Fourteenth Amendment, the justices avoided the embarrassment of not having these strictures apply to the national government by an act of "reverse incorporation." The due process clause of the Fifth Amendment was held to have an "equal protection component" identical in every way to the actual equal protection clause of the Fourteenth. See *Bolling* v. *Sharpe,* 347 U.S. 497 (1954).

CHAPTER · 19

RACE AND THE LAW

WE know that whatever else its framers intended it to mean, the Fourteenth Amendment, and especially the equal protection clause, was directed to the plight of the newly freed black persons in the South. As we have seen, the Black Codes set up a system of virtual apartheid in which blacks were not citizens and did not enjoy ordinary legal capacities such as owning property, making wills, or entering into contracts. Congress initially responded to these Black Codes with the Civil Rights Act of 1866. This addressed the question of unequal legal status, and the equal protection clause was certainly intended to constitutionally legitimize this statute and to settle, once and for all, the question of citizenship. All those born or naturalized in the United States were citizens of the United States *and* of the state in which they resided.

But what more was guaranteed by the language of equal protection? Were the states simply prohibited from depriving persons of ordinary legal capacities because of their race, or were the states precluded from making *any* legal distinctions between their citizens based on race? And did equal protection forbid states from classifying persons based on factors other than race. Was the equal protection clause a broad, general restriction on state governments, going well beyond matters of racial discrimination?

As we have seen, the framers could not have thought that their handiwork prohibited all legal distinctions based on race, or it would have been unnecessary for many of them to initiate the process that added the Fifteenth Amendment in 1869. It hardly would have been necessary to go through the cumbersome process of amending to insure that no one was discriminated against in voting because of race if, in fact, the equal protection clause already forbade such discrimination. Thus, on the one hand, the equal protection clause clearly required the states to refrain from discriminating among persons on grounds of race in conferring ordinary legal status, but, on the other hand, did not of its own force preclude all such discriminations. This moves us forward a little way, but not very far.

In the latter half of the nineteenth century the Supreme Court's approach to these matters was conservative. That is, the Court tended to read the equal protection clause as "constitutionalizing" the provisions of the Civil Rights Act of 1866, insuring that blacks would have legal equality but not banning all state classifications of persons on grounds of color. The decision in *Plessy v. Ferguson,* 163 U.S. 537 (1896), epitomizes this approach. *Plessy* involved a Louisiana law passed in 1890, which required "equal but separate accommodations" for white and black railroad passengers. Speaking for the Court, Justice Henry B. Brown, who had been a young assistant U.S. attorney in Michigan at the time of the ratification of the Fourteenth Amendment, wrote that "the object of the [Fourteenth] Amendment was undoubtedly to enforce the absolute equality of the two races before the law, but in the nature of things it could not have been intended to abolish all distinctions based on color, or to enforce social, as distinguished from political equality, or a commingling of the two races upon terms satisfactory to either. Laws permitting, and even requiring, their separation in places where they are liable to be brought into contact do not necessarily imply inferiority of either race to the other, and have been generally, if not universally, recognized as within the competency of the state legislatures in the exercise of their police power."

While Justice Brown was probably right in thinking the framers of the equal protection clause did not mean it to outlaw all state-imposed distinctions based on race, the framers hardly would have been comfortable with the elaborate edifice of state laws requiring racial separation that grew under the protection of the theory of the equal protection clause that Brown articulated. Historian C. Vann Woodward has traced the development of this network of segregative requirements in a little book titled, *The Strange Career of Jim Crow.* The first phase of the modern civil rights movement in the middle decade of the twentieth century had to do precisely with overcoming this nineteenth century interpretation of the equal protection clause, developing in its place the doctrine that race is a suspect criterion of classification when used by government (at least when it is used invidiously), and can only be justified by the most compelling and overriding state interests.

The cases examined in this chapter trace the development of the idea of race as a suspect classification. They illustrate the delicacy of determining those situations in which race may properly be used by government as a criterion of classification.

Korematsu v. *United States*
323 U.S. 214, 65 S.Ct. 193, 89 L.Ed. 194 (1944)

The *Korematsu* case marks a very unhappy chapter in American history. The exclusion of ethnic Japanese from certain areas on the west coast, and their subsequent detention in "relocation camps," has been examined recently by a national commission and found (albeit with the benefit of hindsight) to have been an unjustified overreaction. The Supreme Court, however, faced the question of excluding the ethnic Japanese in the war time context of 1944 without the benefit of that hindsight. Justice Black's opinion for the Court evinces the deepest distaste for the use of racial classifications, and Black is clear that invidious governmental classifications based on race are, as a matter of Fourteenth Amendment equal protection and Fifth Amendment due process, very difficult to justify. Thus *Korematsu* stands for the proposition that only the most compelling sort of state interest can justify racial discriminations. With the Second World War still raging, and looking back on the period immediately after Pearl Harbor in which America's basic conceptions about its security had been shaken to their foundations, the majority found itself unable to say that a compelling state interest did not exist.

Mr. Justice Black delivered the opinion of the Court.

The petitioner, an American citizen of Japanese descent, was convicted in a federal district court for remaining in San Leandro, California, a "Military Area," contrary to Civilian Exclusion Order No. 34 of the Commanding General of the Western Command, U.S. Army, which directed that after May 9, 1942, all persons of Japanese ancestry should be excluded from that area. No question was raised as to petitioner's loyalty to the United States. The Circuit Court of Appeals affirmed, and the importance of the constitutional question involved caused us to grant certiorari.

It should be noted, to begin with, that all legal restrictions which curtail the civil rights of a single racial group are immediately suspect. That is not to say that all such restrictions are unconstitutional. It is to say that courts must subject them to the most rigid scrutiny. Pressing public necessity may sometimes justify the existence of such restrictions; racial antagonism never can. . . .

Exclusion Order No. 34, which the petitioner knowingly and admittedly violated, was one of a number of military orders and proclamations, all of which were substantially based upon Executive Order No. 9066, 7 Fed. Reg. 1407. That order, issued after we were at war with Japan, declared that "the successful prosecution of the war requires every possible protection against espionage and against sabotage to national-defense material, national-defense premises, and national-defense utilities. . . ."

We uphold the exclusion order as of the time it was made and when the petitioner violated it. In doing so, we are not unmindful of the hardships imposed by it upon a large group of American citizens. . . . But hardships are part of war, and war is an aggregation of hardships. All citizens alike, both in and out of uniform, feel the impact of war in greater or lesser measure. Citizenship has its responsibilities as well as its privileges, and in time of war the burden is always heavier. Compulsory exclusion of large groups of citizens from their homes, except under circumstances of direst emergency and peril, is inconsistent with our basic governmental institutions. But when under conditions of modern warfare our shores are threatened by hostile forces, the power to protect must be commensurate with the threatened danger.

It is said that we are dealing here with the case of imprisonment of a citizen in a concentration camp solely because of his ancestry, without evidence or inquiry concerning his loyalty and good disposition towards the United States. Our task would be simple, our duty clear, were this a case involving the imprisonment of a loyal citizen in a concentration camp because of racial prejudice. Regardless of the true nature of the assembly and relocation centers—and we deem it unjustifiable to call them concentration camps with all the ugly connotations that term implies—we are dealing specifically with nothing but an exclusion order. To cast this case into outlines of racial prejudice, without reference to the real military dangers which were presented, merely confuses the issue. Korematsu was not excluded from the Military Area because of hostility to him or his race. He *was* excluded because we are at war with the Japanese Empire, because the properly constituted military authorities feared an invasion of our West Coast and felt constrained to take proper security measures, because they decided that the military urgency of the situation demanded that all citizens of Japanese ancestry be segregated from the West Coast temporarily, and finally, because Congress, reposing its confidence in this time of war in our military leaders—as inevitably it must—determined that they should have the power to do just this. There was evidence of disloyalty on the part of some, the military authorities considered that the need for action was great, and time was short. We cannot—by availing ourselves of the calm perspective of hindsight—now say that at that time these actions were unjustified.

Affirmed.

Justices Frankfurter and Roberts wrote concurring opinions. Justices Murphy and Jackson wrote dissenting opinions.

Brown v. *Board of Education*
347 U.S. 483, 74 S.Ct. 686, 98 L.Ed. 873 (1954)

Brown v. *Board of Education* is the most famous Supreme Court decision of modern times. Yet today it is infrequently read. Most people think they know what it says, but do they? Chief Justice Warren, writing for a unanimous Court, did not hold that the Constitution was color blind or that racial classifications could never be used by government. What he did hold was that the doctrine of "separate but equal" deriving from *Plessy* v. *Ferguson* "has no place" in education. On its face, the *Brown* opinion applied only to schools and contained no broader theory of equal protection. But as *Brown* was later applied, it came to stand for the principle that racial classifications may not be used by government, except when they pass the strictest judicial scrutiny and are justified by a compelling state interest. Such a compelling interest, it has developed, might be the tailoring of a judicial or legislative remedy for some past invidious racial discrimination. Absent this, the contemporary doctrine is that race may not be used by government as a criterion for classification. The reference for this doctrine is always to *Brown* v. *Board of Education.* Yet in *Brown* we have a classic example of a decision enunciated in very limited terms coming to stand for a much broader constitutional rule. It also is interesting to note that *Brown* itself contained no direction to the lower courts or to the states as to implementation or remedial orders. That came a year later in *Brown* II, 349 U.S. 294 (1955). Here the Court, after hearing arguments from the original participants in *Brown* as to the proper posture for it to take with respect to implementation of that decision, decreed that desegregation should proceed "with all deliberate speed." Both *Brown* itself and the arguments with respect to implementation were the handiwork of the NAACP, and the leading advocate was Thurgood Marshall, later to become an Associate Justice.

Mr. Chief Justice Warren delivered the opinion of the Court.

These cases come to us from the States of Kansas, South Carolina, Virginia, and Delaware. They are premised on different facts and different local conditions, but a common legal question justifies their consideration together in this consolidated opinion.

In each of the cases, minors of the Negro race, through their legal representatives, seek the aid of the courts in obtaining admission to the public schools of their community on a nonsegregated basis. In each instance, they had been denied admission to schools attended by white children under laws requiring or permitting segregation according to race. This segregation was alleged to deprive the plaintiffs of the equal protection of the laws under the Fourteenth Amendment. In each of the cases other than the Delaware case, a three-judge federal district court denied relief to the plaintiffs on the so-called "separate but equal" doctrine announced by this Court in *Plessy* v. *Ferguson,* 163 U.S. 537. Under that doctrine, equality of treatment is accorded when the races are provided substantially equal facilities, even though these facilities be separate. In the Delaware case, the Supreme Court of Delaware adhered to that doctrine, but ordered that the plaintiffs be admitted to the white schools because of their superiority to the Negro schools.

The plaintiffs contend that segregated public schools are not "equal" and cannot be made "equal," and that hence they are deprived of the equal protection of the laws. . . .

In approaching this problem, we cannot turn the clock back to 1868 when the Amendment was adopted, or even to 1896 when *Plessy* v. *Ferguson* was written. We must consider public education in the light of its full development and its present place in American life throughout the Nation. Only in this way can it be determined if segregation in public schools deprives these plaintiffs of the equal protection of the laws.

Today, education is perhaps the most important function of state and local governments. Compulsory school attendance laws and the great expenditures for education both demonstrate our recognition of the importance of education to our democratic society. It is required in the performance of our most basic public responsibilities, even service in the armed forces. It is the very foundation of good citizenship. Today it is a principal instrument in awakening the child to cultural values, in preparing him for later professional training, and in helping him to adjust normally to his environment. In these days, it is doubtful that any child may reasonably be expected to succeed in life if he is denied the opportunity of an education. Such an opportunity, where the state has undertaken to provide it, is a right which must be made available to all on equal terms.

We come then to the question presented: Does segregation of children in public schools solely on the basis of race, even though the physical facilities and other "tangible" factors may be equal, deprive the children of the minority group of equal educational opportunities? We believe that it does. ...

... To separate them from others of similar age and qualifications solely because of their race generates a feeling of inferiority as to their status in the community that may affect their hearts and minds in a way unlikely ever to be undone. ... Whatever may have been the extent of psychological knowledge at the time of *Plessy* v. *Ferguson,* this finding is amply supported by modern authority. Any language in *Plessy* v. *Ferguson* contrary to this finding is rejected.

We conclude that in the field of public education the doctrine of "separate but equal" has no place. Separate educational facilities are inherently unequal. Therefore, we hold that the plaintiffs and others similarly situated for whom the actions have been brought are, by reason of the segregation complained of, deprived of the equal protection of the laws guaranteed by the Fourteenth Amendment.

Because these are class actions, because of the wide applicability of this decision, and because of the great variety of local conditions, the formulation of decrees in these cases presents problems of considerable complexity. On reargument, the consideration of appropriate relief was necessarily subordinated to the primary question—the constitutionality of segregation in public education. We have now announced that such segregation is a denial of the equal protection of the laws. In order that we may have the full assistance of the parties in formulating decrees, the cases will be restored to the docket, and the parties are requested to present further argument on Questions 4 and 5 previously propounded by the Court for the reargument this Term. The Attorney General of the United States is again invited to participate. The Attorneys General of the states requiring or permitting segregation in public education will also be permitted to appear as *amici curiae* upon request to do so by September 15, 1954, and submission of briefs by October 1, 1954.

It is so ordered.

Swann v. Charlotte-Mecklenburg
402 U.S. 1, 91 S.Ct. 1267, 28 L.Ed.2d 554 (1971)

What had the Supreme Court meant by desegregation in *Brown II?* At the time, most commentators assumed the Court intended a cessation of the state enforced racial separation that seventeen states had maintained before the *Brown* decision. But *Brown II* was followed by a period of "massive resistance" in which a number of southern states tried to avoid doing anything to alter their dual school systems. Federal district courts throughout the South became the front line on which desegregation battles were fought school system by school system. The district court judges had to come up with remedial orders. As they did so, and as they attempted to move recalcitrant local authorities to alter "traditional" practices, desegregation began to take on a new meaning. In *Swann,* the Supreme Court held that it was not enough for states to stop segregating. If they had segregated in the past, they now labored under an affirmative obligation to create unitary school districts, which implied a certain degree of racial balance in the schools. Districts with a history of a dual school system must become "unitary," and if this requires the transportation of children from their own neighborhoods to other neighborhoods in order to achieve acceptable levels of racial balance (busing), then, said the majority, so be it.

Mr. Chief Justice Burger delivered the opinion of the Court.

We granted certiorari in this case to review important issues as to the duties of school authorities and the scope of powers of federal courts under this Court's mandates to eliminate racially separate public schools established and maintained by state action. *Brown* v. *Board of Education,* 347 U.S. 483 (1954).

This case and those argued with it arose in states having a long history of maintaining two sets of schools in a single school system deliberately operated to carry out a governmental policy to separate pupils in schools solely on the basis of race. That was what Brown v. Board of Education was all about. These cases present us with the problem of defining in more precise terms than heretofore the scope of the duty of school authorities and district courts in implementing *Brown I* and the mandate to eliminate dual systems and establish unitary systems at once. Meanwhile district courts and courts of appeals have struggled in hundreds of cases with a multitude and variety of problems under this Court's general directive. Understandably, in an area of evolving remedies, those courts had to improvise and experiment without detailed or specific guidelines. . . .

By the time the Court considered *Green* v. *County School Board,* 391 U.S. 430, very little progress had been made in many areas where dual school systems had historically been maintained by operation of state laws. In *Green,* the Court was confronted with a record of a freedom-of-choice program that the District Court had found to operate in fact to preserve a dual system more than a decade after *Brown II.* While acknowledging that a freedom-of-choice concept could be a valid remedial measure in some circumstances, its failure to be effective in *Green* required that

"The burden on a school board today is to come forward with a plan that promises realistically to work *now* . . . until it is clear that state-imposed segregation has been completely removed." *Green,* at 439. . . .

The objective today remains to eliminate from the public schools all vestiges of state-imposed segregation. Segregation was the evil struck down by *Brown I* as contrary to the equal protection guarantees of the Constitution. That was the violation sought to be corrected by the remedial measures of *Brown II.* That was the basis for the holding in *Green* that school authorities are "clearly charged with the affirmative duty to take whatever steps might be necessary to convert to a unitary system in which racial discrimination would be eliminated root and branch." 391 U.S., at 437–438.

If school authorities fail in their affirmative obligations under these holdings, judicial authority may be invoked. Once a right and a violation have been shown, the scope of a district court's equitable powers to remedy past wrongs is broad, for breadth and flexibility are inherent in equitable remedies. . . .

In seeking to define even in broad and general terms how far this remedial power extends it is important to remember that judicial powers may be exercised only on the basis of a constitutional violation. Remedial judicial authority does not put judges automatically in the shoes of school authorities whose powers are plenary. Judicial authority enters only when local authority defaults. . . .

The school authorities argue that the equity powers of federal district courts have been limited by Title IV of the Civil Rights Act of 1964. . . . The language and the history of Title IV shows that it was not enacted to limit but to define the role of the Federal Government in the implementation of the *Brown I* decision. It authorizes the Commissioner of Education to provide technical assistance to local boards in the preparation of desegregation plans, to arrange "training institutes" for school personnel involved in desegregation efforts, and to make grants directly to schools to ease the transition to unitary systems. It also authorizes the Attorney General, in specified circumstances, to initiate federal desegregation suits. Section 2000c(b) defines "desegregation" as it is used in Title IV:

" 'Desegregation' means the assignment of students to public schools and within such schools without regard to their race, color, religion, or national origin, but 'desegregation' shall not mean the assignment of students to public schools in order to overcome racial imbalance."

Section 2000c−6, authorizing the Attorney General to institute federal suits, contains the following proviso:

"nothing herein shall empower any official or court of the United States to issue any order seeking to achieve a racial balance in any school by requiring the transportation of pupils or students from one school to another or one school district to another in order to achieve such racial balance, or otherwise enlarge the existing power of the court to insure compliance with constitutional standards."

On their face, the sections quoted support only to insure that the provisions of Title IV of the Civil Rights Act of 1964 will not be read as granting new powers. The proviso . . . [is] designed to foreclose any interpretation of the Act as expanding the *existing* powers of federal courts to enforce the Equal Protection Clause. There is no suggestion of an intention to restrict those powers or withdraw from courts their historic equitable remedial powers. The legislative history of Title IV indicates that Congress was concerned that the Act might be read as creating a right of action under the Fourteenth Amendment in the situation of so-called "de facto segregation," where racial imbalance exists in the schools but with no showing that this was brought about by discriminatory action of state authorities. In short, there is nothing in the Act which provides us material assistance in answering the question of remedy for state-imposed segregation in violation of *Brown I*. The basis of our decision must be the prohibition of the Fourteenth Amendment that no State shall "deny to any person within its jurisdiction the equal protection of the laws."

The scope of permissible transportation of students as an implement of a remedial decree has never been defined by this Court and by the very nature of the problem it cannot be defined with precision. No rigid guidelines as to student transportation can be given for application to the infinite variety of problems presented in thousands of situations. Bus transportation has been an integral part of the public education system for years, and was perhaps the single most important factor in the transition from the one-room schoolhouse to the consolidated school. Eighteen million of the nation's public school children, approximately 39% were transported to their schools by bus in 1969–1970 in all parts of the country.

The importance of bus transportation as a normal and accepted tool of educational policy is readily discernible in this and the companion case. The Charlotte school authorities did not purport to assign students on the basis of geographically drawn zones until 1965 and then they allowed almost unlimited transfer privileges. The District Court's conclusion that assignment of children to the school nearest their home serving their grade would not produce an effective dismantling of the dual system is supported by the record.

Thus the remedial techniques used in the District Court's order were within the court's power to provide equitable relief; implementation of the decree is well within the capacity of the school authority.

At some point, these school authorities and others like them should have achieved full compliance with this Court's decision in *Brown I*. The systems will then be "unitary" in the sense required by our decisions in *Green*. . . .

For the reasons herein set forth, the judgment of the Court of Appeals is affirmed as to those parts in which it affirmed the judgment of the District Court. The order of the District Court dated August 7, 1970, is also affirmed. It is so ordered.

Milliken v. *Bradley*
418 U.S. 717, 94 S.Ct. 3112, 41 L.Ed.2d 1069 (1974)

Where were the outer limits on the kinds of remedies the Supreme Court would authorize lower courts to impose on school districts in the pursuit of racial balance? In early 1974, attention focused on the case of *Milliken* v. *Bradley*, which involved the school system of Detroit, Michigan. The record in the case amply indicated purposeful segregative behavior on the part of the Detroit school authorities. The hard reality, however, was that there were not many white children within the city of Detroit who could be bused. Thus following the logic of *Swann* v. *Charlotte-Mecklenburg*, an impossible situation was created. There had been de jure segregation in the past, so the district must become "unitary," and this necessitated some degree of racial balance. But the ethnic resources did not exist within the district to obtain any sort of racial balance that might satisfy the requirement. In the briefs, civil rights organizations such as the "INK Fund," represented by Jack Greenberg, the Mexican-American Legal Defense and Educational Fund, the National Education Association, and the Jewish Rights Council, argued that the only recourse in such circumstances was to allow the district court judge to craft a remedial order that reached beyond the limits of the school district in question and sequestered students of the requisite ethnic background from the surrounding districts—whether or not these districts were tainted by a history of de jure segregation. For the first time the United States, represented by Solicitor General Robert Bork, entered a case as *amicus curiae* opposing a school desegregation remedy. The majority of a deeply divided Court agreed with Bork and thus established outer limits on remedial action in pursuit of racial balance. Unless outlying school districts can be implicated in the segregative behavior of an inner-city district, they may not be drawn in for remedial purposes.

Mr. Chief Justice Burger delivered the opinion of the Court.

We granted certiorari ... to determine whether a federal court may impose a multi-district, areawide remedy to a single-district *de jure* segregation problem absent any finding that the other included school districts have failed to operate unitary school systems within their districts, absent any claim or finding that the boundary lines of any affected school district were established with the purpose of fostering racial segregation in public schools, absent any finding that the included districts committed acts which effected segregation within the other districts, and absent a meaningful opportunity for the included neighboring school districts to present evidence or be heard on the propriety of a multidistrict remedy or on the question of constitutional violations by those neighboring districts. ...

The record before us, voluminous as it is, contains evidence of *de jure* segregated conditions only in the Detroit schools; indeed, that was the theory on which the litigation was initially based and on which the District Court took evidence. ... With no showing of significant violation by the 53 outlying school districts and no evidence of any interdistrict violation or effect, the court went beyond the original theory of the case as framed by the pleadings and mandated a metropolitan area remedy. To approve the remedy ordered by the court would impose on the outlying districts, not shown to have committed any constitutional violation, a wholly impermissible remedy based on a standard not hinted at in *Brown I* and *II* or any holding of this Court. ...

We conclude that the relief ordered by the District Court and affirmed by the Court of Appeals was based upon an erroneous standard and was unsupported by record evidence that acts of the outlying districts effected the discrimination found to exist in the schools of Detroit. Accordingly, the judgment of the Court of Appeals is reversed and the case is remanded for further proceedings consistent with this opinion leading to prompt formulation of a decree directed to eliminating the segregation found to exist in Detroit city schools, a remedy which has been delayed since 1970.

Reversed and remanded.

Mr. Justice White, with whom Mr. Justice Douglas, Mr. Justice Brennan, and Mr. Justice Marshall join, dissenting. ...

. . . .

Regretfully, and for several reasons, I can join neither the Court's judgment nor its opinion. The core of my disagreement is that deliberate acts of segregation and their consequences will go unremedied, not because a remedy would be infeasible or unreasonable in terms of the unusual criteria governing school desegregation cases, but because an effective remedy would cause what the Court considers to be undue administrative inconvenience to the State. The result is that the State of Michigan, the entity at which the Fourteenth Amendment is directed, has successfully insulated itself from its duty to provide effective de-segregation remedies by vesting sufficient power over its public schools in its local school districts. If this is the case in Michigan, it will be the case in most States. . . .

Mr. Justice Marshall, with whom Mr. Justice Douglas, Mr. Justice Brennan, and Mr. Justice White join, dissenting.

In *Brown* v. *Board of Education* . . . this Court held that segregation of children in public schools on the basis of race deprives minority group children of equal educational opportunities and therefore denies them the equal protection of the laws under the Fourteeenth Amendment. This Court recognized then that remedying decades of segregation in public education would not be an easy task. Subsequent events, unfortunately, have seen that prediction bear bitter fruit. But however imbedded old ways, however ingrained old prejudices, this Court has not been diverted from its appointed task of making "a living truth" of our constitutional ideal of equal justice under law. . . .

After 20 years of small, often difficult steps toward that great end, the Court today takes a giant step backwards. Notwithstanding a record showing widespread and pervasive racial segregation in the educational system provided by the State of Michigan for children in Detroit, this Court holds that the District Court was powerless to require the State to remedy its constitutional violation in any meaningful fashion. Ironically purporting to base its result on the principle that the scope of the remedy in a desegregation case should be determined by the nature and the extent of the constitutional violation, the Court's answer is to provide no remedy at all for the violation proved in this case, thereby guaranteeing that Negro children in Detroit will receive the same separate and inherently unequal education in the future as they have been unconstitutionally afforded in the past.

I cannot subscribe to this emasculation of our constitutional guarantee of equal protection of the laws and must respectfully dissent. . . .

To begin with, the record amply supports the District Court's findings that the State of Michigan, through state officers and state agencies, had engaged in purposeful acts which created or aggravated segregation in the Detroit schools. . . .

Aside from the acts of purposeful segregation committed by the State Legislature and the State Board of Education, the District Court also concluded that the State was responsible for the many intentional acts of segregation committed by the Detroit Board of Education, an agency of the State. . . .

. . . .

Most significantly for present purposes, the State has wide-ranging powers to consolidate and merge school districts, even without the consent of the districts themselves or of the local citizenry. . . .

Desegregation is not and was never expected to be an easy task. Racial attitudes ingrained in our Nation's childhood and adolescence are not quickly thrown aside in its middle years. But just as the inconvenience of some cannot be allowed to stand in the way of the rights of others, so public opposition, no matter how strident, cannot be permitted to divert this Court from the enforcement of the constitutional principles at issue in this case. Today's holding, I fear, is more a reflection of a perceived public mood that we have gone far enough in enforcing the Constitution's guarantee of equal justice than it is the product of neutral principles of law. In the short run, it may seem to be the easier course to allow our great metropolitan areas to be divided up each into two cities— one white, the other black—but it is a course, I predict, our people will ultimately regret. I dissent.

Justice Stewart wrote a concurring opinion and Justice Douglas wrote a dissenting opinion.

CASE STUDY: BUSING TO ACHIEVE RACIAL BALANCE

We have seen that in the period between *Brown* II (1955) and *Swann* (1971) the prevailing conception of "desegregation" on the Supreme Court evolved from one stressing the cessation of state-mandated segregation in schools to one requiring some degree of racial balance—even if this meant the assignment of pupils to particular schools on the basis of race and transportation beyond neighborhood schools (busing). Professional civil rights advocates continued to be virtually united in support of busing as a remedy for past state-imposed segregation, but popular opposition continues to run broadly and deeply within American society.

In the wake of the decision in *Swann,* a number of proposals were introduced in Congress to limit court-ordered busing to achieve racial balance or to stop it altogether. As with the issues of school prayer and abortion (see Chapter 23), such efforts involved the legislative branch responding to initiatives taken by courts. Therefore, the question of legislative interference with the judicial branch cut across and complicated the policy debate. In 1972, Senator Robert P. Griffin, of Michigan, proposed an amendment to the Higher Education Act of 1965, which would have provided that "no court of the United States shall have jurisdiction to make any decision, enter any judgment or issue any order the effect of which would be to require pupils be transported to or from school on the basis of their race, color, religion, or national origin." This involved a clear limitation of the power of the judiciary and failed in the Senate by a vote of 50 to 47. But Congress did adopt a milder amendment to the Higher Education Act in June of 1972. This included a "moratorium" on court orders having "the purpose of achieving racial balance among students with respect to race, sex, religion, or socio-economic status."
economic status."

The response of the judiciary to this, interestingly, was to ignore it. In *Drummond* v. *Acree,* 409 U.S. 1228 (1972), Justice Powell, then writing as a circuit judge, took the position that the statutory provision was aimed at "desegregation plans that seeked to achieve racial balance." Since court-ordered busing plans sought to enforce the mandate of *Swann* v. *Charlotte-*

Mecklenburg for "unitary school districts," the congressional action did not apply to these. That the requirement of "unitariness" in *Swann* was itself defined in terms of some degree of racial balance did not alter the matter for Powell. If Congress had really been seeking to stop all busing orders, he argued, "it could have used clear and explicit language appropriate to that result."

In the 1974 amendments to the Education Act, Congress returned to the matter of busing. "Excessive transportation of students" to achieve "the elimination of the vestiges of a dual school system" was condemned. This was followed by a declaration of policy to the affect that "the neighborhood is the appropriate basis for determining public school assignments." And that the "failure of an educational agency to attain a balance, on the basis of race, color, sex, or national origin, of students among its schools shall not constitute a denial of equal opportunity or equal protection of the laws." Finally, the Amendment explicitly stated that no federal court or agency was to "order the implementation of a plan which would require the transportation of any student to a school other than the school closest or next to his place of residence." This seemed to constitute an explicit congressional prohibition of busing, but the courts have interpreted it in the light of an introductory statement urged by critics of the provision as necessary to insure its constitutionality. This provided that the anti-busing provisions were not "intended to modify or diminish the authority of the courts of the United States to fully enforce the Fifth and Fourteenth Amendments." Thus the 1974 congressional action had no more impact on judicial behavior than the 1972 action.

Each Congress since 1974 has seen further efforts to limit the kinds of "desegregation" remedies that courts could order. In 1976, for instance, a series of riders to appropriation bills sought to bar the use of federal funds "to require . . . transportation of any student to a school other than the school which is nearest the student's home. . . ." Unsuccessful efforts have been made to legislate cut-offs of federal funds from districts which engage in large scale busing, but these have been defeated on the argument that to make the school district the object of a sanction actually aimed at the federal courts is unfair. In July of 1979, the first of several proposed constitutional amendments which would have barred busing reached the floor of the House. Such amendments, however, would involve the sorts of explicit prohibitions on courts issuing certain kinds of orders that had been turned back repeatedly in the years since. Anti-busing amendments have thus far fallen far short of achieving the necessary two-thirds majorities.

As with school prayer and several other of the more hotly contested contemporary issues in the politics of civil rights and civil liberties, there seems to be a durable congressional majority opposed to busing, but no durable majority, let alone an extraordinary two-thirds majority necessary for constitutional amendment, which would explicitly and unambiguously limit the power of the federal courts to issue busing orders.

CHAPTER · 20

CONGRESSIONAL ENFORCEMENT OF CIVIL RIGHTS

IT was a decade from *Brown* v. *Board of Education* to the entry of Congress into the serious business of expanding legal equality in America. But once involved, Congress and the Court have interacted briskly. After several false starts in the Civil Rights Act of 1957 and 1960 (both largely concerned with making it easier for blacks to seek judicial remedies for violation of the constitutional rights by states), Congress, in 1964, finally enacted a law that created significant new statutory rights. This law forbade racial discrimination in places of public accommodation engaged in interstate commerce (Title II); it banned employment discrimination on race and certain other factors in government and by employers holding federal contracts (Title VI); and it did the same for employers involved in interstate commerce (Title VII). The commerce clause rationale underlying the Act was upheld by the Supreme Court in *Heart of Atlanta Motel* v. *United States,* 379 U.S. 241 (1964).

Beginning with the famous reapportionment decisions of *Baker* v. *Carr,* 369 U.S. 186 (1962), and *Reynolds* v. *Simms,* 377 U.S. 533 (1964), in which majorities held that the equal protection clause of the Fourteenth Amendment prohibited legislative districts that substantially departed from the rule of "one man one vote," both the Supreme Court and the national Congress have been involved in continuing efforts to alter the pattern of American electoral arrangements. What we have witnessed is a process by which the Court and the Congress, interacting in a dialectical fashion and spurred on by interest group advocates, are opening the electoral process further and further to groups at the fringes—the poor, the ethnic minorities, and the young.

In 1965, Congress, with the support of President Johnson, passed the Voting Rights Act. Aimed primarily at the problem of blacks in the southern states (where the use of a variety of restrictive registration devices by racist officials had held down the number of black voters), this statute singled out certain states and counties based on low levels of electoral participation. It banned the use of literacy tests in those jurisdictions, and it provided strict supervision by the Attorney General and the Federal District Court of the District of Columbia of voter registration and the conduct of elections in those areas. The Voting Rights Act was based squarely on the power of Congress to implement the Fifteenth Amendment and was sustained as constitutional by the Supreme Court in *South Carolina* v. *Katzenback,* 383 U.S. 301 (1966). The Act, and its vindication by the Court, involved the abandonment of certain traditional federal understandings about the conduct of elections and establishing the qualifications of electors, but it affectively broke southern resistance to black voter registration.

In 1970, Congress moved again to expand electoral participation and to provide uniform federal rules in the place of varying state regulations without regard to the special problem of racial discrimination in voting. In the cases that follow, we will examine both constitutional questions and questions of statutory interpretation that have arisen with respect to the Civil Rights Act of 1964 (*Griggs* v. *Duke Power Co.*), the 1970 amendments to the Voting Rights Act (*Oregon* v. *Mitchell*), and the Voting Rights Act of 1965 (*Mobile* v. *Bolden*).

Griggs v. *Duke Power Co.*
401 U.S. 424, 91 S.Ct. 849, 28 L.Ed.2d 158 (1971)

In 1964, as we have seen, Congress passed the first meaningful federal civil rights act since the Reconstruction period. Among other things, the Act prohibited racial discrimination in employment by government, by private businesses engaged in interstate commerce, and by private entities (such as colleges and universities) receiving federal funds. But how was the Court to determine whether there *was* discrimination in employment? Need the plaintiffs show actual intentional discriminatory behavior on the part of the employer? Or was it sufficient to show that the employment practices followed by a particular organization had a disproportionate impact on a racial minority, and that such employment practices served no legitimate purpose in terms of determining who could perform what jobs? In *Griggs,* the Court seems to have accepted the proposition that a showing of disproportionate impact is sufficient to establish a violation of Title VII of the Act, which prohibits discrimination by private employers engaged in interstate commerce. It is interesting that the Court has declined to accept disproportionate impact as sufficient indication of a denial of Fourteenth Amendment equal protection by a state agency, and it is unclear whether disproportionate impact is a sufficient indication of a violation by employers covered by Title VI of the Act, which prohibits discrimination by agencies receiving federal funds.

Mr. Chief Justice Burger delivered the opinion of the Court.

We granted the writ in this case to resolve the question whether an employer is prohibited by the Civil Rights Act of 1964, Title VII, from requiring a high school education or passing of a standardized general intelligence test as a condition of employment in or transfer to jobs when (a) neither standard is shown to be significantly related to successful job performance, (b) both requirements operate to disqualify Negroes at a substantially higher rate than white applicants, and (c) the jobs in question formerly had been filled only by white employees as part of a longstanding practice of giving preference to whites.

The objective of Congress in the enactment of Title VII is plain from the language of the statute. It was to achieve equality of employment opportunities and remove barriers that have operated in the past to favor an identifiable group of white employees over other employees. Under the Act, practices, procedures, or tests neutral on their face, and even neutral in terms of intent, cannot be maintained if they operate to "freeze" the status quo of prior discriminatory employment practices.

The Court of Appeals' opinion, and the partial dissent, agreed that, on the record in the present case, "whites register far better on the Company's alternative requirements" than Negroes. . . . This consequence would appear to be directly traceable to race. Basic intelligence must have the means of articulation to manifest itself fairly in a testing process. Because they are Negroes, petitioners have long received inferior education in segregated schools and this Court expressly recognized these differences. . . .

Congress has now provided that tests or criteria for employment or promotion may not provide equality of opportunity merely in the sense of the fabled offer of milk to the stork and the fox. On the contrary, Congress has now required that the posture and condition of the job-seeker be taken into account. It has— to resort again to the fable—provided that the vessel in which the milk is proffered be one all seekers can use. The Act proscribes not only overt discrimination but also practices that are fair in form, but discriminatory in operation. The touchstone is business necessity. If an employment practice which operates to exclude Negroes cannot be shown to be related to job performance, the practice is prohibited.

On the record before us, neither the high school completion requirement nor the general intelligence test is shown to bear a demonstrable relationship to successful performance of the jobs for which it was used. Both were adopted, as the Court of Appeals noted, without meaningful study of their relationship to job-performance ability. Rather, a vice president of the Company testified, the requirements were instituted on the Company's judgment that they generally would improve the overall quality of the work force.

The evidence, however, shows that employees who have not completed high school or taken the tests have continued to perform satisfactorily and make progress in departments for which the high school and test criteria are now used. The promotion record of present employees who would not be able to meet the new criteria thus suggests the possibility that the requirements may not be needed even for the limited purpose of preserving the avowed policy of advancement within the Company. In the context of this case, it is unnecessary to reach the question whether testing requirements that take into account capability for the next succeeding position or related future promotion might be utilized upon a showing that such long-range requirements fulfill a genuine business need. In the present case the Company has made no such showing. . . .

The Court of Appeals held that the Company had adopted the diploma and test requirements without any "intention to discriminate against Negro employees." . . . We do not suggest that either the District Court or the Court of Appeals erred in examining the employer's intent; but good intent or absence of discriminatory intent does not redeem employment procedures or testing mechanisms that operate as "built-in headwinds" for minority groups and are unrelated to measuring job capability.

The Company's lack of discriminatory intent is suggested by special efforts to help the undereducated employees through Company financing of two-thirds the cost of tuition for high school training. But Congress directed the thrust of the Act to the *consequences* of employment practices, not simply the motivation. More than that, Congress has placed on the employer the burden of showing that any given requirement must have a manifest relationship to the employment in question.

The facts of this case demonstrate the inadequacy of broad and general testing devices as well as the infirmity of using diplomas or degrees as fixed measures of capability. History is filled with examples of men and women who rendered highly effective performance without the conventional badges of accomplishment in terms of certificates, diplomas, or degrees. Diplomas and tests are useful servants, but Congress has mandated the commonsense proposition that they are not to become masters of reality.

Nothing in the Act precludes the use of testing or measuring procedures; obviously they are useful. What Congress has forbidden is giving these devices and mechanisms controlling force unless they are demonstrably a reasonable measure of job performance. Congress has not commanded that the less qualified be preferred over the better qualified simply because of minority origins. Far from disparaging job qualifications as such, Congress has made such qualifications the controlling factor, so that race, religion, nationality, and sex become irrelevant. What Congress has commanded is that any tests used must measure the person for the job and not the person in the abstract.

The judgment of the Court of Appeals is, as to that portion of the judgment appealed from, reversed.

Oregon v. Mitchell
400 U.S. 112, 91 S.Ct. 260, 27 L.Ed.2d 272 (1970)

The Voting Rights Act of 1965, which addressed interference with the exercise of the franchise on grounds of race, was based on the power of Congress to implement the Fifteenth Amendment. In the Voting Rights Act Amendment of 1970, Congress moved beyond the task of remedying Fifteenth Amendment violations to the task of relaxing access to the franchise generally. The Act did several things. First, it suspended the use of literacy tests for all elections, state or national, throughout the country for a period of five years. Second, it prohibited the states from enforcing their durational residency requirements for presidential elections (requiring that voters could register any time up to thirty days before a presidential election). Third, and most controversially, Congress sought to provide for the eighteen-year-old vote for both federal and state elections. A deeply divided Supreme Court sustained the ban on literacy tests and the prohibition of residency requirements for presidential elections. By a vote of five to four the Court upheld the eighteen-year-old vote as applied to federal elections, but, again divided five-four, disallowed the congressional mandating of the eighteen-year-old vote for state and local elections.

Mr. Justice Black announcing the judgments of the Court in an opinion expressing his own view of the cases.

I. [T]he responsibility of the States for setting the qualifications of voters in congressional elections was made subject to the power of Congress to make or alter such regulations if it deemed it advisable to do so. This was done in Art. I, § 4. . . .

The breadth of power granted to Congress to make or alter election regulations in national elections, including the qualifications of voters, is demonstrated by the fact that the Framers of the Constitution and the state legislatures which ratified it intended to grant to Congress the power to lay out or alter the boundaries of the congressional districts. . . .

There can be no doubt that the power to alter congressional district lines is vastly more significant in its effect than the power to permit 18-year-old citizens to go to the polls and vote in all federal elections.

In short, the Constitution allotted to the States the power to make laws regarding national elections, but provided that if Congress became dissatisfied with the state laws, Congress could alter them. . . . The Voting Rights Act Amendments of 1970 now before this Court evidence dissatisfaction of Congress with the voting age set by many of the States for national elections. I would hold, as have a long line of decisions in this Court, that Congress has ultimate supervisory power over congressional elections. Similarly, it is the prerogative of Congress to oversee the conduct of presidential and vice-presidential elections and to set the qualifications for voters for electors for those offices. It cannot be seriously contended that Congress has less power over the conduct of presidential elections than it has over congressional elections.

On the other hand, the Constitution was also intended to preserve to the States the power that even the Colonies had to establish and maintain their own separate and independent governments, except insofar as the Constitution itself commands otherwise. . . . No function is more essential to the separate and independent existence of the States and their governments than the power to determine within the limits of the Constitution the qualifications of their own voters for state, county, and municipal offices and the nature of their own machinery for filling local public offices. Moreover, Art. I § 2, is a clear indication that the

Framers intended the States to determine the qualifications of their own voters for state offices. . . .

In enacting the 18-year-old vote provisions of the Act now before the Court, Congress made no legislative findings that the 21-year-old vote requirement was used by the States to disenfranchise voters on account of race. I seriously doubt that such a finding, if made, could be supported by substantial evidence. Since Congress has attempted to invade an area preserved to the States by the Constitution without a foundation for enforcing the Civil War Amendments' ban on racial discrimination, I would hold that Congress has exceeded its powers in attempting to lower the voting age in state and local elections. On the other hand, where Congress legislates in a domain not exclusively reserved by the Constitution to the States, its enforcement power need not be tied so closely to the goal of eliminating discrimination on account of race. . . .

II. . . . In enacting the literacy test ban Congress had before it a long history of the discriminatory use of literacy tests to disfranchise voters on account of their race. [A]s to the Nation as a whole, Congress had before it statistics which demonstrate that voter registration and voter participation are consistently greater in States without literacy tests.

Congress also had before it this country's history of discriminatory educational opportunities in both the North and the South. . . . There is substantial, if not overwhelming, evidence from which Congress could have concluded that it is a denial of equal protection to condition the political participation of children educated in a dual school system upon their educational achievement. . . . Faced with this and other evidence that literacy tests reduce voter participation in a discriminatory manner not only in the South but throughout the Nation, Congress was supported by substantial evidence in concluding that a nationwide ban on literacy tests was appropriate to enforce the Civil War amendments. . . .

III. . . . In enacting [the residency and absentee voting provisions], Congress was attempting to insure a fully effective voice to all citizens in national elections. What I said in Part I of this opinion applies with equal force here. Acting under its broad authority to create and maintain a national government, Congress un-questionably has power under the Constitution to regulate federal elections. . . .

Justice Douglas dissented from the judgment that the congressional attempt to mandate the eighteen-year-old vote in state and local elections was un-constitutional. He thought the implementation clause of the Fourteenth Amendment vested Congress with power to do whatever it thought necessary to advance electoral equality. Justice Brennan also wrote an opinion dissenting on this point, which Justices White and Marshall joined. Brennan suggested that for states not to grant the eighteen-year-old vote actually might be a denial of equal protection. Justice Stewart, with whom Chief Justice Burger and Justice Blackmun joined, dissented from the judgment that Congress could mandate the eighteen-year-old vote for elections for national offices. They argued that Article I left basic voter qualifications to the states and noted that the enfranchisement of blacks and women had both been assumed to require constitutional amendment (the Fifteenth and the Nineteenth). Justice

Harlan would have sustained only the ban on literacy tests, and this on Fifteenth Amendment grounds.

Mobile v. Bolden
446 U.S. 55, 100 S.Ct. 1490, 64 L.Ed.2d (1980)

This case is another excellent illustration of the interplay between Congress and the Court on voting rights. Black residents of Mobile, Alabama, represented by Jack Greenberg and the INK Fund, challenged the form of government and elections in that city. The election of the three commissioners-at-large, it was argued, deprived the black minority of the practical political capacity to elect a black commissioner, which that minority probably would have had under a system in which the commissioners were elected from separate districts within the city. The plaintiffs prevailed in the federal district court and were upheld by the Fifth Circuit Court of Appeals. In the Supreme Court they were supported by the Carter administration in an *amicus ceri* brief from Solicitor General Wade McCree and by an *amicus ceri* brief from the prestigious Lawyers' Committee for Civil Rights under Law. The question before the justices was whether, in order to show a Fifteenth Amendment violation, it was necessary to identify a discriminatory motivation in the questioned electoral arrangement, or whether a disproportionate impact on a racial minority was alone sufficient to establish a claim of unconstitutionality. A deeply divided Court held that a showing of discriminatory motivation was a necessary ingredient of a Fifteenth Amendment violation. An interesting footnote to the case, however, was that when the Voting Rights Act of 1965, scheduled to expire in August of 1982, was up for reenactment, a vigorous debate developed over the standard that should be required to identify a law that denied or abridged the right to vote protected under the Act. Civil rights activists argued for a "result oriented" standard, holding that the discriminatory intent test announced by *Mobile* v. *Bolden* was unduly restrictive. Supporters of the discriminatory intent test responded that a simple "results" test would lead to the establishment of de facto proportional representation. That is, if minorities were not achieving ethnic specific representation, they would be entitled to sue for a change in the electoral arrangements in order to obtain this. A carefully crafted compromise was finally achieved in which "the extent to which members of a protected class (a racial minority) have been elected to office is one circumstance which may be considered" by courts in determining whether there has been a violation of the Act. It was added that "nothing in this [law] establishes a right to have members of a protected class elected in numbers equal to their proportion in the population." President Reagan signed the extension of the Voting Rights Act into law on June 29, 1982. Note that *Mobile* v. *Bolden* held the discriminatory motivation requirement applicable both to the Fifteenth Amendment and to Section II of the Voting Rights Act of 1965.

Mr. Justice Stewart announced the judgment of the Court and delivered an opinion, in which The Chief Justice, Mr. Justice Powell, and Mr. Justice Rehnquist joined.

The city of Mobile, Ala., has since 1911 been governed by a City Commission consisting of three members elected by the voters of the city at large. The question in this case is whether this at-large system of municipal elections violates the rights of Mobile's Negro voters in contravention of federal statutory or constitutional law.

The appellees brought this suit in the Federal District Court for the Southern District of Alabama as a class action on behalf of all Negro citizens of Mobile. Named as defendants were the city and its three incumbent Commissioners, who are the appellants before this Court. The complaint alleged that the practice of electing the City Commissioners at large unfairly diluted the voting strength of Negroes in violation of § 2 of the Voting Rights Act of 1965. . . .

In Alabama, the form of municipal government a city may adopt is governed by state law. Until 1911, cities not covered by specific legislation were limited to governing themselves through a mayor and city council. In that year, the Alabama Legislature authorized every large municipality to adopt a commission form of government. Mobile established its City Commission in the same year, and has maintained that basic system of municipal government ever since.

The three Commissioners jointly exercise all legislative, executive, and administrative power in the municipality. They are required after election to designate one of their number as Mayor, a largely ceremonial office, but no formal provision is made for allocating specific executive or administrative duties among the three. As required by the state law enacted in 1911, each candidate for the Mobile City Commission runs for election in the city at large for a term of four years. . . .

Section 2 of the Voting Rights Act provides:

"No voting qualification or prerequisite to voting, or standard, practice, or procedure shall be imposed or applied by any State or political subdivision to deny or abridge the right of any citizen of the United States to vote on account of race or color." . . .

Assuming, for present purposes, that there exists a private right of action to enforce this statutory provision, it is apparent that the language of § 2 no more than elaborates upon that of the Fifteenth Amendment, and the sparse legislative history of § 2 makes clear that it was intended to have an effect no different from that of the Fifteenth Amendment itself. . . .

The Court's early decisions under the Fifteenth Amendment established that it imposes but one limitation on the powers of the States. It forbids them to discriminate against Negroes in matters having to do with voting. . . .

Our decisions, moreover, have made clear that action by a State that is racially neutral on its face violates the Fifteenth Amendment only if motivated by a discriminatory purpose. . . .

The Court's more recent decisions confirm the principle that racially discriminatory motivation is a necessary ingredient of a Fifteenth Amendment violation. . . .

We turn finally to the arguments advanced in Mr. Justice Marshall's dissenting opinion. The theory of this dissenting opinion . . . appears to be that every "political group," or at least every such group that is in the minority, has a federal constitutional right to elect candidates in proportion to its numbers. Moreover, a political group's "right" to have its candidates elected is said to be a "fundamental interest," the infringement of which may be established without proof that a State has acted with the purpose of impairing anybody's access to the political process. This dissenting opinion finds the "right" infringed in the present case because no Negro has been elected to the Mobile City Commission.

Whatever appeal the dissenting opinion's view may have as a matter of political theory, it is not the law. The Equal Protection Clause of the Fourteenth Amendment does not require proportional representation as an imperative of political organization. The entitlement that the dissenting opinion assumes to exist simply is not to be found in the Constitution of the United States. . . .

Justice Blackmun concurred in the result and Justice Stevens concurred in the judgment. Justice Brennan dissented, arguing that a showing of discriminatory intent should not be required, while Justice White dissented on the argument that there was ample proof of discriminatory intent.

Mr. Justice Marshall, dissenting.

The American ideal of political equality, conceived in the earliest days of our colonial existence and fostered by the egalitarian language of the Declaration of Independence, could not forever tolerate the limitation of the right to vote to white propertied males. Our Constitution has been amended six times in the movement toward a democracy for more than the few, and this Court has interpreted the Fourteenth Amendment to provide that "a citizen has a constitutionally protected right to participate in elections on an equal basis with other citizens in the jurisdiction." . . .

The Court does not dispute the proposition that multimember districting can have the effect of submerging electoral minorities and overrepresenting electoral majorities. It is for this reason that we developed a strong preference for single-member districting in court-ordered reapportionment plans. . . . Furthermore, and more important for present purposes, we decided a series of vote-dilution cases under the Fourteenth Amendment that were designed to protect electoral minorities from precisely the combination of electoral laws and historical and social factors found in the present cases. In my view, the plurality's treatment of these cases is fanciful. Although we have held that multimember districts are not unconstitutional *per se*, there is simply no basis for the plurality's conclusion that under our prior cases proof of discriminatory intent is a necessary condition for the invalidation of multimember districting. . . .

CASE STUDY: AFFIRMATIVE ACTION

"Affirmative action to achieve racial balance." This phrase has become the focus of deep and persistent division within contemporary American society.

Is it morally required or morally repugnant? In approaching this question it is important to distinguish at the outset what one is talking about.

In one sense, affirmative action means that an institutional actor—a government agency, a university, a business, a labor union—has an obligation to do something more than cease discriminating on grounds of race. It has an obligation to actively seek minority persons for its work force at all levels. Since minorities have been discriminated against in the past, it cannot be assumed that minority persons will be found by following "normal" hiring practices. Therefore, the institution must reach out—it must advertise in new places, it must seek to tap new wells of "person power," and it must undertake training programs aimed at bringing minority persons up to the speed at which they can compete for positions. Finally, the institution must examine its hiring standards to see if these include criteria which operate against hiring of minority persons without any relation to job performance.

This conception of affirmative action is sharply distinguished from an alternative conception which focuses on results. By this second approach, affirmative action is only demonstrated in terms of quotas or percentages of new employees, or goals for the total employment force. If racial goals or quotas are going to be set and taken seriously, however, this inescapably involves using race, at least to some extent, as a criterion of selection.

Titles VI and VII of the Civil Rights Act of 1964 apply to government employers, private employers holding government contracts, and private employers engaged in interstate commerce. On their face, the legislation seems to contemplate affirmative action in the first sense of aggressively seeking minority employees. This was also the sense in which the term "affirmative action" was used in the crucial executive orders of the Johnson Administration (notably Executive Order Number 11246), which fixed the bureaucratic responsibility for enforcing the nondiscrimination provisions of the Civil Rights Act among government contractors. This conception of affirmative action, however, was reshaped in successive Labor Department and Department of Health, Education, and Welfare regulations, which emphasize goals, numbers, and minority "set-asides."

But use of racial quotas and goals as public policy raised a constitutional question. There was, lurking in the constitutional background of the late 1970s, the dissenting opinion of the First Justice Harlan in the Civil Rights Cases, which argued that the Constitution should be "color blind." And while the Supreme Court in *Swann* had licensed the use of racial classifications in school assignments as an appropriate device for remedying the evils of past state enforced segregation, it was not altogether clear to what extent other governmental agencies could discriminate on racial lines in an effort to achieve benign ends. Did the Constitution permit "reverse discrimination"? Did it allow for "color conscious" policy outside the area of school integration orders?

The Supreme Court first confronted these questions in the case of *University of California's Regents* v. *Bakke,* 438 U.S. 265 (1978). Here the medical school of the University of California at Davis had set aside sixteen places in an entering class of one hundred for minority students. Minority status was operationally defined in racial terms. In the course of the litigation it was stipulated by the Regents that Bakke, who was white, would have been admitted to the entering class had it not been for the minority "set-aside."

The Court was deeply divided in this case, as it has been in succeeding responses to questions of "reverse discrimination." One group of four justices, including Brennan, Marshall, White, and Blackmun, argued that the Davis affirmative action program violated neither the equal protection clause of the Fourteenth Amendment nor Title VI of the Civil Rights Act of 1964, which prohibits discrimination on grounds of race by both public and private institutions receiving federal funds. Another group of four justices, including Chief Justice Burger, Stewart, Rehnquist, and Stevens, thought that it was unnecessary to consider the constitutional question, since they believed that the Davis program contravened the "no-racial-discrimination provision" of Title VI.

There was no opinion for the Court. Justice Powell cast the tie breaking vote and announced the judgment of the Court in an opinion which argued that Title VI and the Equal Protection Clause imposed essentially identical obligations, and that by making race alone the dispositive criteria for admission under the minority set-aside, Davis had employed a racial classification that could not survive strict scrutiny. But Powell went on to suggest that had Davis used race along with other factors (say, poverty) in determining eligibility for the relaxed admissions standards applied to the set-aside slots, the program would have been both constitutional and legal under Title VI.

With constitutional experts still trying to unsnarl the implications of *Bakke,* the Court in 1979 confronted the case of *United Steel Workers* v. *Weber,* 443 U.S. 193. This involved an affirmative action plan worked out by a private employer and a labor union whereby half of the openings for in-plant training programs were reserved for black workers. The question was whether this violated the no-racial discrimination provision of Title VII of the Civil Rights Act. Justice Brennan wrote the majority opinion and held that, since the underlying purpose of the Civil Rights Act had been to advance the economic and social position of blacks in America, the no-discrimination language had to be read against that background. When this is done, it was argued, the program before the Court clearly was not a violation of the statute.

In *Fullilove* v. *Klutznick,* 448 U.S. 448 (1980), the question of reverse discrimination was before the justices once again. Here a federal law, the Public Works Employment Act of 1977, provided that a certain share of federal construction business should be set aside for minority contractors. Once more there was no opinion for the Court. Chief Justice Burger announced the judgment of the Court—that the congressional use of a racial classification was not unconstitutional in this instance. His opinion was joined by Justices White and Powell.

Burger argued that the use of a racial classification by Congress was constitutional as long as it was carefully limited and tailored to remedy some past discrimination. The Chief Justice rejected the contention that "Congress must act in a wholly 'color-blind' fashion." However, he seemed to suggest that there were severe limitations on the use of racial classifications for benevolent purposes.

Justices Marshall, Brennan, and Blackmun concurred in the judgment. Justice Stevens dissented on the grounds that the ten percent minority set-aside adopted by Congress did not meet the criteria for limited and precise action directed at particular past discrimination, which the Chief Justice had set up in the plurality opinion. Justices Stewart and Rehnquist dissented and would have adopted the Harlan position that the Constitution is color blind.

The community of professional rights advocates has been split on the issue of affirmative action, with some Jewish groups, notably the American Jewish Congress, now taking positions opposed to their traditional allies, the NAACP and the ACLU. And when the Reagan administration announced, in April of 1983, that affirmative action rules for federal contractors would be relaxed somewhat, the dispute flared anew.

CHAPTER · 21

SEX AND THE LAW

THE process that culminated in *Brown* v. *Board of Education* involved the Supreme Court's reinterpreting the equal protection clause in a way that preserved the broad, underlying antislavery purpose of the framers by freeing it from the limitations of their particular nineteenth century perspective. But were there other meanings to equal protection, meanings beyond its significance for government classifications of people based on race? The approach of late nineteenth and early twentieth century Supreme Court majorities to this question was cautious.

In the *Slaughter-House Cases,* 16 Wallace 36 (1873), the Court was confronted by the claim of a group of New Orleans butchers that a Louisiana statute of 1869, which had granted a monopoly of the slaughter of livestock in that city, deprived them of federally protected rights under the Fourteenth Amendment because they could no longer pursue that part of their livelihood involving the slaughter of animals. Speaking through Mr. Justice Samuel F. Miller, the majority rejected these claims. In Miller's view, the purpose of the Fourteenth Amendment had been to insure the equal legal capacities of black people. He did not see the Amendment as creating a broad category of new individual rights against state government, and especially he did not see the equal protection clause as forbidding states from making discriminations among their citizens on grounds other than race. Miller clearly reflected the dominant opinion on the Court in the latter decades of the nineteenth century in suggesting that a broad interpretation of the Fourteenth Amendment would project national power into the affairs of the states to such an extent as to disrupt and even nullify the essentially federal character of the American governmental arrangement. The framers of the Fourteenth Amendment, according to Miller, had been aiming to remedy a particular problem, not to impose broad limitations on the states in legislating to protect the health, welfare, and morals of their citizens.

There was vigorous dissent in the *Slaughter-House Cases.* Justices Stephen J. Field and Joseph P. Bradley each wrote, arguing that the Fourteenth Amendment *should* be understood as having created certain broad general rights, inhering in all persons, defensible against the states. The first fruit of this suggestion was the development, in the latter years of the nineteenth and early years of the twentieth centuries, of the doctrine of "substantive due process" referred to in Chapter 2. According to this interpretation, Supreme Court majorities were persuaded to find in the due process clause of the Fourteenth Amendment a general liberty of economic contract or entrepreneurship, which could be burdened or infringed upon by states only on showings of special need.

Beyond this, however, the Field and Bradley dissents of the *Slaughter-House Cases* did not bear fruit until the twentieth century. In Chapter 22 we will examine how the old notion of substantive due process has been resuscitated recently to protect not economic liberty, but personal autonomy in matters of sexual relations and child rearing. Even more important has been the way in which the Court in the 1960s and 1970s was willing to expand the equal protection clause into new areas.

Race was, of course, the paradigmatic "suspect classification." And while gender classifications have never been formally declared suspect, Supreme Court majorities came to require careful scrutiny of, and extraordinary justification for, governmental regulations that classify persons on the basis of sex. Gender classifications may not require the "compelling state interest" needed to justify racial classifications, but they do require something more than the ordinary level of reasonableness that any state law which classifies people must reach.

The three decisions examined in this chapter—*Reed* v. *Reed, Frontiero* v. *Richardson,* and *Craig* v. *Boren*—trace how the Court has articulated the standard a state legislature must meet when it distinguishes between men and women for some regulatory purpose. In addition, we will examine the affect and controversy surrounding Title XI of the Education Act Amendments of 1972. This will involve us with the statutory phase of the contemporary effort to protect women's rights in American society.

Reed v. Reed
404 U.S. 71, 92 S.Ct. 251, 30 L.Ed.2d 225 (1971)

To what extent are distinctions between the sexes—gender discriminations, as the Supreme Court prefers to call them—prohibited by the equal protection clause of the Fourteenth Amendment? Traditionally, if a classification based on sex had a "rational basis"—that is, if it furthered the legitimate state purpose and if the means chosen by the legislature were related to the achievement of that purpose—the distinction passed constitutional muster. *Goesaert* v. *Cleary,* 335 U.S. 464 (1948), is an excellent example of the traditional approach. Here the state of Michigan provided that no woman could obtain a bartender's license unless she was the wife or daughter of the male owner of the bar. In rejecting an equal protection challenge, Justice Frankfurter wrote that "Michigan could, beyond question, forbid all women from working behind a bar." And since this was so, the exception of some women from the ban, based on intimate relation to the owner of the bar, was not irrational. The beginning of a change came in the case of *Reed* v. *Reed*. Here the state of Idaho gave preference to men over women when it was necessary to appoint an administrator for an estate. ACLU stalwart Melvin L. Wulf was on the brief for the female appellant, along with the leading feminist lawyers Ruth Bader Ginsberg, Pauli Murray, and Dorothy Kenyon. *Amicus curiae* briefs in support of their position came from the city of New York, the American Veterans Committee, and from the National Federation of Business and Professional Women's Clubs (this one bearing the name of Senator Birch Bayh, Democrat of Indiana).

Mr. Chief Justice Burger delivered the opinion of the Court.

Richard Lynn Reed, a minor, died intestate in Ada County, Idaho, on March 29, 1967. His adoptive parents, who had separated sometime prior to his death, are the parties to this appeal. Approximately seven months after Richard's death, his mother, appellant Sally Reed, filed a petition in the Probate Court of Ada County, seeking appointment as administratrix of her son's estate. Prior to the date set for a hearing on the mother's petition, appellee Cecil Reed, the father of the decedent, filed a competing petition seeking to have himself appointed administrator of the son's estate. The probate court held a joint hearing on the two petitions and thereafter ordered that letters of administration be issued to appellee Cecil Reed. . . .

. . . Having examined the record and considered the briefs and oral arguments of the parties, we have concluded that the arbitrary preference established in favor of males by § 15–314 of the Idaho Code cannot stand in the face of the Fourteenth Amendment's command that no State deny the equal protection of the laws to any person within its jurisdiction.

Idaho does not, of course, deny letters of administration to women altogether. Indeed, under § 15–312, a woman whose spouse dies intestate has a preference over a son, father, brother, or any other male relative of the decedent. Moreover, we can judicially notice that in this country, presumably due to the greater longevity of women, a large proportion of estates, both intestate and under wills of decedents, are administered by surviving widows.

Section 15–314 is restricted in its operation to those situations where competing applications for letters of administration have been filed by both male and female members of the same entitlement class established by § 15–312. In such situations, § 15–314 provides that different treatment be accorded to the applicants on the basis of their sex; it thus establishes a classification subject to scrutiny under the Equal Protection Clause.

In applying that clause, this Court has consistently recognized that the Fourteenth Amendment does not deny to States the power to treat different classes of persons in different ways. . . .

. . . The Equal Protection Clause of that amendment does, however, deny to

States the power to legislate that different treatment be accorded to persons placed by a statute into different classes on the basis of criteria wholly unrelated to the objective of that statute. A classification "must be reasonable, not arbitrary, and must rest upon some ground of difference having a fair and substantial relation to the object of the legislation, so that all persons similarly circumstanced shall be treated alike." ...

Clearly the objective of reducing the workload on probate courts by eliminating one class of contests is not without some legitimacy. The crucial question, however, is whether § 15–314 advances that objective in a manner consistent with the command of the Equal Protection Clause. We hold that it does not. To give a mandatory preference to members of either sex over members of the other, merely to accomplish the elimination of hearings on the merits, is to make the very kind of arbitrary legislative choice forbidden by the Equal Protection Clause of the Fourteenth Amendment; and whatever may be said as to the positive values of avoiding intrafamily controversy, the choice in this context may not lawfully be mandated solely on the basis of sex. ...

The judgment of the Idaho Supreme Court is reversed and the case remanded for further proceedings not inconsistent with this opinion.

Reversed and remanded.

Frontiero v. *Richardson*
411 U.S. 677, 93 S.Ct. 1764, 36 L.Ed.2d 255 (1973)

Reed v. *Reed* raised the question of whether the Court was really applying a simple "rational basis" test to the Idaho statute. Chief Justice Burger said that he was, but close reading of the opinion suggests that since there was a rational basis for Idaho's practice—it was not irrational to assume that, in the normal run of things, men were more likely to have experience with financial affairs than women—the Court must have been applying, covertly, a higher standard. This issue surfaced with a vengeance in *Frontiero*. Justice Brennan announced the judgment of the Court and read an opinion in which three others joined. Brennan would have held sex to be a suspect category and applied the highest level of equal protection scrutiny. He could not, however, carry a majority of the Court with him on this point, and while *Frontiero* certainly indicates the path from *Reed* v. *Reed* leads to a higher level of equal protection scrutiny for gender discriminations than for other kinds of discriminations, the precise nature and justification for this scrutiny remains obscure.

Mr. Justice Brennan announced the judgment of the Court in an opinion in which Mr. Justice Douglas, Mr. Justice White, and Mr. Justice Marshall join.

The question before us concerns the right of a female member of the uniformed services to claim her spouse as a "dependent" for the purposes of obtaining increased quarters allowances and medical and dental benefits [on] an equal footing with male members. Under [the] statutes, a serviceman may claim his wife as a "dependent" without regard to whether she is in fact dependent upon him for any part of her support [but a] servicewoman [may] not claim her husband as a "dependent" [unless] he is in fact dependent upon her for over one-half of his support. ...

At the outset, appellants contend that classifications based upon sex, like classifications based upon race, alienage, and national origin, are inherently suspect and must therefore be subjected to close judicial scrutiny. We agree and, indeed, find at least implicit support for such an approach in our unanimous decision only last Term in *Reed*. ... [T]he Court [there] implicitly rejected appellee's apparently rational explanation of the statutory scheme, and concluded that, by ignoring the individual qualifications of particular applicants, the challenged statute provided "dissimilar treatment for men and women who [are] similarly situated." [This was a] departure from "traditional" rational-basis analysis with respect to sex-based classifications is clearly justified.

There can be no doubt that our Nation has had a long and unfortunate history of sex discrimination. Traditionally, such discrimination was rationalized by an attitude of "romantic paternalism" which, in practical effect, put women, not on a pedestal, but in a cage. As a result of notions such as these, our statute books gradually became laden with gross, stereotyped distinctions between the sexes and, indeed, throughout much of the 19th century the position of women in our society was, in many respects, comparable to that of blacks under the pre-Civil War slave codes. Neither slaves nor women could hold office, serve on juries, or bring suit in their own names, and married women traditionally were denied the legal capacity to hold or convey property or to serve as legal guardians of their own children. And although blacks were guaranteed the right to vote in 1870, women were denied even that right [until] adoption of the 19th Amendment half a century later.

It is true, of course, that the position of women in America has improved markedly in recent decades. Nevertheless, it can hardly be doubted that, in part because of the high visibility of the sex characteristic, women still face pervasive, although at times more subtle, discrimination in our educational institutions, in the job market and, perhaps most conspicuously, in the political arena. Moreover, since sex, like race and national origin, is an immutable characteristic determined solely by the accident of birth, the imposition of special disabilities upon the members of a particular sex because of their sex would seem to violate "the basic concept of our system that legal burdens should bear some relationship to individual responsibilty." ... And what differentiates sex from such nonsuspect statuses as intelligence or physical disability, and aligns it with the recognized suspect criteria, is that the sex characteristic frequently bears no relation to ability to perform or contribute to society. As a result, statutory distinctions between the sexes often have the effect of invidiously relegating the entire class of females to inferior legal status without regard to the actual capabilities of its individual members. ...

[The] Government concedes that the differential treatment accorded men and women under these statutes serves no purpose other than mere "administrative convenience." [It] maintains that, as an empirical matter, wives in our society frequently are dependent upon their husbands, while husbands rarely are dependent upon their wives. Thus, the Government argues that Congress might reasonably have concluded that it would be both cheaper and easier simply conclusively to presume that wives of male members are financially dependent upon their husbands, while burdening female members with the task of establishing dependency in fact. The Government offers no concrete evidence, however, tending to support its view that such differential treatment in fact saves the Government any money. In order to satisfy the demands of strict judicial scrutiny, the Government must demonstrate, for example, that it is actually cheaper to grant increased benefits with respect to *all* male members, than it is to determine which male members are in fact entitled to such benefits and to grant increased benefits only to those members whose wives actually meet the dependency requirement.

Reversed.

Justice Stewart concurred in the judgment of the Court. Justice Powell, with whom Chief Justice Burger and Justice Blackmun joined, also wrote an opinion concurring in the judgment. Justice Rehnquist dissented, arguing that sex was not a suspect classification, that the proper test was "rational basis," and that by this test Air Force practice did not constitute a denial of equal protection.

Craig v. Boren
429 U.S. 190, 97 S.Ct. 451, 51 L.Ed.2d. 574 (1976)

A logician might protest the notion of ambiguity being made explicit; yet this does describe the relationship between *Frontiero* and *Craig* v. *Boren*. In *Frontiero,* Justice Brennan could not attract five votes for the proposition that sex should be regarded as a suspect classification similar to race. On the other hand, in *Craig* v. *Boren,* he was able to marshall a majority behind an opinion making clear that gender discriminations required some higher level of equal protection scrutiny than the traditional examination for a rational basis. There must be, Brennan argued, a close "fit" between the legitimate end pursued by the legislature and the means adopted by it to reach that end. Thus it is fair to say that while not a suspect classification, sex is a "semi-" or "proto-" suspect classification requiring some degree of midrange scrutiny.

Mr. Justice Brennan delivered the opinion of the Court.

The interaction of two sections of an Oklahoma statute . . . prohibits the sale of "non-intoxicating" 3.2% beer to males under the age of 21 and to females under the age of 18. The question to be decided is whether such a gender-based differential constitutes a denial to males 18–20 years of age of the Equal Protection of the Laws.

[To] withstand constitutional challenge, previous cases establish that classifications by gender must serve important governmental objectives and must be substantially related to achievement of those objectives. . . . Clearly, the protection of public health and safety represents an important function of state and local governments. However, appellees' statistics in our view cannot support the conclusion that the gender-based distinction closely serves to achieve that objective and therefore the distinction cannot under Reed withstand equal protection challenge.

The appellees introduced a variety of statistical surveys. First, an analysis of arrest statistics for 1973 demonstrated that 18–20-year-old male arrests for "driving under the influence" and "drunkenness" substantially exceeded female arrests for that same age period. Similarly, youths aged 17–21 were found to be overrepresented among those killed or injured in traffic accidents, with males again numerically exceeding females in this regard. Third, a random roadside survey in Oklahoma City revealed that young males were more inclined to drive and drink beer than were their female counterparts. Fourth, Federal Bureau of Investigation nationwide statistics exhibited a notable increase in arrests for "driving under the influence." Finally, statistical evidence gathered in other jurisdictions [was] offered to corroborate Oklahoma's experience by indicating the pervasiveness of youthful participation in motor vehicle accidents following the imbibing of alcohol. . . .

Even were this statistical evidence accepted as accurate, it nevertheless offers only a weak answer to the equal protection question presented here. The most focused and relevant of the statistical surveys, arrests of 18–20-year-olds for alcohol-related driving offenses, exemplifies the ultimate unpersuasiveness of this evidentiary record. Viewed in terms of the correlation between sex and the actual activity that Oklahoma seeks to regulate—driving while under the influence of alcohol—the statistics broadly establish that .18% of females and 2% of males in that age group were arrested for that offense. While such a disparity is not trivial in a statistical sense, it hardly can form the basis for employment of a gender line as a classifying device. Certainly if maleness is to serve as a proxy for drinking and driving, a correlation of 2% must be considered an unduly tenuous "fit." . . .

There is no reason to belabor this line of analysis. It is unrealistic to expect either members of the judiciary or state officials to be well versed in the rigors of experimental or statistical technique. But this merely illustrates that proving broad sociological propositions by statistics is a dubious business, and one that inevitably is in tension with the normative philosophy that underlies the Equal Protection Clause. . . .

. . . [S]ocial science studies that have uncovered quantifiable differences in drinking tendencies dividing along both racial and ethnic lines strongly suggest the need for application of the Equal Protection Clause in preventing discriminatory treatment that almost certainly would be perceived as invidious. In sum, the principles embodied in the Equal Protection Clause are not to be rendered inapplicable by statistically measured but loose-fitting generalities concerning the drinking tendencies of aggregate groups. We conclude that [this] gender-based differential [is] a denial of the Equal Protection of the Laws to males aged 18–20. . . . .

Reversed.

Justices Powell and Stevens wrote concurring opinions. Justice Stewart wrote an opinion concurring in the judgment. Justice Rehnquist wrote a dissenting opinion, again arguing his view that the appropriate test for gender distinctions is "rational basis."

Cannon v. University of Chicago
648 F. 2d 1104 (1982)

In this case we are not dealing with a decision of the Supreme Court of the United States but of the United States Court of Appeals for the Seventh Circuit. Whether the Supreme Court will review *Cannon* v. *University of Chicago* has not yet been decided, but the case is so interesting that it warrants inclusion here. Title IX of the Education Act Amendments of 1972 provided that no persons could be subjected to discrimination "on basis of sex" by any educational institution receiving federal financial assistance. This, of course, left the question of what constituted discrimination. As we saw in the areas of voting rights (*Mobile* v. *Bolden*) and employment (*Griggs* v. *Duke Power*), two methods for determining discrimination are urged on the judiciary: the first requires a showing of an actual discriminatory intent by someone in setting up a particular institutional arrangement; the second requires only a showing that the institutional arrangement has a disproportionate impact on persons within the protected category. In *Mobile* v. *Bolden,* the legislative enactment at issue was the Voting Rights Act of 1965, and in *Griggs* v. *Duke Power,* it was Title VII of the Civil Rights Act of 1964. The protected categories were racial minorities. In *Cannon,* the statutory guarantee was Title IX and the protected category was women. As in *Mobile* v. *Bolden,* the *Cannon* holding was that the statute required a showing of discriminatory motivation; a showing of disproportionate impact was not sufficient to establish a violation.

Pell, Circuit Judge.

Plaintiff-appellant Geraldine G. Cannon comes before this court for a third time in her effort to gain admission to the defendants' medical schools. She was denied admission for the 1975 academic year and has been involved in litigation over the denials at all levels of the federal judiciary since that time. In her complaints, appellant claimed that the defendants' failure to admit her violated the age and sex discrimination prohibitions of . . . Title IX of the Educational Amendments of 1972. . . .

The present appellees, Northwestern University Medical School and the Pritzker School of Medicine at The University of Chicago, were two of the ten medical schools to which appellant unsuccessfully applied in 1975. Her undergraduate grade point average (GPA) in science and math related courses was 3.17 of a possible 4.00. The average GPA in these courses of the accepted applicants at the Pritzker School was 3.70 and at least 50% of all applicants to Northwestern had higher GPAs than appellant. On the science portion of the medical college admission test, appellant scored in the lower half of the applicant group to the defendant schools. On the quantitative portion of the test, she scored in the bottom half of the applicants to Northwestern and in the bottom 20% of the applicants to the University of Chicago.

In 1975, only 110 of over 6700 applicants were accepted at Northwestern while only 104 of 5427 applicants were accepted at Chicago. The Dean of the Pritzker School stated in an affidavit that at least 2000 applicants with better academic qualifications than appellant were rejected. At Northwestern, only seven applicants with lower academic qualifications were admitted: five blacks and two women. During the period from 1971 to 1975, 18.1% of the applicants to Pritzker School were women while 18.3% of the entering classes were women, and 2.2% of all women applicants were admitted while 2.1% of all male applicants were admitted.

Appellant's suits ... are based upon the admission policies of the defendant schools which in 1975 either discouraged individuals over the age of 30 from applying, or, in the case of Northwestern, prohibited the admission of any applicant over the age of 35 who did not possess an advance[d] academic degree. At the time of her application, appellant was 39 years old and had no such degrees. She asserts that because women historically interrupt their higher education to pursue a family and other domestic responsibilities more often than men, these age policies disparately affected women. Appellant claims that the defendants' age policies therefore resulted in sexual discrimination violative of Title IX.

The complaints appellant filed in these actions contain no express allegations that her applications to the defendants' medical schools were purposefully or intentionally rejected because of her sex. It is clear from the text of her complaints that appellant's cause of action was based solely upon the alleged disparate impact the defendants' age policies had upon women. With regard to the Title IX claims, the complaints allege simply:

A material criterion for defendants' denial of plaintiff's application for admission to the September 1975 entering class at [the defendants'] Medical School[s] was her age which, in the circumstances of application to medical school, is a criterion disproportionately characteristic of her sex and does not validly predict any lack of success in the education program or activity of the school[s]. This conduct on the part of defendants is in violation of ... Title IX of the Education Amendments of 1972, ... which provides:

"No person in the United States shall, on the basis of sex, be excluded from participation in, be denied the benefits of, or be subjected to discrimination under any education program or activity receiving Federal financial assistance," ...

This claim of disparate impact, even when coupled with the allegations made in appellant's brief to this court that the defendants knew of this impact while enforcing their age policies, is insufficient to establish a violation of Title IX. ... An illegal intent to discriminate cannot be posited solely upon a mere failure to equalize an apparent disparate impact. ...

In short, appellant has alleged nothing more than that a facially neutral age policy had a disparate impact upon women due to the domestic role they have traditionally assumed prior to continuing their education. No allegations have been made from which it can be inferred that it was more likely than not that discriminatory considerations were involved in the defendant's actions. . . . The disparate effect alone, even if established, would not warrant relief under Title IX. . . .

CASE STUDY: DRAFT REGISTRATION FOR MALES ONLY

Shaken by the collapse of an American ally and the emergence of a hostile power in Iran, and by the Soviet invasion of Afghanistan, President Carter decided in 1980 that it was necessary to reactivate the Selective Service registration process. Draft registration had been ended by Gerald Ford's presidential proclamation in 1975. Prior to that, in 1973, the Selective Service Act had been amended to preclude actual conscription. Authority to order registration remained in the executive, but this authority was only to require the registration of males.

President Carter sought funds from Congress to reinstitute registration and also to recommend to Congress that it amend the Selective Service Act to permit registration of women as well as men. Congress allocated the funds for registration of males but declined to amend the Act to permit the registration of women. A lawsuit was quickly brought by several men challenging the constitutionality of the "males-only" registration, and a three-judge federal district court in Philadelphia ultimately held that the Act's gender-based discrimination violated the equal protection component of the due process clause of the Fifth Amendment.

The case arrived at the Supreme Court as *Robert L. Goldberg, et al.,* v. *Bernard Rostker, Director of Selective Service*. It was decided on June 25, 1981. Justice Rehnquist delivered the opinion of the Court and sustained the "males-only" registration requirement. Rehnquist reasoned that Congress had "specifically recognized and endorsed exclusion of women from combat" roles in military service. He further noted that the constitutionality of excluding women from combat was unchallenged in the lawsuit. Given the exclusion of women from combat, Rehnquist went on, it was reasonable for Congress to conclude that in raising manpower to meet a military emergency (in which providing forces for combat was the primary objective), registering males only would be a substantially more expeditious way of meeting the emergency than requiring registration of both sexes.

Justice Rehnquist rejected the characterization of the Selective Service Act, in an *amicus curiae* brief presented by the National Organization for Women, as a law that precluded "women as a class from performing tasks or jobs of which they are capable, . . ." Women were not excluded from military service, simply not required to register for a draft. Noting that it was certainly possible for a small number of women to be drafted for noncombat roles, Rehnquist concluded that Congress "simply did not consider it worth the added burden of including women in draft and registration plans."

Justice White wrote a dissenting opinion in which Justice Brennan joined. White noted the many military specialties for which women were suited and presently employed. He argued further that in an emergency draft there would be large numbers of noncombat positions to be filled by draftees. Moreover, the exclusion of women from registration did not rest on any congressional finding that their inclusion would have an *adverse* affect on military preparedness, and the congressional conclusion that including women was just not worth the trouble did not rise to the magnitude of governmental interest which would justify a gender distinction. Justice White was not clear about what equal protection test he would apply to the Selective Service Act, but whatever the test, the Act did not meet it. White accused the majority of being overly deferential in accepting the congressional justification for males-only registration.

What is most interesting about the case is that all involved accepted the proposition that it was constitutional for Congress to decide that women as a group could be excluded from combat roles. Justice Rehnquist's argument that Congress was entitled to make a prudential judgment as to the efficiency of registering males only, as opposed to both men and women, would collapse if the constitutionality of excluding females from combat were not admitted. Are all females unsuited to combat service, or just a portion of them? And if the latter, should not admission to combat roles be by individualized judgment? Does the exclusion of all women from combat represent precisely the sort of archaic stereotyping of sex roles that Justice Brennan attacked in his opinion in *Craig* v. *Boren*?

Or is society entitled to its traditional views in this matter? Under the Carter administration, the American military came to make use of women in greater numbers in near combat positions than any other military establishment in the world. The Reagan administration, after some adverse public reaction in the late 1970s, has scaled back this use of women. But at what point is a traditional view suspect if it denies individualized treatment? At what point must it be accepted as an expression of the deep-seated cultural commitments of the people, as registered through their elected representatives, and thus entitled to respect as public policy? *Rostker* v. *Goldberg* disposed of the immediate question of the registration requirement, but the larger question of which gender discriminations are proper and which are improper with respect to military service is far from settled.

CHAPTER · 22

FUNDAMENTAL RIGHTS AND SUSPECT CLASSIFICATIONS

IN Chapters 19 and 20, we saw that race, when used as a criterion of classification by government, constitutes a "suspect classification" that triggers the highest level of equal protection scrutiny and can only be justified by some "compelling state interest." It has been argued that any governmental discrimination that impacts adversely on a suspect class (a discrete and insular minority which has been subjected to unjustified discrimination historically) should trigger the same scrutiny given to racial classifications. There is, however, another trigger for high-level equal protection scrutiny—whether the governmental regulation in question impinges on a "fundamental right" protected by the Constitution. In this chapter we will examine *Harper* v. *Virginia Board of Elections* as an example of this "fundamental rights" stand of equal protection doctrine.

In the preceding chapter we learned that gender, while not a fully suspect classification, does trigger a mid-range form of equal protection scrutiny where the means chosen by the legislature must be substantially related to the legitimate legislative purpose. In this chapter we will examine several other classifications the Court has found to be fully suspect. In *Ambach* v. *Norwick*, we find the Court grappling with the question of when government may require citizenship as a criterion of eligibility for some employment or benefit and thus discriminate against aliens. In *Lalli* v. *Lalli*, we will observe how the Court has grappled with the matter of illegitimacy, noting that "nonmarital children" are a suspect class. Finally, in *Massachusetts Board of Retirement* v. *Murgia*, we will see the Court declining to identify classifications based on age as suspect.

With respect to the *Harper* case, and the fundamental rights stand of equal protection doctrine, the key question is how the Court identifies fundamental rights. With respect to the later suspect classification cases, the key question is the similarity of the problems dealt with—illegitimacy, alienage, and age. To what extent are these classifications (and the gender classification) analogous to the paradigmatic suspect classification of race? It was in the area of race where the new equal protection doctrine of higher levels of analysis was initially developed, so it is not unreasonable to ask how closely other suspect classifications resemble the paradigmatic case.

Harper v. Virginia State Board of Elections
383 U.S. 663, 86 S.Ct. 1079, 16 L.Ed.2d 169 (1966)

Harper is an example of the "fundamental rights" strand of equal protection analysis. In this case the equal protection violation did not flow from a discrimination based on a suspect or even semi- or para-suspect classification. The Virginia poll tax for state elections applied to all. Rather, the high-level equal protection scrutiny was appropriate because the requirement bore on the right to vote. The right to vote, Justice Douglas argued, is among the most fundamental of constitutionally protected rights, and any governmentally imposed condition which burdens this right must be justified by a compelling state interest (or something approaching that). In dissent, Justice Black argued that the poll tax had deep roots in American history and that generations of politically literate people had accepted the governmental interest in such taxes as legitimate.

Mr. Justice Douglas delivered the opinion of the Court.

These are suits by Virginia residents to have declared unconstitutional Virginia's poll tax. . . .

While the right to vote in federal elections is conferred by Art. I, § 2, of the Constitution . . . the right to vote in state elections is nowhere expressly mentioned. It is argued that the right to vote in state elections is implicit, particularly by reason of the First Amendment and that it may not constitutionally be conditioned upon the payment of a tax or fee. . . . We do not stop to canvass the relation between voting and political expression. For it is enough to say that once the franchise is granted to the electorate, lines may not be drawn which are inconsistent with the Equal Protection Clause of the Fourteenth Amendment. That is to say, the right of suffrage "is subject to the imposition of state standards which are not discriminatory and which do not contravene any restriction that Congress, acting pursuant to its constitutional powers, has imposed." . . .

We conclude that a State violates the Equal Protection Clause of the Fourteenth Amendment whenever it makes the affluence of the voter or payment of any fee an electoral standard. Voter qualifications have no relation to wealth nor to paying or not paying this or any other tax. Our cases demonstrate that the Equal Protection Clause of the Fourteenth Amendment restrains the States from fixing voter qualifications which invidiously discriminate. Thus without questioning the power of a State to impose reasonable residence restrictions on the availability of the ballot. . . .

Long ago in *Yick Wo* v. *Hopkins*, 118 U.S. 356, 370, the Court referred to "the political franchise of voting" as a "fundamental political right, because preservative of all rights." Recently in *Reynolds* v. *Sims*, 377 U.S. 533, 561–562, we said: "Undoubtedly, the right of suffrage is a fundamental matter in a free and democratic society. Especially since the right to exercise the franchise in a free and unimpaired mannner is preservative of other basic civil and political rights, any alleged infringement of the right of citizens to vote must be carefully and meticulously scrutinized." . . .

It is argued that a State may exact fees from citizens for many different kinds of licenses; that if it can demand from all an equal fee for a driver's license, it can demand from all an equal poll tax for voting. But we must remember that the interest of the State, when it comes to voting, is limited to the power to fix qualifications. . . . To introduce wealth or payment of a fee as a measure of a voter's qualifications is to introduce a capricious or irrelevant factor. The degree of the discrimination is irrelevant. . . .

We agree, of course, with Mr. Justice Holmes that the Due Process Clause of the Fourteenth Amendment "does not enact Mr. Herbert Spencer's Social Statics" (*Lochner* v. *People of State of New York*, 198 U.S. 45, 75). Likewise, the Equal Protection Clause is not shackled to the political theory of a particular era. In determining what lines are unconstitutionally discriminatory, we have never been confined to historic notions of equality, any more than we have restricted due process to a fixed catalogue of what was at a given time deemed to be the limits of fundamental rights. . . . Notions of what constitutes equal treatment for purposes of the Equal Protection Clause *do* change. . . .

[W]ealth or fee paying has, in our view, no relation to voting qualifications; the right to vote is too precious, too fundamental to be so burdened or conditioned.

Reversed.

Mr. Justice Black dissenting.

A study of our cases shows that this Court has refused to use the general language of the Equal Protection Clause as though it provided a handy instrument to strike down state laws which the Court feels are based on bad governmental policy. The equal protection cases carefully analyzed boil down to the principle that distinctions drawn and even discriminations imposed by state laws do not violate the Equal Protection Clause so long as these distinctions and discriminations are not "irrational," "irrelevant," "unreasonable," "arbitrary," or "invidious." These vague and indefinite terms do not, of course, provide a precise formula or an automatic mechanism for deciding cases arising under the Equal Protection Clause. The restrictive connotations of these terms, however, . . ., are a plain recognition of the fact that under a proper interpretation of the Equal Protection Clause States are to have the broadest kind of leeway in areas where they have a general constitutional competence to act. In view of the purpose of the terms to restrain the courts from a wholesale invalidation of state laws under the Equal Protection Clause it would be difficult to say that the poll tax requirement is "irrational" or "arbitrary" or works "invidious discriminations." State poll tax legislation can "reasonably," "rationally" and without an "invidious" or evil purpose to injure anyone be found to rest on a number of state policies including (1) the State's desire to collect its revenue, and (2) its belief that voters who pay a poll tax will be interested in furthering the State's welfare when they vote. Certainly it is rational to believe that people may be more likely to pay taxes if payment is a prerequisite to voting. And if history can be a factor in determining the "rationality" of discrimination in a state law, ... then whatever may be our personal opinion, history is on the side of "rationality" of the State's poll tax policy. Property qualifications existed in the Colonies and were continued by many States after the Constitution was adopted. Although I join the Court in disliking the policy of the poll tax, this is not in my judgment a justifiable reason for holding this poll tax law unconstitutional. Such a holding on my part would, in my judgment, be an exercise of power which the Constitution does not confer upon me. ...

The people have not found it impossible to amend their Constitution to meet new conditions. The Equal Protection Clause itself is the product of the peoples' desire to use their constitutional power to amend the Constitution to meet new problems. ...

Justice Harlan also wrote a dissenting opinion in which Justice Stewart joined.

Ambach v. *Norwick*
441 U.S. 68, 99 S.Ct. 1589, 60 L.Ed.2d 49 (1979)

Alienage—not being a citizen of the United States—is another classification that has been formally designated "suspect." But while the Court has said it applies "close judicial scrutiny" to distinctions based on citizenship, it seems clear that the standard applied is not that of compelling state interest. In some instances, states and the federal government have been allowed to make distinctions based on citizenship and in other instances not. In *Ambach,* the state of New York required all school teachers to be citizens or to register their intention to become citizens. The Court upheld this as rationally related to a valid state objective. In 1973, however, a divided Court had invalidated Connecticut's exclusion of aliens from the practice of law (*In re Griffiths,* 413 U.S. 717), and a New York law requiring citizenship for positions in the permanent civil service of the state (*Sugarman* v. *Dougall,* 413 U.S. 634).

Mr. Justice Powell delivered the opinion of the Court.

New York Education ... forbids certification as a public school teacher of any person who is not a citizen of the United States, unless that person has manifested an intention to apply for citizenship. [Appellees Norwick and Dachinger—both married to American citizens—] meet all of the educational requirements New York has set for certification as a public school teacher, but they consistently have refused to seek citizenship in spite of their eligibility to do so. ...

The decisions of this Court regarding the permissibility of statutory classifications involving aliens have not formed an unwavering line over the years. [The] Court's decisions gradually have restricted the activities from which States are free to exclude aliens. [But our recent decisions] have not abandoned the general principle that some state functions are so bound up with the operation of the State as a governmental entity as to permit the exclusion from those functions of all persons who have not become part of the process of self-government. ... The exclusion of aliens from such governmental positions would not invite as demanding scrutiny from this Court. ...

In determining whether, for purposes of equal protection analysis, teaching in public schools constitutes a governmental function, we look to the role of public education and to the degree of responsibility and discretion teachers possess in fulfilling that role. Each of these considerations supports the conclusion that public school teachers may be regarded as performing a task "that go[es] to the heart of representative government." ... Public education, like the police function, "fulfills a most fundamental obligation of government to its constituency." ...

As the legitimacy of the State's interest in furthering the educational goals outlined above is undoubted, it remains only to consider whether [New York's law] bears a rational relationship to this interest. The restriction is carefully framed to serve its purpose, as it bars from teaching only those aliens who have demonstrated their unwillingness to obtain United States citizenship. Appellees, and aliens similarly situated, in effect have chosen to classify themselves. They prefer to retain citizenship in a foreign country with the obligations it entails of primary duty and loyalty. They have rejected the open invitation extended to qualify for eligibility to teach by applying for citizenship in this country. The people of New York [have] made a judgment that citizenship should be a qualification for teaching [in] the public schools. ...

Reversed.

Justice Blackmun, with whom Justices Brennan, Marshall, and Stevens joined, dissented. Blackmun argued that citizenship was not rationally related to successful teaching.

Lalli v. *Lalli*
439 U.S. 259, 99 S.Ct. 518, 58 L.Ed.2d 503 (1978)

The Supreme Court has held illegitimacy to be a suspect classification, but the rational relationship between legislative ends and means does not appear as strict for illegitimacy as it is, say, for race. That is, while illegitimacy is suspect when used as a criterion of classification by government, it does not appear that the "compelling state interest" requirement must be met in order for a classification based on illegitimacy to be sustained. In *Lalli,* New York had established a procedure whereby an illegitimate child, if recognized by the natural father in a judicial proceeding during the father's lifetime, could inherit in intestate successions (situations in which the natural parent did not leave a will) just like children born in wedlock. Justice Powell sustained the New York arrangement against a challenge that New York could have secured its objective of proof of paternity in ways less burdensome for illegitimate children. While recognizing that this was true, Powell, in the plurality opinion, argued that only a reasonable relationship between end and means is necessary in the illegitimacy context, not a showing that means chosen is the least burdensome on the suspect class.

Mr. Justice Powell announced the judgment of the Court in an opinion, in which The Chief Justice and Mr. Justice Stewart join.

This case presents a challenge to the constitutionality of [a section] of New York's Estates, Powers, and Trusts Law, which requires illegitimate children who would inherit from their fathers by intestate succession to provide a particular form of proof of paternity. Legitimate children are not subject to the same requirement.

The primary state goal underlying the challenged aspects of [New York's law] is to provide for the just and orderly disposition of property at death. We long have recognized that this is an area with which the States have an interest of considerable magnitude.

This interest is directly implicated in paternal inheritance by illegitimate children because of the peculiar problems of proof that are involved. Establishing maternity is seldom difficult. ... Proof of paternity, by contrast, frequently is difficult when the father is not part of a formal family unit. ...

As the State's interests are substantial, we now consider the means adopted by New York to further these interests. In order to avoid the problems described above, [New York settled on] a requirement designed to ensure the accurate resolution of claims of paternity and to minimize the potential for disruption of estate administration. Accuracy is enhanced by placing paternity disputes in a judicial forum during the lifetime of the father. ...

The administration of an estate will be facilitated, and the possibility of delay and uncertainty minimized, where the entitlement of an illegitimate child to notice and participation is a matter of judicial record before the administration commences. Fraudulent assertions of paternity will be much less likely to succeed, or even to arise, where the proof is put before a court of law at a time when the putative father is available to respond, rather than first brought to light when the distribution of the assets of an estate is in the offing.

Appellant contends that [New York] excludes "significant categories of illegitimate children" who could be allowed to inherit "without jeopardizing the orderly settlement" of their intestate fathers' estates. He urges that those in his position—"known" illegitimate children who, despite the absence of an order of filiation obtained during their fathers' lifetimes, can present convincing proof of paternity—cannot rationally be denied inheritance as they pose none of the risks [the law] was intended to minimize.

We do not question that there will be some illegitimate children who would be able to establish their relationship to their deceased fathers without serious disruption of the administration of estates and that, as applied to such individuals, [the law] appears to operate unfairly. But few statutory classifications are entirely free from the criticism that they sometimes produce inequitable results. Our inquiry under the Equal Protection Clause does not focus on the abstract "fairness" of a state law, but on whether the statute's relation to the state interests it is intended to promote is so tenuous that it lacks the rationality contemplated by the Fourteenth Amendment. . . .

The New York courts have interpreted [its law] liberally and in such a way as to enhance its utility to both father and child without sacrificing its strength as a procedural prophylactic. For example, a father of illegitimate children who is willing to acknowledge paternity can waive his defenses in a paternity proceeding, or even institute such a proceeding himself. In addition, the courts have excused "technical" failures by illegitimate children to comply with the statute in order to prevent unnecessary injustice. . . .

Even if, as Mr. Justice Brennan believes, [New York's law] could have been written somewhat more equitably, it is not the function of a court "to hypothesize independently on the desirability or feasibility of any possible alternative[s]" to the statutory scheme formulated by New York. . . . "These matters of practical judgment and empirical calculation are for [the State]. . . . In the end, the precise accuracy of [the State's] calculations is not a matter of specialized judicial competence; and we have no basis to question their detail beyond the evident consistency and substantiality."

We conclude that the requirement imposed by [New York] on illegitimate children who would inherit from their fathers is substantially related to the important state interests the statute is intended to promote. We therefore find no violation of the Equal Protection Clause.

The judgment of the New York Court of Appeals is affirmed.

Justice Stewart concurred, while Justices Blackmun and Rehnquist concurred only in the judgment. Justice Brennan, with whom Justices White, Marshall, and Stevens joined, dissented, arguing that proof of a "formal acknowledgement of paternity" would be a sufficient protection of a state's interest in accurate and efficient determination of paternity, and for New York to go further was not justified by any compelling state interest.

Massachusetts Board of Retirement v. Murgia
427 U.S. 307, 96 S.Ct. 2562, 49 L.Ed.2d 520 (1976)

In *Murgia*, we encounter the question of state classifications based on age. The Court has not declared such classifications "suspect" or even partially suspect. But Justice Marshall's dissent is particularly interesting in that he argued against the "rigid two-tier system" he sees the Court applying in the equal protection area. While age is certainly different as a human characteristic from race, or illegitimacy, or alienage, Marshall would have afforded age classifications some higher degree of scrutiny than for "mere rationality." But, given the "mid-range" equal protection scrutiny afforded to gender classifications (where the requirement is for "substantial rationality"), is Justice Marshall's characterization of the Court as "two-tier" really accurate?

Per Curiam.

This case presents the question whether the provision of [Massachusetts law] that a uniformed State Police Officer "shall be retired [upon] his attaining age fifty" denies appellee police officer equal protection of the laws. [Murgia] was an officer in the Uniformed Branch of the Massachusetts State Police. The Massachusetts Board of Retirement retired him upon his 50th birthday. [There is a] requirement that uniformed state officers pass a comprehensive physical examination biennially until age 40. After that, until mandatory retirement at age 50, uniformed officers must pass annually a more rigorous examination. [Murgia] had passed such an examination four months before he was retired, and there is no dispute that, when he retired, his excellent physical and mental health still rendered him capable of performing the duties of a uniformed officer. [The] testimony clearly established that the risk of physical failure, particularly in the cardiovascular system, increases with age, and that the number of individuals in a given age group incapable of performing stress functions increases with the age of the group. The testimony also recognized that particular individuals over 50 could be capable of safely performing the functions of uniformed officers. [A witness] further testified that evaluating the risk of cardiovascular failure in a given individual would require a detailed number of studies.

We need state only briefly our reasons for agreeing that strict scrutiny is not the proper test for determining whether the mandatory retirement provision denies appellee equal protection. [E]qual protection analysis requires strict scrutiny of a legislative classification only when the classification impermissibly interferes with the exercise of a fundamental right or operates to the peculiar disadvantage of a suspect class. Mandatory retirement at age 50 under the Massachusetts statute involves neither situation. This Court's decisions give no support to the proposition that a right of governmental employment per se is fundamental. [Nor] does the class of uniformed state police officers over 50 constitute a suspect class for purposes of equal protection analysis. [While] the treatment of the aged in this Nation has not been wholly free of discrimination, such persons, unlike, say, those who have been discriminated against on the basis of race or national origin, have not experienced a "history of purposeful unequal treatment" or been subjected to unique disabilities on the basis of stereotyped characteristics not truly indicative of their abilities. . . .

We turn then to examine this state classification under the rational basis standard. This inquiry employs a relatively relaxed standard reflecting the Court's awareness that the drawing of lines that create distinctions is peculiarly a legislative task and an unavoidable one. Perfection in making the necessary classifications is neither possible nor necessary. Such action by a legislature is presumed to be valid. In this case, the Massachusetts statute clearly meets the requirements of the Equal Protection Clause, for the State's classification rationally furthers the purpose identified by the State: Through mandatory retirement at age 50, the legislature seeks to protect the public by assuring physical preparedness of its uniformed police. Since physical ability generally declines with age, mandatory retirement at 50 serves to remove from police service those whose fitness for uniformed work presumptively has diminished with age. . . .

Mr. Justice Marshall dissenting.

Although there are signs that its grasp on the law is weakening, the rigid two-tier model still holds sway as the Court's articulated description of the equal protection test. Again, I must object to its perpetuation. The model's two fixed modes of analysis, strict scrutiny and mere rationality, simply do not describe the inquiry the Court has undertaken—or should undertake—in equal protection cases. Rather, the inquiry has been much more sophisticated and the Court should admit as much. It has focused upon the character of the classification in question, the relative importance to individuals in the class discriminated against of the governmental benefits that they do not receive, and the state interests asserted in support of the classification. [Although] the Court outwardly adheres to the two-tier model, it has apparently lost interest in recognizing further "fundamental" rights and "suspect" classes. In my view, this result is the natural consequence of the limitations of the Court's traditional equal protection analysis. If a statute invades a "fundamental" right or discriminates against a "suspect" class, it is subject to strict scrutiny. If a statute is subject to strict scrutiny, the statute always, or nearly always is struck down. Quite obviously, the only critical decision is whether strict scrutiny should be invoked at all. It should be no surprise, then, that the Court is hesitant to expand the number of categories of rights and classes subject to strict scrutiny, when each expansion involves the invalidation of virtually every classification bearing upon a newly covered category.

But however understandable the Court's hesitancy to invoke strict scrutiny, all remaining legislation should not drop into the bottom tier, and be measured by the mere rationality test. For that test, too, when applied as articulated, leaves little doubt about the outcome; the challenged legislation is always upheld. It cannot be gainsaid that there remain rights, not now classified as "fundamental," that remain vital to the flourishing of a free society, and classes, not now classified as "suspect," that are unfairly burdened by invidious discrimination unrelated to the individual worth of their members. Whatever we call these rights and classes, we simply cannot forgo all judicial protection against discriminatory legislation bearing upon them, but for the rare instances when the legislative choice can be termed "wholly irrelevant" to the legislative goal. ...

[While] depriving any government employee of his job is a significant deprivation, it is particularly burdensome when the person deprived is an older citizen. [Whether] older workers constitute a "suspect" class or not, it cannot be disputed that they constitute a class subject to repeated and arbitrary discrimination in employment. [Of course], distinctions exist between the elderly and traditional suspect classes such as Negroes, and between the elderly and "quasi-suspect" classes such as women or illegitimates. [The] elderly are not isolated in society, and discrimination against them is not pervasive but is centered primarily in employment. The advantage of a flexible equal protection standard, however, is that it can readily accommodate such variables. ...

CASE STUDY: AGE DISCRIMINATION

We have seen that the Court has declined to identify age as a suspect classification or, thus far at least, to subject age discriminations to the mid-range equal protection scrutiny employed for gender distinctions. Congress, however, has moved against age discrimination with the Age Discrimination Act of 1975 (42 U.S.C. 6101). And with groups such as the Gray Panthers and the Association of Retired Persons active in the state legislatures and lobbying administrative agencies, there has been a good deal of activity on the "age front" in recent years.

With the Age Discrimination Act, Congress added to a growing list of characteristics protected against discrimination, which now includes race, sex, and national origin. Peter H. Schuck, in an extensive analysis of the Act, "The Graying of the Civil Rights Laws," 89 *Yale Law Journal* 27 (1979), noted how the Act was modeled on previous nondiscrimination legislation, especially that precluding racial discrimination (the Civil Rights Act of 1964). The difficulty, however, is that in the real world of affairs age can be a fair and appropriate basis for decision making whereas race almost never is. Thus rather than banning all discriminations based on age, the Act, as a practical matter, will have to be read as precluding certain discriminations but allowing others.

Since Congress never faced this problem, and did not provide decision rules for determining the licit and illicit in age discrimination, the task will necessarily fall to the courts. As Schuck put it, "judicial policy making under the ADA, however incompetent it may prove to be, nevertheless appears to be inevitable." This will give rise to charges of "judicial arrogation of power," but the basic mischief was for "Congress to enact a law based largely upon conflicting premises and then to refuse to define or even guide its policy except through broad intimations of sentiment. . . ."

The problems with age discrimination reflect the larger theoretical problem of reasoning by analogy from the special case of race. Highly skilled interest group elites, maneuvering in Congress and before the courts in search of doctrinal initiatives beneficial to the minorities they represent, take full and aggressive advantage of analogies to race. It is no accident that the Gray Panthers are not the Gray Cougars. But unless the nation is prepared to dispense with most distinctions based on age, as we are prepared to dispense with most discriminations based on race, then to shape policy in general terms *as if we were* merely leads to confusion and carries with it the danger of bringing the courts into contempt. The anomalous nature of the Age Discrimination Act is best revealed by the fact that Congress declined to apply its provisions to its own employment practices.

PART V

RIGHTS OF PRIVACY

THE concern over individual privacy is deeply rooted in America, but it has not always been described in the terms we use today. The Fourth Amendment's prohibition against unreasonable searches and seizures, discussed in Chapter 14, was based on the deep concern of the framers of the Bill of Rights for the privacy of the home. While the word "privacy" was not used, deeply rooted in the Anglo-American legal tradition, is the notion of the "home as a castle" from which all could be excluded and within which one's business is one's own.

One reason why privacy, beyond physical protection of the home, was not very frequently discussed by American courts and lawyers until the twentieth century, was because, as a practical matter, privacy was so easy to obtain and maintain in the United States. The country was vast, the population (by today's standards) was tiny, and it was always possible to move far enough away that you did not "see your neighbor's smoke." In addition, government—federal and state—was small during the nineteenth century. Bureaucratized police forces, elaborate tax collection agencies, welfare, social security, and medical insurance record keeping are all essentially twentieth century developments. In the nineteenth century, except in the case of very prominent individuals, there was neither the interest nor the capacity in government to gather great amounts of information and maintain elaborate records.

In the same way, the private sector of the nineteenth century (at least until its last few decades) was characterized by a multiplicity of small business and communications firms. Local newspapers were not integrated into national and international networks, which transmitted information virtually instantly, and where the same item or photograph could be displayed simultaneously across state lines or even continents.

Thus, one important reason for the quickened concern with individual privacy in the twentieth century was the change in the institutional setting both of government and the private sector. Another is the increased difficulty of maintaining personal privacy in a large and more highly compacted society where both government and private institutions are armed with computers. But our increased concern with privacy reflects not only altered governmental, economic, demographic, and technological circumstances. It also reflects a change in sensibility on the part of some persons within our society.

Put simply, by the middle of the twentieth century, some people in America had come to believe that certain matters involving sexual activity, reproduction, and family arrangements, which had traditionally been thought of as matters over which the community, through law, exercised legitimate jurisdiction, were really nobody's business but their own. There was, in other words, an increasing demand for privacy defined as autonomy of individual choice in those spheres of behavior considered peculiarly personal.

It is against this background, of a society vastly altered in the middle twentieth century, plus heightened levels of consciousness about certain aspects of the personal lives of individuals, that we must approach the growing body of civil liberties law lumped together under the rubric of "privacy."

SELECTED READINGS

Dionispoulos, P. Allan and Ducat, Craig R. *The Right to Privacy.* (St. Paul, Minn.: West Publishing Co., 1976). While already a little dated, this remains a useful introduction.

Ernst, Morris L. and Schwartz, Alan U. *Privacy: The Right to Be Let Alone.* (New York: The MacMillan Co., 1962). Excellent background on the development of the idea of privacy in Anglo-American law. Ernst was one of the greatest civil liberties lawyers of his time.

Marchand, Donald A. *The Politics of Privacy, Computers, and Criminal Justice Records.* (Arlington, Va.: Information Resources Press, 1980). Criminal justice records present certain particularly delicate privacy problems with respect to maintenance and access. Professor Marchand considers not only the technical and legal aspects of his subject, but the political/bureaucratic as well.

Miller, Arthur R. *The Assault on Privacy.* (Ann Arbor: The University of Michigan Press, 1971). Professor Miller, of the Harvard Law School, is an architect and theoretician of contemporary privacy law.

Pratt, Walter F. *Privacy in Britain.* (Lewisburg, Pa.: Bucknell University Press, 1979). Extremely useful for comparative purposes.

Westin, Alan F. *Databanks in a Free Society.* (New York: Quadrangle/The New York Times Book Co., 1972). Specifically treating the privacy problems of data bank creation in both public and private sectors.

Westin, Alan F. *Information Technology in a Democracy.* (Cambridge: Harvard University Press, 1971). A first-rate collection of essays on the implications of computers for privacy in particular and democratic politics in general.

Westin, Alan F. *Privacy and Freedom.* (New York: Atheneum, 1967). The best one-volume treatment of the subject. Especially noteworthy is Westin's treatment of "organizational privacy."

CHAPTER · 23

PRIVACY AS PERSONAL
AUTONOMY

THE decade of the 1960s has sometimes been described as encompassing a "sexual revolution." Certainly the frankness and detail with which sex was publicly discussed and portrayed in the 1960s was in sharp contrast to preceding decades. A perception grew, and became widespread at least among the intellectual elites of American society, that the kinds of legal restrictions on sexual activities accepted in American society in the past were no longer tolerable. But to say they were no longer tolerable was not the same as saying they were unconstitutional. Battles raged in state legislatures and in the media over restrictive laws on contraception, abortion, and homosexuality. Victories were won in some state legislatures, but others remained steadfastly traditional and resisted the demands of liberal reformers.

It first became clear that the Supreme Court of the United States was prepared to fashion new constitutional law to protect certain aspects of sexual and familial choice from community intervention in the case of *Griswold* v. *Connecticut* in 1965. Here the Court held that Connecticut's regulation of the use of birth control devices violated the privacy of the defendants. The justices failed, however, to make clear precisely which provision of the Constitution was violated by Connecticut's law.

It was the Supreme Court's 1973 decision in *Roe* v. *Wade,* an abortion case, which held that some protection of sexual and familial autonomy inhered in the due process clause of the Fourteenth Amendment in the word "liberty." With this decision, the notion of substantive due process had been resuscitated—not to protect "liberty of contract" as in the late nineteenth and early twentieth centuries, but to protect the personal intimate liberties having to do with reproduction and child rearing.

How far the Court is prepared to take this new substantive due process is unclear. But by declining to hear *Doe* v. *Commonwealth's Attorney,* it could be argued that the justices flinched at extending the logic of *Wade* to homosexual activity between consenting adults.

Griswold v. *Connecticut*
381 U.S. 479, 85 S.Ct. 1678, 14 L.Ed.2d. 510 (1965)

In this case Justice Douglas, speaking for the Court, struck down a Connecticut statute that criminalized the use of artificial birth control devices. The problem for Douglas was to identify what provision of the Constitution of the United States was violated by the Connecticut law. In Chapter 2, we saw how the Supreme Court in the late nineteenth and early twentieth century had read into the Fifth and Fourteenth Amendments a concept of liberty of contract or entrepreneurship that limited government regulation of business enterprise. This doctrine of "substantive due process" had fallen into desuetude by the 1940s, and though never formally abandoned by the Supreme Court, it had been ignored and stigmatized by scholars and judges alike. The epitome of this old, bad doctrine of substantive due process was the case of *Lochner* v. *New York,* 198 U.S. 45 (1905). Here Justice Holmes, in a brilliant two page dissent, rejected the entire theory on which the majority opinion rested. Since the late 1930s, it had been widely held in the constitutional law community that the Holmes' dissent represented the better part of wisdom. Therefore, Justice Douglas did not wish to base his opinion in *Griswold* on an undifferentiated concept of liberty in the Fourteenth Amendment. He was at pains to protest that he was not reading into liberty a new concept of individual autonomy of sexual relations, which would be vulnerable to the same sort of attack as the old notion of liberty of economic contract. In order to avoid "Lochnerizing" (a reference to the majority opinion in the case above), Justice Douglas resorted to many different provisions of the Constitution.

Mr. Justice Douglas delivered the opinion of the Court.

Appellant Griswold is Executive Director of the Planned Parenthood League of Connecticut. Appellant Buxton is a licensed physician and a professor at the Yale Medical School who served as Medical Director for the League at its Center in New Haven—a center open and operating from November 1 to November 10, 1961, when appellants were arrested.

They gave information, instruction, and medical advice to *married persons* as to the means of preventing conception. They examined the wife and prescribed the best contraceptive device or material for her use. Fees were usually charged, although some couples were serviced free.

The statute whose constitutionality is involved in this appeal ... provides:

"Any person who uses any drug, medicinal article or instrument for the purpose of preventing conception shall be fined not less than fifty dollars or imprisoned not less than sixty days nor more than one year or be both fined and imprisoned." ...

"Any person who assists, abets, counsels, causes, hires or commands another to commit any offense may be prosecuted and punished as if he were the principal offender."

The appellants were found guilty as accessories and fined $100 each, against the claim that the accessory statute as so applied violated the Fourteenth Amendment. ...

Coming to the merits, we are met with a wide range of questions that implicate the Due Process Clause of the Fourteenth Amendment. Overtones of some arguments suggest that *Lochner* v. *State of New York*, 198 U.S. 45, should be our guide. But we decline that invitation. ... We do not sit as a super-legislature to determine the wisdom, need, and propriety of laws that touch economic problems, business affairs, or social conditions. This law, however, operates directly on an intimate relation of husband and wife and their physician's role in one aspect of that relation.

The association of people is not mentioned in the Constitution nor in the Bill of Rights. The right to educate a child in a school of the parents' choice—whether public or private or parochial—is also not mentioned. Nor is the right to study any particular subject or any foreign language. Yet the First Amendment has been construed to include certain of those rights. ...

We have had many controversies over these penumbral rights of "privacy and repose." ... These cases bear witness that the right of privacy which presses for recognition here is a legitimate one.

The present case, then, concerns a relationship lying within the zone of privacy created by several fundamental constitutional guarantees. And it concerns a law which, in forbidding the *use* of contraceptives rather than regulating their manufacture or sale, seeks to achieve its goals by means having a maximum destructive impact upon that relationship. Such a law cannot stand in light of the familiar principle, so often applied by this Court, that a "governmental purpose to control or prevent activities constitutionally subject to state regulation may not be achieved by means which sweep unnecessarily broadly and thereby invade the area of protected freedoms." ...

We deal with a right of privacy older than the Bill of Rights—older than our political parties, older than our school system. Marriage is a coming together for better or for worse, hopefully enduring, and intimate to the degree of being sacred. It is an association that promotes a way of life, not causes; a harmony in living, not political faiths; a bilateral loyalty, not commercial or social projects. Yet it is an association for as noble a purpose as any involved in our prior decisions.

Reversed.

Mr. Justice Goldberg, whom The Chief Justice and Mr. Justice Brennan join, concurring.

I agree with the Court that Connecticut's birth control law unconstitutionally intrudes upon the right of marital privacy, and I join in its opinion and judgment. ... My conclusion that the concept of liberty is not so restricted and that it embraces the right of marital privacy though that right is not mentioned explicitly in the Constitution is supported both by numerous decisions of this Court, referred to in the Court's opinion, and by the language and history of the Ninth Amendment. In reaching the conclusion that the right of marital privacy is protected, as being within the protected penumbra of specific guarantees of the Bill of Rights, the Court refers to the Ninth Amendment. I add these words to emphasize the relevance of that Amendment to the Court's holding.

. . . .

The Ninth Amendment reads, "The enumeration in the Constitution, of certain rights, shall not be construed to deny or disparage others retained by the people." . . .

The . . . specific guarantees in the Bill of Rights have penumbras, formed by emanations from those guarantees that help give them life and substance. . . .

. . . .

The entire fabric of the Constitution and the purposes that clearly underlie its specific guarantees demonstrate that the rights to marital privacy and to marry and raise a family are of similar order and magnitude as the fundamental rights specifically protected.

Although the Constitution does not speak in so many words of the right of privacy in marriage, I cannot believe that it offers these fundamental rights no protection. The fact that no particular provision of the Constitution explicitly forbids the State from disrupting the traditional relation of the family—a relation as old and as fundamental as our entire civilization—surely does not show that the Government was meant to have the power to do so. . . .

Justices Harlan and White concurred in the judgment. Justice Black, whom Justice Stewart joined, dissented, arguing that neither Douglas nor Goldberg had succeeded in grounding the judgment in constitutional text.

Roe v. *Wade*
410 U.S. 113, 93 S.Ct. 705, 35 L.Ed.2d 147 (1973)

In this most controversial decision of the Supreme Court since *Brown* v. *Board of Education,* Justice Blackmun sought, like Douglas in *Griswold,* to avoid the charge of "Lochnerizing." The holding of the Court was that women possessed a constitutional liberty to choose abortion that was infringed upon unreasonably by the current abortion laws of most of the states. The challenge for Blackmun, as for Douglas earlier, was to explain where this liberty resided in the Constitution. In the first part of his opinion, Justice Blackmun experimented with Douglas' diffuse right of privacy, with its roots in various provisions of the Constitution. Later in the opinion, however, he refers to this right of privacy as "founded in the Fourteenth Amendment's concept of personal liberty. . . ." It seemed clear to most commentators after *Roe* v. *Wade* that substantive due process was back in the new form of an unspecified liberty of sexual and/or familial relations, which resided in the word liberty in the Fifth and Fourteenth Amendments.

Mr. Justice Blackmun delivered the opinion of the Court.

This Texas federal appeal and its Georgia companion, present constitutional challenges to state criminal abortion legislation. The Texas statutes under attack here are typical of those that have been in effect in many States for approximately a century. . . .

....

Our task, of course, is to resolve the issue by constitutional measurement free of emotion and of predilection. We seek earnestly to do this, and, because we do, we have inquired into, and in this opinion place some emphasis upon, medical and medical-legal history and what that history reveals about man's attitudes toward the abortive procedure over the centuries. We bear in mind, too, Mr. Justice Holmes' admonition in his now vindicated dissent in Lochner v. New York . . .:

> "It [the Constitution] is made for people of fundamentally differing views, and the accident of our finding certain opinions natural and familiar, or novel, and even shocking, ought not to conclude our judgment upon the question whether statutes embodying them conflict with the Constitution of the United States."

The Constitution does not explicitly mention any right of privacy. In a line of decisions, however, . . . the Court has recognized that a right of personal privacy, or a guarantee of certain areas or zones of privacy, does exist under the Constitution. In varying contexts the Court or individual Justices have indeed found at least the roots of that right in the First Amendment, *Stanley* v. *Georgia*, . . .; in the Fourth and Fifth Amendments, *Terry* v. *Ohio*, . . . [and] *Katz* v. *United States* . . .; in the penumbras of the Bill of Rights, *Griswold* v. *Connecticut* . . .; in the Ninth Amendment, . . .; or in the concept of liberty guaranteed by the first section of the Fourteenth Amendment. . . .

This right of privacy, whether it be founded in the Fourteenth Amendment's concept of personal liberty and restrictions upon state action, as we feel it is, or, as the District Court determined, in the Ninth Amendment's reservation of rights to the people, is broad enough to encompass a woman's decision whether or not to terminate her pregnancy. The detriment that the State would impose upon the pregnant woman by denying this choice altogether is apparent. Specific and direct harm medically diagnosable even in early pregnancy may be involved. Maternity, or additional offspring, may force upon the woman a distressful life and future. Psychological harm may be imminent. Mental and physical health may be taxed by child care. There is also the distress, for all concerned, associated with the unwanted child, and there is the problem of bringing a child into a family already unable, psychologically and otherwise, to care for it. In other cases, as in this one, the additional difficulties and continuing stigma of unwed motherhood may be involved. All these are factors the woman and her responsible physician necessarily will consider in consultation.

On the basis of elements such as these, appellants and some *amici* argue that the woman's right is absolute and that she is entitled to terminate her pregnancy at whatever time, in whatever way, and for whatever reason she alone chooses. With this we do not agree. Appellants' arguments that Texas either has no valid interest at all in regulating the abortion decision, or no interest strong enough to support any limitation upon the woman's sole determination, is unpersuasive. The Court's decisions recognizing a right of privacy also acknowledge that some state regulation in areas protected by that right is appropriate. As noted above, a state may properly assert important interests in safeguarding health, in maintaining medical standards, and in protecting potential life. At some point in pregnancy, these respective interests become sufficiently compelling to sustain regulation of the factors that govern the abortion decision. The privacy right involved, therefore, cannot be said to be absolute. In fact, it is not clear to us that the claim asserted by some *amici* that one has an unlimited right to do with one's body as one pleases bears a close relationship to the right of privacy previously articulated in the Court's decisions. . . .

We therefore conclude that the right of personal privacy includes the abortion decision, but that this right is not unqualified and must be considered against important state interests in regulation. . . .

In view of all this, we do not agree that . . . Texas may override the rights of the pregnant woman that are at stake. We repeat, however, that the State does have an important and legitimate interest in preserving and protecting the health of the pregnant woman, whether she be a resident of the State or a non-resident who seeks medical consultation and treatment there, and that it has still *another* important and legitimate interest in protecting the potentiality of human life. These interests are separate and distinct. Each grows in substantiality as the woman approaches term and, at a point during pregnancy, each becomes "compelling."

With respect to the State's important and legitimate interest in the health of the mother, the "compelling" point, in the light of present medical knowledge, is at approximately the end of the first trimester. This is so because of the now established medical fact, . . . that until the end of the first trimester mortality in abortion is less than mortality in normal childbirth. It follows that, from and after this point, a State may regulate the abortion procedure to the extent that the regulation reasonably relates to the preservation and protection of maternal health. Examples of permissible state regulation in this area are requirements as to the qualifications of the person who is to perform the abortion; as to the licensure of that person; as to the facility in which the procedure is to be performed, that is, whether it must be a hospital or may be a clinic or some other place of less-than-hospital status; as to the licensing of the facility; and the like.

This means, on the other hand, that, for the period of pregnancy prior to this "compelling" point, the attending physician, in consultation with his patient, is free to determine, without regulation by the State, that in his medical judgment the patient's pregnancy should be terminated. If that decision is reached, the judgment may be effectuated by an abortion free of interference by the State.

With respect to the State's important and legitimate interest in potential life, the "compelling" point is at viability. This is so because the fetus then presumably has the capability of meaningful life outside the mother's womb. State regulation protective of fetal life after viability thus has both logical and biological justifications. If the State is interested in protecting fetal life after viability, it may go so far as to proscribe abortion during that period except when it is necessary to preserve the life or health of the mother. . . .

. . . .

This holding, we feel, is consistent with the relative weights of the respective interests involved, with the lessons and example of medical and legal history, with the lenity of the common law, and with the demands of the profound problems of the present day. The decision leaves the State free to place increasing restrictions on abortion as the period of pregnancy lengthens, so long as those restrictions are tailored to the recognized state interests. The decision vindicates the right of the physician to administer medical treatment according to his professional judgment up to the points where important state interests provide compelling justifications for intervention. Up to those points the abortion decision in all its aspects is inherently, and primarily, a medical decision, and basic responsibility for it must rest with the physician. If an individual practitioner abuses the privilege of exercising proper medical judgment, the usual remedies, judicial and intraprofessional, are available. . . .

Justice Stewart concurred. Justice White, with whom Justice Rehnquist joined, dissented. Justice Rehnquist dissented separately.

Mr. Justice Rehnquist, dissenting. . . .

I have difficulty in concluding, as the Court does, that the right of "privacy" is involved in this case. [Texas] bars the performance of a medical abortion by a licensed physician on a plaintiff such as Roe. A transaction resulting in an operation such as this is not "private" in the ordinary usage of that word. Nor is the "privacy" which the Court finds here even a distant relative of the freedom from searches and seizures. . . .

If the Court means by the term "privacy" no more than that the claim of a person to be free from unwanted state regulation of consensual transactions may be a form of "liberty" protected by the Fourteenth Amendment, there is no doubt that similar claims have been upheld in our earlier decisions on the basis of that liberty. I agree [that "liberty"] embraces more than the rights found in the Bill of Rights. But that liberty is not guaranteed absolutely against deprivation, but only against deprivation without due process of law. The test traditionally applied in the area of social and economic legislation is whether or not a law such as that challenged has a rational relation to a valid state objective. [*Williamson* v. *Lee Optical Co.*] The Due Process Clause of the Fourteenth Amendment undoubtedly does place a limit, albeit a broad one, on legislative power to enact laws such as this. If the Texas statute were to prohibit an abortion even where the mother's life is in jeopardy, I have little doubt that such a statute would lack a rational relation to a valid state objective. . . . But the Court's sweeping invalidation of any restrictions on abortion during the first trimester is impossible to justify under that standard, and the conscious weighing of competing factors which the Court's opinion apparently substitutes for the established test is far more appropriate to a legislative judgment than to a judicial one. . . .

Doe v. *Commonwealth's Attorney*
403 F. Supp. 1199 (1975)

How far is the Supreme Court prepared to go with this new doctrine of sexual liberty or autonomy? *Doe* v. *Commonwealth's Attorney* was a challenge to Virginia's sodomy statute. The argument was that homosexual acts between consenting adults were the sort of intimate relations protected against state interference by the concept of sexual privacy enunciated in *Griswold* and *Roe* v. *Wade.* Judge Brian, for the special, three-judge federal district court, gave that argument short shrift, relying heavily on language from Justice Harlan's concurrence in *Griswold* v. *Connecticut.* Harlan had stressed the importance of the marriage bond to the finding of unconstitutionality in that case. It is important to note, however, that there was no stress on the marriage bond as crucial to the kind of personal choice protected in *Roe* v. *Wade.* The Supreme Court declined to review *Doe,* even though the case was before it on appeal, and the Court is technically required to take the case if it presents a substantial federal question. Justices Brennan, Marshall, and Stephens apparently thought such a question was presented, since they would have set the case for oral argument. Four votes are required, however, and while it may be difficult to see why the logic of *Roe* v. *Wade* does not raise at least a question with respect to laws banning homosexuality, the fourth vote was not there.

Bryan, Senior Circuit Judge:

> Virginia's statute making sodomy a crime is unconstitutional, each of the male plaintiffs aver, when it is applied to his active and regular homosexual relations with another *adult male, consensually* and *in private.* They assert that local State officers threaten them with prosecution for violation of this law, that such enforcement would deny them their Fifth and Fourteenth Amendments' assurance of due process, the First Amendment's protection of their rights of freedom of expression, the First and Ninth Amendments' guarantee of privacy, and the Eighth Amendment's forbiddance of cruel and unusual punishments. A declaration of the statute's invalidity in the circumstances is prayed as well as an injunction against its enforcement. Defendants are State prosecuting officials and they take issue with the plaintiffs' conclusions. With no conflict of fact present, the validity of this enactment becomes a question of law. . . .
>
> In *Griswold v. Connecticut,* . . . plaintiffs' chief reliance, the Court has most recently announced its views on the question here. Striking down a State statute forbidding the use of contraceptives, the ruling was put on the right of marital privacy—held to be one of the specific guarantees of the Bill of Rights—and was also put on the sanctity of the home and family. Its thesis is epitomized by the author of the opinion, Mr. Justice Douglas, in his conclusion:
>
> "We deal with a right of privacy older than the Bill of Rights—older than our political parties, older than our school system. Marriage is a coming together for better or for worse, hopefully enduring and intimate to the degree of being sacred. It is an association that promotes a way of life, not causes; a harmony in living, not political faiths; a bilateral loyalty, not commercial or social projects. Yet it is an association for as noble a purpose as any involved in our prior decisions." . . .
>
> That *Griswold* is premised on the right of privacy and that homosexual intimacy is denunciable by the State is unequivocally demonstrated by Mr. Justice Goldberg in his concurrence, . . . in his adoption of Mr. Justice Harlan's dissenting statement in *Poe v. Ullman,* . . .:

"Adultery, *homosexuality* and the like are sexual intimacies *which the State forbids* ... but the intimacy of husband and wife is necessarily an essential and accepted feature of the institution of marriage, an institution which the State not only must allow, but which always and in every age it has fostered and protected. *It is one thing when the State exerts its power either to forbid extramarital sexuality* ... or to say who may marry, but it is quite another when, having acknowledged a marriage and the intimacies inherent in it, it undertakes to regulate by means of the criminal law the details of that intimacy." ... Justice Harlan's words are nonetheless commanding merely because they were written in dissent. To begin with, as heretofore observed, they were authentically approved in *Griswold*. ...

With his standing, what he had further to say in *Poe v. Ullman*, ... is worthy of high regard. On the plaintiffs' effort presently to shield the practice of homosexuality from State incrimination by according it immunity when committed in private as against public exercise, the Justice said this:

"Indeed to attempt a line between public behavior and that which is purely consensual or solitary would be to withdraw from community concern a range of subjects with which every society in civilized times has found it necessary to deal. The laws regarding marriage which provide both when the sexual powers may be used and the legal and societal context in which children are born and brought up, as well as *laws forbidding adultery, fornication and homosexual practices which express the negative of the proposition,* confining sexuality to lawful marriage, form a pattern so deeply pressed into the substance of our social life that any Constitutional doctrine in this area must build upon that basis." ...

With no authoritative judicial bar to the proscription of homosexuality—since it is obviously no portion of marriage, home or family life—the next question is whether there is any ground for barring Virginia from branding it as criminal. If a State determines that punishment therefor, even when committed in the home, is appropriate in the promotion of morality and decency, it is not for the courts to say that the State is not free to do so. ...

Although a questionable law is not removed from question by the lapse of any prescriptive period, the longevity of the Virginia statute does testify to the State's interest and its legitimacy. It is not an upstart notion; it has ancestry going back to Judaic and Christian law. The immediate parentage may be readily traced to the Code of Virginia of 1792. All the while the law has been kept alive, as evidenced by periodic amendments, the last in the 1968 Acts of the General Assembly of Virginia, ...

The prayers for a declaratory judgment and an injunction invalidating the sodomy statute will be denied.

District Judge Mehinger dissented.

CASE STUDY: "HUMAN LIFE" AMENDMENTS

No decision of the Supreme Court since *Brown* v. *Board of Education* has generated as much resistance as *Roe* v. *Wade*. But unlike the opposition to the command that state enforced segregation of public education cease, the opposition to *Roe* has not dissipated over the years. One reason is that opposition to *Brown* was regional, while opposition to *Roe* is nationwide. Further, there was no compelling moral argument supporting school segregation, whereas both sides in the abortion debate are fired by intense moral visions that, far from blurring, have only sharpened over the years. It seems likely that in making its decision in *Roe,* the majority of the Court operated on the implicit conviction that while the country might be divided for a time, the wisdom and correctness of the abortion decision would come to be supported by a broad consensus, as had been the case with the Court's initiative against racial segregation.

Opposition to the abortion decision has proceeded along two axes. First, there have been a number of attempts to limit and condition the availability of abortions without banning them outright (abortion in the first trimester of pregnancy was held impermissible by the Court in *Roe*). Second, there have been efforts to amend the Constitution to undo, in one way or another, *Roe* v. *Wade.*

In *Planned Parenthood of Missouri* v. *Danforth,* 428 U.S. 52 (1976), the Court, divided five to four, invalidated a provision of Missouri's law requiring an unmarried woman under eighteen to obtain the consent of a parent before obtaining an abortion in nonemergency circumstances. The Court also rejected a parallel provision barring a married woman from obtaining a nonemergency abortion without her husband's consent. In *Belotti* v. *Baird,* 443 U.S. 622 (1976), the Court confronted a Massachusetts statute that required the consent of both parents for the nonemergency abortion of an unmarried pregnant minor, but provided that if parental consent was refused, a state judge could authorize the abortion "for good cause shown." The Court struck down this law but was deeply divided in its reasoning. Justice Powell, joined by Chief Justice Burger and Justices Stewart and Rehnquist, argued that while the Massachusetts scheme was unconstitutional, a state might constitutionally "provide some guidance" and "provide for adult involvement" in the abortion decision of minors. Justice Stephens, joined by Brennan, Marshall, and Blackmun, attacked Powell's opinion as advisory and addressed to "hypothetical questions" rather than the Massachusetts scheme before the Court.

Finally, in *H.L.* v. *Matheson,* 450 U.S. 398 (1981), the Court, still deeply divided, *sustained* against a facial attack for unconstitutionality a Utah law requiring physicians to notify the parents or guardian of any minor upon whom a nonemergency abortion was to be performed. Writing for the majority, Chief Justice Burger noted that the law granted no "veto power over the minor's abortion decision." Burger argued that the law was reasonably calculated to protect minors as a class; left undecided was whether the law could be constitutionally applied to a "mature or emancipated" minor. Justice Marshall in dissent, joined by Brennan and Blackmun, thought Utah's burdening of "the minor's privacy right" to be undue and therefore unconstitutional.

The efforts to reverse *Roe* v. *Wade* by a constitutional amendment have been well publicized. What is not so well understood is that there are two approaches to amendment: One, following Justice Rehnquist's lead in his dissent in *Roe* v. *Wade,* would provide that nothing in the Constitution shall bar states from regulating the practice of abortion (a return to the *status quo ante Roe*). A second approach, associated with the name of Senator Jesse Helms of North Carolina, seeks to amend the Constitution positively to protect human life "from the moment of conception."

After the initial battles over the constitutional amendments ended in frustration for the anti-abortion forces, flank attacks were undertaken in Congress on the use of public funds for many types of abortions. In a six-to-three decision in 1977, the Court held that there was no constitutional compulsion for the expenditure of federal funds for nontherapeutic abortions for women in financial need. And in 1980, the Court divided five-four in rejecting constitutional attacks on provisions of the so-called Hyde Amendment, which limited the availability of public funding for many medically indicated abortions.

In 1981 a new approach was taken by some members of Congress in an attack on *Roe* v. *Wade.* A "human life statute" was proposed (S. 158 and H.R. 900, 97th Cong., 1st Sess.). This bill included a congressional finding of fact that "present day scientific evidence indicates a significant likelihood that actual human life exists from conception. Based on this "finding" the Congress sought to declare, under its power to enforce the Fourteenth Amendment, that deprivation of life without due process of law meant life from the moment of conception. Such an assertion of congressional authority would have to rest on the much discussed but altogether unclear congressional power to substantively interpret the constitutional provisions. In other words, the Congress would make constitutional law rather than simply enforce and implement the Court's reading of the Constitution. See *Katzenbach* v. *Morgan,* 384 U.S. 641 (1966).

Many in the right to life movement doubted the constitutionality of such legislation, and with the opening of the 98th Congress in January 1982, the focus of activity returned to constitutional amendment. Proposals to simply overrule *Wade* have fallen by the wayside. Today's initiatives include either amendments that would prohibit all abortion, or amendments that would allow abortion if needed to save the mother's life. As on the issue of school prayer, conservative pressure has been rising on the Reagan administration to commit its resources more vigorously in the battle against "pro-choice" forces. The President is deeply committed against abortion on demand, but the disarray among the "pro life" forces—the variety of proposals they have brought forward and their natural fractiousness—makes constitutional amendment in this area unlikely. Neither is there any likelihood of social peace over this issue. The future seems one of continuing guerrilla warfare in the passes and foothills of American public law.

CHAPTER · 24

FREEDOM FROM POLITICAL SURVEILLANCE

THE problems of physical searches, electronic eavesdropping, and the use of informants have been discussed in Chapters 14 and 15. In this chapter we will examine the special problems presented by the activities of the federal government in monitoring and combating terrorism and the activities within the United States of foreign intelligence services. That is, we will be concerned with the infringements on privacy that may occur as a result of efforts by the federal government to protect national security.

Today, national security interests within the United States are defined much more narrowly than they were a decade ago. Excessive intelligence collection by the FBI, sometimes coupled with actual interference with the affairs of domestic political groups, resulted in a series of scandals and reforms in the late 1970s. But these reforms have far from settled all of the disputes or answered all of the questions in this very controversial area.

Through the case of *Laird* v. *Tatem,* we will examine the controversy over the government collecting information about extremist political groups. We will then turn to the case of *U.S.* v. *U.S. District Court,* where the Court rejected a national security justification for warrantless searches in the absence of foreign involvement. Finally, we shall examine the Foreign Intelligence Surveillance Act of 1978, which provided a judicial check on warrantless electronic surveillance for foreign intelligence purposes.

Laird v. *Tatum*
408 U.S. 1, 92 S.Ct. 2318, 33 L.Ed.2d. 154 (1972)

This case had its beginnings in an article by former Army Captain Christopher Pyle, which appeared in the magazine, *The Washington Monthly,* in the January issue of 1970. Pyle, now a teacher of constitutional law and a civil liberties activist, had been an instructor at the Army Intelligence School at

Fort Holibird, Maryland and had acquired extensive knowledge of the "Conus Intelligence Program." Military intelligence groups around the country policed security procedures at military installations and among defense contractors doing classified work. In the Conus program, these intelligence groups were used to observe and report on the activity of various domestic political groups in the mid-1960s, with antiwar and other "New Left" activists being the main targets. When he left the Army, Pyle not only publicized the program but interested Melvin Wulf of the ACLU in the matter. In the fullness of time, plaintiffs were recruited and a law suit was brought. The question before the Supreme Court was whether the gathering of information by the government, without anything more, gave rise to a cause of action by the plaintiffs. That is, had the plaintiffs sustained or were they in immediate danger of sustaining the kind of injury that can be the basis of a law suit. The Court, speaking through Chief Justice Burger, concluded that they did not. While the case is in the form of a dispute over "justiciability," it implies a negative answer to the question of whether government information gathering about the political activities of persons is a violation of the Constitution. It is important to note, as the Chief Justice did in his opinion, that had the record shown the government was preparing to use the information collected in ways that would adversely affect the plaintiffs, a different answer might have been forthcoming.

Mr. Chief Justice Burger delivered the opinion of the Court.

Respondents brought this class action in the District Court seeking declaratory and injunctive relief on their claim that their rights were being invaded by the Army's alleged "surveillance of lawful civilian political activity." The petitioners in response describe the activity as "gathering by lawful means, ... maintaining and using in their intelligence activities, ... information relating to potential or actual civil disturbances [or] street demonstrations." ... On the basis of the pleadings, the affidavits before the court, and the oral arguments advanced at the hearing, the District Court granted petitioners' motion to dismiss, holding that there was no justiciable claim for relief.

On appeal, a divided Court of Appeals reversed and ordered the case remanded for further proceedings. We granted certiorari to consider whether, as the Court of Appeals held, respondents presented a justiciable controversy in complaining of a "chilling" effect on the exercise of their First Amendment rights where such effect is allegedly caused, not by any "specific action of the Army against them, [but] only [by] the existence and operation of the intelligence gathering and distributing system, which is confined to the Army and related civilian investigative agencies." ... We reverse. ...

In recent years this Court has found in a number of cases that constitutional violations may arise from the deterrent, or "chilling," effect of governmental regulations that fall short of a direct prohibition against the exercise of First Amendment rights. ... In none of these cases, however, did the chilling effect arise merely from the individual's knowledge that a governmental agency was engaged in certain activities or from the individual's concomitant fear that, armed with the fruits of those activities, the agency might in the future take some *other* and additional action detrimental to that individual. Rather, in each of these cases, the challenged exercise of governmental power was regulatory, proscriptive, or compulsory in nature, and the complainant was either presently or prospectively subject to the regulations, proscriptions, or compulsions that he was challenging. ... The decisions in these cases fully recognize that governmental action may be subject to constitutional challenge even though it has only an indirect effect on the exercise of First Amendment rights. At the same time, however, these decisions have in no way eroded the

"established principle that to entitle a private individual to invoke the judicial power to determine the validity of executive or legislative action he must show that he has sustained or is immediately in danger of sustaining a direct injury as the result of that action. ..." The respondents do not meet this test; their claim, simply stated, is that they disagree with the judgments made by the Executive Branch with respect to the type and amount of information the Army needs and that the very existence of the Army's data-gathering system produces a constitutionally impermissible chilling effect upon the exercise of their First Amendment rights. That alleged "chilling" effect may perhaps be seen as arising from respondents' very perception of the system as inappropriate to the Army's role under our form of government, or as arising from respondents' beliefs that it is inherently dangerous for the military to be concerned with activities in the civilian sector, or as arising from respondents' less generalized yet speculative apprehensiveness that the Army may at some future date misuse the information in some way that would cause direct harm to respondents. Allegations of a subjective "chill" are not an adequate substitute for a claim of specific present objective harm or a threat of specific future harm; "the federal courts established pursuant to Article III of the Constitution do not render advisory opinions." ...

We, of course, intimate no view with respect to the propriety or desirability, from a policy standpoint, of the challenged activities of the Department of the Army; our conclusion is a narrow one, namely, that on this record the respondents have not presented a case for resolution by the courts. ...

Reversed.

Justice Brennan, joined by Justices Stewart and Marshall, dissented on the issue of justiciability. Justice Douglas, joined by Justice Marshall, dissented separately, arguing that the Army surveillance was "massive" and that the "present controversy is not a remote, imaginary conflict. ..."

United States v. *United States District Court*
407 U.S. 297, 92 S.Ct. 2125, 32 L.Ed.2d. 752 (1972)

Commonly called the *Keith* case, the issue in *U.S.* v. *U.S. District Court* was the President's power to order warrantless wiretaps. Recall that the *Katz* case had brought electronic surveillance under the protection of the Fourth Amendment. In 1968, responding to *Katz,* the Congress had enacted the

Crime Control and Safe Streets Act. Included in that legislation were regulations for the issuance of warrants for telephone taps and electronic bugs. It had been stated in the Act, however, that nothing contained in these warrant regulations would disturb the President's power under the Constitution to order electronic surveillance for national security purposes. But what was the scope of this presidential power? The Court in the *Keith* case held that it did not extend to domestic security matters. Absent the element of *foreign* threat to national security, warrants must be sought for all electronic surveillance. Joining the attack on the government's national security wire tapping in this case were such leading activist lawyers as Arthur Kinoy, a professor of law at Rutgers University and a frequent ACLU volunteer counsel, and William Kunstler, a long time defender of left radicals. Among the groups submitting *amicus curiae* briefs were the ACLU, the American Friends Service Committee, and the Black Panther Party.

Mr. Justice Powell delivered the opinion of the Court.

The issue before us is an important one for the people of our country and their Government. It involves the delicate question of the President's power, acting through the Attorney General, to authorize electronic surveillance in internal security matters without prior judicial approval. Successive Presidents for more than one-quarter of a century have authorized such surveillance in varying degrees, without guidance from the Congress or a definitive decision of this Court. This case brings the issue here for the first time. Its resolution is a matter of national concern, requiring sensitivity both to the Government's right to protect itself from unlawful subversion and attack and to the citizen's right to be secure in his privacy against unreasonable Government intrusion.

This case arises from a criminal proceeding in the United States District Court for the Eastern District of Michigan, in which the United States charged three defendants with conspiracy to destroy Government property. ... One of the defendants, Plamondon, was charged with the dynamite bombing of an office of the Central Intelligence Agency in Ann Arbor, Michigan.

During pretrial proceedings, the defendants moved to compel the United States to disclose certain electronic surveillance information and to conduct a hearing to determine whether this information "tainted" the evidence on which the indictment was based or which the Government intended to offer at trial. In response, the Government filed an affidavit of the Attorney General, acknowledging that its agents had overheard conversations in which Plamondon had participated. The affidavit also stated that the Attorney General approved the wiretaps "to gather intelligence information deemed necessary to protect the nation from attempts of domestic organizations to attack and subvert the existing structure of the Government." ...

Title III of the Omnibus Crime Control and Safe Streets Act, 18 U.S.C. §§ 2510–2520, authorizes the use of electronic surveillance for classes of crimes carefully specified in 18 U.S.C. § 2516. Such surveillance is subject to prior court order. Section 2518 sets forth the detailed and particularized application necessary to obtain such an order as well as carefully circumscribed conditions for its use.

The Act represents a comprehensive attempt by Congress to promote more effective control of crime while protecting the privacy of individual thought and expression. Much of Title III was drawn to meet the constitutional requirements for electronic surveillance enunciated by this Court in ... *Katz* v. *United States*. ...

Together with the elaborate surveillance requirements in Title III, there is the following proviso, 18 U.S.C. § 2511 (3):

> "Nothing contained in this chapter ... shall limit the constitutional power of the President to take such measures as he deems necessary to protect the Nation against actual or potential attack or other hostile acts of a foreign power, to obtain foreign intelligence information deemed essential to the security of the United States, or to protect national security information against foreign intelligence activities. *Nor shall anything contained in this chapter be deemed to limit the constitutional power of the President to take such measures as he deems necessary to protect the United States against the overthrow of the Government by force or other unlawful means, or against any other clear and present danger to the structure or existence of the Government.* The contents of any wire or oral communication intercepted by authority of the President in the exercise of the foregoing powers may be received in evidence in any trial hearing, or other proceeding only where such interception was reasonable, and shall not be otherwise used or disclosed except as is necessary to implement that power." (Emphasis supplied.)

The Government relies on § 2511 (3). It argues that "in excepting national security surveillances from the Act's warrant requirement Congress recognized the President's authority to conduct such surveillances without prior judicial approval." ... The section thus is viewed as a recognition or affirmance of a constitutional authority in the President to conduct warrantless domestic security surveillance such as that involved in this case.

We think the language of § 2511 (3), as well as the legislative history of the statute, refutes this interpretation. The relevant language is that:

> "Nothing contained in this chapter ... shall limit the constitutional power of the President to take such measures as he deems necessary to protect ..."

against the dangers specified. At most, this is an implicit recognition that the President does have certain powers in the specified areas. Few would doubt this, as the section refers—among other things—to protection "against actual or potential attack or other hostile acts of a foreign power." But so far as the use of the President's electronic surveillance power is concerned, the language is essentially neutral. ...

Section 2511 (3) certainly confers no power, as the language is wholly inappropriate for such a purpose. It merely provides that the Act shall not be interpreted to limit or disturb such power as the President may have under the

Constitution. In short, Congress simply left presidential powers where it found them. . . .

We begin the inquiry by noting that the President of the United States has the fundamental duty, under Art. II, § 1, of the Constitution, to: "preserve, protect and defend the Constitution of the United States." Implicit in that duty is the power to protect our Government against those who would subvert or overthrow it by unlawful means. In the discharge of this duty, the President—through the Attorney General—may find it necessary to employ electronic surveillance to obtain intelligence information on the plans of those who plot unlawful acts against the Government. The use of such surveillance in internal security cases has been sanctioned more or less continuously by various Presidents and Attorneys General since July 1946. . . .

As the Fourth Amendment is not absolute in its terms, our task is to examine and balance the basic values at stake in this case: the duty of Government to protect the domestic security, and the potential danger posed by unreasonable surveillance to individual privacy and free expression. If the legitimate need of Government to safeguard domestic security requires the use of electronic surveillance, the question is whether the needs of citizens for privacy and free expression may not be better protected by requiring a warrant before such surveillance is undertaken. We must also ask whether a warrant requirement would unduly frustrate the efforts of Government to protect itself from acts of subversion and overthrow directed against it. . . .

But we do not think a case has been made for the requested departure from Fourth Amendment standards. The circumstances described do not justify complete exemption of domestic security surveillance from prior judicial scrutiny. Official surveillance, whether its purpose be criminal investigation or ongoing intelligence gathering, risks infringement of constitutionally protected privacy of speech. Security surveillances are especially sensitive because of the inherent vagueness of the domestic security concept, the necessarily broad and continuing nature of intelligence gathering, and the temptation to utilize such surveillances to oversee political dissent. We recognize, as we have before, the constitutional basis of the President's domestic security role, but we think it must be exercised in a manner compatible with the Fourth Amendment. In this case we hold that this requires an appropriate prior warrant procedure. . . .

We cannot accept the Government's argument that internal security matters are too subtle and complex for judicial evaluation. Courts regularly deal with the most difficult issues of our society. There is no reason to believe that federal judges will be insensitive to or uncomprehending of the issues involved in domestic security cases. Certainly courts can recognize that domestic security surveillance involves different considerations from the surveillance of "ordinary crime." If the threat is too subtle or complex for our senior law enforcement officers to convey its significance to a court, one may question whether there is probable cause for surveillance.

Nor do we believe prior judicial approval will fracture the secrecy essential to official intelligence gathering. The investigation of criminal activity has long involved imparting sensitive information to judicial officers who have respected the confidentialities involved. Judges may be counted upon to be especially conscious of security requirements in national security cases. . . .

We emphasize, before concluding this opinion, the scope of our decision. As stated at the outset, this case involves only the domestic aspects of national security. We have not addressed, and express no opinion as to, the issues which may be involved with respect to activities of foreign powers or their agents.

The judgment of the Court of Appeals is hereby

Affirmed.

Chief Justice Burger concurred only in the result. Justice Douglas wrote a concurring opinion and Justice White wrote an opinion.

The Foreign Intelligence Surveillance Act of 1978
50 U.S.C. 1801, 92 Stat. 1783

In the wake of the *Keith* case there remained the question of a possible need for restraint on the power of the President to order warrantless electronic surveillance for foreign intelligence purposes. The hearings and report of the Church Committee of the Senate on abuses of power by American intelligence agencies had heightened national consciousness on these issues in the mid-1970s. In 1978, as a direct result of the work of the Church Committee and the Pike Committee in the House of Representatives, the Foreign Intelligence Surveillance Act (FISA) was passed. This legislation, while recognizing the power of the President under the Constitution to undertake electronic surveillance for foreign intelligence purposes without Fourth Amendment warrants, provided a new procedure for clearance of such surveillance by specially designated federal judges. Sitting in secret as a so-called "FISA Court," the federal judge must determine if a government application for surveillance is for a legitimate foreign intelligence collection purpose and if minimization procedures will be followed with respect to U.S. persons (citizens and resident aliens). This statute completed the process begun in *Katz* and made all electronic eavesdropping on communication where both sender and receiver are within the United States subject to some form of judicial supervision.

SEC. 102. (a) (1) Notwithstanding any other law, the President, through the Attorney General, may authorize electronic surveillance without a court order under this title to acquire foreign intelligence information for periods of up to one year if the Attorney General certifies in writing under oath that—

(A) the electronic surveillance is solely directed at—

(i) the acquisition of the contents of communications transmitted by means of communications used exclusively between or among foreign powers, . . .; or

(ii) the acquisition of technical intelligence, other than the spoken communications of individuals, from property or premises under the open and exclusive control of a foreign power, . . .;

(B) there is no substantial likelihood that the surveillance will acquire the contents of any communication to which a United States person is a party; . . . .

SEC. 103. (a) The Chief Justice of the United States shall publicly designate seven district court judges from seven of the United States judicial circuits who shall constitute a court which shall have jurisdiction to hear applications for and grant orders approving electronic surveillance anywhere within the United States under the procedures set forth in this Act, except that no judge designated under this subsection shall hear the same application for electronic surveillance under this Act which has been denied previously by another judge designated under this subsection. If any judge so designated denies an application for an order authorizing electronic surveillance under this Act, such judge shall provide immediately for the record a written statement of each reason for his decision and, on motion of the United States, the record shall be transmitted, under seal, to the court of review established in subsection (b).

(b) The Chief Justice shall publicly designate three judges, one of whom shall be publicly designated as the presiding judge, from the United States district courts or courts of appeals who together shall comprise a court of review which shall have jurisdiction to review the denial of any application made under this Act. If such court determines that the application was properly denied, the court shall immediately provide for the record a written statement of each reason for its decision and, on petition of the United States for a writ of certiorari, the record shall be transmitted under seal to the Supreme Court, which shall have jurisdiction to review such decision. . . .

SEC. 104. (a) Each application for an order approving electronic surveillance under this title shall be made by a Federal officer in writing upon oath or affirmation to a judge having jurisdiction under section 103. Each application shall require the approval of the Attorney General based upon his finding that it satisfies the criteria and requirements of such application as set forth in this title. It shall include—

(1) the identity of the Federal officer making the application;

(2) the authority conferred on the Attorney General by the President of the United States and the approval of the Attorney General to make the application;

(3) the identity, if known, or a description of the target of the electronic surveillance;

(4) a statement of the facts and circumstances relied upon by the applicant to justify his belief that—

(A) the target of the electronic surveillance is a foreign power or an agent of a foreign power; and

(B) each of the facilities or places at which the electronic surveillance is directed is being used, or is about to be used, by a foreign power or an agent of a foreign power;

(5) a statement of the proposed minimization procedures;

(6) a detailed description of the nature of the information sought

and the type of communications or activities to be subjected to the surveillance;

(7) a certification or certifications by the Assistant to the President for National Security Affairs or an executive branch official or officials designated by the President from among those executive officers employed in the area of national security or defense and appointed by the President with the advice and consent of the Senate—

(A) that the certifying official deems the information sought to be foreign intelligence information;

(B) that the purpose of the surveillance is to obtain foreign intelligence information;

(C) that such information cannot reasonably be obtained by normal investigative techniques;

(D) that designates the type of foreign intelligence information being sought according to the categories described in section 101 (e); and

(E) including a statement of the basis for the certification that—

(i) the information sought is the type of foreign intelligence information designated; and

(ii) such information cannot reasonably be obtained by normal investigative techniques;

(8) a statement of the means by which the surveillance will be effected and a statement whether physical entry is required to effect the surveillance;

(9) a statement of the facts concerning all previous applications that have been made to any judge under this title involving any of the persons, facilities, or places specified in the application, and the action taken on each previous application;

(10) a statement of the period of time for which the electronic surveillance is required to be maintained, and if the nature of the intelligence gathering is such that the approval of the use of electronic surveillance under this title should not automatically terminate when the described type of information has first been obtained, a description of facts supporting the belief that additional information of the same type will be obtained thereafter; and

(11) whenever more than one electronic, mechanical or other surveillance device is to be used with respect to a particular proposed electronic surveillance, the coverage of the devices involved and what minimization procedures apply to information acquired by each device. ... and (11) of subsection (a), but shall state whether physical entry is required to effect the surveillance and shall contain such information about the surveillance techniques and communications or other information concerning United States persons likely to be obtained as may be necessary to assess the proposed minimization procedures.

(c) The Attorney General may require any other affidavit or certification from any other officer in connection with the application.

(d) The judge may require the applicant to furnish such other information as may be necessary to make the determinations required by section 105.

SEC. 105. (a) Upon an application made pursuant to section 104, the judge shall enter an ex parte order as requested or as modified approving the electronic surveillance if he finds that—

(1) the President has authorized the Attorney General to approve applications for electronic surveillance for foreign intelligence information;

(2) the application has been made by a Federal officer and approved by the Attorney General;

(3) on the basis of the facts submitted by the applicant there is probable cause to believe that—

(A) the target of the electronic surveillance is a foreign power or an agent of a foreign power: *Provided,* That no United States person may be considered a foreign power or an agent of a foreign power solely upon the basis of activities protected by the first amendment to the Constitution of the United States; and

(B) each of the facilities or places at which the electronic surveillance is directed is being used, or is about to be used, by a foreign power or an agent of a foreign power;

(4) the proposed minimization procedures [are adequate]. . . .

CASE STUDY: THE GIANT EARS OF NSA

The National Security Agency (NSA) was created by secret presidential directive in 1952. It brought together experts in communications monitoring and communications security from the various military services and consolidated their activity in a high-security compound at Fort Meade in Maryland. NSA has responsibility for monitoring communications and other electronic signals in the air around the world for foreign intelligence purposes. NSA is also responsible for cracking the codes used by foreign governments to communicate to themselves and for preserving the security of American codes. From a series of earth stations and orbiting satellites, the NSA is able to monitor everything from the telemetry of Soviet missile tests to the communication of Argentine fighter pilots with their bases.

Sophisticated computers at Fort Meade keep track of patterns of communications and other electronic signals and allow for selective retrieval for interpretation. It is possible to observe an increase in the signal activity of Iranian armed forces preparatory to an attack on Iraq, or overhear the conversations of foreign officials on radio telephones from their limousines. This ever increasing technical capacity of NSA poses two kinds of problems for the privacy of individual Americans.

First, there is the fear that the ears of NSA might be turned inward on the electronic communications of Americans. Most long distance telephone calls, for instance, are now transmitted through the air by microwave rather than over long lines. These microwave transmissions are technically available to NSA, although the agency does not at present monitor them and stoutly maintains that it never will do so.

Second, since international telephone traffic is routed through the air to and from satellites, it is possible for NSA to monitor this traffic, and the agency does so routinely. This monitoring is for foreign intelligence purposes, but the communications of Americans also are sometimes overheard in the course of this monitoring process. It emerged during the Church Committee hearings in the mid-1970s, for example, that in the early 1970s NSA had cooperated with the FBI by placing on a "watch list" the names of a number of American political dissidents, including Jane Fonda and Huey Newton. NSA was upbraided for this and emerged from the episode apparently chastened. No domestic intelligence or domestic law enforcement names or items are included on watch lists today. But this does not end the problem.

James Bamford in his study of the NSA, *The Puzzle Palace,* (Boston: Houghton Mifflin, 1982), poses the issue dramatically. What happens if the routine monitoring of overseas telephone calls produces as an unintended by-product information of extreme domestic law enforcement interest? Suppose information is developed that an American organization is backing revolution in Haiti or has launched a new drive to provide weapons for the Irish Republican Army? And what of the discovery that a Congressman is demanding and receiving money from a foreign government? Should such information be suppressed on the grounds that it involves United States persons (citizens and resident aliens) and was collected without the warrant or probable cause required by the Fourth Amendment? Or should it be turned over to domestic law enforcement on the grounds that since there was no targeting of U.S. persons, and the information was a by-product of routine monitoring for foreign intelligence, it should be regarded as serendipitous, like a piece of incriminating physical evidence being washed in on a beach or emerging from a snowbank in the spring.

NSA has adopted strict "minimization procedures" to reduce the possibility of U.S. persons being overheard or having their conversations recorded and stored. Nonetheless, debate will continue over what the agency should do with the unsought domestic by-product of its foreign intelligence monitoring. One proposal is to use the FISA Court—the special federal district judges empowered under the Foreign Intelligence Surveillance Act of 1978 to authorize electronic eavesdropping within the United States for foreign intelligence purposes. The routine monitoring of overseas telephone calls by NSA takes place outside the FISA framework, but it can be argued that when unintended domestic intelligence information is obtained, the permission of the FISA Court might be sought for disclosure of that information relevant to the law enforcement agency.

The inescapable reality is that foreign intelligence collection and domestic law enforcement are inevitably intertwined, at least to some extent, and we will never have altogether satisfactory "boundary maintenance" between the two spheres of activity.

CHAPTER · 25

EPILOGUE: CONTROVERSIES AND CROSSCURRENTS

WE began this book by observing that what we often glibly refer to as "our civil rights and liberties" is really a special kind of public policy. Like all public policy, rights policy is a product of controversy, but, as we have seen, some aspects of rights policy are more controversial than others. To put it another way, some controversies involve more fundamental kinds of choices than others. We may debate the question of how great a likelihood of disorder justifies police interference with a speaker in a public forum; but the controversy is over where to draw the line, not the basic issue of protecting speakers in streets and parks. In the course of this book, by contrast, we also have encountered a small number of controversies that do involve basic fundamental choices in rights policy. These go far beyond line drawing in particular cases; they are true storm centers in the atmosphere of constitutional politics.

Having come to the end of our journey through the law and politics of rights and liberties, it is useful to refocus briefly on these basic conflicts. The objective is not to stake out positions (although we are all likely to have to do that sooner or later), but rather to see clearly the underlying values that collide or are in tension. What makes these particular conflicts basic—difficult and even desperate—is not only that they go beyond differences of degree and line drawing, but that they involve important and perfectly legitimate values that are mutually exclusive. These controversies will continue to agitate and confound us because they involve powerful crosscurrents of human desires, commitments, and perceptions of reality, which cannot be easily bridged or compromised. How they are eventually fought out will have a good deal to do with the kind of society and polity we will enjoy (or deplore) a few decades hence.

One such fundamental conflict has to do with the extension of First Amendment protections to sexually explicit and abusive expression. Many critics charge that this extension trivializes the First Amendment and risks bringing into contempt a protection that is fundamental to the integrity of our political process. Others respond that the true test of our attachment to First Amendment principles is to extend them to unpopular, gross, and offensive modes of expression. At issue here are differing views of what the speech protection was designed to protect, of what social functions it was meant to perform. Was it principally intended to safeguard political speech, so that opposition to those in office could be mounted and a republican form of government maintained? Or was it principally intended to guarantee individuals the capacity to gratify themselves verbally and pictorially in ways that please them and without any larger justification than that it does so? Underlying this choice are differing views as to the nature of the good society. Those who would restrict obscene and abusive utterances tend to regard past social practice in the area of public manners and morals as correct and worthy of maintaining or (to the extent it has been abandoned) restoring. Opponents of this view regard traditional limitations on verbal and pictoral utterance as stifling, inhumane, and unexceptedly restrictive of the human spirit. Partisans of this position abhor "repression" and look to the liberation of the individual personality from archaic social constraints as a key to a better world. Such are the currents and tidal rips that run below the surface of court decisions, legal briefs, and articles in law reviews.

Another basic controversy in the First Amendment area involves the right to know. While the 1970s saw formidable arguments mounted for openness and disclosure in government at all levels, the 1980s are increasingly yielding examples of where the "public's right to know" collides with other important values. Sometimes these conflicting values are themselves civil liberties concerns. The tension between the right of the press under the First Amendment to cover the judicial process and the rights of defendants under the Fifth and Sixth Amendments to fair trials is a dramatic example. Another value that often collides with the right to know is the value of governmental efficiency or, perhaps better, public performance. We want to know what government is doing but not at the expense of unlimited inefficiencies or diseconomies. These concerns underlie the debate on amending the Freedom of Information Act and the Privacy Act to exempt additional categories of materials from exposure. The debate is troublesome precisely because some of us believe that good government requires that little, if anything, be kept secret, while others of us believe that a distinction between general policy (which must always be public) and specifics of implementation (which must sometimes be secret) is basic to good government.

And what of the arguments swirling around the relationship of religion to the public order? How far can the Supreme Court go in affording exemptions from otherwise valid and binding laws on the basis of religious motives for noncompliance? This question goes straight to core assumptions of persons concerning the proper nature of the political community and the obligations of individuals to it. If such exemptions are afforded only to conventional theistic believers who are members of established religious bodies, this powerfully favors some folk over others who may feel equally indisposed to obey a particular law, but cannot ground their objection in conventional belief and cannot shelter behind a familiar denominational attachment. To many people it appears as clear as day that in a secular polity no one should be exempted, and laws should apply uniformly. To others it is equally obvious that religious scruples are of a special quality, set apart from other commitments of belief and conscience. Proponents of this view argue that the framers of the First Amendment recognized this difference by the inclusion of the free exercise clause. The difficulty in this reasoning, their critics point out, is that it appears to put the free exercise clause at cross purposes with the establishment clause, which excludes preferential treatment for religion by government. One resolution is to exempt all those who object to obeying laws on any conscientious ground. But this might negate the very basis of the state as a human organization by giving everyone the "right" to ignore laws they disagree with strongly. And so it goes.

Consider the increasingly acrimonious controversy over the use of exclusionary rules to protect Fourth and Fifth Amendment values against police misbehavior, even when this results in the loss to the truth finding process of perfectly reliable physical evidence or voluntary statements by the accused to authorities. The justices of the Supreme Court are deeply divided on the issue. Majorities continue to apply broad exclusionary rules, while it is increasingly suggested that exclusionary rules may not, in fact, operate as very powerful disincentives to police misconduct. Civil liberties interest groups, however, are almost unanimously arrayed against any alteration in the exclusionary practices developed over the past two decades. What, it is asked, could be put in the place of exclusionary rules to restrain the police? Underlying this debate, surely, is a fundamental difference in the way criminal offenders are viewed. Many Americans are convinced that the economic social arrangement of society is unjust, and that much of the crime committed by the poor and the young (and that accounts for most street crime) is the product of this injustice. In this view, the unfairness to those already victimized and powerless is compounded if police are not held in the strictest check when gathering evidence for prosecution. Other Americans are confident of the basic fairness of the social structure and of the criminal law. They are concerned to avoid convicting the innocent, and they do not wish to license freewheeling invasion of privacy by police. Beyond this, however, they are concerned that the system work efficiently to achieve crime control.

Even more far reaching—and likely to preoccupy constitutional politicians for years to come—is the issue of extending the "racial paradigm" of equal protection into other equal protection contexts such as sex discrimination. To what extent, critics ask, are sex differences really analogous to race? They are similar in that they are unchangeable, and women have been discriminated against in the past. But "gender" is not analogous to race in that women constitute a slight majority within the population and have not been restricted to the lower socio-economic strata of American society. As for aliens, the group is certainly a minority, which has been discriminated against, but the status is not permanent. Resident aliens may overcome and alter the status by being naturalized as citizens. Illegitimacy offers another set of variations on the racial model of strict equal protection scrutiny. The illegitimate child cannot alter his status by himself; but neither is his status unalterable. It is within the capacity of the natural parent to legitimate the child. Finally, age is clearly not alterable. Yet unlike race or illegitimacy, and a little more like sex, age is a factor that is reasonably and legitimately the basis for many kinds of governmental classifications.

Finally, shall personal privacy be understood to extend to matters of sexual preference? This issue will be fought in court rooms, seminar rooms, and legislative chambers for many years to come. How, many ask, can the Supreme Court reconcile its decisions that intimate matters of abortion, contraception, and family choice are protected by the concept of "liberty" in the Fifth and Fourteenth Amendments, but not recognize that homosexual choices must be protected by the same reasoning. Since the rejection of the abortion decision by some segments of the public has been massive, there is every reason to suppose that opposition to creating a new constitutional protection for homosexual behavior will encounter similar political and intellectual resistance.

These matters involve fundamental, moral, and philosophical issues, and for that reason go beyond being simply controversies. There are no clear answers to these questions, no "solutions" to these controversies, no harmonizing of the crosscurrents to be achieved just by consulting the constitutional text or its history. Persons take positions on these issues in accordance with basic convictions about our society, which in turn reflect differing assumptions about the desirable future shape of society and about human nature itself.

Only the constitutionally uninitiated (and you are no longer such) could suppose the outcomes of any of such conflicts to be foreordained or dictated by a set of constitutional or philosophical principles on which we all agree. Voltaire wrote that "to hold a pen is to be at war," and this is precisely what constitutional lawyers, scholars, and publicists ("rights-and-liberties professionals") are up to most of the time—prosecuting intellectual war. Rather than recoil from the difficulties and indeterminacy of basic controversies in the area of rights and liberties, you should look on them as both an agenda and invitation to struggle.

APPENDIX:
THE CONSTITUTION OF
THE UNITED STATES

We the people of the United States, in Order to form a more perfect Union, establish Justice, insure domestic Tranquility, provide for the common defence, promote the general Welfare, and secure the Blessings of Liberty to ourselves and our Posterity, do ordain and establish this CONSTITUTION for the United States of America.

Article I

Section 1. All legislative Powers herein granted shall be vested in a Congress of the United States, which shall consist of a Senate and House of Representatives.

Section 2. The House of Representatives shall be composed of Members chosen every second Year by the People of the several States, and the Electors in each State shall have the Qualifications requisite for Electors of the most numerous Branch of the State Legislature.

No Person shall be a Representative who shall not have attained to the Age of twenty-five Years, and been seven Years a Citizen of the United States, and who shall not, when elected, be an Inhabitant of that State in which he shall be chosen.

Representatives and direct Taxes shall be apportioned among the several States which may be included within this Union, according to their respective Numbers, which shall be determined by adding to the whole Number of free Persons, including those bound to Service for a Term of Years, and excluding Indians not taxed, three fifths of all other Persons. The actual Enumeration shall be made within three Years after the first Meeting of the Congress of the United States, and within every subsequent Term of ten Years, in such Manner as they shall by Law direct. The Number of Representatives shall not exceed one for every thirty Thousand, but each State shall have at Least one Representative; and until such enumeration shall be made, the State of New Hampshire shall be entitled to chuse three, Massachusetts eight, Rhode-Island and Providence Plantations one, Connecticut five, New-York six, New Jersey four,

Pennsylvania eight, Delaware one, Maryland six, Virginia ten, North Carolina five, South Carolina five, and Georgia three.

When vacancies happen in the Representation from any State, the Executive Authority thereof shall issue Writs of Election to fill such Vacancies.

The House of Representatives shall chuse their Speaker and other Officers; and shall have the sole Power of Impeachment.

Section 3. The Senate of the United States shall be composed of two Senators from each State, chosen by the Legislature thereof, for six Years; and each Senator shall have one Vote.

Immediately after they shall be assembled in Consequence of the first Election, they shall be divided as equally as may be into three Classes. The Seats of the Senators of the first Class shall be vacated at the Expiration of the second Year, of the second Class at the Expiration of the fourth Year, and of the third Class at the Expiration of the sixth Year, so that one-third may be chosen every second Year; and if Vacancies happen by Resignation, or otherwise, during the Recess of the Legislature of any State, the Executive thereof may make temporary Appointments until the next Meeting of the Legislature, which shall then fill such Vacancies.

No Person shall be a Senator who shall not have attained to the Age of thirty Years, and been nine Years a Citizen of the United States, and who shall not, when elected, be an Inhabitant of that State in which he shall be chosen.

The Vice President of the United States shall be President of the Senate, but shall have no vote, unless they be equally divided.

The Senate shall chuse their other Officers, and also a President pro tempore, in the absence of the Vice President, or when he shall exercise the Office of the President of the United States.

The Senate shall have the sole Power to try all Impeachments. When sitting for that purpose, they shall be on Oath or Affirmation. When the President of the United States is tried, the Chief Justice shall preside: And no person shall be convicted without the Concurrence of two thirds of the Members present.

Judgment in Cases of Impeachment shall not extend further than to removal from Office, and disqualification to hold and enjoy any Office of honor, Trust, or Profit under the United States: but the Party convicted shall nevertheless be liable and subject to Indictment, Trial, Judgment, and Punishment, according to Law.

Section 4. The Times, Places and Manner of holding Elections for Senators and Representatives, shall be prescribed in each state by the Legislature thereof; but the Congress may at any time by Law make or alter such Regulations, except as to the Places of Chusing Senators.

The Congress shall assemble at least once in every Year, and such Meeting shall be on the first Monday in December, unless they shall by Law appoint a different Day.

Section 5. Each House shall be the Judge of the Elections, Returns and Qualifications of its own Members, and a Majority of each shall constitute a Quorum to do Business; but a smaller number may adjourn from day to day, and may be authorized to compel the Attendance of absent Members, in such Manner, and under such Penalties, as each House may provide.

Each House may determine the Rules of its Proceedings, punish its Members for disorderly Behaviour, and, with the Concurrence of two thirds, expel a Member.

Each House shall keep a Journal of its Proceedings, and from time to time publish the same, excepting such Parts as may in their Judgment require Secrecy; and the Yeas and Nays of the Members of either House on any question shall, at the Desire of one fifth of those Present, be entered on the Journal.

Neither House, during the Session of Congress, shall, without the Consent of the other, adjourn for more than three days, nor to any other Place than that in which the two Houses shall be sitting.

Section 6. The Senators and Representatives shall receive a Compensation for their Services, to be ascertained by Law, and paid out of the Treasury of the United States. They shall in all Cases, except Treason, Felony, and Breach of the Peace, be privileged from Arrest during their Attendance at the Session of their respective Houses, and in going to and returning from the same; and for any Speech or Debate in either House, they shall not be questioned in any other Place.

No Senator or Representative shall, during the Time for which he was elected, be appointed to any civil Office under the Authority of the United States, which shall have been created, or the Emoluments whereof shall have been increased, during such time; and no Person holding any Office under the United States shall be a Member of either House during his continuance in Office.

Section 7. All Bills for raising Revenue shall originate in the House of Representatives; but the Senate may propose or concur with Amendments as on other Bills.

Every Bill which shall have passed the House of Representatives and the Senate, shall, before it become a Law, be presented to the President of the United States; If he approve he shall sign it, but if not he shall return it, with his Objections, to that House in which it shall have originated, who shall enter the Objections at large on their Journal, and proceed to reconsider it. If after such Reconsideration two thirds of that House shall agree to pass the Bill, it shall be sent, together with the Objections, to the other House, by which it shall likewise be reconsidered, and if approved by two thirds of that House, it shall become a Law. But in all such Cases the Votes of both Houses shall be determined by Yeas and Nays, and the Names of the Persons voting for and against the Bill shall be entered on the Journal of each House respectively. If any Bill shall not be returned by the President within ten Days (Sundays excepted) after it shall have been presented to him, the Same shall be a Law, in like Manner as if he had signed it, unless the Congress by their Adjournment prevent its Return, in which Case it shall not be a Law.

Every Order, Resolution, or Vote to which the Concurrence of the Senate and House of Representatives may be necessary (except on a question of Adjournment) shall be presented to the President of the United States; and before the Same shall take Effect, shall be approved by him, or being disapproved by him, shall be repassed by two thirds of the Senate and House of Representatives, according to the Rules and Limitations prescribed in the Case of a Bill.

Section 8. The Congress shall have Power To lay and collect Taxes, Duties, Imposts and Excises, to pay the Debts and provide for the common Defence and general Welfare of the United States; but all Duties, Imposts and Excises shall be uniform throughout the United States;

To borrow money on the credit of the United States;

To regulate Commerce with foreign Nations, and among the several States, and with the Indian Tribes;

To establish an uniform Rule of Naturalization, and uniform Laws on the subject of Bankruptcies throughout the United States;

To coin Money, regulate the Value thereof, and of foreign Coin, and fix the Standard of Weights and Measures;

To provide for the Punishment of counterfeiting the Securities and current Coin of the United States;

To establish Post Offices and post Roads;

To promote the Progress of Science and useful Arts, by securing for limited Times to Authors and Inventors the exclusive Right to their respective Writings and Discoveries;

To constitute Tribunals inferior to the Supreme Court;

To define and punish Piracies and Felonies committed on the high Seas, and Offenses against the Law of Nations;

To declare War, grant Letters of Marque and Reprisal, and make Rules concerning Captures on Land and Water;

To raise and support Armies, but no Appropriation of Money to that Use shall be for a longer Term than two Years;

To provide and maintain a Navy;

To make Rules for the Government and Regulation of the land and naval forces;

To provide for calling forth the Militia to execute the Laws of the Union, suppress Insurrections and repel Invasions;

To provide for organizing, arming, and disciplining the Militia, and for governing such Part of them as may be employed in the Service of the United States, reserving to the States respectively, the Appointment of the Officers, and the Authority of training the Militia according to the discipline prescribed by Congress;

To exercise exclusive Legislation in all Cases whatsoever, over such District (not exceeding ten Miles square) as may, by Cession of particular States, and the acceptance of Congress, become the Seat of Government of the United States, and to exercise like Authority over all Places purchased by the Consent of the Legislature of the State in which the Same shall be, for the Erection of Forts, Magazines, Arsenals, dock-Yards, and other needful Buildings;—And

To make all Laws which shall be necessary and proper for carrying into Execution the foregoing Powers, and all other Powers vested by this Constitution in the Government of the United States, or in any Department or Officer thereof.

Section 9. The Migration or Importation of such Persons as any of the States now existing shall think proper to admit, shall not be prohibited by the Congress prior to the Year one thousand eight hundred and eight, but a tax or duty may be imposed on such Importation, not exceeding ten dollars for each Person.

The privilege of the Writ of Habeas Corpus shall not be suspended, unless when in Cases of Rebellion or Invasion the public Safety may require it.

No Bill of Attainder or ex post facto Law shall be passed.

No Capitation, or other direct, Tax shall be laid unless in Proportion to the Census or Enumeration herein before directed to be taken.

No Tax or Duty shall be laid on Articles exported from any State.

No Preference shall be given by any Regulation of Revenue to the Ports of one State over those of another: nor shall Vessels bound to, or from, one State, be obliged to enter, clear, or pay Duties in another.

No Money shall be drawn from the Treasury, but in Consequence of Appropriations made by Law; and a regular Statement and Account of the Receipts and Expenditures of all public Money shall be published from time to time.

No Title of Nobility shall be granted by the United States: And no Person holding any Office of Profit or Trust under them, shall, without the Consent of the Congress, accept of any present, Emolument, Office, or Title, of any kind whatever, from any King, Prince, or foreign State.

Section 10. No State shall enter into any Treaty, Alliance, or Confederation; grant Letters of Marque and Reprisal; coin Money; emit Bills of Credit; make any Thing but gold and silver Coin a Tender in Payment of Debts; pass any Bill of Attainder, ex post facto Law, or Law impairing the Obligation of Contracts, or grant any Title of Nobility.

No state shall, without the Consent of the Congress, lay any Imposts or Duties on Imports or Exports, except what may be absolutely necessary for executing its inspection Laws: and the net Produce of all Duties and Imposts, laid by any State on Imports or Exports, shall be for the Use of the Treasury of the United States; and all such Laws shall be subject to the Revision and Control of the Congress.

No State shall, without the Consent of Congress, lay any duty of Tonnage, keep Troops, or Ships of War in time of Peace, enter into any Agreement or Compact with another State, or with a foreign Power, or engage in War, unless actually invaded, or in such imminent Danger as will not admit of delay.

Article II

Section 1. The executive Power shall be vested in a President of the United States of America. He shall hold his Office during the Term of four Years, and, together with the Vice President, chosen for the same Term, be elected, as follows:

Each State shall appoint, in such Manner as the Legislature thereof may direct, a Number of Electors, equal to the whole Number of Senators and Representatives to which the State may be entitled in the Congress: but no Senator or Representative, or Person holding an Office of Trust or Profit under the United States, shall be appointed an Elector.

The Electors shall meet in their respective States, and vote by Ballot for two Persons, of whom one at least shall not be an Inhabitant of the same State with themselves. And they shall make a List of all the Persons voted for, and of the Number of Votes for each; which List they shall sign and certify, and transmit sealed to the Seat of the Government of the United States, directed to the President of the Senate. The President of the Senate shall, in the Presence of the Senate and House of Representatives, open all the Certificates, and the Votes shall then be counted. The Person having the greatest Number of Votes shall be the President, if such Number be a Majority of the whole Number of Electors appointed; and if there be more than one who have such Majority, and have an equal Number of Votes, then the House of Representatives shall immediately chuse by Ballot one of them for President; and if no Person have a Majority, then from the five highest on the List the said House shall in like Manner chuse the President. But in chusing the Pesident, the Votes shall be taken by States, the Representation from each State having one Vote; a quorum for this Purpose shall consist of a Member or Members from two-thirds of the States, and a Majority of all the States shall be necessary to a Choice. In every Case, after the Choice of the President, the Person having the greatest Number of Votes of the Electors shall be the Vice President. But if there should remain two or more who have equal votes, the Senate shall chuse from them by Ballot the Vice President.

The Congress may determine the Time of chusing the Electors, and the Day on which they shall give their Votes; which Day shall be the same throughout the United States.

No person except a natural-born Citizen, or a Citizen of the United States, at the time of the Adoption of this Constitution, shall be eligible to the Office of President; neither shall any Person be eligible to that Office who shall not have attained to the Age of thirty-five Years, and been fourteen Years a Resident within the United States.

In Case of the Removal of the President from Office, or of his Death, resignation, or Inability to discharge the Powers and Duties of the said Office, the same shall devolve on the Vice President, and the Congress may by Law provide for the Case of Removal, Death, Resignation, or Inability, both of the President and Vice President, declaring what Officer shall then act as President, and such Officer shall act accordingly, until the Disability be removed, or a President shall be elected.

The President shall, at stated Times, receive for his Services a Compensation, which shall neither be increased nor diminished during the Period for which he shall have been elected, and he shall not receive within that Period any other Emolument from the United States, or any of them.

Before he enter on the Execution of his Office, he shall take the following Oath or Affirmation:—"I do solemnly swear (or affirm) that I will faithfully execute the Office of President of the United States, and will, to the best of my Ability, preserve, protect, and defend the Constitution of the United States."

Section 2. The President shall be Commander in Chief of the Army and Navy of the United States, and of the Militia of the several States, when called into the actual Service of the United States; he may require the Opinion, in writing, of the principal Officer in each of the executive Departments, upon any subject relating to the Duties of their respective Offices, and he shall have Power to Grant Reprieves and Pardons for Offences against the United States, except in Cases of Impeachment.

He shall have Power, by and with the Advice and Consent of the Senate, to make Treaties, provided two thirds of the Senators present concur; and he shall nominate, and by and with the Advice and Consent of the Senate, shall appoint Ambassadors, other public Ministers and Consuls, Judges of the Supreme Court, and all other Officers of the United States, whose Appointments are not herein otherwise provided for, and which shall be established by Law: but the Congress may by Law vest the Appointment of such inferior Officers, as they think proper, in the President alone, in the Courts of Law, or in the Heads of Departments.

The President shall have Power to fill up all Vacancies that may happen during the Recess of the Senate, by granting Commissions which shall expire at the End of their next Session.

Section 3. He shall from time to time give to the Congress Information of the State of the Union, and recommend to their Consideration such Measures as he shall judge necessary and expedient; he may, on extraordinary occasions, convene both Houses, or either of them, and in Case of Disagreement between them, with respect to the Time of Adjournment, he may adjourn them to such Time as he shall think proper; he shall receive Ambassadors and other public Ministers; he shall take Care that the Laws be faithfully executed, and shall Commission all the Officers of the United States.

Section 4. The President, Vice President and all civil Officers of the United States, shall be removed from Office on Impeachment for, and Conviction of, Treason, Bribery, or other high Crimes and Misdemeanors.

Article III

Section 1. The judicial Power of the United States, shall be vested in one supreme Court, and in such inferior Courts as the Congress may from time to time ordain and establish. The Judges, both of the supreme and inferior Courts, shall hold their Offices during good Behaviour, and shall, at stated Times, receive for their Services, a Compensation, which shall not be diminished during their Continuance in Office.

Section 2. The judicial Power shall extend to all Cases, in Law and Equity, arising under this Constitution, the Laws of the United States, and Treaties made, or which shall be made, under their Authority;—to all Cases affecting Ambassadors, other public Ministers and Consuls;—to all Cases of admiralty and maritime Jurisdiction;—to Controversies to which the United States shall be a Party;—to Controversies between two or more States;—between a State and Citizens of another State;—between Citizens of the same State claiming Lands under Grants of different States, and between a State, or the Citizens thereof, and foreign States, Citizens or Subjects.

In all Cases affecting Ambassadors, other public Ministers and Consuls, and those in which a State shall be Party, the supreme Court shall have original Jurisdiction. In all the other Cases before mentioned, the supreme Court shall have appellate Jurisdiction, both as to Law and Fact, with such Exceptions, and under such Regulations as the Congress shall make.

The trial of all Crimes, except in Cases of Impeachment, shall be by Jury; and such Trial shall be held in the State where the said Crimes shall have been committed; but when not committed within any State, the Trial shall be at such Place or Places as the Congress may by Law have directed.

Section 3. Treason against the United States, shall consist only in levying War against them, or in adhering to their Enemies, giving them Aid and Comfort. No Person shall be convicted of Treason unless on the Testimony of two Witnesses to the same overt Act, or on Confession in open Court.

The Congress shall have power to declare the Punishment of Treason, but no Attainder of Treason shall work Corruption of Blood, or Forfeiture except during the Life of the Person attainted.

Article IV

Section 1. Full Faith and Credit shall be given in each State to the public Acts, Records, and judicial Proceedings of every other State. And the Congress may by general Laws prescribe the Manner in which such Acts, Records and Proceedings shall be proved, and the Effect thereof.

Section 2. The Citizens of each State shall be entitled to all Privileges and Immunities of Citizens in the several States.

A Person charged in any State with Treason, Felony, or other Crime, who shall flee from Justice, and be found in another State, shall on demand of the executive Authority of the State from which he fled, be delivered up, to be removed to the State having Jurisdiction of the crime.

No Person held to Service or Labour in one State, under the Laws thereof, escaping into another, shall, in Consequence of any Law or Regulation therein, be discharged from such Service or Labour, but shall be delivered up on Claim of the Party to whom such Service or Labour may be due.

Section 3. New States may be admitted by the Congress into this Union; but no new State shall be formed or erected within the Jurisdiction of any other State; nor any State be formed by the Junction of two or more States, or parts of States, without the Consent of the Legislatures of the States concerned as well as of the Congress.

The Congress shall have Power to dispose of and make all needful Rules and Regulations respecting the Territory or other Property belonging to the United States; and nothing in this Constitution shall be so construed as to Prejudice any Claims of the United States, or of any particular State.

Section 4. The United States shall guarantee to every State in this Union a Republican Form of Government, and shall protect each of them against Invasion; and on Application of the Legislature, or of the Executive (when the Legislature cannot be convened) against domestic Violence.

Article V

The Congress, whenever two thirds of both Houses shall deem it necessary, shall propose Amendments to this Constitution, or, on the Application of the Legislatures of two thirds of the several States, shall call a Convention for proposing Amendments, which, in either Case, shall be valid to all Intents and Purposes, as part of this Constitution, when ratified by the Legislatures of three fourths of the several States, or by Conventions in three fourths thereof, as the one or the other Mode of Ratification may be proposed by the Congress; Provided that no Amendment which may be made prior to the Year One thousand eight hundred and eight shall in any Manner affect the first and fourth Clauses in the Ninth Section of the first Article; and that no State, without its Consent, shall be deprived of its equal Suffrage in the Senate.

Article VI

All Debts contracted and Engagements entered into, before the Adoption of this Constitution, shall be as valid against the United States under this Constitution, as under the Confederation.

This Constitution, and the Laws of the United States which shall be made in Pursuance thereof; and all Treaties made, or which shall be made, under the Authority of the United States, shall be the supreme Law of the Land; and the Judges in every State shall be bound thereby, any Thing in the Constitution or Laws of any State to the Contrary notwithstanding.

The Senators and Representatives before mentioned, and the Members of the several State Legislatures, and all executive and judicial Officers, both of the United States and of the several States, shall be bound by Oath or Affirmation to support this Constitution; but no religious Test shall ever be required as a qualification to any Office or public Trust under the United States.

Article VII

The Ratification of the Conventions of nine States shall be sufficient for the Establishment of this Constitution between the States so ratifying the same.

Done in Convention by the Unanimous Consent of the States present the Seventeenth Day of September in the Year of our Lord one thousand seven hundred and Eighty seven, and of the Independence of the United States of America the Twelfth. In Witness whereof We have hereunto subscribed our Names.

Articles in Addition to, and Amendment of, the Constitution of the United States of America, Proposed by Congress, and Ratified by the Legislatures of the Several States, Pursuant to the Fifth Article of the Original Constitution.

Amendment I [1791]

Congress shall make no law respecting an establishment of religion, or prohibiting the free exercise thereof; or abridging the freedom of speech, or of the press; or the right of the people peaceably to assemble, and to petition the Government for a redress of grievances.

Amendment II [1791]

A well regulated Militia, being necessary to the security of a free State, the right of the people to keep and bear Arms, shall not be infringed.

Amendment III [1791]

No Soldier shall, in time of peace, be quartered in any house, without the consent of the Owner, nor in time of war, but in a manner to be prescribed by law.

Amendment IV [1791]

The right of the people to be secure in their persons, houses, papers, and effects, against unreasonable searches and seizures, shall not be violated, and no Warrants shall issue, but upon probable cause, supported by Oath or affirmation, and particularly describing the place to be searched, and the persons or things to be seized.

Amendment V [1791]

No person shall be held to answer for a capital or otherwise infamous crime, unless on a presentment or indictment of a Grand Jury, except in cases arising in the land or naval forces, or in the Militia, when in actual service in time of War or public danger; nor shall any person be subject for the same offence to be twice put in jeopardy of life or limb; nor shall be compelled in any criminal case to be a witness against himself, nor be deprived of life, liberty, or property, without due process of law; nor shall private property be taken for public use, without just compensation.

Amendment VI [1791]

In all criminal prosecutions, the accused shall enjoy the right to a speedy and public trial, by an impartial jury of the State and district wherein the crime shall have been committed, which district shall have been previously ascertained by law, and to be informed of the nature and cause of the accusation; to be confronted with the witnesses against him; to have compulsory process for obtaining witnesses in his favor, and to have the Assistance of Counsel for his defence.

Amendment VII [1791]

In Suits at common law, where the value in controversy shall exceed twenty dollars, the right of trial by jury shall be preserved, and no fact tried by a jury, shall be otherwise re-examined in any Court of the United States, than according to the rules of the common law.

Amendment VIII [1791]

Excessive bail shall not be required, nor excessive fines imposed, nor cruel and unusual punishments inflicted.

Amendment IX [1791]

The enumeration in the Constitution, of certain rights, shall not be construed to deny or disparage others retained by the people.

Amendment X [1791]

The powers not delegated to the United States by the Constitution, nor prohibited by it to the States, are reserved to the States respectively, or to the people.

Amendment XI [1798]

The Judicial power of the United States shall not be construed to extend to any suit in law or equity, commenced or prosecuted against one of the United States by Citizens of another State, or by Citizens or Subjects of any Foreign State.

Amendment XII [1804]

The Electors shall meet in their respective States and vote by ballot for President and Vice President, one of whom, at least, shall not be an inhabitant of the same States with themselves; they shall name in their ballots the person voted for as President, and in distinct ballots the person voted for as Vice-President, and they shall make distinct lists of all persons voted for as President, and of all persons voted for as Vice-President, and of the number of votes for each, which lists they shall sign and certify, and transmit sealed to the seat of the government of the United States, directed to the President of the Senate;—The President of the Senate shall, in the presence of the Senate and House of Representatives, open all the certificates and the votes shall then be counted;—The person having the greatest number of votes for President, shall be the President, if such number be a majority of the whole number of Electors appointed; and if no person have such majority, then from the persons having the highest numbers not exceeding three on the list of those voted for as President, the House of Representatives shall choose immediately, by ballot, the President. But in choosing the President, the votes shall be taken by states, the representation from each state having one vote; a quorum for this purpose shall consist of a member or members from two-thirds of the states, and a majority of all the states shall be necessary to a choice. And if the House of Representatives shall not choose a President whenever the right of choice shall devolve upon them, before the fourth day of March next following, then the Vice-President shall act as President, as in the case of the death or other constitutional disability of the President.—The person having the greatest number of votes as Vice-President, shall be the Vice-President, if such number be a majority of the whole number of Electors appointed, and if no person have a majority, then from the two highest numbers on the list, the Senate shall choose the Vice-President; a quorum for the purpose shall consist of two-thirds of the whole number of Senators, and a majority of the whole number shall be necessary to a choice. But no person constitutionally ineligible to the office of President shall be eligible to that of Vice-President of the United States.

Amendment XIII [1865]

Section 1. Neither slavery nor involuntary servitude, except as a punishment for crime whereof the party shall have been duly convicted, shall exist within the United States, or any place subject to their jurisdiction.

Section 2. Congress shall have power to enforce this article by appropriate legislation.

Amendment XIV [1868]

Section 1. All persons born or naturalized in the United States, and subject to the jurisdiction thereof, are citizens of the United States and of the State wherein they reside. No State shall make or enforce any law which shall abridge the privileges or immunities of citizens of the United States; nor shall any State deprive any person of life, liberty, or property, without due process of law; nor deny to any person within its jurisdiction the equal protection of the laws.

Section 2. Representatives shall be apportioned among the several States according to their respective numbers, counting the whole number of persons in each State, excluding Indians not taxed. But when the right to vote at any election for the choice of electors for President and Vice President of the United States, Representatives in Congress, the Executive and Judicial officers of a State, or the members of the Legislature thereof, is denied to any of the male inhabitants of such State, being twenty-one years of age, and citizens of the United States, or in any way abridged, except for participation in rebellion, or other crime, the basis of representation therein shall be reduced in the proportion which the number of such male citizens shall bear to the whole number of male citizens twenty-one years of age in such State.

Section 3. No person shall be a Senator or Representative in Congress, or elector of President and Vice President, or hold any office, civil or military, under the United States, or under any State, who, having previously taken an oath, as a member of Congress, or as an officer of the United States, or as a member of any State legislature, or as an executive or judicial officer of any State, to support the Constitution of the United States, shall have engaged in insurrection or rebellion against the same, or given aid or comfort to the enemies thereof. But Congress may by a vote of two-thirds of each House, remove such disability.

Section 4. The validity of the public debt of the United States, authorized by law, including debts incurred for payment of pensions and bounties for services in suppressing insurrection or rebellion, shall not be questioned. But neither the United States nor any State shall assume or pay any debt or obligation incurred in aid of insurrection or rebellion against the United States, or any claim for the loss or emancipation of any slave; but all such debts, obligations, and claims shall be held illegal and void.

Section 5. The Congress shall have the power to enforce, by appropriate legislation, the provisions of this article.

Amendment XV [1870]

Section 1. The right of citizens of the United States to vote shall not be denied or abridged by the United States or by any State on account of race, color, or previous condition of servitude—

Section 2. The Congress shall have power to enforce this article by appropriate legislation.

Amendment XVI [1913]

The Congress shall have power to lay and collect taxes on incomes, from whatever source derived, without apportionment among the several States, and without regard to any census or enumeration.

Amendment XVII [1913]

The Senate of the United States shall be composed of two Senators from each State, elected by the people thereof, for six years; and each Senator shall have one vote. The electors in each State shall have the qualifications requisite for electors of the most numerous branch of the State legislatures.

When vacancies happen in the representation of any State in the Senate, the executive authority of such State shall issue writs of election to fill such vacancies: *Provided,* That the legislature of any State may empower the executive thereof to make temporary appointments until the people fill the vacancies by election as the legislature may direct.

This amendment shall not be so construed as to affect the election or term of any Senator chosen before it becomes valid as part of the Constitution.

Amendment XVIII [1919]

Section 1. After one year from the ratification of this article the manufacture, sale, or transportation of intoxicating liquors within, the importation thereof into, or the exportation thereof from the United States and all territory subject to the jurisdiction thereof for beverage purposes is hereby prohibited.

Section 2. The Congress and the several States shall have concurrent power to enforce this article by appropriate legislation.

Section 3. This article shall be inoperative unless it shall have been ratified as an amendment to the Constitution by the legislatures of the several States, as provided in the Constitution, within seven years from the date of the submission hereof to the States by the Congress.

Amendment XIX [1920]

The right of citizens of the United States to vote shall not be denied or abridged by the United States or by any State on account of sex.

Congress shall have power to enforce this article by appropriate legislation.

Amendment XX [1933]

Section 1. The terms of the President and Vice President shall end at noon on the 20th day of January, and the terms of Senators and Representatives at noon on the 3d day of January, of the years in which such terms would have ended if this article had not been ratified; and the terms of their successors shall then begin.

Section 2. The Congress shall assemble at least once in every year, and such meeting shall begin at noon on the 3d day of January, unless they shall by law appoint a different day.

Section 3. If, at the time fixed for the beginning of the term of the President, the President elect shall have died, the Vice President elect shall become President. If a President shall not have been chosen before the time fixed for the beginning of his term, or if the President elect shall have failed to qualify, then the Vice President elect shall act as President until a President shall have qualified; and the Congress may by law provide for the case wherein neither a President elect nor a Vice President elect shall have qualified, declaring who shall then act as President, or the manner in which one who is to act shall be selected, and such person shall act accordingly until a President or Vice President shall have qualified.

Section 4. The Congress may by law provide for the case of the death of any of the persons from whom the House of Representatives may choose a President whenever the right of choice shall have devolved upon them, and for the case of the death of any of the persons from whom the Senate may choose a Vice President whenever the right of choice shall have devolved upon them.

Section 5. Sections 1 and 2 shall take effect on the 15th day of October following the ratification of this article.

Section 6. This article shall be inoperative unless it shall have been ratified as an amendment to the Constitution by the legislatures of three-fourths of the several States within seven years from the date of its submission.

Amendment XXI [1933]

Section 1. The eighteenth article of amendment to the Constitution of the United States is hereby repealed.

Section 2. The transportation or importation into any State, Territory, or possession of the United States for delivery or use therein of intoxicating liquors, in violation of the laws thereof, is hereby prohibited.

Section 3. This article shall be inoperative unless it shall have been ratified as an amendment to the Constitution by conventions in the several States, as provided in the Constitution, within seven years from the date of the submission hereof to the States by the Congress.

Amendment XXII [1951]

No person shall be elected to the office of the President more than twice, and no person who has held the office of President, or acted as President, for more than two years of a term to which some other person was elected President shall be elected to the office of the President more than once.

But this Article shall not apply to any person holding the office of President when this Article was proposed by the Congress, and shall not prevent any person who may be holding the office of President, or acting as President, during the term within which this Article becomes operative from holding the office of President or acting as President during the remainder of such term.

Amendment XXIII [1961]

Section 1. The District constituting the seat of Government of the United States shall appoint in such manner as the Congress may direct:

A number of electors of President and Vice President equal to the whole number of Senators and Representatives in Congress to which the District would be entitled if it were a State, but in no event more than the least populous State; they shall be in addition to those appointed by the States, but they shall be considered, for the purposes of the election of President and Vice President, to be electors appointed by a State; and they shall meet in the District and perform such duties as provided by the twelfth article of amendment.

Section 2. The Congress shall have power to enforce this article by appropriate legislation.

Amendment XXIV [1964]

Section 1. The right of citizens of the United States to vote in any primary or other election for President or Vice President, for electors for President or Vice President, or for Senator or Representative in Congress, shall not be denied or abridged by the United States or any State by reason of failure to pay any poll tax or other tax.

Section 2. The Congress shall have the power to enforce this article by appropriate legislation.

Amendment XXV [1967]

Section 1. In case of the removal of the President from office or his death or resignation, the Vice President shall become President.

Section 2. Whenever there is a vacancy in the office of the Vice President, the President shall nominate a Vice President who shall take the office upon confirmation by a majority vote of both houses of Congress.

Section 3. Whenever the President transmits to the President pro tempore of the Senate and the Speaker of the House of Representatives his written declaration that he is unable to discharge the powers and duties of his office, and until he transmits to them a written declaration to the contrary, such powers and duties shall be discharged by the Vice President as Acting President.

Section 4. Whenever the Vice President and a majority of either the principal officers of the executive departments, or of such other body as Congess may by law provide, transmit to the President pro tempore of the Senate and the Speaker of the House of Representatives their written declaration that the President is unable to discharge the powers and duties of his office, the Vice President shall immediately assume the powers and dutes of the office as Acting President.

Thereafter, when the President transmits to the President pro tempore of the Senate and the Speaker of the House of Representatives his written declaration that no inability exists, he shall resume the powers and duties of his office unless the Vice President and a majority of either the principal officers of the executive departments, or of such other body as Congress may by law provide, transmit within four days to the President pro tempore of the Senate and the Speaker of the House of Representatives their written declaration that the President is unable to discharge the powers and duties of his office. Thereupon Congress shall decide the issue, assembling within 48 hours for that purpose if not in session. If the Congress, within 21 days after receipt of the latter written declaration, or, if Congress is not in session, within 21 days after Congress is required to assemble, determines by two-thirds vote of both houses that the President is unable to discharge the powers and duties of his office, the Vice President shall continue to discharge the same as Acting President; otherwise, the President shall resume the powers and duties of his office.

Amendment XXVI [1971]

Section 1. The right of citizens of the United States, who are 18 years of age or older, to vote shall not be denied or abridged by the United States or any state on account of age.

Section 2. The Congress shall have the power to enforce this article by appropriate legislation.

INDEX OF CASES

Cases that appear in this text are represented by italicized page entries.